Highland Games and Hippodromes

–

Scottish Identity and Influence at the Dawn of the American Pro Wrestling Industry

By
Ian Douglass

Edited by Oliver Lee Bateman

Copyright Ian Douglass 2026. All Rights Reserved.

Published by:
Darkstream Press

www.darkstreampress.com

All rights reserved. This book may not be reproduced in whole or in part in any form without written permission from the author.

This book is set in Garamond.

10 9 8 7 6 5 4 3 2 1

ISBN 979-8-218-88406-2

This book is dedicated to the memories of

Claire Elmer Douglass

May 6, 1926 — February 20, 2019

And

Richard Scott Douglass

December 23, 1950 — August 26, 2025

The best grandfather and uncle that any guy could ever have.

Table of Contents

Foreword	2
Wrestling Styles Index	4
One – A Man of Vast Power	6
Two – Scottish Hercules	22
Three – Champion Athlete of the World	39
Four – A Showman's Fat Woman	56
Five – A Scotch Hippodromer	70
Six – The Clever Knowing Ones	88
Seven – More Fun Than Fury	106
Eight – A Little Tin Bucket	124
Nine – Judge, Handicapper, Referee	142
Ten – Tearing His Kilt	160
Eleven – Five-Style Champion	179
Twelve – The Little Scot	196
Thirteen – The Consummate Idiots	212
Fourteen – Character and Conduct	230
Fifteen – Forgotten His Cunning	248
Sixteen – A Pity 'Tis True	265
Seventeen – Looking for Easy Game	283
Eighteen – The Terrible Turk	301
Nineteen – The Ringer	320
Twenty – On a Charge of Swindling	338
Twenty-One – The Hottest Thing Going	356
Epilogue	374
Afterword	385
Editor's Note	392
Acknowledgements	401
Credits	402
About the Author	403

FOREWORD

When I became a professional wrestler who proudly proclaimed his allegiance to his home country of Scotland, it never ceased to amaze me how many wrestling fans from around the world proudly expressed their Scottish identity, even if they had never visited Scotland in their lives. I was honored and flattered by their expressions of national solidarity with me, but I also wondered how they came to identify so passionately with a country that they had never visited.   Then again, I also recall the days of my youth in Prestwick, when I watched wrestling on television and cheered for "Rowdy" Roddy Piper. I knew based on his accent, or his lack of one, that he wasn't from Glasgow like he claimed. Still, when I learned that Piper wasn't actually from Scotland, it was a lot like learning that Santa Claus wasn't real.

But that was the thing… Piper clearly had a deep love for Scotland; no one simply learns how to play the bagpipes for the hell of it. The fondness and devotion that it takes to play that instrument comes from a strong sense of connection to Scotland, which Piper definitely had.

Having spent the majority of my wrestling career in the United States, I have often felt like a foreign outsider in the wrestling business. At least I used to feel that way until I took my first look at Highland Games and Hippodromes and learned about how Scottish immigrants who were quite proud of their heritage shaped the foundation of the professional wrestling business that I thrive in today.

Highland Games and Hippodromes

What you're about to read is a deep dive into how Highland Games athletes and wrestlers like Donald Dinnie, Duncan Ross, and others were able to establish many of the pro wrestling norms that we now take for granted.

Once you read this book, you'll fully understand that the modern professional wrestling business that we all know and love might be totally different today if it weren't for the Scottish pioneers who helped to shape it. And as I continue to forge ahead and achieve new milestones in my own wrestling career, I'll know that I'm carrying on a proud Scottish tradition of achieving greatness in the wrestling world.

Drew McIntyre
WWE Undisputed Heavyweight Champion
1/9/2026

Wrestling Styles Index

This index is intended to provide brief explanations of a few of the many wrestling styles that are frequently mentioned in this book. It should be understood that the majority of the definitions offered here were supplied by wrestler Duncan A. McMillan in 1905, and therefore represent his understanding of these wrestling styles as they were contested in the years covered by this book, which are approximately 1870 to 1905.

With that being stated, there are several instances in this book where the styles named do not neatly cohere with the descriptions provided by McMillan. Therefore, a certain amount of lenience on the part of the reader would be much appreciated.

Catch-as-catch-can

A fall is earned by pinning the opponent's shoulders to the mat. In order to earn the fall, a wrestler can "catch" his opponent by any means necessary, as long as he avoids using any illegal methods. Strangling is usually banned, as are tactics like punching, kicking, and scratching.

Greco-Roman

A fall is earned by pinning the opponent's shoulders to the mat. Wrestlers are not allowed to trip or grab each other by the legs, nor are they allowed to grasp any portion of an opponent's body below the hips.

Collar-and-elbow

Usually contested with both wrestlers standing upright, and wearing a harness and belt. The bout begins with each wrestler holding the harness of the other. A fall is earned when either two hips and one shoulder or two shoulders and one hip of a wrestler are pinned to the mat. Wrestlers are not allowed to release the harnesses of their opponents; letting go of the harness results in a forfeit.

Side Hold
A precursor to American folkstyle wrestling, the side-hold wrestling of the era resembled catch-as-catch-can wrestling, but the matches began with both wrestlers grasping each other while standing side-by-side. A fall was usually counted when two hips and a shoulder of one of the wrestlers were pinned to the ground.

Cornish
Similar to catch-as-catch-can wrestling, but contested while the wrestlers wore loose canvas coats. A fall was awarded when two shoulders and a hip or two hips and a shoulder were pinned to the mat. Opponents were permitted to grab each other anywhere on their coats, but were not permitted to hold two collars in one hand, or to cross collars.

Scottish Backhold
The wrestlers grip each other around the back, and can use any means to trip their opponents to the ground. Under most circumstances, a fall is awarded as soon as one wrestler is thrown from his feet. In some situations, a condition was added that a wrestler was required to control his thrown opponent on the ground for a specific length of time in order to be awarded a fall.

Cumberland
Very similar to Scottish backhold wrestling, with the primary difference being that Cumberland wrestling usually occurs in more traditional wrestling tights or singlets as opposed to kilts.

Sir John Astley's Style
Very similar to Scottish backhold wrestling, but with no tripping permitted. A fall is awarded when one wrestler loses his footing.

1 – A Man of Vast Power

To suggest that Scottish ethnic identity had no influence on early 19th century North American life would be to ignore the plain facts. By the 1840s, dozens of Highland societies and social clubs had formed in both the United States and Canada, and organized Highland Games bearing all of the modern hallmarks were hosted by those organizations with regularity.

From a glance at the events featured at one such Highland gathering held in Hamilton, Ontario, Canada in October 1846, it is clear that well-rounded athleticism was prioritized in the search for athletic champions at these ethnic festivals. Less demanding events sought to identify the "best-playing bagpiper" and the "best-dressed Highlander," along with the "best dancer of the Highland Fling in the Highland Costume," and "the best singer of a popular or ancient Gaelic song."

For the athletically-minded contestants, the most physically demanding events included the hurling of a putting stone, the tossing of a sledgehammer, leaping over a bar from a standing position, and the completion of a 400-yard foot race.

It's also worth acknowledging that the wearing of a familial tartan and kilt was an expectation, if not a requirement, as many advertisements for Highland Games included the guidance that it was "earnestly requested that all members appear as much in the costume of their forefathers as practicable."

It was no accident that the expression of Scottish ethnicity and cultural traditions became a geographical imperative during this era. The 19th century did much to establish the norms that shaped the modern North American conception of Scottish identity, and the event that did the most to aggressively push Scots out of their homeland and into North America's many states and provinces was the ongoing Highland Clearances, and especially its aggressive second phase.

Highland Games and Hippodromes

During the Highland Clearances, which began in approximately 1750 and reached their end at some point between 1860 and 1886 depending on which historical expert you solicit for an opinion, the reframing of landlord-tenant agreements in the Scottish Highlands, and the subsequent overcrowding of allocated crofting zones — or tenant-farming communities — led to the assisted evictions of many Highland families. These evictions were often packaged with the pre-paid resettlement of the evicted Scots in North America.

These scenarios were frequently interpreted as a betrayal of Scottish clansmen by their chiefs. Even though possession of a surname associated with a clan would later come with a presumption of shared descent from the chief of the clan, most clan-affiliated surnames were assumed as a sign of loyalty to the chief of whichever clan offered residency and protection in exchange for military service in times of clan-on-clan warfare, or when the clan chief pledged manpower in the support of a larger military endeavor.

This gradual and nonetheless thorough emptying of several districts of the Highlands into select regions of North America increased the presence and influence of a very pure Scottish identity and its cultural byproducts. It also resulted in claims to Scottish identity that have taken on a rather curious character as the passage of time has separated the descendants of these original waves of Scottish immigrants from the factors that prompted their migrations.

Just as important to note is how much the allure of claiming Scottish ancestry in North America has to do with its easy adoptability, along with the broad appeal of its outwardly exotic elements. To a great many people whose family lines were relocated principally to the United States and Canada in both the pre- and post-colonial eras, English ancestry has come to be perceived as ordinary, and consequently, as boring.

In comparison to English ancestry, Scottish identity comes with a connection to atypical styles of dress, an attention-grabbing accent (if not an entirely different language), and forms of cuisine and music that are seldom seen in North

America. The bagpipes are certainly an acquired sonic taste, and there is an element of bravery linked to displaying the popular styles of dress and consuming much of the food.

The willingness to be publicly observed while wearing a kilt, often construed as a skirt in North America, is as much a claim to bravery as it is a fashion statement for any man daring enough to be seen wearing one. Likewise, the eagerness to subject oneself to a type of food like haggis — an organ-meat casserole usually composed of a sheep's stomach containing pieces of the same sheep's heart, liver, and lungs — also requires an ample reserve of fearlessness.

Exotic components aside, one of the most appealing characteristics of Scottish ancestry is the historic connection created through clan membership, and all of the incentives that coincide with it. While the remaining vestige of the ancient Scottish clan system is a shadow of what it used to be, it is a system that still imparts a sense of instant belonging and kinship to the bearers of Scottish surnames, along with the right to display a clan's badge or coat of arms, and wear clothing bearing the clan's tartan.

This ability to forge an instantaneous sense of belonging to a specific European ethnic group — several of which still retain official clan chiefs recognized by the Court of the Lord Lyon — confers a strong sense of national identity to people with Scottish surnames, or to those who choose to identify with upstream family members who bore them.

While the ownership of a Scottish surname is certainly helpful, the adoption of a Scottish identity by most Americans and Canadians often requires little other than a discovery of some sliver of Scottish heritage, and the wearing of a product knitted from the appropriately colored spool of fabric.

Extending beyond this, the "new Scot" may ultimately purchase any of a dozen other items bearing the clan's crest or badge, each of which communicates that the bearer of those emblems has pledged a form of fealty to an ancient family that never needs to be proven through any action other than the outward display of the clan's approved artwork.

Highland Games and Hippodromes

All of this, combined with the fact that virtually all Scottish residents of Scotland speak either English or Scots — both of which are Germanic language offshoots — makes Scottish identity a very convenient guise for North Americans to slip into when the situation benefits them, and the adopter seldom risks any form of social embarrassment or cultural rejection for doing so.

In professional wrestling circles, the first wrestler to bring Scottish iconography before a fully global audience was Canadian grappler Roderick Toombs, who was far better known by his stage name of "Rowdy" Roddy Piper. Given the diversity of Toombs' genealogy, he becomes an ideal subject for detailing just how far a claim to a wholly Scottish ancestry is capable of stretching without snapping.

Roddy Piper's father was Stanley Baird Toombs, who was born in Ontario, Canada, and claimed Irish descent. By contrast, Piper's mother was born in the United States and claimed to be of Scottish descent.

Thanks to a Canadian census question that required residents to list what they believed the original races of their family members to have been, which in this case was closer to a question of ethnic identity, it is evident that Piper's grandfather was born in Ontario just like Piper's father Stanley, and also claimed to be of Irish descent, while Piper's paternal grandmother was born in the United States and professed herself to be of Scottish descent.

By contrast, Piper's maternal grandfather, Ernest Anderson, was born in New Zealand to two parents that were both legitimately Scottish, while his maternal grandmother Charlotte was born of two parents that were both from Germany.

In essence, if Piper's ancestry was determined solely by the birthplaces of his grandparents, it wouldn't be incorrect to identify him as half-Canadian, one-quarter American, and one-quarter New Zealander. However, this formula wouldn't represent a good-faith effort to understand the practical applications of ethnicity, and it would be more rational to credit Piper with being at least one-quarter Scottish.

More importantly, taking this overly simplistic approach would fail to account for what were likely some complex cultural elements that were at play within the Toombs family. It's plainly evident that *someone* in Roddy Piper's extended family — probably someone on his mother's side of the pedigree chart — emphasized an adherence to Scottish identity.

After all, while Roddy Piper's absence of a Scottish accent is obvious to anyone who ever listened to him talk — which is a promotional tactic he was well-versed in — and he appears to be at least two generations removed from an ancestor who was actually born on Scottish soil, it's quite rare that someone learns to play the bagpipes with as much skill as Piper clearly could without being steered toward the instrument by someone with an ethnically rooted incentive.

Bagpipe mastery aside, in lieu of bearing an authentic Scottish surname on a driver's license or passport, Piper's genetic credentials would place him well within the threshold required to claim what passes for a Scottish identity on the North American continent. Part of this may be owed to the fact that so many North Americans cherish their capacity to claim some modicum of Scottish ancestry that few are willing to police the practice.

In the world of professional wrestling, where exotic ethnic and national identities have been historically adopted for the sake of appealing to specific audience segments, the depiction of Roddy Piper as Scottish took on a distinctly different form from most of the cultural portrayals from the same era. This is evidenced through a brief analysis of Piper's role as one of world-famous wrestler Hulk Hogan's opponents during the latter's first transcendent World Wrestling Federation championship reign from the mid-1980s.

It wouldn't be entirely unreasonable to rank Piper as the most important foil for Hogan during the establishment of Hulkamania as a pop-cultural phenomenon, although proponents of Andre the Giant, Paul Orndorff, and Randy Savage could certainly make rational arguments in their respective favors.

Even so, for as much as the foundation of Hogan's championship reign was rooted in the dominance of an American superhero against U.S. foreign adversaries in the ring, the threat of Piper ostensibly scoring a victory for Scotland over the American champion was never introduced as a reason to support Hogan. This is markedly different from the moments when Hogan faced opponents who were either legitimately or falsely presented as representatives of the Soviet Union, Iran, Mongolia, Japan, Uganda, or even the French-speaking provinces of Canada.

Of the mainstream Scottish wrestling acts that emerged in the aftermath of the proliferation of the internet, which made it easier than ever for North Americans to embrace Scottish culture, acquire Scottish goods, and surround themselves with Scottish trinkets, The Highlanders and Drew McIntyre are noteworthy.

Seemingly due to the portrayal of Scots in the Academy-Award-winning 1995 film *Braveheart* as uncivilized, kilted primitives in comparison to the effete Englishmen who'd subjugated and exploited them, the depictions of Scots as savage, rebellious underdogs added to the attraction of identifying with them.

In particular, Drew Galloway — popularly known as Drew McIntyre — ultimately morphed into the epitome of the masculine Scot. As a tall wall of lean muscle, adorned in a kilt, who carried a literal Claymore sword to the ring with him, McIntyre resembled the idealized image of a Highland Games participant, dripping with all of the sex appeal of a model from the cover of a women's romance novel set in the Scottish Highlands.

Despite McIntyre's prominent presence as an authentic Scot on the truly global professional wrestling landscape of the early 21st century, many of the Highland conventions that he has brandished so effectively first took shape in the heart of the 19th century, when the pro wrestling industry was in its infancy. It was in the late 1800s and very early 1900s that the uniqueness of the Scottish immigrant experience helped to sculpt what pro wrestling as a whole would ultimately become, while leaving Caledonian fingerprints all over the mold of what would evolve into a lasting form of sports entertainment.

If it's impossible to fairly discuss the early explosion of professional wrestling's popularity without the contributions of Scottish athletes, then it is utterly unthinkable to appraise the topic without including the name of Donald Dinnie in the first sentence.

Dinnie was born in Birse, Scotland on July 10, 1837. Beginning in his early teens, Dinnie seemed to win every athletic competition he participated in, unsurprisingly excelling in the traditional slate of Highland sporting events, including *all* of the running, jumping, and throwing competitions.

In the process of touring his native land, Dinnie played an integral role in defining the very concept of a professional athlete in the mid-to-late 19th century. With ample prize money often advertised to be awarded to the winners of the individual events held at Highland Games throughout Scotland, it was probably considered unlikely, at least at first, that a single individual would emerge from amongst the Scots to sweep the first place positions in all events, thereby collecting *all* of the first place prize money for himself.

Still, this is precisely what Dinnie did throughout many years of touring his home country. The number of Highland Games events he is suspected to have won in his lifetime is estimated to have stretched as high as 11,000, translating into tens of thousands of pounds in earnings in an era when each pound carried the equivalent purchasing power of $160 U.S. dollars in 2020.

By devoting himself solely to the pursuit of athletic excellence, Dinnie was able to win prize money at these Caledonian festivals week after week, and year after year, for well over a decade. Understandably, the Scottish press was very interested in what sort of nutrition and training plan it took to transform Dinnie into an unbeatable physical marvel that haunted the nightmares of every other aspiring Highland athlete.

Donald Dinnie preparing to put a shot

"I just trained on hard work and oatmeal porridge," Dinnie would tell reporters several decades later. "I kent naething about what you call your scientific preparation of athletes. It may be well enough in its way, but I think a good deal of it is elaborate nonsense. With us laddies it was just porridge and milk all the time. When it wasn't porridge and milk it was oatcake and milk, with variations in the shape of neep (turnip) or kale brose. I got the hard work earning my living as a stone mason. In the dinner hour and in my spare time of an evening I was jumping or running, lifting weights, or taking dumbbell exercise. I'm a great believer in dumbbells, but even my play time meant hard work to practise, and get myself up to my best form."

The first major wrestling that Donald Dinnie indulged in seems to have occurred when he was approximately 25 years old. In October 1862 — over the course of winning 10 events and the grand prize at the Crossroads Highland Gathering — Dinnie won what was probably a Scottish backhold wrestling competition by defeating William Gilbert of Leochel.

Still, wrestling was not yet ubiquitous at such events. For example, September 1864 marked the first time that the Kincardine O'Neil Highland Gathering offered an open wrestling contest, "which excited a good deal of interest among the spectators" according to *The Aberdeen Journal*.

Dinnie was not present to partake in the wrestling of the day; he was busy dominating the action at the gathering of the Braemar Highland Society. It's perhaps owed to this relative paucity of opportunities to wrestle competitively that Dinnie's mastery of grappling did not reach an equivalent level to that of the other sports in which his explosive power always seemed to carry him to victory. There's also the matter of the different styles of wrestling contested in each locale coming into play.

The report of Dinnie's match results from the Bridge of Allan Games suggests as much, seeing as how he performed true to form by dominating all of the heavy throwing events, only to lose a wrestling bout to William Jamieson, "champion of England," according to *The Glasgow Daily Herald*.

To his credit, Jamieson had legitimately won several multi-round wrestling tournaments in England over more than a decade of wrestling activity at that point in his life. While he may not have been the wrestling champion of all England, Jamieson had competed in and won single-day wrestling events in his native country that stretched to anywhere from four to six rounds.

Not only did Jamieson have more overall competitive wrestling experience than Dinnie, but he likely had a greater degree of sport-specific endurance than the Scotsman, making it easier than expected to outmaneuver him and trap him. Most Scottish backhold bouts lasted one minute or less, since they were usually decided by a simple throw or takedown. Other wrestling events that necessitated a pinfall to conclude them could extend for several minutes to even hours.

The results of the Vale of Leven National Games held in September 1866 at Alexandria, Dumbartonshire, are worth evaluating primarily because they offer a clear description of Dinnie's style of wrestling at the time, and also because they provide evidence that Dinnie occasionally participated in the Highland Fling dance competition.

The notion that Dinnie — whose muscular size and development was practically unmatched for his era — was apparently nimble enough to outdance competitors with far less weight on their frames, speaks to the extraordinary level of agility, grace, and body control he must also have possessed.

Following a dancing demonstration that landed him in second place, Dinnie reportedly won all of the throwing competitions before manhandling both William Taft and William McKenzie on his way to a first-place finish in wrestling.

"Dinnie overthrew the two others successively, falling up them with a crash that might have settled ordinary men for life," stated *The Glasgow Daily Mail*. "His style of wrestling is to remain with his feet firmly on the ground and overthrow his man by sheer strength."

Judging from this description of Dinnie's approach to wrestling and his prior loss at the hands of Jamieson, it's also possible that Dinnie was lacking regular wrestling competitors of a world class quality — at least in Scotland — and therefore grappled down to the level of his competition. In most of his wrestling interactions, Dinnie was able to bully his way through the field simply by leaning on his overwhelming power advantage.

To clarify the point, it's more likely than not that grappling down to the level of his competition for Dinnie meant that most of his early wrestling training occurred in the company of his brothers, Lubin and Montague, who often wrestled and competed alongside him at Highland events.

The records reflect that Dinnie's brothers, who were also masons, were capable of putting up respectable power displays of their own. *The Dundee Courier* printed the results of a hammer throwing competition in June of 1865, at which Donald Dinnie won the event with a toss of more than 92 feet, while Lubin finished in third place with a respectable throw of 81 feet.

Similarly, the results from the 1867 Highland Games at Aboyne confirm that all three Dinnies were in attendance. Donald dominated the overall scoring by winning nine of the 10 events he entered. If Lubin and Montague competed in any events other than wrestling, they did not place among the top three finishers in any of them. However, the Dinnie brothers swept the podium positions in wrestling, with *The Aberdeen Journal* noting that they "conquered all other competitors."

Dinnie was not alone in falling prey to stylistic weaknesses when venturing into unfamiliar terrain. For example, when Dinnie found himself at a Highland-themed wrestling event in June of 1867, it was reported that confusion reigned at the outset, "arising from the fact that the competitors coming from far distant places had each his own set of rules, which, being different from each other, it was impossible for the judge to reconcile in every case with his own opinions."

The Dumbarton Herald and County Advertiser covered the event, and detailed how Dinnie overcame a Cumberland wrestler by the name of Collins, who objected to the way Dinnie broke his hold, which was an infraction of the rules according to Collins' understanding. In order to satisfy all parties, three falls were required until Dinnie finally conquered Collins to the contentment of all onlookers.

However, in the finals, Dinnie had serious difficulty defeating a wrestler by the name of Francis from the Scottish town of Hawick. Despite weighing less than eight stone — or 112 pounds — the "suppleness and tact" of Francis enabled him to make it all the way to the finals of the tournament, where he challenged Dinnie courageously before finally being thrown.

The fact that Dinnie could be threatened by undersized wrestlers in his own country should not be construed as an accusation that Dinnie was an altogether unskilled wrestler. Even against Scottish competitors whose power rivaled Dinnie's own, like James Fleming of Tullymet, Dinnie was often dominant. The duo traded victories in the throwing events during the games of the Dundee Highland Society, but once the grappling began, the much older Dinnie had a clear edge.

"The wrestling created immense amusement, and displayed in a most unmistakable manner Dinnie's strength," reported *The Aberdeen Journal.* "All comers were by him quickly disposed of, and even Fleming was worsted in the briefest possible space."

In a matter of a few years, even though the variety of wrestling conducted at Highland Games events may not have been identical across all of the gatherings, it had rapidly become one of the most popular spectator events of these Highland festivals, if not *the* most popular event outright. While attendees of the games were curious to see the winners of all the Highland events — athletic or otherwise — the desire to see who could physically dismantle their opponents in legalized combat quickly became the highlight of the competitions.

It was in 1869 that Dinnie was advertised to appear at the Great Northern Games in Newcastle, England, and the novelty of having the great Scottish athlete set to participate in the region's wrestling competition merited significant attention. In fact, the article advertising the Northern Games captured the attention of readers with the promise of "Newcastle Wrestling" as a headline.

"Donald Dinnie, the celebrated champion athlete, the winner of upwards of 1,000 prizes, will be present in full Highland costume and contend for the majority of the prizes, including the wrestling," teased *The Newcastle Daily Chronicle*.

On the first day of the Great Northern Games, the status of Dinnie as something akin to a special attraction was made evident by the formal debut of the caber toss as an official event in Newcastle upon Tyne. The contest required the end-over-end hurling of a wooden pole weighing at least 100 pounds, and at least 16 feet in length.

Evidently, the event had been added more so to display Dinnie's hitherto matchless might and unique Highland sports prowess than as a vehicle for true competition, as only one Englishman even dared to contend with the specially trimmed and extremely unwieldy tree when it was presented to the assembled competitors for tossing.

"Jamieson, the celebrated wrestler, accompanied by Dinnie, was the first to compete, and after several unsuccessful efforts he succeeded in throwing it over," observed *The Newcastle Daily Journal*. "Dinnie then took hold of the pole and tossed it over with apparent ease. A heavier and longer pole was then brought into the ring, and Jamieson made several attempts to throw it over, but failed. Donald, after three unsuccessful efforts, at last succeeded, and was rewarded with loud and general applause, thereby winning the prize."

Dinnie also reigned supreme in the throwing of the four-stone weight to successfully conclude his first day of competition. This was fortunate for him, because the next day's events exposed Dinnie's relative lack of all-purpose wrestling skills when he was plunged into an experienced pool of 64 grapplers who hailed primarily from Northern England.

In the first round, Dinnie enjoyed a considerable weight advantage over Jasper Edmonds of Low Walker, and *The Daily Chronicle* averred that the size disparity alone was enough to cause "much amusement" amongst the observers.

Dinnie disposed of Edmonds promptly when he "lifted his man carefully up and laid him down on the grass."

The degree of difficulty surged in the second round. Dinnie was matched against William Pearson, who managed to take the Scottish strongman down to the ground. The crowd seemed to think Pearson would be skilled enough to complete the fall on Dinnie, but Dinnie "settled his man, turning him over by sheer force."

Dinnie with a belt of medals adorning his waist

In the round of 16, Dinnie was matched with John Yeates of Shankhouse, and *The Daily Chronicle* described them as being "a well matched pair in appearance," but stopped short of intimating that they might be of anything approaching equivalent skill levels. As a veteran of multiple Northern Games, Yeates had a habit of making admirable showings before falling in the latter rounds as the prowess of his opponents increased. Against Dinnie, he seemed to have little difficulty, and this was a point that the reporting of *The Daily Chronicle* seemed to stress.

"So far as wrestling was concerned, the Highland champion could make little defence against the play of Yeates, and the latter won an easy victory," concluded the *The Chronicle*.

Following up on his victory over the legend, Yeates fell swiftly to William Jamieson — the prior English conqueror of Dinnie in wrestling — in the quarterfinal round. Jamieson eventually advanced to the finals and defeated John Emmerson of Weardale three falls to one to win the "open to the world" wrestling championship of the Great Northern Games.

In defense of Dinnie, he was preoccupied with other events of the day; the Highland champion won both the 17-pound shot put and the running high jump; he heaved the heavy ball more than 41 feet, and cleared a bar set five feet and four inches from the ground "in capital style." For good measure, Dinnie also "threw the 20-foot caber in splendid style" even though no official contest was underway, as this final feat was seemingly done solely for the sake of entertaining the crowd.

The Newcastle Courant printed an editorial specifically about the wrestling event, and included the detail that there were 4,000 spectators present. The publication also seemed to use Dinnie's failure to advance to the quarterfinal round of the wrestling tournament as an opportunity to crow about the skill of wrestlers in Northern England.

"... if any district should be prouder than another of its wrestling powers, it is the counties of Cumberland, Westmoreland, Northumberland, and Durham," insisted the editorial's unnamed author. "Donald Dinnie, the Highland athlete, entered the lists with our local men, but even his

Herculean strength had to yield to their superior skill. Still Dinnie is a remarkable man. Standing about six feet in height, and weighing over 15 stones, he is one of the best built men which any country ever produced, while his agility is almost beyond comprehension."

Curiously, it seems that Dinnie's identity as a Highlander was not universally agreed upon, at least according to a few finicky sources. In 1863, Dinnie was described in *The Manchester Guardian* as "a sore thorn in the sides of the Highlanders, as he is not of them, being a modest-looking Lowland lad, firmly knit, and evidently a man of vast power of arm."

Dinnie's hometown of Birse, which is a few miles from the more populous yet still small town of Aboyne, lies squarely in an area of Aberdeenshire that is east of the traditional Highland-Lowland divide. Consequently, it would be fair to classify Dinnie as a Lowlander based on its precise geography.

However, if there was any clash over the way the term applied to Dinnie, his dominance of Highland competitions and the seeming unanimity that 19th century Scots seemed to employ in appointing Highland customs as representing true Scottish culture and character made Dinnie a de facto Highlander and national hero. This became especially true when Dinnie was promoted as his nation's foremost athletic export during his first tour of North America.

2 – Scottish Hercules

By the time Donald Dinnie made landfall in the United States from Scotland in 1870, he was a bonafide legend in his native land. In fact, he had already won 15 consecutive national Highland Games championships, and didn't appear to be in any serious jeopardy of losing his claim to the throne.

One of the first public announcements that Dinnie would be traveling to the United States was linked to his participation in the annual gathering of the Caledonian Club of Detroit, Michigan, for which the waterbound site of Belle Isle Park had been selected.

"It may be interesting to the public to learn something about the wonderful performances of this modern Hercules," invited the July 10, 1870 edition of *The Detroit Free Press*. "He was born at Aboyne, Aberdeenshire in 1838, and commenced his career as an athlete in 1857. Since then, he has gained upward of fifteen hundred prizes, one thousand of them being for throwing the hammer, putting the stone, tossing the caber, running, leaping, wrestling, etc."

The article went on to credit Dinnie with 62 silver medals and "the champion gold medal awarded by the Glasgow Celtic Society for throwing the hammer in 1867." The writer also elaborated that 40 of those medals were championship medals that required their possessor to hold them for three successive years before they became the honoree's permanent property.

"[Dinnie] is acknowledged to be one of the best specimens of muscular development that has ever appeared in Scotland," gushed the article, providing a thorough physical description of the great champion. "The following are some of his dimensions: height, six feet one inch; round the chest, forty-five and a half inches; arm, fifteen and a half inches; thigh, twenty-five and a half inches; weight, two hundred and ten pounds."

The *Free Press* concluded by listing Dinnie's personal bests in all manner of lifts, throws, and leaps.

The writer of the article was apparently off by at least one year in ascribing major athletic achievements to Dinnie. However, if the estimate of the quantity of Dinnie's trophy collection at the time was even remotely accurate, Dinnie would have needed to have averaged 100 major victories every year for the previous 15 years.

Donald Dinnie at age 40

Dinnie's U.S. introduction included his best results in nine different throwing and leaping events while making no real mention of his wrestling prowess. While tallying this many victories may sound like an impossibility, recognizing that an athlete of Dinnie's caliber and standing would have been fully capable of winning 10 or more Highland Games events within a single outing, combined with his tireless streak of activity, the 1,500-victory claim becomes far more realistic than it initially sounds.

All of this information came by way of a standard press release that was replicated in several Midwestern newspapers, including *The Daily Milwaukee News*, ahead of Dinnie's early August appearance in Wisconsin.

As would be expected, Dinnie was the star attraction of the August 4 games held at the 5th annual picnic of the Chicago Caledonian Club. *The Chicago Tribune* described it as a national celebration, although doubtless the number of American-born Scots outnumbered the natives amongst the attendees.

The promotion of Dinnie as a "Scottish Hercules" in most of the press clippings that heralded his arrival seemingly left quite a few attendees feeling disappointed when they eventually laid eyes on him. *The Tribune* writer described how Dinnie was "hailed with applause," yet many of the fans "expressed disappointment in not finding him an overgrown giant in form and being."

"Donald is not a bull-necked gladiator, but at first sight presents himself as a somewhat slender-looking man for an athlete," described *The Tribune*. "This impression is quickly corrected as soon as he divests himself of the 'garb of old Gaul,' and enters the lists in a primitive kind of costume which is a very slight improvement on what Mother Eve might have fashioned for her goodman. He is not of such dimensions as the popular notion had fashioned for him, but his form is a perfect model of symmetry and manly beauty. He has no superabundant flesh — every muscle and fiber being formed for use, as was exemplified in the ease and grace with which all his movements were executed."

In these descriptions, Dinnie was depicted similarly to how Eugen Sandow — the "Father of Modern Bodybuilding"

— would be characterized years later, although Dinnie predated him on the world scene by several decades.

Dinnie didn't even come close to equaling any of his advertised high marks during his outing at the Chicago Caledonian Club's picnic, but he still put considerable distance between himself and any of the other competitors in attendance, who were seemingly there to serve as a control group against which Dinnie's prowess could be compared.

As for the events of the day, Dinnie apparently won every contest he entered, and had little trouble separating himself comfortably from the also-rans in most of them. He hurled the hammer 83 feet, which was nearly 26 feet further than the runner up. His 34-foot shot put effort was seven feet better than the throw of his nearest rival. He also dominated the caber toss as the only man present who could even lift the 17-foot tree, which needed to be cut to 14 feet for the remaining men to make respectable attempts at tossing it.

Living up to his reputation of all-round athletic dominance, Dinnie won nine total events, including every throwing, running, and leaping event, with the exception of the pole vault, which he likely did not enter. This assumption is based on the fact that a loss by Dinnie in any event would have undoubtedly been chronicled.

For example, when Dinnie ultimately *did* lose his first event after arriving in the U.S. — in this instance, the hop, skip, and jump competition held during the 12th annual games of the Caledonian Club of Harrisburg, Pennsylvania — *The Morning Patriot* was right there to report it. The newspaper added that a knee injury contributed to Dinnie's loss, and summarily prompted him to bow out of all subsequent events.

This injury proved to be merely a minor setback for Dinnie. A few weeks later at the Caledonian Club Games in New York, the de facto national championship amongst the Highland competitors in the United States at the time, Dinnie was back to being an overpowering force.

In front of a Jones' Wood crowd that ranged from 10,000 to 15,000 in estimated attendees, the 33-year-old Dinnie put on a show in the middle of Manhattan. He won the shot put events with both the heavy stone and light stone, and also won at tossing the heavy hammer and light hammer. He then won the short race and the running high leap, while finishing second in the hop, skip, and jump, and third in the long jump.

The New York Times commented that Dinnie refused to participate in the caber toss, apparently on the grounds that the 16-foot caber used for the games was too light to be worth his time. Even though Dinnie conceded placement in the official caber-tossing event to the other competitors, he did inspire awe in the attendees by lifting a 27-foot caber, being the only man of sufficient strength to do so, simply to demonstrate that he could easily have won the official caber toss if he had been in the mood to compete.

None of Dinnie's appearances during his inaugural North American tour indicate that he spent any time wrestling. However, in 1872, one competitor seemed keen on the idea of coaxing Dinnie out onto the wrestling carpet. Charles Bell, of Saginaw, Michigan, went so far as to publish a public challenge to Dinnie in the press, which received the following reply:

Mr. Campbell,

Sir: Yours to hand. In reply I may state that I am sorry it is no use of my trying to wrestle at present, or for some months to come, as my hand is entirely useless in taking hold; but if Bell is reasonable I will come over next summer and wrestle him in his *own style* for any sum. I expect to get a match with McLennan at hammer-throwing next summer, so it will be more inducement to cross the ocean. If you can, possibly get up a match with Bell at that same time, as it is unreasonable of him to challenge a lame man. I thank you much for offering to back me so well, and I trust you may be able to get a match with him for next season. I shall be willing to allow him one fall the start out of the five, in the Cumberland style.

You can make public use of this if you wish.

Yours respectfully, in haste,

Donald Dinnie

P.S. — We sail for "Auld Scotis" tomorrow.

Highland Games and Hippodromes

True to his word, Dinnie did participate in some wrestling during his 1873 return visit to the United States, albeit against James Fleming over the course of a long athletic duel in St. Joseph, Missouri. After easily defeating Fleming in the hammer throw, but losing to him in the cumulative distance of seven hurls of the shot put despite having the single longest throw of the group, Dinnie settled in to wrestle Fleming "Scottish style," and bested him in consecutive falls.

After the wrestling concluded, Dinnie apparently wished to leave no doubt as to who was the stronger of the two men. To accomplish this, Dinnie demonstrated what amounted to a 152-pound dumbbell snatch with one arm, holding the weight over his head for 30 full seconds before allowing it to crash to the ground while the crowd applauded him.

"Some idea of the muscular force required in the accomplishment of the act may be learned when we state that ordinary men had difficulty in moving the dumbbell from off the ground," explained *The St. Joseph Gazette*.

The pairing of Dinnie and Fleming in Missouri was no accident, as Fleming had emerged as the primary challenger to Dinnie in strength-based competitions in Scotland, and was one of very few men who could rival him in that department. This being the case, the pair frequently served as the advertised headliners of Scottish Games events in their home country, and in several instances, showcase events were often reserved exclusively for the two of them to compete in, which permitted the other athletes to amass some victories in the standard events.

This being the case, Dinnie and Fleming were often limited to competing in only the throwing contests, which were turned into a sideshow for the two men to thrill the assembled crowds with their power. Likewise, they were excluded from the open wrestling tournaments and were *only* permitted to wrestle each other in what amounted to the true wrestling championship matches contested at these gatherings, which were isolated and separated from the formal tournaments.

Highland Games and Hippodromes

Or, to phrase it in a way that could be understood contemporarily, the open wrestling tournament at these Caledonian events served as the undercard to the featured main-event bouts between Dinnie and Fleming, in what amounted to the headlining grappling clashes at these Highland-themed gatherings.

One of the men that Dinnie was certainly on the radar of when it came to both wrestling contests and the customary Highland events was Duncan C. Ross. When Donald Dinnie issued an open challenge to any man in the world in a series of athletic contests, Ross responded from his home in Toronto in November of 1878 with a public acceptance of that challenge.

"If Dinnie will put up a deposit, I will arrange a match, to consist of nine competitions, I to select four and he four, the ninth to be decided upon by the toss of a coin, for $1,000 to $2,000," said Ross. "I will allow him $200 expenses to come to America, the amount he has offered me to go to Scotland, he knowing that on account of some financial transactions, I will not go to Scotland, but will meet him at Ottawa, Canada or New York."

Dinnie took a full month to reply, but when his response hit the news desks, it incited great excitement on both sides of the Atlantic. In summation, Dinnie agreed to meet Ross in New York during the first week of July 1879. He also named all nine events in which the two men would compete: Throwing and putting the 56-pound stone, throwing the heavy hammer, throwing the light hammer, putting the heavy stone and light stone, tossing the caber, running 100 yards with or without hurdles, and performing a running high leap.

Much to the disappointment of many Scots, the proposed 1879 athletic showdown between Dinnie and Ross did not come to pass; it would be a few more years until the memorable clash between them would take place. By that time, Ross had made significant strides toward bridging whatever gap was perceived to have existed between himself and Dinnie with respect to who the greatest living athlete of Scottish descent truly was.

Highland Games and Hippodromes

The rise of Duncan C. Ross as a competitor worthy of Dinnie's time proves that the usefulness of Scottish culture and the Highland Games in advancing athletic talent to a world-class level applied just as well outside of Scotland as it did within it, and whether the Scots involved in those games were true Scottish natives, or were raised overseas.

The circumstances of Duncan Ross' birth would become a matter of conjecture later in his sports career, and betrays a certain sensitivity surrounding questions of legitimacy in adopting Scottish identity. Depending on the year and location of Ross' appearances, as well as who he was competing against, he would be varyingly identified as a Scot, a Turk, a Canadian, or an American.

The identity of Ross as a "Turk" is entirely owed to the common claim that he had been born in Scutari (Üsküdar), Turkey while the Crimean War was in progress, and while his father was stationed overseas. In order for this story to be true, Duncan's mother would obviously have needed to have been living either with or near to her husband while the latter was serving in a forward area; it was not uncommon for the British military to allow wives to assist their military husbands by performing non-combat duties during times of war.

For whatever it's worth, there were multiple occasions during his career that Ross would insist the tale of his birth being circulated, which stated that he was born within "The Gateway to Asia," was false.

"In our issue of November 16, we introduced [Ross] to our readers, and we, in the course of our chat with the Champion of America, elicited all the facts bearing upon his performances in the land of his adoption," printed *The Australian Star* in November of 1889. "We may, however, again state that Ross, who holds the proud title of all-round champion athlete of the world, is a Scotchman, 33 years of age, and was born at Burnside Cottage, Possil-road, Glasgow, and *not*, as some newspapers have it, at Scutari, in Turkey."

Seemingly, whenever Ross had control of his own life narrative, he would contend that he was born in Glasgow,

Scotland, even though by all accounts he only spent a short segment of his childhood there before his family completed a permanent relocation to Ontario, Canada.

Regardless of the precise location at which Ross entered the world, the fact that he was born on March 16, 1855 to Scottish parents is considered an uncontested fact. Furthermore, the assertion that he became the North American Scottish community's answer to Donald Dinnie is likely to be rejected only out of spite by Ross' detractors, of whom there would eventually be legions.

In fairness, their refusal to heap equivalent praise upon Ross as they would on Dinnie is arguably well-warranted given how Ross's name would eventually be uttered contemptuously, and at times justly, after he came to symbolize all of the worst aspects of the pro wrestling industry.

Before he was being disparaged for disgracing wrestling, Ross was a young man whose climb to the top of the athletic world was remarkably similar to that of Dinnie's. Standing just over six-feet tall and sporting a well-muscled physique, Ross was seemingly dominant at whatever strength events he entered against his fellow Scots at Highland Games held throughout Canada and the Northern United States. The earliest reports of Ross' exploits show him in his early 20s winning hammer-throwing events, putting contests, and even caber tosses at tournaments held throughout the region.

To the extent that the path of Ross' development diverged from Dinnie's, it was caused by Ross' willingness to offer or accept physical challenges for practically any competitive event in which strength, stamina, or agility were being measured. For example, in February 1879, Ross withdrew from a 26-hour walking duel with William Miller in Baltimore after completing *only* 40 miles worth of walking, while Miller went on to complete a grand total of 107 miles.

The withdrawal from Ross was only surprising because he had completed a 54-hour walk against Miller on the same course just two weeks prior. Ahead of that event, Ross was described as a YMCA instructor of athletic exercises in

Baltimore. Coverage of this event also saw Ross labeled as a native of Glasgow, Scotland, who was a holder of 33 gold and silver medals that he had earned "in Caledonian field games." It was a tally that was a far cry from that of Donald Dinnie's, but Ross was only getting started.

The same reports described Ross as "weighing fully 200 pounds," although he officially weighed in at 184 pounds for his first ironman walking duel, and would tip the scales at just 177 pounds before the rematch two weeks later.

Regardless, Ross lost both walking events to Miller, and quickly engaged in what would become his habit of leveling public accusations against the organizers of any major events at which he tasted defeat. More than a few newspapers printed Ross' complaint that both walking events had been "frauds," and that the $500 purse that he and Miller had been competing for had been "a myth." He also threatened a lawsuit against organizer Major Ferguson for unfairly dividing the proceeds from the events.

In some of the reports of the walking contests, Ross was described as the "champion athlete of Canada," in contrast to Miller, who was simply said to be "the wrestler."

The fact that Scottish identity was like a veil that Ross could easily slip in and out of was evident at the "International Athletic Contest" in Baltimore's Darley Park in May of that same year. Ross and his partner E.W. Johnston were introduced as the Scottish team, and they competed against the Irish team of James Daly and John Maloney for "the championship of the United States."

The 21-event competition concluded after only 19 events due to the insurmountable margin that Ross and Johnston had established over their Irish opponents in events like hammer throwing, and the triple jump. Ironically, wrestling was one of the two events that was cancelled, along with the half-mile run.

By the fall of 1879, Ross was engaging one-on-one athletic contests with a heavy emphasis on wrestling, including a series of bouts against James Daly. In Hamilton, Ontario, both men were required to grapple in "Irish, Scotch, and English" styles after the pair finished throwing a hammer and shot-putting three different weights, and then posting their best possible marks at the high jump and long jump.

Later that month, Ross defeated Daly in a five-fall, five-style wrestling invitational for $1,000 and a wrestling championship of an unspecified title. Ross won the first fall in catch-as-catch-can style, only to lose the next two falls to Daley using the Cumberland and collar-and-elbow techniques. Battling from behind, Ross leveled the score by winning the Scotch-style event, and then won the deciding Greco-Roman fall to take home the money and the offered title belt.

Ross continued to wrestle with greater frequency, and also introduced wrestling to some of the Caledonian events of North America in bouts that were indistinguishable from the typical pro wrestling challenge matches of the era. In effect, rather than hosting invitational tournaments in the Scottish backhold style, Ross would use the Highland Games as a backdrop for him to hold one-on-one bouts in front of crowds that exceeded those that could be contained by comparatively smaller venues like local gathering halls and theaters.

Moreover, by appearing as the sole Scottish wrestler in one-on-one bouts waged in front of large audiences that were composed primarily of individuals who self-identified as Scots, Ross was able to effectively leverage his ethnicity far more masterfully than many other wrestlers of the era, as he could always count on huge numbers of Scots to be present and supportive of him at these gatherings.

As a case in point, *The New York Times* expressed a great deal of interest in the conclusion to a match between Ross and Daly held on August 24, 1880 in Providence, Rhode Island. As the featured attraction of a Scottish games event hosted by the Providence Caledonian Club, Ross and Daly waged a five-fall war aboard a boat seated on the calm waters of the lake at Park Garden. It was a vessel that had previously been featured in a presentation of Gilbert and Sullivan's *HMS Pinafore*, which had debuted just two years earlier in 1878.

A bout that had been intended to last as many as five falls only lasted three, and not because either Ross or Daly had dominated the action and captured three straight falls. Instead, it was due to the outrageous ending to the Scotch-style fall, after the Irish and Greco-Roman rounds had concluded with the score tied at one fall apiece.

Duncan C. Ross bares his chest

"After brief skirmishing, both men struggled over the edge of the boat and sank beneath the surface of the water, amid intense excitement," highlighted *The Times*. "Both appeared in a few seconds, and as Ross reached a plank thrust out to save him, Daly caught him by the foot and sought to drag him back. Ross struck him violently in the face, and Daly retaliated with vigor before they were lifted out. Both men were greatly excited, and Daly sustained an injury to his leg which prevented his return to the carpet. The referee refused to make any decision, and the contest was postponed."

Instead of simply disqualifying both men or ruling the bout a draw, the match between Ross and Daly was resumed three days later in front of an impressive assemblage of 4,000 onlookers, with the continuation of the Scotch-style fall that had seen both men attempt to drown one another.

"Daly struggled hard to gain the mastery, and at times it seemed as though he would succeed, but Ross' great muscular strength, combined with extreme agility, carried the day, and he soon had the Irish giant on his back," printed *The Boston Globe*.

Then, when Daly rallied to take the fourth fall, Ross recovered the momentum to win the final round, which was another round contested in Scotch-style.

"At the close, Ross put Daly on his shoulder and tried to hold him, but the latter squirmed out of the situation and got Ross on his back," added *The Globe*. "The Scotchman made an almost superhuman effort, and quick as lightning, turned the tables, holding Daly down, despite his efforts to escape, until the umpire called time."

Just days later, Ross wrote a letter to *The Boston Globe* in which he boasted that he had "not yet met with defeat" in any of the matches he had competed in, and was "willing to wrestle any wrestler in the world" with the sum of $500 to be awarded to the winner. He also signed the letter "Duncan C. Ross, Heavy Weight Champion," although he neglected to specify precisely what he was claiming to be the champion of.

If Ross was positioning himself to be the all-styles heavyweight wrestling champion of the world, that illusion was shattered during his very next outing on the mat.

Just four days after his challenge was printed in *The Boston Globe*, Ross had the same publication reporting how he was defeated by Henry Dufur at Riley's Opera House in Marlboro, Massachusetts.

Dropping the first fall to Dufur by way of a grapevine hold that was transitioned into a hiplock, Ross' frustrations grew ever greater during the second fall. Failing to secure a fall

Highland Games and Hippodromes

against Dufur despite grabbing his neck and taking him down several times, "Ross threw off his jacket and refused to wear it any longer." This action apparently provoked a ruling from the referee, who allowed Ross to continue competing without the jacket, as wearing it "was not stipulated in the agreement."

Now grappling without the presumed inconvenience of a cumbersome jacket, Ross took Dufur down and turned him with a "double neck lock." When Dufur attempted to break the hold by bridging out of it, "the bridge was broken by Ross raising Dufur from the carpet and throwing him down with much force, winning the second fall in ten minutes."

The men traded the next two falls, and after Dufur tallied the final fall, Ross immediately challenged Dufur to a rematch. This was followed by another published invitation for a match, presenting Ross as a notoriously poor loser in a way that was not unlike his responses to losses in sports contests outside of wrestling.

Expressing that he was "a stranger in the states" even though he had clearly spent several months of each of the prior three years in the U.S., Ross proposed New York, Providence, and Montreal as potential locations for a rematch between the two. A rematch in Marlboro was out of the question to Ross, who suggested that poor officiating he had received in Marlboro contributed to his loss to Dufur when he said "the treatment I received does not warrant my return."

Further evidence to the fact that championship claims of the day were remarkably flexible is the fact that Ross still insisted on titling himself as "Heavy Weight Champion" in his latest letters, even though Dufur was now claiming the title of "champion collar-and-elbow wrestler of the world." The outcome of their rematch would cast even greater doubt upon who the true champion was.

The Buffalo Daily Republic reported that on October 11, 1880, "Scottish champion" Duncan C. Ross bested Dufur for $500 and the championship belt after Ross "secured two catch-as-catch-can falls and a fair side hold fall" to win the best-of-five bout.

Highland Games and Hippodromes

The numerous variations in wrestling styles and the lack of homogeneity in the competitions gifted wrestlers and other athletes with considerable leeway when making title claims. For example, while Ross may not have been the most popularly recognized world heavyweight wrestling champion, he could still claim supremacy in different styles of wrestling, cite his undisputed championships as an all-around athlete, or situationally claim to be the champion of Canada, America, or the Scottish people.

As a case in point, one month after Ross' victory of Dufur, Donald Dinnie challenged him to "a grand international athletic contest for the championship of the world." Without learning of the specifics, it's unknown whether this proposed duel would have included any wrestling whatsoever. Moreover, when *The San Francisco Chronicle* reported of Dinnie's challenge to Ross' world title, the staff of the paper admitted to their own confusion, stemming from their belief that William Miller was the acknowledged world champion of athletics, even though many East Coast publications applied that title to either Ross or Dinnie at the time.

The one public boast from Ross that Dinnie seemed to take major exception to was the open challenge Ross issued in October 1880 to any man who fancied himself a champion of "Scotch wrestling." Dinnie, who at times seemed like he couldn't have cared any less about how the balance of his wrestling skills were assessed, was notoriously protective of his reputation as an elite Scottish-style grappler.

"In the first place, I accept his challenge at Scotch wrestling, and, as he is only a beginner in the athletic way, I will allow him two falls start out of nine, and will meet him in New York if he allows reasonable expenses," wrote Dinnie. "I also wish to inform him that he can have the same start out of any nine heavy athletic feats for which he is so renowned. A reply will be punctually attended to by Donald Dinnie."

In response, Ross offered that he would "wrestle any man in the world if a proper forfeit is put up," while adding that he did not believe that Dinnie would return to the U.S.

and accept his challenge. What's interesting about this reply is that wrestling had little to do with the original challenge presented to Dinnie by Ross, as their budding rivalry had more to do with establishing who was the best athlete of Scottish descent on either side of the Atlantic Ocean.

When Dinnie and Ross eventually did cross paths, wrestling became a fixture of their meetings, either as an adjunct to a series of other athletic events, or as an alternative means of determining who was the better man between them. Ross was still busy battling Henry Dufur in December 1880, and a rematch between the two underscored the extent to which the winners of these "world championship" bouts were determined primarily by the style and order of the wrestling conducted during each evening.

The New York Times reported that during an early December rematch between the pair in Fall River, Massachusetts, Dufur won "a prize belt, the championship of the world, $400, and a special purse of $200." Dufur seized the victory by winning two collar-and-elbow falls and one side-hold fall, and Ross won both of the catch-as-catch-can falls.

The obvious inference is that Ross could just as easily have left Fall River with the money and the world championship if only he was as adept at either of the other two wrestling styles as he had been in catch-as-catch-can wrestling, or if he had been fortunate enough to get more catch-as-catch-can falls added to the agenda.

Eventual disclosures from pro wrestling whistleblowers would confirm that this deduction was not only true, but factored into the planning of each match for the sake of reputational protection.

Later that month, on December 18, Ross appeared at a benefit event for the Boston Baseball Club in the role of a strongman attraction who would "elevate the dumbbells against all comers." Then he took a step down in competition to once again wrestle J.C. Daly at the Infantry Hall in Providence, Rhode Island.

The bout lasted through four of its five falls, although it's arguable that Ross won every fall that was held; *The Boston Globe* reporter insisted that Daly was awarded the second fall on a technicality "but did not win it." Apparently, Daly was overwhelmed by frustration while being physically manhandled by Ross, and began to act erratically.

"During the third bout, Daly lost his temper and struck the referee because the latter refused to make a decision in his favor," added *The Globe*. "Ross, provoked beyond endurance by Daly's disgraceful actions and talk, sprang at Daly and struck him in turn. The two wrestlers then sprang for each other, and the great audience surged toward the platform to interfere, while thirty policemen, who were detailed at the hall, at the word of command sprang onto the platform, ranged themselves across it, and drew their clubs ready to repel the expected attack of the crowd."

The presence of so many armed policemen quieted the rioters, and when the match continued, Daly pummeled Ross with "several severe blows with his fist." Ross retaliated in kind, and when Daly rose from the carpet and attempted to punch Ross, the police intervened. *The Globe* concluded its coverage by admitting that the "disgraceful affair" had "caused great excitement."

Duncan Ross had very quickly catapulted himself to prominence on multiple sporting fronts, and a grander victory than he ever imagined was on the horizon. Unfortunately, the way Ross would choose to conduct himself in the aftermath of his successes would result in all of his conquests being warily regarded as being too good to be true.

3 – Champion Athlete of the World

Duncan Ross opened 1881 by wrestling Henry Dufur to yet another draw in Providence. Ross then traveled to New York to face Edwin Bibby in a catch-as-catch-can bout for what was billed as a bout for the "championship of America." With the best-of-five contest knotted at two falls apiece, Bibby won the 12-minute final fall, at which point Ross predictably "protested against the decision of the referee, Ed Plummer."

The follow-up coverage by *The New York Times* framed the victory by Bibby as a massive upset, owed primarily to the size disparity between the two men. After describing Ross as a giant who stood just over 6'1" and weighed 205 pounds, *The Times* portrayed Bibby as a comparatively diminutive 5'6" and 155 pounds. Undeniably, it was an embarrassing loss to suffer for a man like Ross, who frequently labeled himself as the heavyweight champion of all athletic pastimes, only to be cleanly defeated by a man he outweighed by 50 full pounds.

Unbeknownst to anyone at the time was the fact that the American catch-as-catch-can championship won by Bibby would quickly achieve an unsurpassed level of prestige in the United States, and would rapidly evolve into North America's most coveted "world wrestling championship."

Ross' next major bout — at the Athenaeum of St. Paul, Minnesota against Clarence Whistler of Kansas City — was described by *The Saint Paul Globe* as a "miserable fiasco." After tugging Ross down to the carpet and holding him there for one hour and 35 minutes without securing a pinfall, Whistler was awarded the opening-fall victory when "Ross declared that he would give a fall rather than prolong the contest any longer."

"The twenty minutes allowed by the rules had elapsed when Mr. Whistler announced that as Ross had been so magnanimous as to give him the first fall, he would reciprocate with interest, and give him the two falls, collar-and-elbow," continued *The Globe*. "Ross protested and insisted that the match should take place according to the programme. Loud calls from the audience supported the demand, but the referee decided Mr. Whistler had the privilege of surrendering. Ross then claimed the rest of twenty minutes between each bout, which was allowed by the referee, and the audience was compelled to wait for forty minutes longer."

Clarence Whistler

In other words, the Athenaeum crowd had been subjected to more than an hour and a half of wrestling without a satisfying finish to the fall, only to learn that they would be robbed of two additional scheduled rounds while Ross was permitted to rest for a full hour.

As soon as the action resumed to begin the next catch-as-catch-can round, Whistler pounced on Ross and quickly pinned him in four minutes, sending Ross back to his corner to rest for another 20 minutes. By the time the final intermission concluded, the Athenaeum crowd had now seen a total of four minutes of wrestling in the previous hour and 25 minutes.

This set the stage for Ross to engage in an animated debate with the referee, insisting that "according to the rules of Greco-Roman wrestling, a fall would only count with three points down." The referee presented a printed copy of the official rules to Ross, and showed him that only both shoulders were required to be down for a pinfall to count.

"Then Ross demanded that the articles of agreement be read," continued *The Globe*. "This was done, and they specified that the match should take place between the hours of 6 and 12 p.m. Ross then claimed, amid a shower of hisses, that the match was off, as the hour of 12 had passed. The time-keeper's watch was consulted, and indicated that it was two minutes from 12. The referee decided that if Ross refused to proceed, he would declare the match won by Whistler. Ross donned his coat while the audience hissed and hooted. He entered a protest against any money being paid over, after which Mr. Johnstone declared Clarence Whistler the winner of the match and stakes."

The sportswriter from *The Globe* included the detail that he expected that the bout "will probably be the last one that will be witnessed in St. Paul," essentially predicting that the lingering disappointment from the bout would completely kill off the wrestling business in that Twin Cities area.

The full backstory behind the Ross-Whistler debacle would be revealed over the course of the following two years. Meanwhile, after leaving Minnesota, Ross pressed onward.

Losing his prior American championship match with Edwin Bibby did nothing to deter Ross from referring to himself as the champion of America, and he was promoted as such when he faced "champion of Ireland" Lou Moore at the Liederkranz Hall in Louisville, Kentucky. The five-fall effort went the full distance, with Ross finally trapping Moore in an arm-and-leg hold to achieve the final victory in just a shade under two hours.

Even before this bout with Moore occurred, Clarence Whistler insisted in a letter to the editor of *The Courier Journal* that Ross would "get the conceit taken out of him" if he ever dared to challenge his Kansas City opponent ever again. Surprisingly, the next action taken against Whistler by Ross would be of a legal variety that spilled into the opening month of 1882.

On January 3, 1882, *The Courier-Journal* reported that Clarence Whistler had been placed under arrest as the result of a bail writ that had been "sworn out by Duncan C. Ross." It was in response to a claim made by Ross that Whistler had absconded from their November match with money that Ross had been rightfully owed.

"According to the rules, the man who won the match was to take not only the stakes, but the gate money," clarified *The Courier-Journal*. "The match was won by Whistler and was so decided. Ross, however, was not satisfied, and claimed $100 as his share of the gate money. The disputed money was put in the bank by Mr. Muldoon, who backed Whistler in the match, until the difficulty was settled. Late last night, Ross swore out a bail writ against Whistler to get the $100, which he claims is due him. Mr. Muldoon claims, according to the rules, that Ross was entitled to nothing, and says that he was beat out of $250, as the collateral which Ross put up to secure his stakes proved worthless."

The "Mr. Muldoon" referenced in the report was William Muldoon, a legendary Greco-Roman wrestler in his own right, and one of the most respected grapplers of the era.

Seemingly galled by the idea that Ross was continuing to refer to himself as "the champion athlete of the world," *The Cincinnati Enquirer* itself agreed to put up $100 for "a fair, square, and honest wrestling contest" between Whistler and Ross. No such bout would be forthcoming.

Apparently not honoring the results of any of the bouts he lost in the East, Ross formally adopted Louisville as his hometown, and resumed promoting himself as the wrestling champion of America, just as he did when he faced "champion of Canada" Patrick O'Donnell from Toronto. The irony that Ross spent perhaps the entirety of his youth in Canada and was raised primarily in Toronto was lost on the Louisvillians.

During the bout in question, Ross received the reaction of a hometown hero from the Louisville fans. *The Courier Journal*'s reporter went so far as to make note of Ross' measurements, declaring his height to be 6'0", with a weight of 193 pounds, with a 44-and-a-half-inch chest and 16-and-a-half-inch biceps.

The match extended into a fifth and final fall, at which point Ross grasped O'Donnell tightly in a combination half-nelson-and-leg hold, and then lifted his body from the floor and slammed him three times in succession. The final landing placed O'Donnell's body upon the hard floorboards adjacent to the footlights of MacAuley's Theater, and Ross then threw his full weight on top of O'Donnell while the referee counted the pinfall.

"The crowd then yelled and tossed their hats in the air, and it was some time before the referee could announce the result of the fall," concluded the article. "The time was three minutes. The match lasted one hour and thirty minutes, and was squarely contested and won, being by far the most exciting one ever wrestled in this city, and one of the best on record."

Whatever championship mettle Ross had displayed against O'Donnell, his next outing against William Muldoon exposed his obvious shortcomings as a grappler to the wrestling fans in his adopted home state of Kentucky. Ostensibly believing that he was competent enough at Greco-Roman wrestling to prevent himself from being embarrassed, Ross accepted the challenge of Muldoon — a Greco-Roman savante — which required Muldoon to throw Ross six times in one hour in order to be declared the winner and the Greco-Roman wrestling champion of the United States.

It was odd that one wrestler would have to thrash the other so decidedly in order to be anointed as the champion of a particular wrestling discipline, but Muldoon not only scored six falls on Ross in that style in front of a reported 1,500 fans at

Highland Games and Hippodromes

the Louisville Opera House, but he completed the feat in only 18 minutes.

The reporter present at the event described it as "perhaps the only honest wrestling match that Louisville ever saw; the men were rivals and bitter enemies." Meanwhile, the sports page of *The Cincinnati Enquirer* insulted Louisville sports fans for being duped into throwing their support behind Ross.

Opening the April 5, 1882 edition by saying that what Louisville sports reporters didn't know about "hoss-racing, dog, and chicken-fighting... would more than fill any paper in the town even if its advertisements were crowded out," *The Enquirer*'s sports editor went on to criticize them for not looking up Ross' records in Canada and the Eastern United States "before committing themselves body and soul to his championship."

Not willing to allow his public image to be so thoroughly tarnished by the defeat, Ross sent a letter to the editor of *The Courier Journal* explaining how Muldoon had simply succeeded in his area of wrestling expertise. The humiliated Scotsman then vowed to defeat Muldoon eight times in one hour if side-hold-in-harness was the official style, and sent $200 along with his letter, representing the money Ross would forfeit to Muldoon if he lost the challenge. When Muldoon responded by insisting that the contest should be catch-as-catch-can so that he would at least have a sporting chance, no match between the two men was scheduled for quite some time.

That same month, *The Courier Journal* of Louisville published a piercing exposé on the practice of hippodroming, and placed special emphasis on the hippodroming activities that persisted on a professional wrestling scene that was only increasing in popularity. In seeking to get to the bottom of the corrupt business, the publication corralled a wrestler "who passed through the city a few days ago," and spoke under the condition of anonymity as he was "not at first inclined to give the rest of the wrestling fraternity away."

The Courier Journal's article serves as something akin to a Rosetta Stone for deciphering the actions of the professional wrestlers of the era, and for understanding the telltale signs that should have immediately tipped off wrestling fans — and *especially* sporting men interested in wagering money on the action — as to when a phony bout was about to commence.

"I see that in a recent number the *Police Gazette* says that Muldoon scarcely ever wrestled a square match, but 'hippodromed' all over the country. The same may be said of Bower, Miller, Christol, Owens, McMahon and a number of others; in fact, nearly all the wrestlers; but I am glad to say that a few of them are square," said the unidentified wrestler. "Billy was a square man, and, as long as he remained so, he downed everybody that tackled him. He could then get no one to wrestle him, and, consequently, could not make any more money, and it was then that offers were made to him.

"At first he would not sell a match, but consented to make them 'draws,' which was done, and the money-making business went on. It was shortly after this that the custom of wrestling mixed matches was gotten up, and it was done for this purpose. A man who claimed a certain style as his specialty could win at that style, and allow himself to be thrown in the other styles, so that it was nothing to his discredit when he lost a match."

Continuing, the whistleblower confirmed that nearly every match would be extended to the maximum number of falls in order to build the suspense, while the cities targeted by the wrestlers were locales with a sufficient number of people who could be "easily gulled."

The typical pattern would then play out where one wrestler would arrive in the city to offer an open challenge, while the corresponding letter of acceptance, "which was written by both of them," would soon follow, and the match would be signed. Then, the wrestlers would usually "keep up a cross-fire upon each other" through the local press in order to make the fans believe that they were "bitter enemies."

The unnamed wrestler then went into the short list of bouts that he knew for a fact involved authentic combat. These included a bout between Muldoon and Whistler in New York, during which the promoter had the lights abruptly shut off "because Muldoon was getting decidedly the worst of it," resulting in a draw. A separate bout between Miller and Theo Bauer was said to have continued for 10 hours before both men were so exhausted that they could hardly move, at which point that bout was also declared a draw.

Finally, the anonymous tipster exposed that double-crosses invariably occurred, such as in a bout that Bauer had been expected to lose, and was even paid his share of the money before the curtain went up to begin the show. However, Bauer saw that there was "more money in the house than he expected," at which point he "raised a kick" and refused to lay down in the last round unless his pay was increased. As soon as the receipt of the additional funds was confirmed by Bauer's second, he promptly went down in two minutes after forcibly extending the prior fall to two hours.

"There are numbers of other instances and matches which I could name, with time to think over them," insisted the unknown grappler. "It is, however, a settled fact, that all the wrestlers, who are abusing each other, are very good friends in reality, and put on the disguise of enmity to gull the people more easily."

The Courier Journal then concluded its exposé with a warning directed primarily at the sportsmen who continued to wager large sums on wrestling, stating that the facts obtained in its investigation "do not go to show that the art of wrestling is as noble a pursuit as might be imagined, and, if such is the case, the people should take a wrestling match for just what it is worth, and not 'bank' too much upon its fairness."

No wrestling victory — real or orchestrated — could compete with the boost that Ross received in July 1882. That's when Duncan Ross officially competed against Donald Dinnie for the first time in a Highland Games competition.

Highland Games and Hippodromes

More than a decade later, *The Evening Times* of Glasgow would tell the presumably true tale of the first time Ross and Dinnie physically crossed paths. The interaction was said to have taken place at a parade held just before the games, with Dinnie and Ross assigned to ride in the same carriage.

"Donald took Ross' cushion, and, placing it upon his, sat down, leaving Ross to sit upon the wooden seat," illustrated *The Evening Times*. "The latter expostulated, and demanded the return of the cushion, but Dinnie replied — 'I'm a big man, and must sit above you.'"

Dinnie's reported display of ego shouldn't be taken at face value due to inaccuracies in the article, not least of which is the fact that *The Evening Times* got the location of the meeting incorrect; the event was held in New York rather than Boston. The closing statement of the same article is also a bit of a stretch, because it informed readers that Ross then "beat Dinnie in *every* event," implying that there were many contests between the pair. In fact, there were only two.

Regardless of the phrasing, it *is* correct to say that it was at Mountaineer Grove at Nodine Hill, New York, and under the auspices of the Yonkers Caledonian Club, that Ross performed a feat that had once been unfathomable.

"Much to the surprise of nearly all present, young Ross defeated the champion in the two principal events of the day, as follows," began *The Yonkers Statesman*. "Putting the light stone — Ross, 44 feet 7 ½ inches; Dinnie, 43 feet 7 ½ inches. Throwing the light hammer — Ross, 102 feet 9 ½ inches; Dinnie 101 feet 7 inches. When the referee announced his decision, Ross received a perfect ovation, and was carried off the grounds by his friends."

Again, with Dinnie more than a decade removed from this defeat at the hands of Ross, *The Evening Times* described a scene unfolding where the other athletes in attendance "made considerable sport of Dinnie and his high seat," alluding to the egotistical statement attributed to Dinnie claiming that he must sit above Ross. Fables aside, from that moment forward, it is fair to say that Ross would never confess to occupying a subordinate seat either beside or beneath anyone.

The New York Star declared it to have been the first time Dinnie had ever been defeated "at two of his favorite games," and included an attribution from Dinnie that the legend had only lost due to the intense heat in New York, even though Ross had been forced to contend with the exact same weather.

At the age of 45, Dinnie would have been better served by blaming the loss on his age, since he was 18 years Ross' senior. However, the writer from *The Statesman* took up Dinnie's defense by informing its readers that Dinnie hurled the light hammer 110 feet at a similar event held by the Hudson County Caledonian Club on the prior Tuesday, which was sufficient to make him "still the champion of the world."

Clearly, the writer of the article did not understand how head-to-head competitions work; one competitor is not obligated to exceed another's all-time best mark in order to claim victory over them. For most, the significance of Ross' victory was plainly evident: By defeating Highland Games icon Donald Dinnie at a Caledonian event on U.S. soil, Ross was able to cement his claim to being the Scottish legend's equivalent on the other side of the Atlantic, and demand equal billing to Dinnie at Highland events hosted in North America.

In Scotland, several newspapers ran the report of Dinnie's loss to Ross by reporting the results without further commentary beneath the alliterative headline "Donald Dinnie Defeated."

Following Dinnie's loss to Ross, the men temporarily joined forces to present themselves as a Scottish superteam. The two openly challenged any pair of athletes to compete against them at festivals hosted by various Caledonian clubs, even though those same events invariably pitted Dinnie and Ross against one another as competitors.

When both men appeared along with E.W. Johnston at the Boston Caledonian Club picnic at Spy Grove in late August, *The Boston Globe* described all of the other athletes —

including Dinnie and Ross — as "diminutive looking when compared to him."

The Globe also noted that the amphitheater of Spy Grove was filled with 10,000 spectators who were anxious to watch the customary athletic contests like the throws, runs, and jumps. All of these athletic competitions merely served as a prelude to the main event of the day, which was a special wrestling encounter between Dinnie and Ross.

"Both men had taken part in many of the day's contests, and yet both looked in good form as they reached forward for a body hold," detailed *The Globe*. "Although Ross is a large man, yet his opponent gave assurance of victory in the great strength which his body, arms and legs indicated. The first fall was won by Dinnie in less than two minutes. In the second, Ross took him unawares, and he was sent to the ground, losing the fall. The third bout was won by Dinnie. E.W. Johnston acted as referee. The prize was $50."

This period of time gives rise to the confusing idea that Dinnie successfully captured what was described as "the *Police Gazette* champion medal for mixed wrestling in the United States." The confusion seems to find its root in the fact that Dinnie and Ross faced Thomas Lynch and Captain James C. Daly in a *team* competition for $1,000 and the all-around championship for the world.

The Evening Herald of Fall River, Massachusetts, reported how the two teams agreed to compete in a grueling slate of 15 events, and the entire affair would be capped with a mixed wrestling event, including collar-and-elbow, catch-as-catch-can, and side-hold wrestling.

The scheduled duel finally transpired in front of 2,000 excited onlookers on September 6, 1882 in Renz Park in Philadelphia, but *no* wrestling took place on that day, and neither did nearly half of the promised events. As *The St. Louis Globe-Democrat* reported, the team of Daly and Lynch was, "in this instance, clearly overmatched." At the conclusion of the eighth competition, "Daly objected to the continuance of the sport as announced in the programme," and stated that unless adjustments to the events were made, he would "withdraw from the field."

"Ross was willing to accede to the New Yorker's demands, but Dinnie objected, and the sport thus ended," concluded the article.

Illustration of Captain James C. Daly

This event aside, there is no evidence that Dinnie was advertised to compete in any wrestling-specific world or national championships during 1882. On the basis of the Renz Park affair, he could rightly have claimed a world athletic championship as the teammate of Ross. Still, given the air of general disappointment that encircled the event, it's unlikely that Dinnie would have asserted his ownership of this particular championship with any sort of pride.

In a complaint that would be a precursor to similar allegations that would follow Dinnie and Ross more than a decade later, it was reported by *The Weekly Wisconsin* how Ross and Dinnie were "declared forever barred from participating in games on account of ungentlemanly and unsportsmanlike behavior at recent games."

This ban occurred in the aftermath of an event hosted by the Caledonian Society of Hamilton, Ontario. This prohibition was only enforced at one set of Caledonian games, but it remains fascinating that the two primary athletic attractions of the continent's Scottish athletic circuit were outright banned from competing due to their disreputable behavior when nearly all prior coverage of the men had described them as being of an altogether gentlemanly caliber.

It was around this time that Dinnie's activities began to mirror those of most American wrestlers. Specifically, he would pose challenges in the newspaper that were exclusive to wrestling, like his November submission where he posited his wish to wrestle "any man in America for one or two hours, each man to contest half the time in his own style, and the other half in his opponent's, the winner of the greatest number of falls to take the stakes."

In June 1883, *The Ottawa Daily Citizen* told the tale of a legendary bout between Dinnie and William Muldoon, in a matchup between a Scotch-style wrestler and a Greco-Roman wrestler. The terms of the bout were that they would wrestle half an hour in each style, with only the time spent in active wrestling counting toward the total. A takedown resulting in any part of the opponent's anatomy striking the ground would count as a fall.

The stipulation was added that Dinnie was obligated to throw Muldoon twice as many times in the half hour of Scottish wrestling that favored him as Muldoon threw Dinnie in Greco-Roman falls in order for Dinnie to earn a victory.

Highland Games and Hippodromes

The reason for the stipulation was probably due to the comparative ease with which a bout of Scottish-style wrestling could be won in comparison to a Greco-Roman contest. While the terms "throw" and "fall" were often used interchangeably during that era to acknowledge victories in wrestling bouts, their separate origins are found in the specific wrestling styles they were taken from.

In this instance, a Scottish, or backhold wrestling bout was begun when both wrestlers locked arms with their left arms over the opponent's right shoulder, and with their right arm under each other's left arms, with their hands clasped together behind the opponent's back. Intentionally or inadvertently releasing the hold at this point resulted in disqualification, while tripping, lifting, or otherwise throwing your opponent to the ground immediately earned a victory.

By comparison, Greco-Roman wrestling prohibits grabbing any part of an opponent's anatomy beneath the waist, and a fall is only awarded when both of the adversary's shoulders are pinned to the mat. Given the demands of each style, Dinnie should have had a considerable advantage in amassing victories through his preferred style, but the official results of the bout suggest differently.

"The men worked hard," reported *The Daily Citizen*. "They started with the Scotch style, then wrestled Greco-Roman, and thus alternated until midnight, when Dinnie gave up. He had thrown Muldoon eleven times in 13 minutes 46 seconds actual wrestling time, and Muldoon had thrown Dinnie fifteen times in 16 minutes 45 seconds. Muldoon threw Dinnie each time they wrestled Greco-Roman, and Dinnie lost two falls at his favourite Scotch back hold."

The bout between Donald Dinnie and a young Duncan McMillan in June 1883 at the Mechanics Pavilion of San Francisco came in the aftermath of a month that the two spent dueling in assorted Caledonian events in the San Francisco Bay area. At the annual picnic of the San Francisco Thistle Club, Dinnie and McMillan were two of only three competitors capable of flipping the caber, while McMillan also showed respectably next to Dinnie in several of the established champion's best strength and power events.

In fact, Dinnie's puts of just over 33 feet and 42 feet with the heavy and light stones, respectively, were each only able to surpass McMillan's putting efforts with each stone — 32 feet and 41 feet — by only one foot in each of the contests. In the meantime, McMillan displayed his athletic versatility by winning both the running and standing long jumps, and placing second in the hop, step, and jump.

Dinnie's victories in the throwing events were not as authoritative as they had often been, and things only got worse when his "triumph" in "the great card of attraction" — the advertised wrestling bout between Dinnie and William Farrell — was labeled as "the great disappointment of the day" by the reporter from *The San Francisco Examiner*.

"Farrell understood that they were to wrestle alternate falls in the Cumberland and collar-and-elbow styles, and then toss for choice in the odd fall," reported *The Examiner*. "The first fall was in the Cumberland, or as it was called yesterday, the Scotch style, back holds. In this style, Farrell is no match for Dinnie, and the latter did not add to the luster of his laurels by palpably not trying, or as Reuben Lloyd would say, 'hugger-muggering' with his opponent. They tugged at each other for a couple of minutes, when Dinnie broke holds and took a rest. Then after about two minutes more had been spent in hugging, both men fell to the ground.

"The fall was allowed to Dinnie, though no one could find out why it was so, for neither the back, hips, nor side of Farrell touched the ground. Then Farrell put on his harness for a try at collar-and-elbow, in which style he has an even chance with the Scotch giant. But Dinnie would not wrestle in any style but his own, and neither appeals, reproaches, nor the hisses of some spectators could induce him to give Farrell a hold. Farrell offered to toss for choice of styles, but Dinnie would not concede a point, and the match was never finished."

Considering how the Dinnie-Farrell event appeared to have been intentionally constructed in the mixed-styles format

Highland Games and Hippodromes

that was often a telltale sign that hippodrome was afoot, or at least led to strong suspicions of such, neither of the likeliest scenarios that elicited Dinnie's lack of cooperation casts him in a positive light.

Presuming the contest was legitimate, Dinnie won the first bout in the Scottish style by virtue of a contestable call by the referee and then refused to engage further with Farrell in any of the grappling methods at which Farrell would have held a clear advantage.

In the far more likely scenario that the result of the bout was predetermined, it's unfathomable that the final result of a scripted wrestling match at a Caledonian event would have called for Dinnie to lose. Therefore, it's probable that Dinnie simply refused to display any semblance of vulnerability in any style of wrestling in front of his devoted Scottish followers at a Highland Games setting, preferring instead to disappoint them with an inconclusive finish after he had achieved the only visual victory of the day.

If Dinnie's less-than-impressive showing at the Thistle Club Picnic had left a bitter taste in the mouths of his followers, this could certainly have been overcome by a show of force over the local Highland competitor and wrestler who'd had the nerve to put his stones so uncomfortably close to Dinnie's best marks at that event. Much to the chagrin of any of Dinnie's fans in attendance, the way the bout at Mechanics Hall opened wouldn't have instilled in them any confidence that Scotland's national hero would be achieving redemption.

McMillan won the first collar-and-elbow bout in just under three minutes when he managed to lock his own leg around Dinnie's and "downed the burly Caledonian squarely, and heavily as well" while the fans "cheered enthusiastically."

Dinnie saved some semblance of face by winning the next fall in two-and-a-half minutes, but then surrendered the final fall in under three minutes when McMillan "fell with full force on Dinnie, and both went down, McMillan on top."

On most nights, this would have signaled the end of the wrestling, but after an intervening bout between William

Highland Games and Hippodromes

Muldoon and Celestin Deitmann, Dinnie and McMillan again took center stage to grapple in the Scottish backhold style. Employing the familiar technique of his homeland, Dinnie quickly restored his image at the expense of his fellow Scot. All three falls were won in less than one minute, with Dinnie securing the two quickest falls in 36 seconds and 54 seconds to prove himself the superior backhold wrestler.

Following three rounds of boxing from James McDonald and James Linehan, Dinnie and McMillan came together once more for a third set of bouts in mixed backhold and collar-and-elbow styles. Dinnie won the toss, and threw McMillan in the two backhold bouts to win the mixed wrestle two rounds to one. This also earned him a victory in the total fall count that evening at five to four, and victories in two of the three overall sets of matches by a score of two to one.

As was the intent of the format, each wrestler was permitted to look like the master of his respective style, and no true transfer of prestige resulted. However, Dinnie's primary objective of preserving his status as the best Scottish-style wrestler in the world was achieved.

Although Donald Dinnie was victorious at the Thistle Club's festivities, his days as a prominent professional wrestling figure in the United States were already numbered. Many sporting sleuths were hell-bent on sniffing out hippodrome activity, and Dinnie — a man with a reputation for true athletic excellence that was practically unrivaled — would ironically become the professional wrestler whose name evoked the greatest suspicion of inauthentic combat.

4 – A Showman's Fat Woman

While the star of Duncan Ross had been shining more brightly than ever after his victory over Donald Dinnie in Highland-style hammer throwing, rumblings began to stir that his wrestling matches might not have been honest depictions of physical struggles against his opponents. In January 1883, in response to being insulted by Ross in the press, Clarence Whistler essentially outed Ross, Muldoon, *and* himself for colluding as hippodromers during their St. Paul, Minnesota bout in 1881, while seeking to pin the entirety of the blame on Ross.

"I'll tell you what kind of a hippodrome that was. Ross had been making a heap of talk about being able to down any man in the country, and Muldoon and I concluded to give him a trial," Whistler was quoted in *The New Orleans Picayune*. "We knew what his racket was in wrestling matches, and that we could never get him to come on the stage in a square match. So Muldoon sent for him to come around to the hotel where he was stopping."

According to Whistler's tale, Muldoon lured Ross into a match by assuring Ross that he would be the winner of a best-of-three-falls contest, thereby acquiring "the reputation that no other wrestler had gained" by becoming the first to defeat Whistler in a major bout. Without hesitation, Ross agreed to the terms of the bout and the split of the money.

"Understand now that this whole scheme had all been fixed up, not just for us to make money out of it, but just simply to put a stop to the Scotchman's talk," Whistler continued. "The night of the wrestle, [Ross] came on the stage blooming, and thinking of how the news would be telegraphed to the world that he had downed Whistler. But I soon took the bloom out of him, for I laid him on his back three times so quick that it made his head swim, and he never recovered from it since. That's the kind of hippodrome we had with Duncan Ross."

Highland Games and Hippodromes

In the vernacular, Whistler was alleging that he and Muldoon had fooled Ross into believing that their bout would be a "work," only for Ross to discover once the contest began that he had been beguiled into a "shoot."

Truly, Whistler was exaggerating with respect to the quickness with which he had been able to down Ross. Presuming the entire bout had been real, Ross submitted at the end of the first catch-as-catch-can fall after more than an hour and a half of activity due to Whistler's refusal to cooperate. Whistler then verbally conceded *two* collar-and-elbow falls to Ross just to advance the match to the next catch-as-catch-can bout, and then quickly defeated Ross in just four minutes. It was only then that Ross quit, and the bout was awarded to Whistler.

Regardless, Ross now officially had a hippodroming charge laid at his feet by two of his fellow wrestlers who had sought to absolve themselves in the process. Just as hurtful as the hippodroming accusation was the deduction that Ross was simply not a wrestler of the caliber of Whistler and Muldoon, and the way the Ross-Whistler match unfolded lent credence to that opinion.

In the short term, the allegations did little to slow Ross' momentum, and he was portrayed in Ohio — and especially in Cleveland — as a worldbeater of the first order. When he wrestled John Theurer in that northern Ohio city, the question on the table wasn't whether or not Ross could pin Theurer, but if he could complete the task nine times in 90 minutes.

"At 8:20 o'clock both men appeared in the ring and were introduced to the company by Prof. Ryan. Ross stripped at 202 pounds and Theurer at 148," recounted *The St. Louis Daily Globe-Democrat*. "Ross forced the issue from the beginning, and both men worked with desperation seldom witnessed in a wrestling match. Theurer was constantly on the defensive, but notwithstanding this fact acquitted himself with wonderful credit. Ross worked hard, and used every fair means to outdo his antagonist. He gained three falls in the first forty-five minutes, after which both men took a rest of ten minutes.

Highland Games and Hippodromes

The strain during this period told heavily on Theurer, and Ross demonstrated his superiority by throwing him six times in the following twenty-seven minutes, thus winning the match."

A critical detail tacked on at the very end of the article was that "considerable money changed hands on the result" of the match, and that the "sporting men of the city" turned out in large numbers to wager money on the result.

By this point, Ross' value has sufficiently swelled that he was advertised for a main event bout at New York City's Madison Square Garden against John McMahon, one of the most popular wrestlers in New York. Unfortunately for Ross, he would arrive at the venue on time to discover that the doors to the entertainment mecca that was now in only its fourth year of existence remained locked due to a credentialing complication. This was said to have greatly upset local wrestling fans who "went home grumbling."

"The match cannot go on. The Garden has not paid its license fee," confirmed promoter W.E. Harding. "I have been down to see the District Attorney, Corporation Counsel, and Commissioner French. They said it would be necessary to have a license. Then I telegraphed to Mr. Van Arsdale at the Grand Central Depot, and he said he would see that the license fee was paid today. But the match is postponed indefinitely."

With his chance at a major bout with McMahon spoiled, Ross headed south for Florida to participate in a series of bouts with Theobaud Bauer of France that would ultimately raise further suspicions that all was not as it seemed when it came to Ross and his wrestling career.

The match between Ross and Bauer was held at the grounds of the Florida State Fair at an event hosted by the Scottish Association of Florida, which advertised the bout as the featured attraction within a full slate of Highland Games events. More importantly, it was marketed as the first of at least two matches that would determine who was the rightful Greco-Roman wrestling champion of the world.

"A large crowd attended the wrestling match between the famous champions, Duncan C. Ross and T. Bauer," declared *The Times Union* of Jacksonville. "These two men have a wide world reputation, and proved themselves worthy of such distinction by their splendid exhibition here on the fair grounds. They were stripped of all clothing except drawers and socks, and stood upon a large sheet of canvas, and in the hot sun began to hug and toss each other about as if they possessed the strength of Samson. The first 'bout' lasted 22 minutes; the second was short, and on the third call Bauer failed to respond, and Ross was declared the victorious champion at the Florida State Fair."

Wrestling champion Duncan C. Ross

The Weekly Floridian informed its readers that the injury suffered by Bauer during the second fall of the bout had supposedly prevented him from participating in the remainder of the Highland athletic events, which were joined by many participants, all of whom were "excelled by Ross."

From there, the two men traveled north to Savannah, Georgia, to wrestle at an event that was similarly hosted by the local Caledonian Club. Prior to the bout, the championship belt and *Police Gazette* medal that were now owned by Ross were displayed overnight in the windows of LaFar's clothing store at No. 23 Bull Street in Savannah.

Apparently, the injury that Bauer had supposedly suffered in Florida did not preclude his participation in either this 3:00 p.m. wrestling bout or the events of the 2:00 p.m. Scottish Games that immediately preceded it.

For some reason, the fact that both men would risk their health or physical preparedness in sporting events requiring explosive movements just one hour prior to a wrestling bout with a world championship on the line seemingly failed to rouse suspicions that at least the latter competition might not have been entirely on the level.

As would be expected at an organized Scottish gathering that prioritized keeping the assembled Scots happy, Ross won the bout by winning the final two falls after surrendering the first, and retained his title belt and medal in the process, while Bauer apparently lost his temper at the bout's conclusion, according to *The Savannah Morning News*.

From there, Ross materialized in New Orleans, and in March he published an open challenge that was soon accepted by an "unknown" wrestler, who unbelievably turned out to be Theobaud Bauer. While Ross made a show of claiming to be angry about not knowing who his mystery opponents would be, *The Times-Picayune* revealed that confusion about the matter was circulating because "Ross has traveled with a Bauer," but Ross and Bauer were claiming to be facing each other for "the very first time" when they met in New Orleans.

The concocted cover story was that Bauer was "incensed" because "some other party" had "assumed the name of Bauer in different portions of the country." Ordinarily, a lawsuit would have been forthcoming under such circumstances, but instead the upcoming match would ostensibly be Bauer's opportunity to violently repay Ross for the fraud that he had been perpetuating at the true Theobaud Bauer's expense.

Seeing right through the charade, *The New Orleans Times-Democrat* pointed out how suspicious the supposed happenstantial arrival "of two such renowned athletes as Duncan C. Ross and Thiebaud Bauer" in New Orleans had been, especially when the two of them had just been touring together in the Southeast.

"New Orleans is out of the circuit of such professionals, so we can speak of them only by hearsay; but it certainly has been said of both Ross and Bauer that they do not always do their best in wrestling matches," asserted *The Times-Democrat*. "Both have been accused of deliberately submitting to defeat when they could easily have achieved the victory. Both have been suspected of arranging results beforehand when, on the merits of the case the issue should have been different. We do not know that the general public suffer in consequence of these alleged insecurities. The betting men naturally complain. But one thing is very certain: The general public do not take much interest in a match when they have reason to doubt its genuineness."

The publication further observed that there was little excitement in the Greco-Roman bout due to rumors that Ross and Bauer were "contemplating what is known as a hippodrome," and admonished them to do whatever they could to "set these doubts at rest" while promising them "only a languid notice from our people if there clings to them the faintest odor of suspicion."

Either New Orleans simply hadn't developed a thirst for professional wrestling, or speculation that the Ross-Bauer bout might have been an insincere contest convinced the city's residents who may have otherwise been interested to remain home. Regardless, only 1,500 spectators ventured out to the St. Charles Theatre — a venue that could easily hold 4,000 — to watch the action.

Highland Games and Hippodromes

In stark contrast to the audiences present at the multiple Scottish Games events where the two had met just one month earlier, the inhabitants of the city that had come to represent the heart of what was once colonial French America threw their support decidedly behind the Frenchman Bauer.

After trading falls over the course of an hour, the men readied themselves for the final fall, and then "went after each other savagely." Bauer eventually managed to force Ross onto his knees and seized control.

"As before he proceeded very warily until he got a fine neck hold, when he threw Ross half over on his back," said *The Times-Democrat*. "Like a tiger he leaped over him, and using his head and shoulder forced his man gradually on his back and held him there. The referee announced that he had won the fall, and Bauer jumped up and bowed triumphantly amid a most enthusiastic applause from the audience."

At the conclusion of the 36-minute final bout, Bauer wore a black eye and claimed to have had two of his teeth knocked out, while Ross' body "looked as though he had worn a fly blister" as a consequence of Bauer boring his head and chin into it. The obvious superficial damage that shown on the bodies of both men may have been the reason that "the major portion of the audience seemed to be satisfied that the match was perfectly square."

Someone who had seen Ross handily and repeatedly defeat Bauer in front of crowds that had been thirsting for a Scottish victory might have looked at the way the tables turned in front of a French audience with considerable skepticism. *The Times-Democrat* provided Ross with a ready-made excuse, reminding its readers that the Scottish-Canadian's reputation had been built on catch-as-catch-can wrestling, and not on Greco-Roman wrestling, which was the style in which his bout with Bauer was contested.

Ross' explanation would be similar when he lost a best-of-five mixed-style bout to Henry Dufur in Rochester that April. When the bout went to a decisive fifth fall, which was contested in the side hold style, Ross refused to stand fully upright once the harness was buckled on.

At this point, referee Harding told Ross that he needed to stand up in accordance with the *Police Gazette* rules that governed the bout, and once Ross granted the official's request, he was immediately defeated. Afterwards, the now former *Police Gazette* world champion of mixed wrestling offered the outrageous excuse that he had been ignorant of the *Police Gazette*'s rules governing sidehold wrestling.

When Ross recovered his claim to the *Police Gazette* title in June, by defeating Dufur at the Rochester Grand Opera House, *The Rochester Democrat and Chronicle* opined that the interest in the bout had been negligible, perhaps underscoring the common difficulty of repeating the same match in an identical town without any new interesting elements, and expecting to attract the same number of fans.

The bout, which went "unbacked by money," proceeded in a similar fashion to the first encounter between the two, only this time "the referee was more lenient to Ross' interpretation of the rules" once the deciding sidehold round commenced.

"Three times in succession Ross picked the man from Massachusetts bodily up and threw him to the floor, and the third time succeeded in pushing him over from his side to his back, which the referee decided was a fair fall and which terminated the match, Ross bowing his acknowledgements to the crowd as a winner," added *The Democrat and Chronicle*.

The next set of maneuvers by Ross would go a long way toward establishing him as perhaps the most important figure in tying together a cohesive wrestling region stretching from Ohio into Western New York. The sequence of events began with a 12-man wrestling tournament in Buffalo at the tail end of June, which was preceded by a rather foreboding incident. Ahead of the tournament, Ross was reportedly sparring with E. O. Williams, and inadvertently broke the latter's leg.

Highland Games and Hippodromes

To silence the rumors that he had intentionally disabled a contender ahead of the tournament, Ross called the offices of *The Buffalo Commercial* and explained that Williams had insisted that they train on wet grass, and that Williams' injury had occurred when the Fredonia wrestler slipped, and Ross accidentally fell across his vulnerable leg.

The multi-night tournament that also included men like Dennis Gallagher, James Daly, and Mervine Thompson utilized a point system, and concluded with a Ross victory that earned him the *Police Gazette* trophy, and ostensibly the advertised cash prize of $500.

Ross' win in the *Police Gazette*'s Buffalo tournament was followed by his participation in the three-man mixed wrestling tournament in Cleveland, the results of which could have been predicted by the simple fact that it was promoted by Cleveland's Caledonian Society.

Competing against Thompson and Gallagher, Ross won all six of his bouts in commanding fashion to sweep the tournament and establish himself as an unstoppable force in the city of Cleveland.

As far away as Tennessee, the results of the tournament were offered as an encouragement to Southerners who were sick of receiving "patronizing suggestions" from Northerners to shake off "the lethargy inherited from the slavery system" and get to work. As such, they were encouraged to look to the successes of Ross for motivation, and to travel north to rid themselves of the laziness that the semi-tropical climate of the South had inspired in them.

"The northern climate encourages activity and motion, and in looking through the dispatches on yesterday morning's daily papers, the reader will be struck with the number of energetic people who are engaged in a peculiar industry in several of the northern cities," prompted *The Tennessean*. "Mr. Duncan C. Ross, at Cleveland, is successfully prosecuting the lucrative business of wrestling. Monday night he won the first prize and championship badge at the Caledonian Club's mixed wrestling tournament. The young men who have gone north to grow up with the country will find in the success of this ambitious wrestler a heroic achievement worthy of emulation, and opportunity in a new profession for the acquisition of reputation and riches."

From late November extending into December, a second wrestling tournament was held under the auspices of the Caledonian Society of Cleveland at the City Armory. The festivities were launched by the joyful news from *The Cleveland Evening Post* that Duncan Ross had "announced his intention of settling among us," having just obtained a 10-year lease of McGuire's block on Ontario Street, which he promised to convert into an athletic training facility. Later reports would theorize that Ross spent $6,000 to overhaul the building to his liking.

At the conclusion of this four-man tournament, which also involved Pooler, Thompson, and Gallagher, Ross defeated Gallagher and was presented with the *Police Gazette* medal signifying his supremacy as "the champion mixed wrestler of the world," while the papers also upheld Ross' alleged status as the best all-around athlete on the planet." In summary, Cleveland could not have landed a hotter commodity around which to shape its athletic foundation.

The year would not end nearly as favorably for Donald Dinnie as it had for Ross. The trouble started when Dinnie and Duncan McMillan took their grappling partnership on the road to the Pacific Northwest and presented the public with bouts that failed to pass the smell test for authenticity as far as the Seattle press was concerned.

Anyone from San Francisco who was familiar with both Dinnie and McMillan and the friendly relationship between them surely became suspicious of misconduct when McMillan materialized as the surprise "unknown" challenger of Dinnie for several August bouts in Oregon.

The opening bout between them was billed in *The Sunday Oregonian* as "Scotland vs. America," with the publication identifying McMillan as "an American" who was "no less strong and large, agile and scientific" than Dinnie, at a height of 6'3" and a weight of 210 lbs. In this case, at least for the time being, McMillan, who had been frequently identified as a Scot in past matches on the basis of his conspicuously Scottish last name and authentic Scottish ancestry, would be temporarily cast as an American when facing a native Scot born in the shadow of the Highlands.

Duncan McMillan

After six rounds of wrestling in collar-and-elbow, Scottish backhold, and Greco-Roman, the pair dueled to a tie of three falls apiece. A seventh tussle contested in the Greco-Roman style was deemed necessary to decide the contest. *The Seattle Post Intelligencer* described how McMillan got Dinnie "on his hands and knees," and pulled and hauled him all over the platform for 30 minutes while Dinnie's actions and expression indicated that he was toying with his opponent and "only wishing to show McMillan the utter uselessness of his task, rather than to try and turn the tables and throw himself."

"They finally got up, and after a short struggle McMillan caught Dinnie unawares, throwing him quickly, but fairly, having to force him over on his back, winning the fall, and the match; time of the last fall, 34 minutes, 17 seconds," recorded the *Post-Intelligencer*. "At the conclusion of the match, Manager Stechhan stated that Mr. Dinnie had been seasick on the voyage up, and had not fully recovered from its effects, also that, in consequence, he had not trained any since his arrival."

It was reported that Stechhan's speech "was not received kindly by the audience, hisses being plainly heard, and remarks anything but complimentary, were frequent." Soon thereafter, the *Tacoma Daily Ledger* published an editorial about the base dishonesty of the practice of hippodroming in many sports, and cited the bout between Dinnie and McMillan as a clear example of the practice in action.

"Professional pugilists, oarsmen, pedestrians, and all the other miscellaneous crowd that hang on the skirts of society and earn a precarious living by making matches between each other for the purpose of corralling as much as possible of the coin of the credulous public, are but a very few removes, perhaps not more than one, above the swindlers who eat penitentiary fare and wear government motley," stated *The Ledger*'s editorial. "In nine cases out of ten, the 'events' are 'put up jobs,' the result being pre-arranged, and betting by the members of the ring reduced to a certainty, or as it is termed in the slang of the profession, 'a soft thing.'

"The recent great (?) wrestling match between Donald Dinnie and McMillan, in Portland, is said to have been of this description — with what measure of truth we are not prepared to say. This much, at least, we can safely venture to assert, viz: that the large majority of such exhibitions are hippodrome and so arranged that big money can be made at the time, and the 'pigeon' element of the betting fraternity seduced into further experiments in the way of backing their opinion in future matches, for which the principals are always careful to prepare."

When Dinnie returned to San Francisco to face William Muldoon, *The Ledger* sustained its skepticism about the veracity of what was being presented on the mat. Noting that "The City by the Bay" was presently "crazy over wrestling," the publication averred that the entire region was "agog to see the giants grapple." Yet, it also cautioned the fans that they should guard their hearts and wallets when in the presence of pro wrestlers, because "when the thing is made a trade of, as it is with the above named professional wrestlers, it becomes anything but worthy of encouragement, and certainly should be put down."

"In nine cases out of ten, such affairs are what are known as 'hippodromes,' or, in the more common slang, 'put-up-jobs,' and the fellows stand, to win or lose, according as it happens to suit them, and make gate money," added the article. "Dinnie, at any rate, is nothing better than a showman's fat woman, or living skeleton, or Chinese giant, or any other catch-penny curiosity. Muldoon, who is an ex-policeman, has this, at least, in his favor, that he has never gone around the country as an appanage to a show or circus. He has a crowd of engagements on hand, among which, is one to box a certain Seattleite, of the name of Davis, the match to come off in Portland. There would be no very serious injury to the community if the whole gang were safely laid by the heels in some reasonably comfortable jail."

The accusation being made by *The Ledger*'s writer was that Dinnie's name was far too valuable to the Caledonian circuit to have its integrity risked and diminished through real losses that could reduce the status of his attraction. At the same time, the quality of his overall wrestling talent was several steps beneath the value of his name and brand. As such, any wrestling contest that included Dinnie would *need* to be a hippodrome simply out of the necessity to negate any possibility that he might suffer a reputation-lessening loss.

Highland Games and Hippodromes

It should be noted that in some publications the fact that Dinnie and McMillan were engaged in hippodroming was handled as an open secret. A reporter from *The Reno Gazette* spotted Dinnie and McMillan traveling together at the train depot, and bluntly stated that the two were heading off to Denver "to hippodrome at the Scotch games that are to come off there next Saturday."

Soon, the accusations and evidence that Donald Dinnie was hippodroming would become front-page news, culminating in an embarrassing fiasco that would see him leave North America in disgrace, just as Duncan Ross was becoming the most powerful star of the entire pro wrestling circuit.

Highland Games and Hippodromes

5 – A Scotch Hippodromer

The course of events that would ultimately lead to the confirmation that Donald Dinnie was hippodroming along the West Coast was initiated by the following letter from Dinnie to the editor of *The San Francisco Chronicle*:

SIR: I am surprised at (William) Muldoon's reply to my fair proposition for a wrestling match to prove who is the best wrestler now in America. There are seven different styles of wrestling, and I ask who can determine by any one style the merits of a man? Joe Acton is ready to wrestle any man in America at catch-as-catch-can style, but would not venture Muldoon at Graeco-Roman. I had never seen either of these styles contested until I met Muldoon and Whistler in our late matches; but as I have at least as much agility and strength as either, with half their practice I think I would stand a good chance in the Graeco-Roman alone. How is it, then, that these men with their youth, strength and many claims dare not attempt anything but Graeco-Roman? I still offer to wrestle any man in America in a mixed match, or each man his own style against time, for any reasonable sum; or will agree to any proposal made by the *Chronicle*, *Pacific Life*, or *New York Clipper* regarding the fairest way to decide who is the best wrestler in America. — Donald Dinnie

Allegedly, as *The Chronicle* would report, Dinnie's letter was shown to Muldoon, "who at once began to speak bitterly against Dinnie for having advertised him (Muldoon) to appear at various wrestling matches in Oregon, when his presence was an impossibility." The next day, Muldoon supposedly returned to the offices of *The Chronicle* to say that he had received a telegram from B.F. Schwartz, Dinnie's manager, saying that the purse being offered to the victor of the bout would be $1,000 if Muldoon would travel to Portland for a match with Dinnie, three rounds backhold, two Greco-Roman.

Muldoon then alleged that he wired back a response stating that if the rounds were reversed so that three of the rounds would be Greco-Roman, he would agree to the match.

When these terms were hastily accepted, Muldoon said that this puzzled him "for it was throwing the match right into his hands."

Muldoon added that he remained puzzled about the hasty acceptance of the match on terms that were unfavorable to Dinnie until he read that a lawsuit had been filed by Dinnie and McMillan against Schwartz to recover more than $500 in salary. He then jumped to the conclusion that Schwartz was attempting to draw a big crowd so that he could pay off the debt that he had accrued to Dinnie and McMillan.

Whether or not this was initially intended to be a customary portrayal of posturing through the press for the sake of building the interest of the audience, things played out *very* differently on the night of the match, as *The San Francisco Chronicle* synthesized the accounts of what the Oregon newspapers referred to as "the match that didn't come off."

At Portland's New Market Theater, the large and impatient audience was left waiting for a full 45 minutes past the bout's advertised 8:00 p.m. start time. That's when Muldoon emerged, dressed in tights, and "expressed his willingness and anxiety to begin the contest and claimed not to understand the cause of Dinnie's absence." Fifteen minutes later, Dinnie entered the building through the stage door, and was "greeted with yells, hisses and groans" as he proceeded to the dressing room.

When another 30 minutes passed without the Scottish strongman making his way to the stage, an ex-runner for a sailor boarding house stood in front of the crowd and apprised them as to the cause of the delay, with the newspapers retaining the peculiarities of his voice in their printed account:

"*Ladies hand Gentlemen*: Hi 'ave been requested by Mr. Dinnie to say that there his ha bill howed to 'im by Mr. Stechhan and 'ee refuses to rastle until the haforesaid bloomin' bill his paid and 'ee den't hexpect hanny benefit from this 'ouse and doesn't care for hanny arrival from the money taken hin hat the door; hin fact, don't want hannything from hit vatsomever. Mr. Stechhan 'ired 'im hat ha weekly salary hand has for this match there his over $500 due 'im."

After hearing this, the crowd at the New Market Theater chanted Dinnie's name, but the speaker explained that Dinnie wouldn't be addressing them directly because he was "ha foreign Scotchman and couldn't speak the Henglish language hexactly."

William Muldoon

That's when Muldoon returned to the stage to announce that the delay was caused by a "private quarrel" between Dinnie and the promoter that should not "stand in the way of a public entertainment." Muldoon added that he would be willing to donate every cent of his share of the gate money to a charitable institution if that would enable the show to proceed as scheduled.

The Chronicle surmised that something was "fixed up behind the scenes" because the announcer soon returned to the stage to say that "the bloody misunderstanding between Mr. Stechhan and Donald Dinnie 'ad been misconstrued hand the match will go hon."

The match — if it can be called that — was insulting in its brevity. It was listed in the program as a best-of-five-falls affair, with two falls Greco-Roman, two falls Scottish backhold, and one fall catch-as-catch-can. Once Dinnie and Muldoon finally made physical contact, they concluded their engagement after a brief, one-fall encounter.

"The first bout was to be Graeco-Roman, and Muldoon, acting at once on the aggressive, soon had Dinnie around the waist, lifted him in the air, and brought him heavily down," described *The Chronicle*. "Muldoon might have claimed a fall, but still wrestled on, throwing his man a second time in 1:40, but still said nothing about it and kept on worrying Donald for another six minutes, when the fall was so palpable that Muldoon had to quit, although the *News* asserts that there was neither umpire nor referee."

One way of interpreting the action, which took place without a third party officiating the match, is that Muldoon embarrassed Dinnie by abusing him on the mat for nearly eight minutes, scoring three visible falls, and refusing to relent until he was satisfied that Dinnie appeared to have been thoroughly vanquished.

Apparently, Dinnie took exception to this mistreatment, because the next person to emerge during the intermission was promoter F.W. Stechhan, who took the opportunity to plead his case to the crowd and explain his side of the story.

"[Stechhan] claimed that his arrangements were with Mr. Schwartz, Dinnie's manager, with whom he shared the profits of Dinnie's tour, and that he (Stechhan) was not responsible for debts due Dinnie; that Dinnie's refusal to wrestle on this occasion was simply an effort to blackmail him into paying a debt which he had not incurred," elaborated *The Chronicle*. "The green curtain then fell and the audience refused to leave, setting up a prolonged howl."

As if the evening hadn't already deteriorated into an embarrassment for all involved, Muldoon then stepped onto the stage and said that he had "come to Portland expecting to have an honest contest with Dinnie" and was prepared to continue with the match. Muldoon then stunned the crowd by publicly leveling an accusation at Dinnie and McMillan that the pair had been "hippodroming through the country," effectively stating that none of Dinnie's wrestling matches — at least those with McMillan — were legitimate, and implying that his dominance of Dinnie on the stage that evening had been a reflection of Dinnie's genuine wrestling talent, or lack thereof.

Then, in what was likely the biggest shock of the proceedings, Dinnie stepped out onto the stage and *admitted* that Muldoon's accusation of "hippodroming" on his part was true, but that "the fault lay with the manager, who could draw more money by advertising a 'contest' than by an 'exhibition.'" This was followed by another appearance by Stechhan, who attempted to explain himself to a crowd that "left in huge disgust."

"As may be imagined, the Portlanders were 'mad clear through' about the whole affair and the papers echo the popular feeling with no uncertain sound," printed *The Chronicle*. "In justice to Muldoon it should be said that not the slightest blame is attached to him, all agreeing that he acted squarely and made hosts of friends, but Dinnie is scored most unmercifully. He is called a chromo, a bulldozer, barelegged, a Scotch hippodromer, a swindler and a contemptible cur."

Following his humiliating night at the New Market Theater, Dinnie's situation went from bad to worse when he was arrested the following day, a Wednesday, "for obtaining money under false pretenses," and jailed until his friends could collect a $400 bail to spring him. The instant Dinnie was freed, he was then *rearrested*. A $1,000 bond was put up, and Dinnie was brought before Judge Moreland on Friday, at which point he and McMillan were both required to give testimony as to the nature of their arrangements with Stechhan and Schwartz.

During the disclosures before the court, the following details emerged: Dinnie was contracted to Schwartz on a salary of $100 a week and was required to wrestle as often as Schwartz demanded. Similarly, McMillan testified that he had agreed to wrestle for $50 a week, and that all of the bouts that were presented as authentic contests before a paying public were merely exhibitions with predetermined winners.

All the events in the Portland region had been profitable, with all profits being shared between Stechhan and Schwartz. Things took a sharp turn for the worse when the tour passed through Victoria, British Columbia, and the promoting duo consequently lost money. This resulted in a back salary of $600 being owed to Dinnie, a further $300 to McMillan, and a corresponding rift in the partnership.

What caused the latest Portland show to go awry was that Dinnie had agreed to wrestle for 20 percent of the gate money to ensure that he received something tangible for his efforts, while Muldoon received 50 percent of the gate receipts. Each man had a representative in the box office that pocketed his respective share as the money came in, but once Dinnie's portion of the gate had been secured, he still refused to wrestle the match unless Stechhan immediately compensated Dinnie for the additional $600 that he was owed.

Muldoon emerged from the fray smelling like a rose, at least temporarily. There was no contractual agreement for hippodroming that could be directly tied to Muldoon, nor had he admitted to the practice in a public setting. In the meantime, *The Wood River Times* reported that Judge Moreland of the Portland Police Court ruled that Dinnie was "a self-convicted liar and people were swindled thereby," but the statute for obtaining money under false pretenses "did not provide for punishment of liars."

Highland Games and Hippodromes

Dinnie returned to San Francisco with his reputation damaged, but not entirely in tatters, as there was only so much harm that could be done to the reputation of an athlete whose might was proven beyond a doubt every time he flung a hammer. Still, Dinnie soon departed for Australia to begin 1884, where the Aussies received him as a major sports celebrity who was visiting their shores.

The Australian press praised Dinnie as the "champion all-round athlete of the world" who held "nearly all the records at feats of skill and strength." Still, the Aussies did not turn a total blind eye to current events, as the article in *The Australian Town and Country Journal* that trumpeted Dinnie's arrival also carried the warning that the famous strongman had been "badly worsted by William Muldoon in the many matches which they had," and that Dinnie had also been "mixed up in several very fishy hippodromes during his sojourn on this coast."

While Donald Dinnie spent the beginning of 1884 nursing his reputational wounds in Australia, Duncan Ross reigned as the unquestioned king of the Cleveland athletic scene. The favorable impression that he established among the city's residents was obvious to readers of *The Cleveland Leader*, which expressed that Ross was "in constant receipt of letters from prominent people asking him to give an athletic entertainment in some public hall in the city to which ladies and children can be invited."

Ross had also undertaken the task of managing the boxing career of Mervine Thompson, who had previously wrestled against Ross on the shows along the Lake Erie corridor that had established Ross' supremacy in the region. Other wrestlers from those shows were also now training daily at Ross' gym.

It was retroactively apparent that Ross had probably wielded greater control over the events that enlarged his influence and popularity than originally realized. Still, in light of these questionable connections, the feats that *The Leader* credited Ross with sounded all the more preposterous under the circumstances.

"Cleveland is at present the most prominent sporting center in the country. She has been helped to this position by several circumstances, not the least of which is the very vigorous and thorough manner in which Mr. Duncan C. Ross has crushed out 'hippodroming,'" boasted *The Leader*. "Ross' permanent location in Cleveland has given the interests in athletic entertainments and exhibitions a healthy impetus, and the public are beginning to appreciate the fact."

In effect, at a moment when Clevelanders would have been justified in suspecting that Ross had been orchestrating hippodromes in their midst, *The Leader* offered its wholehearted endorsement that all of Ross' activities had been completely on the level, thereby absolving him of any blame.

At the same time, the general self-assuredness of Ross also makes the outcomes of some of his activities difficult to decipher. For example, while Ross was parading Mervine Thompson around at the South Side Natatorium of Chicago in an effort to drum up interest for a potential fight between Thompson and reigning American bareknuckle boxing champion John L. Sullivan, Ross also took to the mat for a match against 19-year-old Frank Whitmore, who was certainly unknown outside of Chicago. To say the results of the match were surprising would be an understatement.

"Ross had settled down to the conviction that he had a very easy thing. At the conclusion of a twenty-minute struggle, the champion realized that he had met a hard man," averred *The Cincinnati Enquirer*. "He was unable to throw Whitmore. To the surprise of the audience, Whitmore got a neck-lock on Ross and threw him fairly three counts. There was a great excitement when the fall was announced, and Ross protested the decision."

Given the intention of the event, which was both to promote Thompson as a fighter, and also to advertise Ross' own capabilities as a promoter, it makes little obvious sense why Ross would allow himself to be embarrassed by a comparative unknown unless he was setting the stage for a highly publicized rematch.

No such in-ring reunion between Ross and Whitmore ever took place, at least under the aforementioned circumstances. This makes the Whitmore bout one of the blemishes on Ross' record that may reflect a moment when Ross unwittingly bit off more than he could chew in a real match.

In the selection of language that *The Buffalo Commercial* employed to cover Whitemore's upset victory, the publication almost seemed to treat reports of Ross' loss as rumor, referring to Whitmore as "the man who is alleged to have thrown Ross in Chicago."

Safely back in Cleveland, Ross provided the staff of *The Leader* with unfettered access to his gym, and demonstrated for them "the systematic training necessary to develop the muscles that are called into action in a mixed wrestling match." The interview with Ross began with the reporter questioning Ross as to how he had managed to shed 13 pounds in the week since his appearance in Chicago. Ross' reply speaks to the woeful misapprehensions about health and nutrition that typified the 19th century prior to the discoveries of concepts like calories, which occurred a little more than a decade later.

"There is nothing better to remove superfluous flesh than seasickness," insisted Ross. "Something as exacting as that disease in calling out the unnecessary accumulations in the inner man is actually required once in four or five years. Good, lively running in one or two mile spurts, or exercise that exhausts the wind, will remove flesh. The proper diet is rare beef and stale bread. Warm food or drink must not be taken into the stomach."

To his credit, Ross did offer some legitimately helpful advice, insisting that trainees should take care not to overexert themselves, while still repeating longheld false beliefs, like the notion that the perspiration lost during exercise amounts to surplus fatty tissue being eliminated from the body, as opposed to mere water weight.

Highland Games and Hippodromes

"Very often exercise that tends to harden and enlarge the muscles will at the same time carry away surplus fat," continued Ross. "Hitting the sand bag, swinging the dumbbells and clubs, and all such vigorous work will also pull down the weight. A wrestler with any great amount of superfluous flesh upon his bones cannot hope to succeed against a man whose weight is made up of muscles and bones."

Ross also personally demonstrated his favorite methods for developing the strength and power of his upper body, which involved devices that would catch on with the general public in the coming century and beyond.

"Dumbbell practice is the best for developing the muscles of the arm. Very light ones are used. The arm is first extended to its full length and then closed, bringing the iron down to the shoulder. The work is continued vigorously for twenty minutes," Ross explained. "Two or more apparatuses for tightening the grip of the hands and fingers are also employed. One is a sand bag weighing about a hundred pounds, and having four ears, one at each corner. This is tossed in the air as high as possible and caught in the hands. It is vigorous and tedious exercise, but if continued, will eventually give the hands the grip of a vice."

Meanwhile, O.E. Pooler, another wrestler in the room, explained how a wrestler's knees are the first area of the body to weaken during a bout, and suggested that "leaping, kangaroo fashion, across the room," was the most efficient way for a wrestler to strengthen his legs. Likewise, the running of stairs was suggested as the best manner for improving strength in the calf muscles, with the training routine of Henry Dufur offered as a system worthy of emulation.

"(In the) Back of [Dufur's] store is a long flight of stairs leading to another street," said *The Leader*. "After his day's work, the 'Statue of Marlboro' dashes up and down the long steps ten or twelve times in succession. Citizens sometimes stand below and gaze stupidly up at him, wondering whether he is a fool or a lunatic. He contents himself, however, with the knowledge that he is neither, and the calves of his legs are like steel."

The training routine of Colonel James McLaughlin of Detroit was also described, which included placing one of his best horses "within the thills of a sulky" while one of his sons climbed into the seat. From there McLaughlin would grasp the rear bar, and dart off with the horse in a sharp trot, often covering up to 17 miles in a day.

Ross maintained that he was not obligated to engage in training routines that might cause him to burn himself out, since his advantage was owed to the fact that he always kept himself in good condition through consistent daily exercise, and the help of a few ointments that strengthened his exterior.

"The feet are toughened by being coated with Stockholm tar, and the skin of the hand and wrists by a mixture of salt and vinegar," said Ross. "This seems to absorb all the moisture of the skin, and to leave the hands dry and tough. Sometimes tannic acid is used, but it often injures the skin."

One of the major motivations behind *The Leader*'s exploration of Ross' training center was to document the daily grind and diversity of modalities required to mold Ross into the mixed wrestling champion of the world. The timing of the coverage was favorable, in retrospect, because Ross was about to go on a championship run that would further substantiate that lofty claim in the eyes of the public, at least in the Midwest.

First would be a series of bouts with James McLaughlin, who was regarded by many as the regional champion of collar-and-elbow wrestling and "counted as the best wrestler in the world at that style" according to *The Evening Post of Cleveland*. He had also recently defeated Henry Dufur in that grappling style in front of a Detroit crowd, for whom McLaughlin was the unrivaled ruler of the sport.

"The two men had never met in the wrestling arena, and opinion among sporting men was pretty evenly divided as to who would prove the victor," added *The Evening Post*.

"People interested in such matters came here from New York, Chicago, Detroit, Pittsburgh and elsewhere to see the contest, and it is said that large sums were wagered on the result. The Opera House stage was thickly padded for the occasion, and seats sold for $3 each on the floor, $2 in the balcony and $1 in the gallery, $600 being paid to the tragedian Keene to give up the night for the wrestling match."

Ross succeeded in winning the Greco-Roman fall to open the match, and during the announcement of his victory, "Mrs. Duncan C. Ross, a handsome young lady who occupied a proscenium box, passed a basket of beautiful flowers upon the stage, a gift she had promised her husband if he should win the first fall."

This would mark perhaps the first occasion that Ross' wife, Eugenie L. Gerke of Baltimore, Maryland, was mentioned in relation to his career, but it certainly wouldn't be the last. In the meantime, the men donned canvas jackets for the collar-and-elbow bout, and McLaughlin displayed his mastery of the method by downing Ross in only eight minutes.

At this juncture, it's important to recall the presence of the sportsmen wagering large sums of money on the match, because with the score tied, and the remaining fall to be contested in catch-as-catch-can, the smart money was undeniably on McLaughlin, who was advertised as one of the best wrestlers in the world at that style. No doubt, a longshot bet placed on Ross would pay handsomely if he could somehow manage to pull off the miraculous upset.

The third fall was preceded by a conspicuous exchange instigated by McLaughlin, who emerged from his dressing room wearing a jacket for the catch-as-catch-can bout, and demanded that Ross likewise don a jacket. When Ross refused, the referee read the articles of agreement and decided that nothing therein obligated the wrestlers to wear jackets. Therefore, the third round began with one wrestler shirtless, the other wrestler — an unhappy one — dressed in a jacket.

"This bout was a struggle between enormous strength, and wonderful quickness combined with great skill," continued

The Evening Post. "Ross repeatedly evaded a fall by marvelous twists and squirms, while McLaughlin often defied threatening locks by sheer force and weight. After an exciting contest of fifteen minutes, in which victory seemed to hover first over one and then the other, McLaughlin was laid squarely on his back with a full neck lock and Ross won the fall, the match, the stakes, sixty percent of the $2,200 door receipts, and the title of champion of the world at mixed wrestling."

After Ross completed the shocking upset of McLaughlin, the Colonel was summoned to stand before the footlights of the stage. From that position, McLaughlin blamed his loss on the fact that Ross had not worn a jacket, and insisted that he would "meet this man again for $2,000 in two weeks if he will wear a jacket." Ross agreed to those terms as long as it was a best-of-five series, but added that he would *not* wrestle McLaughlin in Detroit under any circumstances.

In the meantime, *The Detroit Free Press* took stock of the financial toll that misplaced bets on the Ross-McLaughlin match had taken on many Detroiters. The Gillman Bros sporting establishment of Detroit — adjacent to their hotel and restaurant at the corner of Woodward and Jefferson avenues — had been the site of considerable wagering on the results of the bout, and the gathered sportsmen received live updates on the results of the bout via telegraph.

"There was considerable money up on the contest, many bets being made on the night of the last Dufur-McLaughlin match," informed *The Free Press.* "The general opinion as to the winner of the match was considerably divided. The friends of Colonel McLaughlin were confident of his ability to throw Ross, but many doubted this on account of the nature of the match. While Detroit's champion has won many laurels at collar-and-elbow, it was thought by a number of sporting gentlemen that he could not throw Ross in the other styles of wrestling."

The article concluded with the somber statement that many Detroiters were "reported to have dropped considerable money in Cleveland last night over the result," which is an indication not only of how widespread the gambling on professional wrestling had grown, but how many opportunities there were to manipulate the results for financial gain.

When gambling houses in multiple large cities were all taking action on the same bouts, and with the wrestlers having the ability to manipulate the outcomes, they could very easily coordinate the placements of favorable bets through third parties from hundreds of miles away. Therefore, what looked like a loss for a wrestler in one city may have resulted in a massive financial windfall for them in another.

The next event would show just how strategic Ross could be about using a documented event from a match that took place in one city to influence the perception of a match result in another city at a later date.

Matsada Sorakichi, the first Japanese wrestler to acquire significant name recognition in the United States, made his way to Cleveland in April 1884 to headline an event with Ross. One of Sorakichi's unique contributions to mixed wrestling bouts was his insistence that his opponents battle in "the traditional Japanese style," which played out in a variation of sumo wrestling mixed with a great deal of headbutting, all of which his North American opponents typically made a great show of proclaiming that they were altogether ignorant of.

This inherent advantage of Sorakichi's was on full display during his bout in Cleveland with Ross. After Ross won the opening catch-as-catch-can round, the men retreated to their respective dressing rooms before returning to the carpet and preparing themselves for their first round of Japanese-style grappling.

"In preparing for this bout, each of the men wrapped about his loins a long band of cloth, which is a sort of a harness used by the Japanese," described *The Leader*. "Informing the seconds that if either of them touched one of the contestants that the fall would be given to his opponent, Referee Curry called time. Slapping his stomach with his right hand, the Jap lowered his head and rushed at Ross, who was advancing as if to shake hands. Before Ross knew what had happened, the Jap butted him with all his force in the short ribs of the right side. With the wind knocked out of him, Ross fell with his hands and feet on the carpet, and the fall was given to the Jap, the time being too short to compute."

Ross objected to the way Sorakichi assaulted him. He turned toward the referee and remarked, "I thought the fellow was going to shake hands with me. He held out his hand, and I was going to take hold of it." The crowd was said to have "laughed loudly" at Ross' complaint.

Matsada Sorakichi

More importantly, Ross conducted an examination of his side and "discovered that one of the short ribs was broken, the ends being plainly perceptible to the touch." Ross insisted on continuing with the bout despite the injury that he assured the audience that he had suffered.

Again, Ross won the catch-as-catch-can bout, which led to yet another round of Japanese-style combat. The round commenced with exhortations from the crowd that Duncan should keep an eye on Sorakichi and not repeat the mistake of attempting to shake hands with him.

"Facing each other, they danced about the platform several times like roosters in a barnyard, and then made a rush," continued *The Leader*. "The Jap aimed for Ross' ribs with his head, but he was wide of the mark. Ducking his head, Ross butted the Jap squarely on the nose. Retreating for an instant the Jap made another rush. Jumping to one side, Ross lowered his head, and striking the Jap in the side with all his force, touched his hands to the carpet. Sorakichi rolled over on his back, and the crowd yelled, but as Ross' hand touched the carpet before the Jap fell, the fall was decided against him."

Although Sorakichi had technically won the one-minute round, his demeanor betrayed his acknowledgement that he had been defeated at his own brand of wrestling, and had won simply on a technicality. Looking despondent, Sorakichi suddenly clutched his side, and then requested to be escorted to his dressing room. It was soon announced that Sorakichi was unfit to continue the bout due to the blow he had suffered to his side, although it seemed far more likely that he was deemed psychologically unfit to proceed due to hurt feelings.

In the dressing room following his victory, Ross apparently overheard someone referring to Sorakichi as a tough man. Ross agreed with this, and further added that Sorakichi was "the worst man he ever took hold of," and "worse than half a dozen McLaughlins," but added that his opponent was "no wrestler," and "simply a butter."

Sometime between the conclusion of Ross' bout with McLaughlin and his bout with Sorakichi, he changed his mind about the venues he refused to compete in. By the middle of April, he was in Detroit defending the mixed heavyweight championship of the world against McLaughlin.

Highland Games and Hippodromes

In contrast to many of the newspapers of the day, *The Detroit Free Press* handled its coverage of the title rematch between the two men who were the preeminent wrestling figures in their respective cities as if it was a work of pure theater. The opening line of the article recounting the event opened by admitting that the large attendance at the Detroit Opera House served as a testament to "the fact that Detroit people rather enjoy to be Barnumized," an allusion to prominent showman, circus magnate, and "perpetrator of hoaxes" P.T. Barnum.

Attention was also called to the fact that young boys roamed the aisles of the Opera House selling photographs of McLaughlin for 25 cents a piece, but *The Free Press* remarked that most of the men present at the venue declined to purchase any souvenirs out of the need to carry no evidence of their whereabouts on that evening.

Through the first four falls, McLaughlin had won rounds one and three, both of which were collar-and-elbow falls, and Ross had been victorious in the second and fourth rounds, the sidehold contests. When the final round — a catch-as-catch-can bout — was about to begin, a "satirical individual" in the audience remarked that MacLaughlin "will now surprise the world by throwing the champion catch-as-catch-can wrestler," if for no other reason than it was an odd fall, which meant that it was now "his turn."

True to the terms agreed upon after their first bout, the men wrestled the catch-as-catch-can round clad in loose jackets. In the midst of the struggle, McLaughlin resorted to unseemly tactics in his efforts to gain an advantage over Ross.

"[McLaughlin] tried for nearly a minute, and then placed his knee upon a portion of Ross' person that is strictly prohibited by the rules, the penalty for transgression being forfeiture of the match," observed *The Free Press*. "In this position, by springing up and down, he caused Ross to drop to the stage. As soon as he was permitted to rise, Ross sprang to his feet, rushed up to McLaughlin and commenced what looked like the imitation of a rough-and-tumble fight. Any such earnest work was not on the programme, however, and he was hauled back and held until his ire subsided. He claimed the foul, plainly witnessed by every spectator, but the claim was denied and the fall given to McLaughlin."

In his dressing room, Ross blamed the loss on a knee that McLaughlin had driven into his ribs — the same ribs injured during his prior bout with Sorakichi — and refused to concede that the loss was a fair one. As a result, Ross continued to refer to himself as the mixed wrestling champion of the world along Lake Erie, while McLaughlin claimed the same title in Detroit. It would remain a moot point, as each man was the acknowledged ruler of his respective domain, and neither would contest the other's claim as long as each remained confined to their preferred regions.

In a few short months, Duncan Ross had made himself an indispensible figure on the Midwestern athletic scene. In Australia, Donald Dinnie would make a valiant effort to replicate that feat while rehabilitating his tarnished reputation. Unfortunately, one errant move in a single wrestling match would touch off a series of struggles and setbacks that would take a long time for Dinnie to overcome.

6 – The Clever Knowing Ones

As Duncan Ross reigned as a wrestling figurehead in the Midwest, he continued with his sustained campaign of calling out John L. Sullivan for a fight with Ross' trainee and client, Mervine Thompson. In a reply offered in May 1884, Sullivan was relatively respectful of Thompson, acknowledging that it was perhaps true that Thompson was "a great wrestler" and would have been capable of throwing Sullivan in a wrestling bout.

However, Sullivan was skeptical about Ross' claim that Thompson could not be knocked out, and conveyed that he was "anxious to test my powers on him." As for Ross, Sullivan dismissed him outright as "a schemer and a hippodromer," and implied that he could not be trusted with the handling of an honest fight.

That same month, Ross defeated Matsada Sorakichi again, this time at the Theatre Comique in Washington, D.C., in front of a half-full house that "possessed some strong lungs which it used to circulate some bad language." Sorakichi was said to appear "in a sick condition," and the finish to the five-fall bout went in the favor of Ross. Multiple falls were disputed during the match, including the final fall, throughout which Sorakichi "did not seem to understand the proceedings," according to *The National Republican*, "and used what few English words he knew in claiming that he was not fairly thrown."

Anyone with a comprehensive knowledge of the relationship between Ross and Sorakichi would probably have been surprised to hear that the two seemed to have such an acrimonious relationship when they faced each other in Washington, or that Sorakichi was still having difficulty understanding the rules of wrestling in the United States.

The Cleveland Leader revealed in April that Sorakichi had been traveling in the entourage of Ross as he moved around the region in a group that also included Mervine Thompson, Dick Pooler, Charles Lange, and Mark Lamb. In fact, Sorakichi had served as Ross' second during his bout in Detroit with McLaughlin, and was confirmed to have "slapped him vigorously on the back" in between rounds "to keep the blood in a healthy circulation."

Illustration of Matsada Sorakichi

Moreover, Sorakichi was the only person who is confirmed to have been accompanying Ross during that trip to Detroit. While Sorakichi butted the walls of the Detroit Opera House with his head, Ross stood by and commented on the display, stating that the headbutts were a basic feature of a Japanese-style wrestling match, and added that Sorakichi had also scared passengers aboard the train car that brought the pair to Detroit by similarly butting the walls of the conveyance.

These initial bouts between Ross and Sorakichi were apparently a dress-rehearsal for their bout at Irving Hall in New York City. *The New York Herald* recounted the prior encounters between the pair in Cleveland and Washington, along with the detail that Sorakichi had supposedly broken Ross' ribs, presumably referring to the alleged injury from their Cleveland encounter.

The men wrestled on a 24-foot platform, and the writer from *The Herald* observed that Sorakichi looked darker and approximately 20 pounds lighter than when he had wrestled in New York during the prior winter. The first round in the catch-as-catch-can style was said to have been "the fiercest bout ever seen in New York" at that style, as it was punctuated by Ross tossing Sorakichi off the platform twice, the two men exchanging slaps to the face, and Ross repeatedly dropping his opponent onto the back of his own head.

Ross won the first fall after 53 minutes, and when the show proceeded to the inevitable fifth fall, Ross pulled off an unbelievable upset. With Sorakichi appearing confident that he would win the final fall, which was contested in Japanese style, he walked onto the platform wearing an embroidered Japanese gown that conferred upon him "the dignity of a foreign ambassador."

Ross somehow "pressed the Jap's knees to the platform" by dint of his "superior strength," certainly astounding the gamblers who thought it impossible that Sorakichi could lose a Japanese-style round.

While Ross was strengthening his control over wrestling in the Lake Erie region of the United States, Donald Dinnie's reputation on the West Coast was either partially salvaged or further damaged depending on how damning one considers proven links to predetermined wrestling matches to be.

In April 1884, in an apparent effort to bury the San Francisco wrestling scene on his way out of town, William

Highland Games and Hippodromes

Muldoon, who had easily been the Bay's top wrestling attraction in his time there, contacted the local press and made a further confession that hippodromes were rampant in the region, but insisted that all of his bouts had been on the level.

"The self-styled Graeco-Roman champion related his experiences in this city, charging almost everybody with crookedness in his line of business, and claiming for himself the credit of always acting fair with the public," reported *The San Francisco Examiner*. "Before the article had reached the public eye, Muldoon had vanished, and could not consequently be held personally responsible for the statement he had made in reference to many of the sporting people of this city."

This left the remaining wrestlers and promoters in the region in a tight predicament, forced to decide whether they should outright deny Muldoon's accusations, or bury him in an adjacent grave.

In particular, promoter Dan McNeil was asked to answer to Muldoon's statement that McNeil had arranged a meeting between Muldoon and Dinnie, and that Dinnie wanted to coordinate matches with Muldoon in a way that would ensure Muldoon "wouldn't be so rough with him," and that heavy falls suffered by Dinnie during a prior bout between the two "had jarred him very much."

"Muldoon lies bigger than a mule," responded McNeil. "He never made any such statement to me, and I never asked him to come in to see Dinnie. The match was all arranged before I ever went to see him. All I had to do with it was to take the business management, after everything else had been arranged. That was after Dinnie had come from Stockton and Sacramento."

McNeil was then asked if all of Muldoon's bouts in San Francisco had been "on their merits." McNeil smiled and said that Muldoon was "the shrewdest athlete who ever came to this Coast," and that he had so much money that he could dictate the terms of all of his matches, which usually resulted in Muldoon leaving with 90 percent of the gate money.

McNeil closed by stating that Muldoon's actions had "ruined sporting affairs on this Coast," and that the local wrestling fans "had been gulled to such an extent that they would no longer patronize the exhibitions."

In the meantime, Monsieur Max, the manager of Le Grande Auguste, was far less diplomatic when asked about Muldoon's statements, stating that Muldoon had never wrestled an authentic match on the West Coast, and that he had leveraged his money to purchase his favorable reputation.

"I have read all about it, and I brand him as a liar," said Max. "The first match with Donald Dinnie was fixed. The Scotchman was to fall. Muldoon sold the house to Len Grover before the match for $800, and he sold the second to Dan McNeill for, I think, $1,000. On the night of the match, Muldoon said if Dinnie did not go according to agreement he would break his neck."

Whether it should be applied to his credit or shame, Muldoon assumed a degree of culpability when he arrived on the East Coast. *The Boston Globe* reported how the newly arrived wrestler had confessed that "none of the matches excepting the first one with Donald Dinnie, were square — all being under an 'agreement' as to the result." Muldoon added that net receipts of his bouts along the Pacific Coast had amounted to $40,000, of which he personally received $25,000, a sum equivalent to roughly $800,000 in 2020.

Roughly 7,000 miles away from a San Francisco wrestling scene that was in disaray, Dinnie wrestled his first bouts in Australia, where the public interest in his presence instantly centered around a match between himself and the foremost native wrestler of Australia, William Miller.

A Melbourne native, Miller had a reputation as a fantastic Greco-Roman wrestler and world-class boxer, and also as a well-rounded athlete, albeit to a far lesser degree than Dinnie. He had also successfully toured North America and shared the stage with several of the most well-known wrestlers there, including William Muldoon, Theobaud Bauer, and Colonel McLaughlin.

Highland Games and Hippodromes

The two powerful men met in April at the Exhibition Building of Melbourne. Billed as a bout between the Australian wrestling champion and the world champion athlete for the "world heavyweight wrestling championship," the bout was constructed as a mixed-styles affair intended to allow Miller and Dinnie to showcase their presumed strengths in Greco-Roman and backhold wrestling, respectively. Curiously, the bout was only scheduled for six falls, making a draw the likeliest possible outcome if each man held serve.

The Argus of Melbourne pointed out that Miller was the stouter man who "looked every inch a gladiator," but that the much older Dinnie "seemed to be composed entirely of bone and sinew, with bunches of muscle on his limbs and arms, and wonderfully-developed shoulders."

Dinnie quickly took Miller down to the carpet during their first Greco-Roman tussle, but being comparatively unskilled on the ground, Dinnie was unable to advance his position, while Miller "looked round coolly while the Scotchman vainly tried to turn him over on his back, the excitement amongst the onlookers being worked up to the highest pitch as the struggle progressed."

"Dinnie relaxed his strain for an instant, and then like lightning the positions were reversed, Miller being in the ascendant, but he too failed to get his opponent back downward, although the crowd cheered on the men wildly," continued *The Argus*. "Both were on their feet again, and when Dinnie, once more getting the back hold, hurled Miller like a child to the ground, a wild Gaelic shout arose above the monotony of cheers. The applause was impartially given, and, if anything, the sympathies of the larger section of the crowd were with the Scotchman, who was struggling under strange conditions."

The "strange conditions" that Dinnie found himself in, apparently, was that he was wrestling on the ground with an opponent who was far more adept than Dinnie when their bodies were positioned horizontally. The reporter from *The Argus* seemingly picked up on this, remarking that when both wrestlers were down, "Miller, with his great power and experience, was all-potent, but when erect, Dinnie's wonderful activity more than counterbalanced his opponent's superior strength."

Miller easily pinned Dinnie to conclude the Greco-Roman round. As expected, Dinnie just as effortlessly won the backhold bout, and the reporter observed "it was apparent that each man was well-nigh invincible in his own style of wrestling, and that there was little hope of the match being anything but a drawn one."

The action proceeded predictably until the third encounter in the Greco-Roman fashion. During that round, both men fell to the carpet in a heap, and Miller forced Dinnie onto his back to capture a third consecutive pinfall victory at his favored style of wrestling. However, when Miller attempted to rise to his feet, he instead fell back to the carpet and clutched his left ankle.

"In an instant the tumult was stopped, for it was evident that in the final effort something had gone wrong," concluded *The Argus*. "Miller's friends ran to his assistance, and he was lifted up; but, after taking a couple of steps, he staggered and again fell, and, on examination, it was evident that his ankle was either badly dislocated, or that the bone was fractured. His late opponent promptly came to his assistance, and, as the men grasped each other heartily by the hand, the appreciation of the crowd for the manliness and fine spirit shown by both men found vent in loud cheers."

Miller was carted away on a shutter, with his opponent being one of the men who was kind enough to carry him out of the venue. With Miller now safely removed from the building, several members of the crowd lingered to hear details about the injury, while others openly questioned whether or not they had just been the latest victims of one of Dinnie's hippodroming efforts.

"In a few instances some of those unhappy people who have been, or believe that they have been, systematically victimised during an unfortunate acquaintance with every sport about which a bet can be booked affirmed their pronounced suspicions as to the accident being 'a put-up thing,'" stated the article. "A moment's reflection would have shown, of course, that Miller had everything to gain and nothing to lose by finishing the match. As a rule, however, these sorts of people, who estimate the intentions of others by their own standard do not reflect about anything, but merely jump hurriedly at silly conclusions."

The ankle was later confirmed to have been fractured, and Miller would be sidelined for nearly a year. Those closest to the scene of the injury insisted to the naysayers that they had personally viewed Miller's ankle and could affirm that it was uncomfortably swollen in appearance.

With all due respect to the reporter from *The Argus*, the conclusions of the crowd were not altogether silly in light of the accusations that Dinnie had left in his wake in the United States. Still, while it is more likely than not that the bout was indeed wrestled with a predetermined outcome in mind, the injury to Miller were proven to be legitimate, and Dinnie's business prospects in Australia would soon suffer due to the loss of the only heavyweight wrestler and athlete on the continent who could competently wield weights alongside him.

In Miller's case, the injury was particularly devastating, as it had been planned for months that he would travel to the U.S. to fight against the uncrowned world heavyweight champion John L. Sullivan. *The Seattle Post-Intelligencer* reported that the compound fracture to Miller's ankle would cost Sullivan upwards of $10,000, and suggested that Sullivan would likely "lick Dinnie" if he saw him, since Dinnie was being directly blamed for breaking Miller's leg.

To add insult to a literal injury, it was reported that Miller's mother passed away the very next day after he had broken his ankle.

The six-round structure of the bout seems as if it was intended to force a draw in order to generate interest in a series that would culminate in the crowning of a respectable world heavyweight wrestling champion. The net result of the match was that it left a world championship vacancy that had no hopes of being filled anytime soon, leaving Dinnie to tour the nation without the ability to make a justifiable claim to championship status.

The following month, Dinnie would visibly take a long step downward in the caliber of his competition. Replacing Miller, who had been the only Australian wrestler of sufficient size and fame to appear as a respectable name alongside Dinnie's on the marquee, was Mons. Victor, a far smaller wrestler.

Suddenly, when faced with the challenge of the comparatively diminutive Victor, Dinnie was now seemingly brave enough to compete exclusively in the Greco-Roman style of wrestling, even though that technique had been his Achilles heel in seemingly all other engagements with skilled grapplers.

At the Victoria Hall, Victor successfully pinned Dinnie in the first fall, probably to interest enough of the bettors present to place a wager in his favor, with the house paying £25 to £50 on the result. After the first fall, it was reported by *The Argus* that during the rest of the encounter Dinnie's opponent "never had the slightest chance of scoring."

"The Scotch wrestler mastered the difficulties of the Graeco-Roman style after the first few minutes wrestling, and then threw Victor three times in succession, thus winning the match," printed *The Argus*. "At the close, Dinnie announced, through his manager, Mr. Joseph Pickersgill, that he would make a match to throw any wrestler in Australia 10 times within the hour, allowing them to choose their own styles. It was explained that Professor Miller, who was injured in a recent match, was of course excepted.

"In alluding to the late match between Dinnie and Miller, Mr. Pickersgill stated that the former was anxious to give his disabled opponent a benefit, and that if other athletes would join in the matter his services were available in any way required. The announcement was received with loud applause, and Dinnie, whose victory was a very popular one, was loudly cheered."

Dinnie's brave pronouncement that he would throw any wrestler in Australia 10 times in an hour while allowing his opponent to choose the styles was indeed a daring gesture, as it was far closer to the spirit of a true open challenge than the majority of the collaboratively drafted letters to the editor submitted by colluding wrestlers in North America.

Whether it was Dinnie or Pickersgill who didn't think very highly of the quality of available wrestlers in 19th century Australia, which had a population of just over two million at the time, the wrestler-manager tandem was going to be in for a rude awakening. When Dinnie toured the town of Sale, with a population well under 5,000 residents, he was challenged by a local by the name of Dr. McDonald during an event held under the auspices of the local Caledonian Society.

The Singleton Argus announced that it had received a private letter delineating how Dinnie had been successfully thrown by McDonald, and that "all the Caledonians assembled in a neighboring hostelry and drank (McDonald's) health in a bumper." It was announced in the same report that Dinnie "had a row with his boss," Joseph Pickersgill, and that Dinnie's company had "seceded from Joseph," while Pickersgill was threatening to send the authorities after Dinnie.

Dinnie's embarrassment at the hands of a rural Aussie wrestler was not the sole reason for the falling out between Dinnie and Pickersgill, although it couldn't possibly have helped. Rather, *The Sporting Judge* reported how it was at the same event in Sale that Dinnie had needed to repeatedly pester Pickersgill for past-due payments, in a scenario that was conspicuously similar to his dispute with Stechhan in Oregon. It was for this reason that Dinnie had no-shown an event in the Gippsland region, and decided to part company with his managers.

"Mssrs. Pickersgill and Willis, on the other hand, allege that they have been very harshly treated, that Dinnie's engagement all through has been a failure, that their expenses have been very heavy — that instead of owing Dinnie money, he, on the contrary, is indebted to them in some hundreds of pounds, and that he has on occasions insisted on his full bond," added *The Judge*. "Then came a smash up. Dinnie did not appear, and Mssrs. Pickersgill and Willis threaten to bring an action against him for breach of contract. And Dinnie and they have fallen to calling one another names and expressing their opinions publicly of one another, to the amusement of outsiders, but the distress of sport."

Incredibly, the next move by Pickersgill was to rent Victoria Hall in order to deliver a lecture entitled "Athletes I have met, notably Donald Dinnie." The one-and-a-half-hour lecture — attended by a reporter from *The Mercury* — concluded with Pickersgill "showing up Dinnie's uncouth manner of treating his patrons, and the manner in which he had led to the breach between himself and the management."

The Mercury cautioned that all of Pickersgill's "allusions to Scotland's champion athlete are absolutely unreportable, as we entertain a wholesome respect for the pains and penalties of the law."

As a direct response to Pickersgill's defamatory lecture, Dinnie wrote a letter to the athletic editor of *The Sportsman*, stating that Pickersgill had written him a letter after his first appearance in Sale lamenting that Dinnie's appearances had been a financial flop, and that they would meet with him to settle up the next morning at 11 a.m. because it was "beyond their intention or patience to waste money or go on losing."

"When we met, he offered me nothing from the previous evening's drawings, but proposed to give me one-half gross receipts till back salary was paid. I refused this, stating that under his management I would not have a chance of ever being paid up," Dinnie wrote. "He refused any other condition; consequently I stated that I should then find work for myself. I offered my services again that evening if former salary was paid, but he at once refused; so with the aid of my Scotch friends in Sale, we set up an entertainment on the Caledonian Society's Grounds, and also a performance in the evening. At a lecture he gave on Friday evening, he represented me as the 'black sheep,' but I leave my countrymen in particular, and also the public in general, to judge this for themselves."

In conclusion, Dinnie submitted that he agreed to appear for the Caledonian organizations in Ballarat and Sale without Pickersgill's management, and was paid a total of £170 for the two nights of work; he had allegedly made only £15 for nine days of work under Pickersgill's management.

The amount with which Dinnie was compensated for his performances had seemingly increased tenfold now that he was free from the oversight of a handler. Still, reports indicate that he had some difficulty paying bills and fines. *The Ovens and Murray Advertiser* recounted how Dinnie was arrested by two constables in Beechworth for having not paid a fine of £3 — with a further £1 6s and 6d worth of costs imposed on him — that he had incurred in the town of Mooroopna "for insulting behaviour to the sergeant of police at that place, in refusing him admission to his entertainment."

"The renowned Scotchman, on receiving the summons, treated it with contempt by not allowing so small a matter to interfere with his appearances in public, and accordingly did not attend the court to answer the charge," explained *The Advertiser*. "The fine not having been paid, a warrant for Dinnie's arrest was issued, and was about to be executed just prior to the entertainment in St. George's Hall commencing, when further proceedings were stayed by the payment of the £4 6s 6d demanded."

Operating under his own management, Dinnie found new opponents to compete against from amongst the available Australians. In July, he wrestled against Thomas of Eaglehawk at the Matthews Bros' Circus in Sandhurst, with five different styles of wrestling being contested, but with a toss being made between each bout that empowered its winner to select from the grappling styles that had not yet been wrestled at the time of the toss.

In the presentation of the bout, great pains were seemingly made to position Dinnie as an expert in Greco-Roman wrestling, a style that had been one of his clear weaknesses in prior appearances, and which also happened to be developing a reputation alongside catch-as-catch-can style as the grappling method that most convincingly marked the true masters of wrestling.

For anyone with knowledge of the way a mixed-styles wrestling encounter generally unfolded, and especially an affair that involved Donald Dinnie, the way this bout played out would certainly have appeared fishy. To wit, Thomas won the toss, and quickly selected Cumberland style to begin the bout, since it was plainly advertised as the style he was most familiar with.

In the style that Thomas professed to be best at, he was demolished in a shade over two minutes. *The Evening News of South Wales* described how "the easy manner in which Thomas was overpowered in this style created some surprise," which led Thomas to explain his abrupt defeat to the audience by stating that he simply "did not get a good hold."

Thomas rallied to win the Cornish-style round in just under 12 minutes, and then, upon seizing the momentum of the bout and being fortunate enough to win the following toss for selection of styles, made the preposterous choice of Scottish style — the system of wrestling that Dinnie was advertised to be undefeated in. It was a choice that no rational competitor would make, and Dinnie immediately hurled Thomas to the ground and held him down for the 30 seconds required to earn the fall.

The next round, contested in Sir John Astley's style, simply required that a grappler be driven to one knee in order to be defeated. Dinnie and Thomas both slipped, resulting in Dinnie's hand and knee touching the ground first. The Scotsman appealed the decision to no avail, and Thomas tied the score in fluke fashion.

"The contest for the remaining style, Graeco-Roman, was regarded as a gift to Dinnie, and so it proved," concluded *The Evening News*. "The contest lasted 2 min 30 sec. Dinnie was then declared the winner amid applause."

In no other scenario would it have been perceived that a win for Dinnie in a Greco-Roman wrestling match would be a foregone conclusion. To his credit, Dinnie seemed to have learned his lesson from the Sale incident, and now clearly ducked challenges that came from unvetted sources.

As a case in point, when Dinnie and his troupe toured the North Shore region of New South Wales, it was revealed by *The Goulbourn Evening Post* that a local wrestler named John Keating emerged from the crowd, challenged Graham at collar-and-elbow wrestling, and effortlessly threw him three times.

"Keating then challenged either Dinnie or Thomas for £50 a side, which was not accepted," continued *The Post*. "Keating challenged Dinnie last week through the columns of the *Evening News* and met with no reply. He stated that he is willing to wrestle Dinnie in three different styles, viz., collar and elbow, Cornish, and Dinnie to choose any other style he likes."

While Dinnie had seemingly acquired an understanding about the dangers of accepting open challenges, he was also apparently slow to learn the lesson that certain conclusions to wrestling matches are inherently unsatisfying when a sizable portion of the assembled onlookers are placing wagers on the outcome, and when the ultimate aim is to drum up repeat business.

On the November night when Dinnie met J. Stables of South Brisbane, the condition was that Stables only needed to win two falls out of seven in order to be deemed the winner of the match. Dinnie won the first fall, but Stables was awarded the second when the umpire decided that Dinnie had lost hold of Stables when in the act of throwing him "and thus committed a breach of regulations."

In theory, the fact that Stables only needed to win one fall of the remaining five in order to achieve victory should have elevated the tension of the bout, but for the remainder of the night Stables was "unable to secure the slightest advantage," and "the spectators manifested signs of impatience." Of note was the fact that the grapplers appeared to be going out of their way to intentionally waste time that "might have served to complete the contest half-a-dozen times over."

At 10 o'clock, the time that had been agreed upon for the cessation of the bout, Graham stepped out to announce the bout was a draw, which was an unpopular decision to say the least.

"This announcement was received with hooting on the part of those in the gallery and body of the hall; and amid some disorder Dinnie stated that he was willing to renew the contest on the understanding that there should be a limit to the time for catching hold," said *The Courier Mail*. "It was far from right, he said, on the part of his opponent, to waste the time in this respect, as he had done from beginning to end of the match."

The Mail added that the disorder increased as the crowd dispersed, with "not a few of those present expressing their opinion in no measured terms that the whole affair was a 'sell.'"

Responding in print to the claim that his match with Stables had been prearranged, Dinnie had a letter circulated in the press stating that it would have been absurd for him to have entertained such a proposal.

"I wished to finish that night, and gave every chance to my opponent to do so, but I believe his judge advised him against taking hold to save some money he had bet on the result," Dinnie explained. "Had not Mr. Stables complained of having sprained his side, I would have insisted on the referee putting us together, but as he promised to double the stakes for a similar match, I consented to give him all the chance of getting well. Mr. Marsden, who acted as referee tells me he is blamed for being in the 'sell,' as it is called, but I never met the gentleman before, and I only lost by the toss of a coin by the referee I chose, Mr. Walters. As it was all chance who was to be referee, it shows how very unreasonable the general public often is. I have my money down to wrestle for stakes only. What do the clever knowing ones say to this?"

If the "clever knowing ones," had the luxury of reading the North American newspapers, they might have glimpsed at least one of the articles that explained how nearly all of the stakes involved in professional wrestling bouts were made-up sums, and that most bouts were conducted solely for an agreed-upon split of the money earned from spectator admissions. With this knowledge in tow, most knowledgeable fans would have been painfully unimpressed by Dinnie's rejoinder.

Donald Dinnie and his collection of medals

Even if Dinnie's followers in Australia didn't know enough about the wrestling game to be skeptical about his grappling exhibitions, they were strikingly critical about other events that were conducted under his management, and his athletic displays in particular.

Highland Games and Hippodromes

The Warwick Examiner and Times not only criticized Dinnie's handling of the Stables affair, but then divulged that the Highland event hosted by Dinnie at the Exhibition Grounds the following Saturday was "far from successful." The paper opined that "want of management was everywhere noticeable," that the event was poorly attended, and that many of the events were held under such unsatisfactory conditions that few athletes even wished to compete in them.

This sentiment was echoed in the pages of *The Queensland Figaro*, which compared Dinnie's latest events to the games that he hosted when under the management of Joseph Pickersgill, and especially an event held in recognition of the Prince of Wales birthday, when Dinnie was "the cynosure of neighbouring eyes."

"That exhibition was given under the auspices of the Queensland Scottish Association, the arrangements were complete, and the prizes on the most liberal scale," elaborated *The Figaro*. "Such matters ensured success. Since then, Dinnie has been exhibiting on his own hook."

The Figaro then elaborated on what went wrong for Dinnie during his event at the Exhibition Grounds, detailing how the program he presented "was so handicapped with conditions of beating fastest records, etc., that the chief events fell through and Dinnie saved his offered money."

In effect, by desiring to maximize his own profits, the parsimonious Dinnie had become severely tightfisted. As such, even the legitimate Highland athletic contests he hosted were beginning to take on a controversial character.

If these unfavorable revelations about Dinnie's games hadn't resulted in enough bad publicity, things would become palpably worse when it was perceived that Dinnie had stiffed a respected Australian athlete with ample name recognition.

During a Caledonian-themed event held in December at the Cremorne Gardens of Melbourne, Dinnie offered a prize of £50 to "anyone who could jump within six inches of the highest record." The challenge was accepted by trained

Australian high jumper D.M. Brown, who cleared a height of 5'5".

"... and on that [Brown] claimed the prize, being under the impression that Dinnie meant to award it to the person who came within 6in. of his best record, which according to his bills, was 5ft. 11in," reported *The Courier Mail*. "Donald intimated he intended to have mentioned the winning height was to be within 6in. of 6ft. 2in., or 5ft. 8in. — 3in. below what he is said to have cleared."

To place the matter into its proper context, Dinnie's requirement that the jump needed to be within six inches of 6'2" meant that he was stipulating that a prize-winning jump at his Highland Games needed to be within six inches of the acknowledged *world* high-jumping record of the time, which was still officially under 6'3".

A disappointed Brown quickly challenged Dinnie to publicly jump against him one-on-one as an alternate means of earning the advertised money, but Dinnie brushed aside the challenge by stating that he no longer jumped competitively "owing to an accident he had met with some time ago."

Try as he might, Donald Dinnie couldn't seem to avoid negative publicity wherever he trod in Australia. Conversely, Duncan Ross could seemingly do no wrong within his Lake Erie stronghold. Things would take a drastic turn when Ross shifted his gaze westward, and a shocking tragedy would soon have the Scottish-Canadian hero contemplating the end of an athletic career that was only just reaching its peak.

7 – More Fun Than Fury

The next high-profile wrestler that Duncan Ross would engage in matches with wouldn't do him any favors in relation to the air of distrust that was beginning to encircle him, and the niggling suspicions that his wrestling was less than authentic.

The man Ross wrestled with was William Muldoon, with whom Ross had already had a contentious relationship. Muldoon and Whistler had famously squabbled with Ross over money that the Scottish-Canadian alleged that they owed him from a bout that Muldoon and Whistler had openly declared to have been a hippodrome, albeit one that they had pretended to coordinate in order to entrap and embarrass Ross.

Under these circumstances alone, it seems foolish for Ross to have had any professional dealings with Muldoon going forward, and this is before considering the more damning accusations that dogged Muldoon following his departure from the West Coast one year earlier, and particularly as it pertains to his bouts with Donald Dinnie.

Nonetheless, Muldoon and Ross apparently patched up their relationship enough to make a business partnership palatable, and the two met at the Grand Opera House in Cincinnati in June, in front of "a tremendous audience" that included much of the upper crust of the Cincinnati community.

Noting that "a better class of people probably never patronized a sporting event," *The Cincinnati Enquirer* listed a series of prominent residents in the crowd, including mayor Thomas Stephens, former mayor William Means, leading Democratic political figure John D. Banks, and several major business figures within the Cincinnati area.

While the majority of mixed-style wrestling matches from the era were painfully dull in their strict adherence to the pattern of each wrestler winning the rounds contested in the grappling styles in which they were favored, the Ross-Muldoon bout went completely against form.

Highland Games and Hippodromes

The Enquirer's reporter exclaimed how "every fall was contrary to the slate the spectators had fixed up," which the paper declared to have been a "marvelous surprise." The writer confirmed that it had been "generally agreed that Muldoon would win the two Greco-Roman falls, Ross the two side-hold falls, and that it would be nip and tuck in the final bout at catch-as-catch-can, with odds in favor of the superb athlete from New York."

"The very first bout wrecked the plans when Ross won one of the Greco-Roman bouts, and the surprise was all the more manifest when Mudoon won one of the side-hold falls," continued the article. "This left all in a state of the wildest excitement when the catch-as-catch-can bout was announced. Even at the beginning of this, it seemed that Muldoon was having it all his own way until the wily Scotchman got him by the legs, threw him over the stage, and then downed him at the entrance of one of the right flies, out of the sight of most of the audience. The exhibition was most exhilarating, and the wildest excitement and cheer ensued when the result was announced."

To clarify, *The Enquirer* was referring to the disputed fall that occurred in the fifth and final round, and which occurred upon the theatrical rigging system of the stage, and outside of the designated area. With the men partially intertwined with the rope-and-pulley system that raised and lowered stage scenery, Ross pressed Muldoon's shoulder to the mat, the referee counted the fall, and the curtain quickly went down.

"In a moment, the stage was filled with outsiders, and opinion was divided on the decision," explained the publication. "Many of Muldoon's friends claimed that the referee had no right to decide (rule) it a fall when the men were in the flies, but should have commanded them to break and try it over again. The referee showed no disposition to change his views, and the match was given to Ross."

Afterwards, the men in the audience who supported Muldoon — presumably with their wagers — were all "claiming that the match was a hippodrome, a cut-and-dried affair, carried out according to programme." It's unknown whether they were suggesting that the bout was phony on the basis of Muldoon having been set up to lose, or whether or not they believed that Muldoon was a willing participant in the scheme.

Regardless, *The Enquirer*'s reporter tied an introspective bow on the affair, asking a series of contemplative questions about what it would mean to professional wrestling as an industry, and the sporting public at large, if the event contested that evening had not been an authentic grappling competition.

"It would seem a little strange that Muldoon should enter into a scheme to wheedle and swindle the public, and at the same time submit to a defeat," stated *The Enquirer*. "If, as Mr. Muldoon's intimate friends declare, the affair was a farce, merely to get a big crowd for another match at Cleveland, the questions arise. Was there ever, or will there ever be, a match wrestled on the square? And is either Muldoon or Ross worthy of further notice from a respectable people and a respectable press?"

The mere presence of Muldoon and Ross together on the same stage at that point in their careers should have been enough to elicit suspicions about the bout's authenticity, but the writer from *The Enquirer* might have arrived at a more definitive conclusion had he been privy to the amount of money that could be made in a room of dignitaries and high rollers by having the correct sequence of longshot bets all pay off on the same night.

With individual bets taken on everything from the lengths of each fall to who would win each fall, as well as the ultimate winner of the bout, a person who correctly bet that Muldoon would lose a Greco-Roman fall — the grappling discipline in which he was the avowed world champion — and also lose a bout he was the overall favorite to win, could probably have made a small fortune on that evening. In reality, it's likely that Muldoon and Ross both did exactly that by placing secret bets through intermediaries.

The Enquirer noted that Muldoon "took his defeat gracefully," knowing that the loss "does not detract from his reputation one whit" because he lost a mixed wrestling bout and was still the reigning Greco-Roman champion. If Muldoon indeed capitalized financially that night the way it is suspected, it was indeed a clever way for him to have his cake and eat it, too.

Duncan Ross cigarette advertisement

In the midst of these events, Ross still maintained his connection with the Caledonian communities of the country through whom he had built his athletic reputation and earned much of the money that had funded his ventures. In July 1884, he made an appearance at a Highland Games event held by the

St. Andrew's Society of Milwaukee that attracted an audience of 12,000, and Ross "electrified his spectators by exhibiting the very muscle and sinew of a brawny Scotchman."

The following month, Ross attended an even larger event hosted by the Caledonian Club in Boston, which drew 18,000 people. With Donald Dinnie safely in Australia, Ross dominated all of the popular throwing events, including the hammer throw and the caber toss.

At both the Boston Caledonian event and a Highland Games event held that same weekend in Erie, Pennsylvania, Ross participated in the only wrestling bouts contested at either affair. It's worth committing to memory that his opponent in Erie was John McBain, "of the Queen's Life Guard, and champion horseback wrestler of the English Army," because the authenticity of any one-on-one bouts participated in by Duncan Ross at Highland gatherings would soon be called into question, and with them the credentials of his opponents. As it stands, there is no evidence that this particular McBain ever participated in another wrestling event in his life.

All things considered, 1884 had been a wonderful year for Ross. A syndicated report that began circulating in September listed Ross amongst the richest athletes in the United States in terms of total earnings. In wrestling matches alone, it was reported that Ross "cleared $30,000," which, if true, would mean that he earned the 2020 equivalent of about $1 million.

The legitimacy of this figure may be either spot-on or far off depending on a few different factors. The person compiling the list certainly included the supposed stakes that Ross was earning from his wrestling matches, which were usually fake numbers used to raise public interest. Undoubtedly, Ross left the majority of those bouts with large shares of the gate money, and may have returned home with totals that approached the advertised stake money depending on how active his intermediaries were in placing bets on his behalf.

Highland Games and Hippodromes

Late in November, Ross made the obligatory public announcement that he was going to be departing from Cleveland and made a final challenge directed at "Capt. J.C. Daly, Col. J.H. McLaughlin, W. Muldoon, Joe Acton, and John McMahon" to meet him in a wrestling bout, although he probably had no illusions about the fact that any of them would be answering his challenge in the affirmative.

As a harbinger of things to come, Ross also challenged Donald Dinnie, "who claims to have defeated all the athletes and wrestlers in Australia," and also directed a challenge that seemingly came out of nowhere to meet Boswick Reed of Toronto "who claims the championship with broadswords." The latter proposal probably represents one of Ross' original attempts to broaden his reach as a performer, which was something he would soon revisit after completing his inevitable move to the West Coast.

Whether or not any responses to Ross' challenges were eventually received is irrelevant, because his next major public appearance was well over 2,000 miles away in San Francisco, California. *The San Francisco Examiner* described how Ross received a hero's welcome via a reception that included 40 guests, where "champagne flowed freely and jolly good fellowship and conviviality was the order of the evening until a late hour."

Ross was an invited guest of the Central Park Association, which was hosting a Caledonian event at which Ross was originally only going to give exhibitions, but "acting under [Ross'] advice," the association decided to offer prizes totalling $555 for the events in which Ross would be participating.

"They consist of throwing the heavy and light hammers, putting the heavy and light stones, tossing the caber, and running high jump," explained *The Examiner*. "Ross claims the all-round athletic championship of the world. He has a most enviable record and is the possessor of dozens of medals and trophies won by exertions. He is a magnificent specimen of physical manhood. He was born in Scotland, March 16,

Highland Games and Hippodromes

1855. His weight is 203 pounds, height 6 feet one-fourth inch, chest measurement 44 ¾ inches, biceps 16 inches, calf 17 inches, and thighs 25 inches. He is a married man."

This is perhaps one of the best examples of the sort of influence Ross brandished in Caledonian circles. Having inherited the mantle from Donald Dinnie as the top draw at Highland Games events in North America, Ross was able to "advise" the Central Park Association to offer the 2020 equivalent of more than $15,000 in events that Ross would be a clear favorite to win.

Predictably, no one at these games posed much of a challenge to Ross in any of the events he entered, and perhaps the most dodgy element to Ross' appearance at the games was the fact that he did not participate in the wrestling event, which was a one-on-one exhibition between Clarence Whistler and Tom Cannon. This represents one of the first times Ross and Whistler were present at the engagement since Whistler had boasted about double-crossing Ross in Minnesota.

If Whistler and Ross had mended their relationship enough to share the carpet with one another yet again, that match would have to wait until Ross' introductory five-styles match with Tom Cannon could be concluded. The bout took place at the California Theater, and it involved a fair amount of intra-match communication between Ross, Cannon, and their seconds that the crowd found humorous.

With the fall count tied at one apiece, Ross and Cannon began their round of sidehold-in-harness grappling. Ross hurled Cannon to the floor "with terrible force," and *The San Francisco Chronicle*'s reporter recorded that Ross' second shouted that it should have been ruled a fall when both of Cannon's shoulders struck the carpet.

"Where are my hips?" sneered Cannon, as he turned his head and looked in disgust at Ross' second.

"It's three points for a fall," explained Theo Bauer, who was serving as the referee. "Two shoulders and one hip or two hips and one shoulder."

Highland Games and Hippodromes

The round continued, and Ross slammed Cannon onto the floor again, requesting that Bauer count the pinfall in his favor.

"It is not necessary to stretch a man out like a log," said Ross to the audience, good-humoredly. "It takes only two points to win a fall."

"*Three* points constitute a fall," corrected Referee Bauer.

Ross went straight back to work, tossed Cannon to the ground again, and finally completed the fall by forcing Cannon's hips to the carpet along with his shoulders.

Cannon won the fourth round, which meant that the final round would decide the bout, and it would be wrestled in the collar-and-elbow style, with harnesses included, and with three points to constitute a fall.

As the wrestlers were being strapped into their harnesses, Ross said to his second: "See that he (Cannon) stands up close."

Throughout the opening moments of the fall, Ross' second indeed nagged Cannon about how he was positioned, prompting Cannon to respond to the annoyance by sarcastically asking him "How do you want me to stand? *This* way?" Cannon then obliged the second by assuming "an outward position."

"Go on and wrestle and don't talk so much," Bauer cautioned him.

After 11 minutes of tussling, Ross threw Cannon to the carpet twice, planted both his shoulders and hips to the floor, and won the match.

In the wake of Ross' win over Cannon, the prospects of a Ross-Whistler match were openly discussed in the San Francisco newspapers. However, before that bout could be confirmed, a very real tragedy struck Ross, which was first reported by *The Cleveland Leader*.

"Mrs. Duncan C. Ross, wife of the well-known athlete, died at their place of residence, No. 171 Ontario Street, last evening," revealed *The Leader*. "Mr. Ross was in San Francisco at the time, but has started for home and will reach the city next Tuesday night. Mrs. Ross had been in poor health ever since coming to Cleveland, but her death was very sudden and unexpected. Her parents live in Baltimore and will arrive today. Two children, a boy of four years and a girl of two, are left. The blow will be a severe one to Mr. Ross. The marriage was a romantic one, Mrs. Ross having wealthy parents and eloping to New York, where the marriage ceremony was performed. A reconciliation followed, and Mrs. Ross but recently returned from a pleasant visit home."

It was later disclosed by several newspapers that no fewer than three attempts were made to steal the remains of Eugenie Gerke Ross from the home of her father, Charles Gerke, resulting in guards being posted by her body to prevent further attempts to steal her corpse prior to its burial.

The San Francisco Examiner reported that Ross, perhaps believing that he had no further reason to sustain any presence in Cleveland, wrote a letter to M.E. Joyce, the treasurer of the Central Park Association, dated December 27, in which he expressed "strong hopes of finally taking up his permanent residence in this city (San Francisco)." In light of this stated desire, Ross' next set of announcements would be downright shocking.

A few weeks following the burial of his wife, the rumor spread through several news outlets that Ross had "given up his saloon business, renounced athletics, and decided to enter the ministry." As far-fetched as this sounded, the rumor was soon verified by a reporter who called Ross directly to ascertain the truth.

"Yes, I am going to give up my saloon, and shall wrestle no more," confirmed Ross. "I have decided to enter the pulpit and am now perfecting my plans for that purpose. I have tonight written a letter to the faculty at Trinity College, a theological seminary at Toronto, for admission, and hope to obtain a favorable reply, and if I do, I shall immediately close up my affairs here and enter. My purpose is to take a two years' course of study in theology, and then enter the ministry."

Highland Games and Hippodromes

Ross was then asked what had prompted him to make such a sudden shift in both his career choice and lifestyle.

"Principally a desire to help my fellow men," Ross answered. "Since my wife's death I have not the heart to resume my wrestling matches, and the saloon business has always been obnoxious to me. Besides, I am now convinced that in this way I can do the most good, and that it is my duty. In my particular business I have seen many things that will be useful in the pulpit. It will not be my purpose to wage war against the saloonist.

"In other words, I shall not pose as a reformed drunkard, for I have never been a drunkard. Neither am I to preach and advocate temperance exclusively. It is rather my design to point out to the young the dangers that lay in wait for them in great cities and to advocate a vigorous war on the disreputable dens that infest the city and the bad characters they shelter and protect. There is a field for such work, and I am confident I shall succeed in it. I hope to get away from the city in two weeks and to enter college the first of February."

Ross' decision to exchange professional sports for the pulpit was met with fervent praise from many newspeople, and especially those who decried the practice of alcohol consumption. One example of this came from *The Berrien Springs Era* of Southwest Michigan, which employed a colorful metaphor relating Ross' wrestling career to what he was likely to encounter in a theological setting.

"Many ambitious and too worldly minded clergymen desert their pulpits and sacred calling for the bar, but it is not often the case that hardened veterans of the bar adopt the clerical profession," printed *The Era*. "A notable case has just occurred of the latter change. Duncan C. Ross, an alleged athlete, has deserted the bar of a saloon he owned at Cleveland and is going to fit himself for the ministry. It is to be hoped the money he has made at his bar may not give out until he shall have acquired enough theological training to enable him to withstand the devil in a catch-as-catch-can struggle."

Highland Games and Hippodromes

Before the month was out, Ross apparently began to waffle on his decision to enter the pulpit. *The Democrat and Chronicle of Rochester* commented on the newest rumors emanating from Cleveland that Ross was having second thoughts about his decision.

"Everybody wished him well and expressed a hope that he would become as good a preacher as he had been a wrestler. But now comes the strange intelligence that Ross has within the past few days renounced his intentions of entering the ministry, and that he will stick to the saloon and athletic work," wrote *The Democrat and Chronicle*. "These erratic and gymnastic feats on the part of the Scotchman led many to believe that all is not well with Duncan's reason, and that perhaps he is not as strong in his mind as he is in his arms. His next proclamation will be awaited with considerable interest by his friends here and elsewhere."

The Kansas City Journal shed additional light on what motivated Ross' hasty decision to take up ministry, but couldn't resist the urge to remind readers who followed the original hippodroming suspicions about Ross closely that "there was a time when Ross was about as tricky and crooked a sport as there was in the ranks of the profession." With that said, *The Journal* noted that Ross had been credited with changing his ways, and attributed this to guilt over his failure to accede to the final wishes of his now-deceased wife.

"His wife was the daughter of a Baltimore merchant, and was a most estimable lady. She fell in love with Ross and ran away from home to marry him," continued *The Journal*. "Her father was very angry with her for wedding him, and never saw her again in life. She died in childbirth a few weeks ago in Cleveland, her husband being in San Francisco at the time. She begged him not to leave her when he went away, but he thought her fears were groundless. He was summoned home the night she died, and met her father for the first time at her coffin side. The father was very favorably impressed with Ross, who is at heart a decent fellow. His resolution to change his model of life is due to a desire to please the father of his wife, and partly through remorse at having left her when most she needed his presence and his aid."

Soon it was reported that Ross had already written a letter to Trinity College of Toronto requesting admission. Yet, either out of a sense of obligation to fulfill his commitments or the desire for one final grand payday, Ross expressed his wish to wrestle Clarence Whistler one final time in San Francisco before retiring from wrestling and athletics for good.

"I have told the *Herald* man that it was evident, from the complications arising, that I will have to carry them through, as those who are interested were determined to compel me to fill the contracts made, otherwise they would enter suit for damages, which they could collect, which would leave me in poor circumstances, and undoubtedly I will have to go to California," said Ross, in a statement relayed through *The Morning Call* of San Francisco.

When pressed about whether or not he still intended to take up the ministry, Ross affirmed "as soon as I finish this job with Whistler I will return, and by that time I hope to have everything in readiness to enter the college." In this case, Ross elaborated that he hoped to enter Auburn Theological Seminary in New York City and enroll in a four-year course of study.

The Sunday Morning Truth of Buffalo took a far more cynical approach to the first sign that Ross was walking back his vow to give up his athletic career. Addressing a statement to "Duncan" in one of its February issues, *The Truth* assured Ross that "all hands understand the roorback was a gratuitous ad," thereby taking the stance that the Ross' one-month retirement from activity was merely a creative means of generating nationwide publicity, and that the tactic had worked magnificently.

Coincidentally, that same month, *The Courier Journal* of Louisville printed an article about all-purpose swindlers. Ironically, the article was prompted by a local fight that was believed to have been contested entirely "on the square," with the writer following this pronouncement by stating that there was a group of athletes who deserved a far worse reputation than boxers.

"Although prize fighters generally have the worst reputation of all sporting men, the contrast between those who have been in the city and the wrestlers who were here at the same time was great," asserted *The Journal*. "Although Duncan C. Ross has generally borne the reputation of being a quiet, inoffensive man, his closing performance in this city displayed his true nature very properly."

The Journal added there had been at least a dozen hippodromes in Louisville, and that anyone who believed that any of the matches was authentic "is certainly very innocent." It then closed with the warning that the people of Louisville "were getting very tired of the professionals who come to the city with a great flourish and arrange a hippodrome contest to swindle them out of their money," and they should "give the city a wide berth and avoid getting into trouble."

Arthur Chambers of *The Kansas City Journal* not only echoed this statement, but specifically listed Duncan Ross and Clarence Whistler as two wrestlers who "call themselves champions" but seldom do anything except talk, and added that "even when two of them do come together the public generally knows that the contest will be a hippodrome."

Chambers' concluding statement was that the public had become "so nauseated" by wrestlers like Ross and Whistler that no one paid any attention to them. However, this was certainly untrue in California, where the public was chafing at the bit to see a match between the two.

Anyone who had their doubts as to whether or not the bout between Ross and Whistler would be genuine was probably intrigued to hear of the unscheduled dealings that Ross had with British fighter Charles Mitchell at the private apartment building owned by Harry Maynard in San Francisco.

On a Wednesday evening at the very end of April 1885, Ross and Mitchell were among a collection of accomplished gentlemen that also included the famous swimmers Arthur

Clampett and W.H. Dailey, of England and California respectively. After many bottles of champagne were downed, and the group became a bit more rambunctious, Mitchell donned his overcoat at 1:00 a.m. and began to shake hands with the group of men with whom he had been drinking for several hours.

Ross displays his medals in a manner reminiscent of Dinnie

"As [Mitchell] was about leaving the room, Ross, who appeared to be in a somewhat surly humor, made the assertion that he had a man in Cleveland, Ohio, who could reduce Mr. Mitchell to a piece of cold clay," recorded *The Examiner*. "The

Englishman turned at this and demanded the name of the party in whom Ross appeared to have such confidence."

"Mervine Thompson," replied Ross.

At this, Mitchell reportedly smirked and shrugged, apparently finding the argument not to be worth his while, but Ross, who seemed intent on pressing the matter, persisted in his efforts to minimize Mitchell's pugilistic capabilities.

"You fighters can lick nothing," prodded Ross. "If I had you in a room I could lick you myself."

"Two pink spots made their appearance on Mitchell's cheeks, and he quietly informed Ross that he was then and there in a room," continued *The Examiner*. "The latter, springing up, threw his coat and advanced toward Mitchell, who was waiting to receive him. The English pugilist did not give Ross the opportunity to strike the first blow, but quickly sent his right with terrific force toward the Scot's cranium, striking him just beneath the right eye and raising the structure above referred to."

"Ross, without waiting for Mitchell's left, retired suddenly to the other end of the room, a distance of fourteen feet, and reclined on the floor. Mitchell approached his fallen opponent and expressed his solicitude as to the result of the blow. For his sympathy, he received a vicious kick in the thigh and retired in good order. After some minutes Ross rose and proclaimed his intention of annihilating Mitchell the following day, and the latter promptly produced a check calling for $500 as a forfeit for a fight. This Ross could not cover. A carriage was summoned and the injured athlete driven to his home and confined to the care of a physician, raw meat and oysters."

When asked later that evening about what happened, Mitchell and the other witnesses to the encounter all told tales that essentially gelled with the aforementioned story. Mitchell summarized the matter with his supposition that Ross had been looking for a reputation, but his aggression was also fueled by the fact that the Scotsman had been "under the influence of wine." W.H. Daily added that Ross was hit "bang in the right eye" and that there was "no fight in Ross after that."

Fortunately for Ross, there was no great shame in being outslugged by a world class fighter while he was in a drunken state, even if *The Examiner* contributed the unflattering detail that Ross' eye needed to be "concealed beneath a circular piece of raw beefsteak" while he recovered from the punch.

Apparently wishing to get all of his athletic desires out of his system before making his way into the ministry, Ross made the peculiar choice to participate in broadsword contests on horseback in San Francisco's Central Park against a variety of men, including a man identified as Owen Davis of the United States Cavalry.

The two men sat on their steeds 150 feet apart from one another, and charged at each other at full speed while wearing iron masks, helmets, and full coats of armor. The battle was fought until a combatant achieved the best score out of a potential total of 21 points, and in a scenario that played out in a manner suspiciously similar to that of almost every best-of-five mixed-styles wrestling contest that Duncan Ross ever participated in, the score was tied at 10-10 entering the final point, with Ross notching the decisive tally to win the duel 11-10.

Notwithstanding the closeness of the final score and the presumed drama of the moment, the event was described as "a hollow show destitute of skill and interest."

Ross' swordfighting contests were labeled as being "more fun than fury," and "a comedy of errors," until he held an exhibition against Captain E.N. Jennings, a local fencing instructor who claimed to have served with the Eighth Royal Irish Hussars.

According to reports, during one of the exhibitions between the two men, Ross struck Jennings with a blow to the back of the head that brought an instant halt to the contest, as Jennings hit the ground and continued to lie there as if dead.

After one of Jennings' friends on the scene informed him that he had only suffered a scalp wound, Jennings averred that he knew his skull had been fractured, and asked his friend to "get a good doctor."

The summoned physician informed the press that Jennings had nearly suffered a fatal blow, as his skull had been fractured "a hair's breadth back of the temporal bone." *The Examiner* reported that if Jennings managed to recover it would be "a miracle."

Well, the miraculous occurred, and before long, Jennings had not only recovered from his "near-fatal injury," but was once again engaging in broadsword contests against Ross, with their challenges and invectives directed against one another through the press in a manner that was once again identical to the model popularized by professional wrestlers.

Wary individuals who had been familiar with the actions of pro wrestlers in general, and the reputation of Duncan Ross in particular, might have immediately speculated that Ross was diversifying the avenues through which he could obtain an income through simulated combat.

A later article published in *The Examiner* explained how Ross and Jennings had met each other as much as one decade earlier "in the East," and Ross had participated in as many as three broadsword contests against "a French cavalryman" named "Colonel Lennon" until the sport was dropped due to a lack of public interest. According to *The Examiner*, things were now quite different, and "considerable interest" was now being manifested toward sword contests now that Ross had leveraged his wrestling and athletics fame for that purpose.

What had once been advertised as the match that would signify Ross' retirement from wrestling took place in June. It was a bout between Ross and Whistler that had been long-awaited on the Pacific Coast, although the matter had been considered long-settled in the Midwest, since Ross had been incapable of doing anything with Whistler when the latter ceased cooperating with him.

Having established himself, justifiably or not, as a swordsman of lethal proficiency, Ross berated Whistler in the press by challenging him to all manner of contests, which even included a plumduff-eating competition.

Of course, Ross was sure to tender a challenge at Whistler to face him with broadswords, which Ross now saw fit to identity as his "native game." Given the reports of what had supposedly happened to Jennings, Whistler was ostensibly making the safer choice by choosing to grapple with Ross rather than facing him with a blade in his hand.

Despite its buildup, the bout between Ross and Whistler was underwhelming according to reports. *The Sacramento Union* characterized it as "a fair exhibition, but nothing more," and assumed this opinion on account of the fact that Whistler dominated Ross in the wrestling styles that the fans tended to care about the most — Greco-Roman and catch-as-catch-can — while Ross struggled considerably in winning the collar-and-elbow and sidehold falls.

The Union chalked it up as a luck-of-the-draw victory by Ross, who was certainly not the better wrestler of the two, but simply the competitor who got lucky because he won the coin flip prior to the deciding fall and selected collar-and-elbow as the grappling method. Then again, the media outlet also seemed to question why Whistler wrestled in such a reserved manner.

"There was a general expectation that Whistler would disable Ross and win the match that way, but as Whistler wrestled like a gentleman, and not like a savage, a great deal of disappointment was expressed by a part of the crowd, who enlivened the proceedings by yelling out, 'Twist an arm off him, Whistler,' 'Break the big duffer's leg,' 'Choke the life out of him,' and similar kindly suggestions in the interest of brutality," illustrated *The Union*.

Duncan Ross had begun 1885 flirting with a permanent relocation to the pulpit, but had instead given birth to a brand new strain of sports entertainment. Ross was clearly ambitious, and it would soon become quite clear that there were no lines he wouldn't cross in order to get what he desired, in both his professional and private lives.

Highland Games and Hippodromes

8 – A Little Tin Bucket

Late in June 1885, Duncan Ross set out to further prove why he demanded to be treated as if he was one of the best athletes in the world even though he had been keeping himself distracted in recent months with both his wrestling and swordfighting exploits. At San Francisco's Central Park, Ross vowed that he would break all of the new records for hammer throwing and shot putting that he alleged had been recently set in Edinburgh, Scotland by George Davidson.

The reason these records of Davidson's are "alleged" is because there don't appear to be any records set by Davidson in Scotland at any point during his lifetime that are acknowledged as all-time-best marks. More to the point, Donald Dinnie had official marks on the books — including a 107-foot, 10-inch hurl of a 16-pound hammer in Aboyne — along with several unofficial marks in exhibitions that surpassed any of the "new records" that would be reported by Ross.

"Ross started on his task by putting a 56-pound weight," stated *The Chronicle*. "He put the weight 26 feet 6 inches, beating the English record by five inches. His second attempt was with the 16 pound hammer. He succeeded in throwing it 109 feet 2 inches, being over six feet further than the record. He next threw a twelve pound hammer to a distance of 131 feet 6 inches, the best previous record being 118 feet six inches. His next endeavor was to throw a twenty-one pound hammer to beat the English record of 79 feet. After several trials, he threw the hammer 82 feet 1 ½ inches. His last effort was the throwing of a sixteen pound shot. In this Ross failed to beat the record of 43 feet 4 ½ inches, by throwing nine inches short."

Understandably, the fact that this unprecedented display of throwing acumen by Ross did not take place during a sanctioned Highland Games event was likely to cause some concerns about the sincerity of the recorded marks. This doubt was apparently anticipated, because *The Chronicle* attached a statement signed by Caledonian Club officers D.A. MacDonald and Daniel McLeod, along with Scottish Thistle Club chieftain A. Foreman, and Central Park superintendent D.R. McNeill.

The statement affirmed that all of the apparatuses employed by Ross prior to his record-setting performance were measured and weighed, along with the insistence that "the ground was level and the measurements were taken from the nearest toe mark to the first break of the weights and hammers."

Even with so many witnesses present, the integrity of the event must still be questioned for several reasons, not the least of which is the fact that Ross somehow succeeded in hurling the light hammer a remarkable six feet further than a supposed world record, and seven feet further than the distance he had thrown it when he had defeated Donald Dinnie in a sanctioned Highland Games event.

Moreover, since all of the witnesses had a vested interest in the promotion of Ross at Caledonian engagements in California, it is difficult to consider any of these throwing marks as credible when they were not tallied during sanctioned events with truly neutral parties in attendance.

The presence of the Central Park superintendent also needs to be acknowledged in light of the fact that by this point Ross either owned or had a managerial interest in a Central Park bar, and was in fact sued by his barkeeper A.J. Chambers just two months later for just under $195 in unpaid wages.

Finally, the fact that Duncan McMillan was one of two men who hurled alongside Ross during the exhibition, the other being J. Carroll, doesn't necessarily improve the impression that some of the results may have been exaggerated. For what it's worth, the Scottish press devoted not even a passing mention to the records that Ross was alleged to have set.

If anyone had thought Ross to be sincere in his vow that his bout with Whistler would signal his retirement from wrestling, or that his ultimate goal was to assume a position of leadership behind the preacher's pulpit in honor of his deceased wife, August would deliver a shocking revelation that signaled precisely how sharply the morality of Ross had seemingly shifted in the opposite direction.

That month, 16-year-old Eva R. Hurlburt, a young lady that *The San Francisco Examiner* described as "tall and slender, dark-eyed and very pretty," stood before the Police Court of San Francisco and revealed the details of the secret sexual relationship that she had been engaging in with Duncan Ross following her own arrest.

Standing before Judge Hale Rix, Hurlburt told the story about how Ross had rented a room for a time at her family's dwelling, which was above the Pioneer Coffee Saloon at 1185 Market Street, of which her father was the proprietor. According to her, Ross seduced her one night before he left their house to move to a new residence at the corner of Market and Eighth streets.

Having thusly been "ruined" by Ross, she continued sneaking out of her father's house during the night and heading off to sleep with the famous athlete. The police officer who arrested the young lady further explained how he noticed Hurlburt's stealthy departure from the coffee saloon at night and notified her father at the first opportunity.

"The following day I saw Mr. Hurlburt, who conducts the coffee saloon, and inquired what time any young girls he employed retired to their homes," testified the officer. "The answer was a query from him as to my reasons for asking such a question. I told him. 'Great God!' he exclaimed, 'Can it be my child who leaves her bed to meet a man?' That same night we watched. At midnight the father visited the girl's room. Her bed was empty. He notified me, and I at once visited the house in which Ross resides, and met the girl coming from her assignation, and arrested her."

With his young lover arrested for sneaking out late at night — but with him having apparently broken no laws whatsoever — Ross appeared alongside his attorney before both Judge Rix and the 16-year-old's parents, who were said to be "convulsed by grief," while Ross requested that "the ruined maiden be allowed to go free" so that she could live with him.

Rather than handing the young lady over to the 30-year-old Ross, whose presumed intent was to marry her, Judge Rix opted to commit Hurlburt to the Magdalen Asylum until she reached the age of 18. As the statutory rape law in California was functionally non-existent at the time, Ross faced no repercussions, save for perhaps some small measure of public embarrassment.

By November, Ross was paying little attention to wrestling and was devoting the majority of his energy to his swordfighting endeavors, either because the latter exhibitions were a more reliable source of money, were easier to fake, or because they were less likely to result in an injury.

Ross and Jennings proceeded to trade the "Donahue Diamond Medal" — emblematic of the "world swordfighting championship" — back and forth. As such, the 30-year-old Ross could now lay claim to having simultaneously held the titles of world athletic champion, world wrestling champion, and world swordfighting champion, at least in a strictly nominal sense.

Remarkably, Ross seemed to delight in playing the role of heel during these swordfighting exhibitions. During a match against Jennings, who Ross had already been accused of nearly killing earlier in the year, Ross was jeered by the crowd for resorting to the use of aggressive and potentially illegal tactics when he struck Jennings upon his right gauntlet.

"On examination, it was found that [Jennings'] arm was seriously hurt, being numb and black and blue from the elbow down to the wrist," stated *The Examiner*. "The wrist bone had been struck and was very painful, and he found himself completely disabled. The glove of his left hand was cut open by one of Ross' blows, and after some minutes' consultation, Jennings announced that he was unable to proceed, and 'Ross might have the medal if he chose to take it at the standings of the score,' which was 3 to 5 in Jennings' favor."

Highland Games and Hippodromes

He was technically behind on the scoreboard, yet Ross accepted the medal that made him the world champion, and then proceeded to defeat Jennings' replacement Captain Voss by battering his cuirass with a sword until it was dented and Voss was disoriented. The police attempted to intervene to no avail, and as the crowd screamed its disapproval at Ross, Voss swung his sword wildly toward Ross' head, missed, and fell from his horse, which immediately ended the duel with Ross as its victor.

Upon hearing of Ross' activities in California, newspapers from areas of the country where fans thought they had been swindled by Ross in the past appended their coverage of his actions with addendums soaked in distrust. *The Inter Ocean* of Chicago, upon hearing that Ross had "permanently taken up his residence in San Francisco," concluded that "California seems to be a good state to hippodrome."

Likewise, *The Salt Lake Herald* followed its report about Ross' wrestling and swordfighting exploits by protesting that if Ross had "stuck to wrestling instead of hippodroming in the manner he did," he would have far more friends. *The Minneapolis Tribune* went so far as to label the relocation of Ross to the West Coast as a form of addition by subtraction, crediting the rise in the number of square wrestling matches in the Midwest to the "absence of Duncan Ross."

Curiously, even though Utah was apparently one of the places where the press was wary of Ross and his exhibitions, he still toured the state with his swordfighting show, and brought along someone fighting under the name of "McGuire" to battle against him. *The Examiner* reported how McGuire won the first bout between the pair in Salt Lake, setting the stage for a rematch, which Ross won "after a desperate encounter."

While Ross was enjoying a financial windfall as the result of his many business ventures, Donald Dinnie had been in dire financial straits, and as the summer of 1885 approached in Australia, the return of William Miller to the nation's wrestling scene certainly came none too soon as far as Dinnie was concerned.

Highland Games and Hippodromes

The majority of the brawny Scot's public appearances had left something to be desired. Dinnie's immense size created an expectation that he would manhandle all of his smaller opponents through sheer might alone, while simultaneously making him a difficult individual to support when such displays left the impression that Dinnie was simply bullying and throwing men who were far smaller and weaker than himself.

What's more, Dinnie's lack of all-purpose wrestling ability was apparently obvious to everyone, and he addressed this in a letter to the press that summer by stating, "I do not pretend to be able to beat everyone at all styles of wrestling, but am still prepared to prove that I can beat all-comers as a general wrestler, and I will allow any man in Australia his choice of four styles out of seven, and if one stone less weight than me they can have choice of three from five. If weighing two stone less, I will allow them choice of four from five styles, and if three stone less they can have choice of all the five styles."

In this respect, Dinnie was offering a significant handicap to compensate for the weight disparity, but shortfalls in weight are often very difficult to compensate for if the level of skill between wrestlers is even vaguely close.

This is exemplified by Dinnie's July match against William Hudson, the former wrestling champion of Australia, over whom Dinnie wielded a nearly five-stone weight advantage, or roughly 70 pounds. The five-styles match took place at the Lyceum Hall in Ballarat.

Dinnie surrendered the first fall — in Cumberland style — to Hudson, albeit a fall that was awarded on an infraction of the rules that did not require Dinnie to visually appear to have lost. Dinnie easily won the second fall in catch-as-catch-can, a style that he usually struggled to amass victories in during prior wrestling encounters.

The third round was described as the "huggie style," and was likely a Scottish backhold bout that was won by a literal throw to the mat. Dinnie *lost* the fall, which would explain why it would have been called something other than a Scottish backhold fall, since Dinnie was still claiming to have been undefeated in the style. Quickly, Dinnie knotted the score at two falls apiece by winning the collar-and-elbow round.

"The score now was equal — two for each man — and the final bout was announced as the Cornish," printed *The Australasian* of Melbourne. "The struggle was the most prolonged of any, there being three intervals. To wind up, however, Dinnie planted his head against Hudson's throat, and dropped him onto his back, thus winning the match by three falls to two. Hudson, on being lifted up, staggered to his corner, which was the signal for a great uproar."

Moments later, Dinnie appeared before the crowd where he "was greeted with mingled hooting and cheering." He then explained that the tactics he used to win the final fall had been well within the rules, but he was willing to wrestle Hudson again in a best-of-nine-falls bout in any style the smaller man might choose.

For context, less than one year earlier, Dinnie had professed to be "thoroughly ignorant of the Cornish style." Now, he was using that same style to pull out timely victories. Regardless, the fact that Dinnie had struggled mightily against a comparatively miniscule man likely lessened the grandeur of the feat.

Since gambling fueled the pro wrestling scene of the era, it was essentially a requirement for all wrestlers to show some semblance of vulnerability against every opponent they faced. To that end, while it would have benefitted Dinnie's reputation as a powerhouse for him to have simply mauled his opponents without surrendering any falls, it wouldn't have been conducive to enticing sportsmen to lay down money, nor would it have generated the intrigue necessary to drum up repeat business.

In essence, it was in Dinnie's best interest as a wrestling and gambling attraction to appear beatable, but repeatedly dropping falls to smaller men did no favors for his reputation as a strongman. To say that Dinnie needed to be seen as taking a step up in the caliber of his competition was an understatement, and William Miller's return to active status accomplished this, and then some.

By now, it was public knowledge that Dinnie needed the financial relief that a series of matches against Miller might provide. In June, *The Evening News of Sydney* printed the tale of how Dinnie was arrested and hauled before the Echuca Police Court for failing to pay his billposter, James Hook. Tacking up signs advertising Dinnie's shows had generated a bill amounting to 17s 6d, which Dinnie had refused to pay because "[Hook] pestered him for money while he was making arrangements for his exhibition at Temperance Hall." The owed money was paid directly to the court clerks as soon as the proceedings concluded.

After a delay that had lasted well over a year, the long-awaited rematch for the world heavyweight wrestling championship — as recognized in Australia — took place on August 1 at Melbourne's Bijou Theatre. The interest in the match was vast; *The Argus* observed that the building "might have been filled twice over," and that fans were being turned away in large numbers half an hour before the festivities began.

Even before the bout started, the Dinnie-Miller rematch was an unqualified financial success. *The Argus* reported that the high-priced reserved seats in the dress circle and on the stage were purchased well in advance of the day.

The rationale behind what qualified the bout as a world-title contest had changed in a year's time. The story now was that it was a world title match on the grounds that Dinnie claimed to have won the wrestling championships in all areas of the world with the sole exception of Australia, where Miller was the unquestioned titleholder. This would have been news to a great many wrestling fans, including those in England, where Dinnie had struggled to advance beyond the opening rounds of wrestling tournaments contested in the native style.

"When the curtain drew up at 10 minutes past 3, and the men stepped onto the stage after Mr. George Leopold had announced them, the contrast between the two was very striking," noted *The Argus*. "Miller, squarely set, and wearing crimson and white hose and lace-up boots, represented massive strength, while Donald Dinnie, lithe, wiry, and tall, was the model of sinewy proportions. The one was remindful of pictures of Roman gladiators, the other suggested the speed and endurance of the pedestrian, especially as he wore running shoes without spikes."

The first round was Greco-Roman, and the two grapplers spent 12 minutes exchanging holds and positions on the mat while the crowd cheered for their respective champions. Presuming the nature of the cheering embodied the same spirit as their original bout, Dinnie's supporters would have consisted primarily of Scottish immigrants and Australians who still clung strongly to their Scottish identities. By contrast, Miller's support came from those who viewed their primary identity as Australian, even though the first steps toward the colony's independence were still another 16 years away.

Miller managed to place Dinnie on the mat, grasped him tightly around his neck, and slowly turned him onto his back.

"The tension on Dinnie's neck was more than he could resist, but when he was put on his back he strove with splendid pluck and stamina to keep his hips from the dreaded contact with the floor by supporting himself on his left leg bent nearly double," described *The Argus*. "The struggle lasted a few moments longer, but with Dinnie's neck still in his iron grip, Miller slowly brought his tremendous weight and muscle to bear upon the prostrate athlete, and it was a relief to those who do not like human suffering prolonged when the referee held up his hands announcing the first fall to Miller. The cheers shook the building."

Thus far, the bout was following the pattern established more than a year ago, with Dinnie unable to contend with the superior Greco-Roman grappler, and forced to rely on his mastery of Scottish wrestling to remain competitive. When the two men assumed the starting backhold position for the second round, Dinnie "forced the work from the commencement."

"Miller was brought to the ground, but his nimbleness in regaining his feet saved him unpleasant consequences," continued *The Argus*. "He warmed up, and catching Dinnie, essayed to throw him, but slipping in the effort, Dinnie very rapidly seized him and threw him cleanly on his back. He turned over and tried to rise on his hands and knees, but Dinnie was too quick for him, and forcing his head down, was working to turn him again on his back, when the referee gave the fall in his favour. The time of the round was 7 minutes. There was long-continued cheering, and the match so far being a tie, the third and final throw, which was to be in the 'mixed style,' was looked forward to with the liveliest interest."

The final catch-as-catch-can round began at 4:00 p.m. and proceeded for 45 minutes. From the very beginning of the round, Miller took the fight to Dinnie, and in his efforts to avoid Miller's takedown attempts, Dinnie "frequently came in contact with spectators and chairs on the stage, whereupon he invariably left off the attack, and returned to the middle of the stage."

After 30 minutes of cat-and-mouse action, Dinnie "began to perspire profusely," and Miller secured a neck hold on Dinnie and attempted to pin him using the method he utilized to win the first fall, except he was unable to get enough of his weight toward the middle of Dinnie's body to force the Scot's hips onto the carpet. Still, Dinnie showed signs that he was gradually succumbing to the pressure supplied by the Aussie, and Miller's fans "began to grow more and more jubilant" as the bout reached its inevitable conclusion.

"The men uneventfully finessed for another quarter of an hour, when Dinnie missed a grip he made at Miller, and the latter hugged him down with the same vice-like pressure upon the neck that had told so well before, and this time the referee was satisfied that two shoulders and one hip were held on the ground, and gave the match in Miller's favour by two falls to one," concluded the report. "The result was received with much enthusiasm, but the audience quickly and quietly dispersed."

As Miller celebrated a world championship victory with "a host of friends who invaded his dressing room as soon as the match was over," Dinnie promptly blamed his loss on "an illness he had in Sydney two months ago" that resulted in him being "rather lighter than he should have been." This "devastating" illness had seemingly done nothing to curtail Dinnie's activities during the prior two months, as he had still made several appearances in both athletic and wrestling events.

Furthermore, Dinnie said he was already looking forward to the rematch between the two men that had been immediately scheduled for August 15 at Victoria Hall. It would be a best-of-five-styles bout that would hypothetically reveal who the more well-rounded and durable of the two grapplers truly was. *The Argus* also called attention to the fact that three of the five wrestling rounds "were to be in the styles in which Donald Dinnie was supposed to excel, and which bring tripping, his special forte, into play."

In the first round of the rematch, wrestled in sidehold, Dinnie secured a tight grip on Miller and threw him "as easily as a ninepin" earning a massive ovation and the first fall of the title match. The next round was a Greco-Roman fall that was described as Miller's "facile princeps," and *The Argus* reiterated that Dinnie was not naturally comfortable with the Greco-Roman style because "wrestling on the floor is allowed."

"The funny part of the [Greco-Roman] performance was that Miller, lifted in Dinnie's arms, would look quite helpless, but as soon as Dinnie attempted to put him on the floor, his feet and legs would become endued with surprising muscular activity, and he would fall right end up instead of lengthwise," illustrated *The Argus*. "He was like an angler's floater, always coming upright when the line is cast. All the while, Dinnie was wearing out his strength, and Miller was patiently biding his time, and letting his superior weight have its full effect by giving Dinnie exhausting chances to throw him, which he could not accomplish."

Miller eventually gained control of Dinnie's head and rolled him onto his shoulders "to the great delight of fully half of the spectators," thereby evening the fall count at one after 17 minutes of Greco-Roman wrestling. The men then pulled on their Cornish canvas jackets and spent 18 minutes trying to trip each other onto the ground. After a long struggle of 18 minutes, Dinnie succeeded in dropping Miller to the floor to go up two falls to one. Hilariously, the reporter from *The Argus* wrote that Dinnie "at once proved himself to be an expert Cornishman" despite the fact that he had been dismissed as being totally unskilled in the art just one year earlier.

The catch-as-catch-can fall followed, and after 23 minutes of continuous action, Miller "put Dinnie on his back while holding his legs like the handles of a wheelbarrow, and secured the fall, and the applause, which had been most liberal all through this, the liveliest part of the programme, was redoubled."

To the fans in attendance, the scenario was clear: The fate of the bout — and what was being termed as the "mixed-styles heavyweight wrestling championship of the world" — now rested on the result of a single Scottish backhold fall. Given the identities of the match participants, the ending of the match was very much a foregone conclusion.

"Dinnie, who was looking as fresh as Miller, though he had been doing more work nearly all through, commenced the bout with much confidence," stated *The Argus*. "He twice threw Miller, but could not keep him down. A third time he put him full length on the stage, and held him there securely for 15 or 20 seconds. The referee stood, watch in hand; the spectators grew rampant with excitement, and the combatants struggled fiercely for the mastery. Miller writhed to keep his body off the floor, and Dinnie, with victory in his grasp, strained every nerve to fasten him to the floor, but in vain.

"Miller threw his opponent off, and the referee, amid some groaning, announced no fall, as 30 seconds had not expired while Miller was touching the stage. The contest was resumed, and very soon Dinnie fairly threw Miller, who rolled over from his back onto his side. Dinnie grappled him, and forced him again on his back, and in spite of all that Miller could do, pinned him until the fall was won and celebrated with tumultuous cheering."

Officially, at least in Australia, Dinnie was now a world heavyweight wrestling champion of sorts. Still, the ever-changing structures of his bouts with Miller, which had been best-of-six, best-of-three, and best-of-five fall encounters with different styles of wrestling featured in each, made it reasonable for the reporter from *The Argus* to write that "the question of supremacy between him and Miller remains where it was before either of their two [recent] matches, one having been won by each."

The Bendigo Advertiser conceded that Dinnie, by dint of his world-title win, had "quite recovered the prestige which he lost," but cautioned that the arrival of Clarence Whistler in Australia might serve to severely limit the length of Dinnie's reign at the top of the heap.

The statement from *The Advertiser* turned out to be rather prescient, because just 14 days later on Saturday, August 29, Dinnie lost his world title to Whistler at Victoria Hall over the course of two programs' worth of matches that came to a rather unsatisfactory conclusion.

The afternoon's program was a best-of-three-falls affair, which began with an interesting disagreement caused by Whistler's desire to wrestle with a bare upper body, while Dinnie insisted that singlets were mandatory.

"The referee could not find anything compelling either wrestler to appear in singlets or undershirts of any kind in the articles of agreement which he held in his hand, and he therefore had no alternative except to direct the men to wrestle as they were," stated *The Age of Melbourne*.

Whistler defeated Dinnie two falls to three in the afternoon program by winning the Greco-Roman and catch-as-catch-can rounds. This created a scenario where Dinnie needed to win the evening's best-of-five series simply to save his title with a tie. Dinnie won the sidehold and Scotch-style falls, while

Whistler predictably obtained the Greco-Roman and catch-as-catch-can bouts. That's when Dinnie decided he was through wrestling for the evening.

"When the men reappeared after a few minutes' interval, the referee announced that Dinnie was unable to go on with the match, as he had injured his left shoulder in the afternoon, and he (the referee) would therefore declare the match a win for Whistler," concluded *The Age*. "The style which was not wrestled was Cornish, and it would probably have proved in favor of Dinnie, who appeared to be the better man in the standing up work, while on the ground Whistler was immeasurably his superior. The audience was tolerably impartial in their applause and remarks, but if anything, they favored Whistler rather than the veteran, whose performances, however, could not fail to suggest to many what he must have been 15 years ago."

In a tragic twist, Dinnie's opportunity to have a lengthy reign as a world heavyweight champion in Australia would die along with Clarence Whistler. After successfully defending his newly won title against Miller, it was reported in the middle of October 1885 that Whistler was confined to his room at Her Majesty's Hotel, suffering from severe chest pain. Over a three-week period, his condition gradually deteriorated, prompting a writer from *The Mount Alexander Mail* to print the dire projection on November 6 that "all hope of [Whistler's] recovery has been abandoned."

"I cannot understand by what carelessness this splendidly formed man has been suffered to perish," lamented *The Mail*'s Melbourne correspondent. "The fact that one of his lungs was adherent was so conspicuous that in his match with Dinnie at the Victoria Hall, at least five weeks before he wrestled Miller, I pointed it out to other spectators on the stage, and some doubt was expressed in consequence of this defect of condition, he would be able to outlast Dinnie."

That same day, Whistler passed away in his hotel room, and on November 7 *The Melbourne Daily Telegraph* printed the preemptively drafted story that Whistler "is now lying at Her

Majesty's Hotel, Swanston Street, so dangerously ill from pleuro-pneumonia, accompanied by a cold… that his death may take place at any moment."

Regrettably, by the time those words were released to the public, Whistler had indeed expired from his illness at the age of 29. The loss of the young wrestling champion was an international tragedy, and it is of comparatively little consequence that his death blurred the world title picture of the Australian wrestling scene, and left both Dinnie and Miller incapable of presenting any matches to the Australian public that could match the intrigue that their bouts with Whistler had occasioned.

At the very beginning of 1886, *The Omaha World* posted a statement that it attributed only to "a man with a little tin bucket in his hand," which means that any statements proceeding from said man should be taken with a heaping helping of salt. If true, the bucket-toting man's comments provide ample insight into how Duncan Ross viewed several of his pro wrestling peers at the time, as well as why he seemed determined to sock away as much money as he possibly could while the opportunity presented itself.

"Duncan Ross was telling me that the sporting world had about gone to pieces," the bucket-bearing man is alleged to have stated, before explaining in the words of Ross how famed fighter John L. Sullivan had "a good body but a poor head," and would "knock himself out before a good man comes along to succeed him." Ross added that his former client and trainee Mervine Thompson "went to pieces," and Ross no longer knew his whereabouts.

To clarify this point, while Ross had once promoted Thompson as the fighter who would remove Sullivan from title contention in the boxing world, Sullivan was by now recognized as the first certified world heavyweight boxing champion, having won the title one year earlier in Cincinnati, Ohio, to move his professional record to 43 wins and no defeats.

Highland Games and Hippodromes

While Mervine Thompson had not truly disappeared, he had definitely proven to be unremarkable as a professional boxer; his record was 4-1-4 at that moment, and his future accumulation of losses would comfortably outpace his acquisition of wins.

Colonel James H. McLaughlin

Ross apparently proceeded with his analysis, stating that William Muldoon had "gone to pieces in every way," and was eking out a meager living by "posing in a specialty company." According to Ross, Col. James McLaughlin blew $8,000 of his hard-earned money "on a Detroit saloon," and then "allowed his place to go to pieces while he rambled around at little towns with one-horse wrestlers."

Perhaps Ross' most interesting analysis was reserved for the newest major star on the wrestling scene, Evan "The

Strangler" Lewis of Wisconsin. According to the unidentified bucket-holder, Ross referred to Lewis as "a fellow who ought to be done up and will be" because of the dangerous holds he used on the mat. This unkind assessment was seemingly owed to the report that Lewis had purportedly "twisted the Jap's leg out of joint," which Ross took exception to on the basis that "certain locks" had no place in wrestling matches.

It was also alleged that Ross regretfully said that Sorakichi had "fallen a victim of vices," although the proximity of the statements seemed to imply that Ross was blaming the injury of Sorakichi at Lewis' hands on the former's reliance on these vices, whatever they might have been.

The bout in question, which took place in Chicago, Illinois, in February of 1886, ended abruptly when Lewis secured a footlock on Sorakichi and the Japanese wrestler screamed in pain. The round was halted, and when the referee determined that Sorakichi could not continue, the bout was concluded and Lewis was declared to be the winner, which was "a decision that did not please anybody except for those familiar with the rules," according to *The Inter Ocean*.

Almost immediately, the bout acquired a reputation for being an obvious "shoot," or authentic contest, as five or six fans reportedly fainted at the sight of Sorakichi's leg after seeing it jarringly twisted in a direction it was not intended to go.

The opinion as to whether or not an injury was actually inflicted may ultimately rest with how severe of an injury it was stated to be. Sorakichi went back to work on the mat one month later; this generally aligns with the healing guidance for a moderate ankle sprain and even mild dislocations of ankles and knees. As Sorakichi's injury was reported to have been a dislocation, it could not have been a severe one if his leg was healthy enough for him to return to wrestle Edwin Bibby in March.

Duncan Ross told the tale of what had happened between Sorakichi and Lewis with a measure of disgust, but it would soon become obvious that there was something about

Highland Games and Hippodromes

the fallout from that episode that inspired him. Seeing the potential for profitability amidst the chaos, Ross would do his best to insert a version of this scene within his own exhibitions, only to watch his credibility take an abrupt nosedive as a result.

9 – Judge, Handicapper, Referee

Perhaps thinking that all publicity was good publicity in the worlds of sports and entertainment, Duncan Ross soon approximated the carnage of the bout between Evan Lewis and Matsada Sorakichi at one of his next jousting exhibitions. Consequently, Ross' exchange with a gentleman known as Sergeant Walsh would conclude with a fiasco that succeeded in attracting national media attention due to its perceived violence.

"Walsh appeared to be the better swordsman and had the sympathy of the audience," printed *The Cincinnati Enquirer*. "Every point he made was loudly cheered, while the scores made by Ross were unnoticed. This seemed to anger Ross, and when the contestants were ordered to retire after the ninth round, instead of doing so, Ross rushed at his adversary savagely, cutting at him right and left with his sword. The force of his attack was such that Walsh's horse was thrown down and fell on top of his rider, who was knocked senseless by the blows from his assailant's sword."

Ross was subsequently yanked from his horse by police officers who arrested him and took him to the police station, while Walsh was carried to his dressing room and "restored to consciousness." Only then that it was discovered that Walsh had not been seriously harmed. Ross was subsequently released, as Walsh insisted that he would not prosecute his assailant.

The incident received much ink from the North American press, with some newspapers demanding that Ross be treated harshly as a result of the brutality he had inflicted upon Walsh. *The Bradford Era* referred to Ross as a "so-called athlete" who deserved to be "muzzled after the fashion that mad dogs are controlled or made safe these days."

"His recent performances wherein he has permitted his temper to get the better of his judgement in friendly contests with professional swordsmen stamp him as a brute and a coward," added *The Era*. "His opponents in every case would have defeated him had Ross not indulged in brute force to cut and slash them down regardless of science or recognized rules. Duncan C. Ross is an insane athlete who should pass the remainder of his days muzzled or behind the bars of a prison or asylum. He should not be permitted to indulge in wrestling or sword contests with opponents whom the public believe are his sane superiors."

As things always seemed to shake out with Ross, there was some clear chicanery afoot. A few news publications compared notes and realized that one of the armor-clad combatants who dueled with Ross in various locales seemed to be operating under a rotating set of names. This led to Ross making an unscheduled return to the offices of *The Plain Dealer* of Cleveland.

"Duncan C. Ross turned up in town yesterday and made a general and very strong denial of the charges against him about hippodroming in this and other towns in the sword fighting contests, and especially that Captain Charles McGuire and Sergeant Walsh are one and the same person," reported *The Dealer*. "Ross left $100 at this office to make good a bet of $1,000 that McGuire and Walsh are not one, and that McGuire is not Walsh, and alleges that he can prove his statement by Alderman Whalen and Special Customs Agent Noonan of Chicago."

Theoretically, Ross could have settled the dispute and won the bet simply by producing separate individuals claiming to have been McGuire and Walsh, and if later reports were accurate, he would have had little difficulty in doing so. Two years later, shotputter John McPherson gave a detailed account of his involvement with Ross to *The Buffalo Courier Express*.

"I was in Philadelphia last summer and was looking around for something to do, when I ran across Ross," said McPherson. "He was anxious, he said, to have a sword contest, and he wanted me to challenge him. Well, he made me a pretty fair offer, and I accepted it, and he gave me $200 to post as a forfeit, in a newspaper office. I went to the office and put up my stuff, and the next day Ross accepted the challenge. I had, at his request, called myself Sergt. Maj. Patrick C. McGuire of Toronto, in which place I was supposed to be a trainer in a military college.

Promotional photo of Duncan Ross as broadsword champion

"The day for the match came, and all the town was crazy over it. Ross was a Scotchman, and all the Scotch inhabitants stuck to him, while I was supposed to be Irish, and had all the Irishmen at my back. Before the match came off I was scared for fear I'd get cut open, that I didn't know what to do, and I nearly gave away the whole business, but Ross had promised not to hurt me, so I thought I'd better stick it out."

Highland Games and Hippodromes

McPherson explained how the very first time he ever donned a suit of armor or held a sword in his hand was right before his duel with Ross began. McPherson parried the blows from Ross as best he could until Ross smashed him over the head and knocked him from his horse, prompting the Scottish fans to scream even louder.

"I was mad and got up and ran after him without looking for my horse," McPherson proceeded. "I chased him across the court and his horse got all tangled up in one of these things they call a long tennis net. I began hammering at him when all the Scotchmen yelled 'a foul!' a foul!' and the whole mob of them made a rush for me. Then all my Irish friends followed them and they had the prettiest free-for-all scrap I ever saw. While they were hammering each other, the police showed up and about 20 men got clubbed before they could stop the fight. Well they say that Ross is a wolf, but he treated me on the square that time and I never had any other dealings with him."

If true, McPherson's account explains how Ross was always able to find a steady string of Walshs and McGuires to spar with him, regardless of what city he found himself in, and in spite of how soundly he thrashed them in bladed combat.

Outside of the realm of athletics, whether real or theatrical, Ross had failed to keep his hands off of women who might one day land him in trouble. For the second time in as many years, Ross found himself reported about in multiple newspapers due to sexual relations with a woman. This time, the problem wasn't that the woman was underage, but that she was married to Ross' agent, Robert Ferguson.

"Ferguson is an English comedian, about 35 years old, who was connected, until six months ago, with one of the Madison Square Theatre companies," elaborated *The Jersey Journal*. "He was employed by Ross in Denver, and at that time the athlete made the acquaintance of Ferguson's wife. She is a pretty brunette, about 20 years old, and is known as Ida Vallance. She is well educated, rich, and an orphan."

Highland Games and Hippodromes

As the tale was explained, Ross traveled with Ferguson and Vallance to Chicago, at which point Ross adjourned to his room at the Continental Hotel. Ferguson continued to Peoria, Illinois, to schedule appearance dates for Ross, and did so thinking that his wife had gone to stay with her relatives in Iowa. Instead, she returned to Chicago to spend the night with Ross, and Ferguson was justifiably surprised and furious when he discovered the betrayal and barged into Ross' room at the Continental to confront him.

"[Ferguson] attempted to draw a revolver and shoot Ross, but the latter was too quick," illustrated *The Journal*. "He seized the angry little Englishman and tore the revolver from him. 'Now, if you don't get out of here,' cried Ross, 'I'll throw you out of that third-story window.' Ferguson hurried to the office of Justice Meech to secure a warrant for Ross' arrest. Ross says the stories about himself and Mrs. Ferguson are entirely untrue and that he expects to be arrested today, but says he has no fear of the result of the hearing."

For the story to have been untrue as Ross claimed, Ferguson would have needed to be willing to humiliate both himself and his wife on a national scale for the sake of achieving mysterious objective worthwhile enough to justify the reputational sacrifice required to attain it.

By the end of 1886, the number of Ross' swordfighting efforts had declined substantially, and the bulk of his attention returned to professional wrestling. Late in the summer, Ross sued the Cheltenham Beach Company for $2,000 worth of swordfighting money that had not been paid to him, seemingly because the broadsword exhibitions had not been the sustained attractions that Ross and his partners had envisioned.

Ross made his grand return to the wrestling circuit of Cleveland in December by wrestling Matsada Sorakichi for the first time in years. The engagement kicked off a pair of matches that were curiously executed if viewed from the standpoint that Ross would have been reingratiating himself with wrestling fans that had grown progressively more skeptical about the veracity of events in which Ross was a participant, whether he was clad in armor or stripped bare.

According to *The Cleveland Leader*, Ross entered his return bout with Sorakichi already beset by two disadvantages. The paper called attention to the comparative pudginess displayed by Ross since his last set of bouts in Cleveland. Evidently, the ability of Ross to conceal his body beneath a suit of armor had negated his need to retain the striations of his muscle fibers through proper diet and exercise. At 217 pounds, Ross was anywhere from 12 to 25 pounds heavier than what had previously been accepted as his physical prime.

Beyond that, Ross also made a show of expressing that he had taken ill, and advised that any vulnerability or fatigue he displayed should be attributed to this temporary affliction. Unless Ross exaggerrated his lethargy for dramatic effect, then the effects of his loss of conditioning were prominently displayed during his bout with Sorakichi.

By the end of the third round — a catch-as-catch-can bout that Sorakichi won to take a two-to-one lead in the tally — Ross staggered back to his corner "badly under the weather," and announced that he should simply walk out on the match. *The Leader* opined that Ross' "extra flesh and lack of training told on him badly."

Although Ross won the fourth round, which was grappled in the Greco-Roman style and lasted for 13 minutes, Ross turned to his second and said that "he was afraid he would have to give up the match, and he was very sick." At the urging of his second, Ross walked to his dressing room, and after the 15-minute intermission expired without the reemergence of Ross, the referee promptly awarded the bout to Sorakichi, "who was apparently as fresh as when the contest opened."

Sorakichi's improvement since his prior set of appearances in Cleveland was described as "a wonder to all," while *The Leader* ultimately chalked up the loss by Ross to the fact that Ross, "has not wrestled in two years," and had his conditioning further hampered by an illness.

Highland Games and Hippodromes

That same month, Ross and Sorakichi had a rematch before a packed house where "fully $1,000 was taken at the door." Before the featured event took place, the audience jeered at "a number of half dressed and very dirty boys who dragged each other around the stage in alleged wrestling bouts."

In light of the dissatisfying conclusion to the previous match between Ross and Sorakichi, which Ross effectively abandoned prior to the fifth and deciding fall in front of an excited crowd, the least likely outcome would have been any sort of decision that would have led one of the combatants to abandon the bout. Yet, for some reason, this is precisely what occurred.

The alleged disagreement between Ross and Sorakichi began when Ross won the coin toss prior to the fifth fall and selected collar-and-elbow as the style of the round. This was a selection that was in discordance with the stated rules for the evening, which stipulated that only two different styles — catch-as-catch-can and Greco-Roman — would be utilized.

"The Jap very properly refused to wrestle in any other styles but those previously agreed upon, and after considerable loud talk the articles of agreement were called for," said *The Cleveland Press*. "Through the oversight of a green *Plain Dealer* reporter who drew up the articles and did not think it necessary to specify the style of the deciding bout, Ross secured a technical advantage and stuck to it like a drowning man to a life-preserver. It was well understood by everybody that the match was to include only the two styles of wrestling, and as the Jap refused to go on, the match was awarded to Ross amid a chorus of howls and hisses."

After making his way through the angry crowd, Sorakichi "banged a fresh young man in the eye who called around the dressing room door to taunt him." It had definitely been a bizarre choice of consecutive match outcomes if the intent had been to re-acclimate Cleveland's wrestling fans to Ross in a positive way.

Highland Games and Hippodromes

The fact that Ross' swordfighting business had seemingly gone belly up was nothing compared to the difficulty that Donald Dinnie had experienced in Australia in 1886. For Dinnie, the year opened with him serving as the host of a Highland sports event that attracted the leading athletes of South Australia to the Adelaide Oval.

Illustration of an aging Donald Dinnie

In the middle of the cricket pitch where the games were being held, Dinnie oversaw an event that *The Sporting Judge* discredited as being "so hopelessly muddled that the proceedings can only be described as a farce," as well as a "most lamentable failure."

What transformed the Highland athletic tournament into a sham was Dinnie's insistence that he act as both competitor and judge, while placing an obvious thumb on the scale in service to himself and his placement at the top of the score sheet.

"Perhaps it may seem strange that a competitor should be allowed to measure his own and his opponents' throws; but the fact is the Scotch athlete, besides being a competitor, is judge, handicapper, referee, and everything," reported *The Judge*. "For a South Australian athlete to beat the champion of the world at his own game was not to be thought of, but there is no denying it — he was honestly, fairly, and squarely defeated last Saturday, and in justice to his victor we hope the matter will not be allowed to rest."

The event that ultimately led to Dinnie being literally booed off the pitch occurred when local shotputter P.B. Roachock — an ethnically Irish athlete bearing the nickname "Paddy" — competed head-to-head against Dinnie in the putting of the 20-pound stone. In order to defeat Dinnie and collect the advertised prize of £50 and a silver medal, Roachock only needed to land his stone within two feet of Dinnie's best throw.

"So well did [Roachock] perform that Dinnie could get no nearer than five inches to his throw, the respective distance being — Roachock, 42ft. 5in.; Dinnie, 42ft. — this being without the 2ft. handicap conceded to the local man," continued *The Judge*. "Dinnie, however, measured his own throw, and announced himself the winner, on what grounds it is hard to conceive. Roachock's friends protested against Dinnie officiating as judge, but the unfairness of the proceeding was unheeded by the 'canny Scot.'"

Roachock then tossed against Dinnie in the throwing of the light weight, with Dinnie's self-imposed two-foot handicap rule in place. Roachock's 48-feet-and-a-half-foot throw was safely within the handicap range of Dinnie's best toss of under 50 feet. However, Dinnie "proclaimed himself victorious," and effectively disqualified Roachock after protesting that the South Australian athlete "had not adhered to the Caledonian rules."

Highland Games and Hippodromes

The gentleman on the grounds deemed by *The Judge* to have been most qualified to render an impartial verdict on the matter — "Mr. Cummins" — insisted that Roachock should have been allowed to adopt whatever throwing style he wished, "but the champion, with that paltry spirit that has marked his career in Australia, refused to concede a point to his opponent, and limited the run to 7 ½ ft. Shortly after, Dinnie left the Oval, amidst a perfect storm of hoots and hisses."

Also adding to the contentious nature of the scene was the lingering threat that a brawl along ethnic lines seemed destined to break out in the middle of the Oval due to "strained relations" between "the Scotch and Irish parties." This seemed to be owed to the fact that "Dinnie's friends from 'Caledonia, stern and wild' also refused to accept any outcome other than Dinnie being proclaimed the victor of his self-adjudicated events against the Irish-Australian local, who'd brought plenty of his own supporters to the Oval with him.

Following the festival, Roachock promptly posted a challenge to Dinnie in several publications that went unheeded by the nearly 50-year-old man who still insisted on advertising himself as the reigning champion athlete of the world.

The Judge closed its coverage of the affair with one final salvo: "We sincerely hope we have seen the last of the great Donald Dinnie, who has made himself extremely unpopular during his stay in our midst."

The animosity between Roachock and Dinnie over the incident at the Adelaide Oval stewed for several months, as the two repeatedly insulted each other through letters submitted to newspapers. The two agreed to settle the matter three months later through an independently judged one-on-one throwing contest where the rules were mutually agreed upon in advance.

As the April contest drew near, Dinnie notified the press that he would need to postpone his competition with Roachock because "he slipped while putting the heavy stone," fell to the ground, and "severely sprained his arm" in the process. Adding to the peculiar nature of the incident was the circumstance that Dinnie's slip had supposedly occurred because he was kicked in the right leg by a horse while in the process of practicing his throw, thereby causing him to stumble.

To a reasonable person, the news of this incident would have prompted several questions, not the least of which was why Dinnie felt compelled to practice hurling heavy stones within kicking range of a horse. Surely an athlete and strongman of his caliber and experience would have recognized the inherent hazard of polishing his throwing form while standing so close to a large, hoofed mammal.

True or false, the story was absurd either because the lie was so fantastic, or because the placement of a horse next to a Donald Dinnie who was preoccupied with the hurling of heavy objects was so sorely mishandled. Equally misguided were Dinnie's suggestions for how the matter could be rectified and Roachock recompensed.

"[Dinnie] writes that, as he does not wish Mr. Roachock to lose his training, if he cannot postpone, he will allow him £20 if he will transfer the match to J. MacDonald, whom he will back to give him 9in. at putting 28lb stone, or 2ft with 28lb and 14lb combined," relayed *The Town and Country Journal of Sydney*. "He trusts Mr. Roachock will not take advantage of the accident, but either allow a few weeks' time or accept terms with MacDonald as proposed."

Dinnie's attempt to provide a substitute to take his place in the throwing duel was rejected, as Roachock, perhaps looking to collect whatever financial relief he could from the situation, decided to collect the £50 forfeit that Dinnie had been obligated to post when accepting Roachock's original challenge.

Astonishingly, this wasn't even close to being the only time Dinnie's name had been printed in *The Town and Country Journal* owing to an incident involving a horse, although the prior occasion painted Dinnie in an infinitely more heroic light. The previous summer, Donald had been walking along Swanston Street in Melbourne when he "observed a runaway horse coming up the street at full gallop."

Highland Games and Hippodromes

"Dinnie at once took up a position in the roadway to seize the horse, though one of his party urged him not to risk his life," described *The Journal*. "As the horse galloped past him, Dinnie clutched at the reins, but the animal swerved, and Dinnie had just time to grasp the shaft of the cart, and after running along for about fifty yards, he caught the bridle and brought the horse to a standstill."

Soon thereafter, Dinnie was embroiled in yet another embarrassing equine controversy, the story of which was syndicated back in the United States. Angry over an unpaid debt, Dinnie decided to swipe the debtor's low-value horse and held it hostage until such time as the debt could be repaid.

"The fiery steed grazed in a paddock attached to Donald's rural pub at Alphington, Victoria, and for a time the braw Scot seemed to have the best of the deal," the report elaborated. "Then commenced a long wrestle between Donald and the remorseless law. After about six trials, sundry executions, and a few summonses for assaulting bailiffs, Donald had to part with £40 odd of accumulated penalties to keep himself out of jail. At latest date, Donald was still guarding those bones of contention which constitute the horse, and another trial was pending. The derned quadruped is valued at £13. That's where the joke comes in."

While Dinnie had spent years in Australia following his exposure as a hippodromer along America's Pacific Coast, his partner in many of those efforts had been slowly growing in prestige and influence. No one would ever have suspected at the time just how influential Duncan McMillan would ultimately be to the furtherance of professional wrestling as a North American institution, not merely as a champion in his own right, but as a man whose career would be inextricably linked with those of four of the most distinguished stars of the era.

The Highland Games hosted by the Scottish Thistle Club at Badger Park in May 1883 was one of the first noteworthy appearances by McMillan. Performing under what would become his common public pseudonym of "D.A.

McMillan of Bodie," he was credited as the competitor who "ran [Dinnie] close in several of his best games." This included the tossing of the caber, making McMillan one of the rare athletes capable of acceptably completing a regulation caber toss at that stage of the development of the Highland Games in North America.

Before Dinnie's West Coast arrival, McMillan had been one of the star participants in Caledonian games that had been held in the region over the prior decade, including winning all of the throwing events held at the Caledonian Club games of 1880. In his promotional biography, McMillan would later claim to have won several other events all over California and Nevada, earning 52 first-place finishes in the process.

In August 1883, *The San Francisco Chronicle* described McMillan as Dinnie's "friend, partner, adviser, and travelling companion." Outside of California, McMillan positioned himself as Dinnie's chief rival in all matters of Scottish interest, while making a show of deference to Dinnie's dominance in Scottish wrestling.

In *The Oregonian*, McMillan was quoted as saying that he was willing to wrestle Dinnie "in any five styles of wrestling for any money that the Scotch champion will put up," with Scottish backhold being the sole style in which McMillan was afraid to face the legend. While willing to make this concession, McMillan still insisted that he could "defeat Dinnie not only in wrestling, but at most of the Scotch games in which the brawny Scot has achieved world-wide fame."

In Dinnie's absence, the bulk of McMillan's activities on the Pacific Coast flew beneath the radar. He still competed in the 1884 Highland Games hosted by the Scottish Thistle Club of San Francisco and gave an admirable account of himself by winning multiple events.

On the mat, McMillan's biggest match of the year was a five-styles bout with James Pascoe that ended in a draw, and concluded with McMillan expressing to the press that he desired to meet William Muldoon on the mat "as soon as possible."

Highland Games and Hippodromes

Muldoon had returned to San Francisco following the allegations of hippodroming that had caused so much disgrace for a genuine athlete like Donald Dinnie to have been embroiled in. When he got back to work, he was involved in an event at the Mechanics Pavilion that had resulted in the submission of an application for the issuance of an arrest warrant for Muldoon "on a charge of obtaining money under false pretenses in connection with a 'wrestling' match." The application was refused due to the court finding no grounds to issue the warrant.

McMillan was still active in San Francisco when Duncan Ross made his return following the death of the latter's wife. The pair appeared together in May 1885 at a special picnic for young boys who competed in several athletic contests that primarily involved running and jumping. The two were present as attractions and participated in no events except for the special tug-of-war, which they won to the surprise of no one, including the reporter from *The San Francisco Examiner* who made note that the two "sturdy Hibernians" formed the backbone of their team.

The very next month, McMillan was a successful participant in the Caledonian Picnic held in Sacramento's East Park. *The Sacramento Union* estimated that 5,000 people attended the event, including "a large number of Scotchmen" wearing "full Highland costume."

McMillan won every throwing event — including the caber toss — and also placed first in the hitch-and-kick, and third in the running hop, step, and jump.

During 1886 — the same year Ross began swordfighting in earnest and Dinnie had been under fire for not hosting honest competitions in Australia — McMillan ventured outside of the San Francisco Bay area and began to define himself in several new markets. This included Salt Lake City, Utah, where McMillan first accepted a job as a millwright, but later took an ownership stake in a saloon in Park City, a community that proudly claimed him. His June bout with

Deputy John Cudihee was said to have ended in disgrace due to McMillan's actions following the match.

The gate receipts at the Salt Lake City Opera House on that June night were estimated to have been $460, with a crowded upper deck, but only a moderately filled downstairs, where tickets were priced at $1.50. When the wrestlers were late to take their places on the stage, the audience "began to amuse itself by howling, whistling and stamping, and a general tattoo to the tune of 'Ma, ma, where's my pa' was beat upon the floor for fifteen or twenty minutes, hoodlums, sports, business men and all joining in swelling the pandemonium with a hearty and graceful abandon."

The Salt Lake Herald recounted that when the wrestlers finally appeared, with McMillan seconded by Frank Hays, "all eyes were centered on McMillan, a magnificent specimen of the genus homo, 6 feet and 2 inches in height, weight 200 pounds (dressed), age 27 years." McMillan's legs were said to have filled his tights with "hard and beautiful proportions," and it was added that he was "a fine looking fellow in face and form."

Cudihee was described as a less impressive specimen, standing 5'10" ⅛ inches and weighing 185 pounds, and lacking "the general grace and poise of his opponent." As they waited to begin, the two men sat in chairs on opposite sides of a stage that had been covered by canvas that sat atop two inches of sawdust.

Through three rounds, McMillan was winning two falls to one, and he was presumed to have been a favorite in the Cornish style, which required both men to wear loose canvas jackets. Just a few minutes into the bout, Cudihee executed a "back him lock" while McMillan was attempting a grapevine, resulting in McMillan being launched high into the air before he crashed to the sawdust-padded canvas.

"Cudihee was up and off to the room in a second, but McMillan lay quiet for a few moments, and when he arose was half dazed, and seemed to wonder where he was," wrote *The Herald* reporter. "Cudihee's left shoulder had lit on his neck, and had given him a bad but temporary hurt. Hays weakly attempted to protest against the decision going to Cudihee, but was rightfully sent back discomfited, and the crowd again went out for 'atmosphere,' with hearty cheers for the town man."

In between the falls, the reporter poked his head into McMillan's dressing room, where there was "gloom and sickness at the stomach" as McMillan "sat with his head on his hands, undoubtedly hurt." When they returned for the sidehold bout, which was Cudihee's stated specialty, it was considered a foregone conclusion that Cudihee would triumph over the larger McMillan. Still, when Cudihee took McMillan down and pinned his shoulders and right hip to the canvas, McMillan violently protested the official's ruling.

"McMillan literally howled and foamed with rage, called the referee a son of a b— repeatedly, and struggled like a mad man to get at him," continued *The Herald*. "It took three of his friends to force him into his room, or there would doubtless have been blood spilt. Smith, who was an athlete himself, and who has met McMillan in the arena, coolly waited for him in the centre of the stage. McMillan swore, fought and yelled that he had not been beaten, he could lick Cudihee, or the referee either, etc., etc., but was finally forced into his room, where no more was seen of him."

Days later, it was reported that McMillan had arrived at the Opera House in the company of several residents from Park City who had bet a whopping amount of money on the bout and "went broke on their man." Although only $460 was estimated to have been earned at the gate after ticket sales were deducted, it was projected that Park City residents had collectively gambled away close to $5,000 on the result of the McMillan-Cudihee bout.

"Every Parkite had money on the result, including Ed Kimball, the then mayor of the town," reported *The Herald* when it revisited the event in 1900. "John J. Daly, Henry Newell, Thomas Kearns, and scores of the well known residents of the camp, came down to see the match and still farther back their man. Ed Kimball and Henry Newell both made several heavy bets, and Tom Kearns himself got up an extra $50 — an amount which meant more to him then than it would now — and everybody shouted till he was hoarse during the fray, none of them for a moment having the least doubt till the affair was finally decided but that McMillan would win."

When McMillan lost, the Park City contingent was said to have been inconsolable, and to add insult to financial injury, McMillan promptly skipped town and "never returned to the Park." Chances are, a decent chunk of the Park City money found its way into McMillan's pockets thanks to strategic third-party wagers.

On his way out of Utah, McMillan faced Charles Moth in a late July bout, and with McMillan now being suspected of being an outright hippodromer, *The Herald* decided to open its report on the match with a prelude about how there had been "so many hippodromes in the way of athletic exhibitions in this city," and how the bout between Moth and McMillan likely attracted a small audience because of those lingering suspicions.

The match was said to have been wrestled "on the square" as far as the effort level was concerned, which worked in the favor of McMillan and Moth, who wrestled until 12:20 a.m., then declared that night to have been a draw, and invited everyone to return two nights later to watch them continue their bout — while paying a second admission fee.

The men engaged in another extended multi-fall contest that was knotted after four falls. McMillan won the toss to decide the style for the fifth fall, and selected Cornish as the last grappling method of the night. *The Herald* writer's choice of words to describe what followed betrays the skepticism that he felt about what transpired.

"Moth's second, Lang, here came upon the stage and had the presumption to state that Moth did not understand the Cornish style, and unless McMillan would choose some other style, he would not wrestle," printed *The Herald*. "Referee McDonald then appeared with the articles of agreement, and stated that the Cornish style had been one of those agreed upon when the match was made; McMillan had the right to choose it, and unless he came up in ten minutes, the match, stakes, and receipts would be awarded to McMillan. This had the desired effect, and at once brought Moth upon the stage."

McMillan immediately brought the show to a close by putting Moth on his back in five minutes. Out in San Francisco, *The Chronicle* would report how "McMillan got away with Moth in a mixed-styles wrestle," and that an unnamed Utah paper had declared that the match smelled like "the biggest kind of a mice," presumably implying a rat. *The Chronicle* then knowingly added that McMillan and Moth would "probably meet again" with Moth coming out on top.

The Chronicle's assessment of the McMillan-Moth encounter was the opener to a section that covered wrestling events that involved grapplers from around North America who were familiar to San Franciscans. Included in the coverage was a comment about the now expected, and to some extent, accepted practice of hippodroming in wrestling.

"Those who speculate on such men — professional wrestlers, pugilists, etc. — must make up their minds to expect an occasional 'double cross' or so, else where would be the sport?" asked *The Chronicle*. "They cannot count on having everything their own way all the time."

By putting what he had learned from wrestling on the West Coast to good use, Duncan McMillan had managed to financially gut an entire community of the Salt Lake area with his hippodroming expertise. This would only be the beginning for him. As the men who he had modeled himself after would continue to struggle onward in their respective corners of the professional wrestling ecosystem, McMillan was going to land in the perfect place to help launch pro wrestling's resurgence alongside its brightest new star.

Highland Games and Hippodromes

10 – Tearing His Kilt

Donald Dinnie wouldn't participate in another wrestling bout that was treated like a major deal by the Australian press until 1887 after English wrestler Tom Cannon reached the Southern Hemisphere. The two men were hastily matched at the Bijou Theater in Melbourne "for £50, the five-style championship of the world, and the *Police Gazette* diamond belt."

The event was advertised as a match for a vacant championship, and it was explained to the fans that Cannon and Dinnie had each been in possession of the championship in the past, "each having defeated Duncan C. Ross in America." Ross certainly would have objected to this seeing as how the only bout between himself and Cannon for a multi-style championship and a *Police Gazette* belt took place on December 10, 1884 at the California Theatre in San Francisco. *Ross* won the match three falls to two.

Likewise, Ross never wrestled Dinnie with the *Police Gazette* wrestling belt at stake; the two were teammates in a *Police Gazette* bout contested with the world athletic championship on the line, which the pair won in an unsatisfying fashion due to the forfeit of Thomas Lynch and James Daly.

Even if the *Police Gazette*'s endorsement of the title was purely imaginary, the title bout between Dinnie and Cannon was certainly the biggest wrestling match in Australia since the tragic passing of Clarence Whistler. *The Albury Banner and Wodonga Express* described the venue as "a crowded house to all parts of the theatre except the dress circle."

The match was even at 2-2 after the first four falls, with Dinnie's usual weakness of Greco-Roman wrestling serving as the style that the final contest would be contested in. Flashing an atypical level of skill in the art against one of its respected masters, Dinnie dragged Cannon down on all fours and tried to flip him onto his shoulders, but when Cannon's shoulders neared the ground, "he, with an eel-like slipperiness, made two turns instead of one, getting face downwards, until he found a chance to regain his feet."

"At times, Cannon, although most of the work was done by Dinnie, who strove determinedly to win, would assume the aggressive, and twice the Caledonian giant was lifted right off the ground and turned a somersault by his powerful opponent without being able to gain the umpire's fiat," continued *The Banner and Express*. "Finally, when the men had been wrestling 14 minutes, Cannon won the fall by getting Dinnie on all fours and then bringing an inflexible hug to bear on his neck, while he leveled his shoulders over till they touched the stage."

Once Cannon was officially awarded the victory and the world championship belt, Dinnie's trainer stepped onto the stage and stated that "no less than seven styles would have to be wrestled before Dinnie could have a fair test in 'mixed' styles." This attempt to invalidate the result of the bout and salvage Dinnie's reputation seemed to pay little respect to the veneer of all-purpose wrestling mastery implied by the existence of a five-style world championship.

In March, Dinnie was granted his wish of a seven-styles championship match with Cannon, with the title downgraded to either "the wrestling championship of Victoria" or "the championship of Australia" depending on the publication covering the event. Either way, the ending to the bout rendered it a debacle.

After cycling through six rounds of Greco-Roman, Scotch, catch-as-catch-can, Cornish, sidehold, and Cumberland wrestling, the match was level at three falls per grappler, with a collar-and-elbow round remaining to determine the champion.

The previous six rounds had collectively totaled well under an hour of match time; the seventh round — theoretically when the fighters would be at their most fatigued, slippery, and prone to error, lasted for one hour and fifteen minutes, and would have extended into the next morning had the match not been declared a draw at the midnight hour. The fans and the members of the press were extremely suspicious of the way the final fall unfolded, to say nothing of the entirety of the events that preceded it.

"Dinnie did not attempt to make play, and Cannon's only effort was again and again unsuccessful. As an exhibition of wrestling this was one of the dullest and most uninteresting imaginable, and the wonder is that so many persons remained until 12 o'clock, especially when the probabilities, taking everything into account, were so strongly in favor of a draw," printed *The Melbourne Leader*. "The whole contest, with the exception of the last walk round, was an interesting one, and showed Dinnie to be the cleverer wrestler at the stand-up styles, while Cannon was the better man when the work was to be done on all fours on the carpet.

"The unsatisfactory termination of the match is not a matter for surprise, as it has long been the custom to end P.R. and wrestling contests in this way, but the spectators on Saturday night had a right to expect something better than what was shown them between the hours of half-past 10 and 12 o'clock."

Shenanigans such as these were indisputably harmful to Dinnie's reputation. Reporting that the forthcoming bout between Dinnie and Harry Dunn had failed to attract much attention, *The Referee* of Sydney added that "in fact, anything that the Scot is connected with is generally regarded as hippodrome business," but qualified the statement by adding "whether or not the stigma applies in the present case, I am not prepared to say."

Wrestling in Her Majesty's Opera House in front of a crowd that *The Punch* of Melbourne described as "very pussy" — which presumably means that it was sparsely attended — Dinnie and Dunn presented a bout that was received as an earnest effort by the fans. Nevertheless, *The Punch* opined that the way the match unfolded proved "beyond a shadow of a doubt that the thing couldn't have been more exciting if it had been faked up."

Just as in the seven-styles bout between Dinnie and Cannon, the men battled through the first six rounds and found themselves at a standstill. At this point, Dinnie and Dunn had already reached the upper limit of the time for which the venue had been rented, and it was announced by the event's organizer that they needed to clear the seats so that the Opera House could be made ready for that night's singing performance.

That's when Mr. Boucicault, the proprietor of the Opera House, who was likely armed with the best of intentions, announced that he would extend the length of the event by 15 minutes to hopefully provide the men with sufficient time to conclude their duel. The catch-as-catch-can round commenced, but the manner in which it ended gave rise to the belief that the organizers of the match had never intended the final round to begin in the first place.

"There was about five minutes' wrestling, and it was the intention of Mr. Boucicault to allow them to go on if there was any prospect of an early finish," said *The Punch*. "An employee of the theatre, however, misapprehending his instructions, turned the lights out punctually at a quarter-past six o'clock, when the wrestlers were together on the floor, and the match was therefore declared to be a draw, amidst some uproar and confusion."

Dinnie's reputation as a credible wrestler may have been taking on water, but he remained a dangerous man for an unskilled combatant to quarrel with in public. In May 1887, Dinnie was charged with the unlawful assault of lithographer James McAlister of Fairfield Park, owing to a disagreement involving dogs and sheep.

McAlister had gone for a morning stroll with his dogs on Sunday, April 17, when he came upon some sheep grazing in a field. Instinctively, the dogs chased the sheep until McAlister called them off, and as he parted, he said he heard the voice of a woman in a nearby house, who used "very foul language."

"Shortly after, the defendant (Dinnie) drove up in a trap, and dismounting, came towards him and without further provocation, struck him over the face and body with his whip," reported *The Age*. "He also received a blow in the chest, which brought him to the ground, where the defendant kicked him. For some time he lay senseless, and on recovering he went to Constable Cummins at Alphington, and from thence to Dr. Fyle, who examined his wounds and gave him a certificate placing him on the sick list of his lodge.

"For the defence, Dinnie said that one of his sheep having been bitten, he was in the act of chastising the dog, when the plaintiff caught him by his kilt, and whilst he was endeavoring to release himself, the plaintiff was thrown down and received the injuries complained of."

Dinnie filed a counter-suit for damages, alleging that McAlister had initiated the episode when he assaulted Dinnie "by catching hold of and tearing his kilt." Both cases were dismissed without costs.

Duncan Ross also spent more of 1887 garnering attention for private affairs than he would have liked. A peculiar tale involving Ross also served to reveal that the athlete and entertainer had failed to make a serious effort to close down his Cleveland drinking establishment as he had promised after the passing of his wife, nor had he made any serious attempts to reduce his own consumption of alcohol. The event in question resulted in the arrest of Ross stemming from a complaint by a man named William Glass.

"[Glass] says that he visited Ross' saloon and applied for a position as cook; that Ross took him in a back room, promising him the place, and while there forced him to submit to having one side of his whiskers and mustache cut off," printed *The St. Louis Globe*. "The man presented a most woe-begone appearance. Ross was charged with disorderly conduct. Duncan must have been in one of his cheerful moods."

As the year unfolded, Ross continued with what can only be described as an unusual strategy of self-booking in what was once considered to be his home region. At the Academy of Music in Cincinnati, Ross lost a best-of-five match to James Faulkner, who he outweighed by nearly 80 pounds.

Highland Games and Hippodromes

The Plain Dealer made it clear that the 80-pound weight disparity was caused by the insistence of Ross that he should show up looking intrusively overweight. The assigned sportswriter wrote that the once-chiseled Ross "looked gigantic by the side of Faulkner, but he was fat and flabby."

When Faulkner won the fifth fall and the match, the audience "made noise enough for two thousand people and cheered Faulkner wildly." The article described it this way because the crowd that night was estimated at a disappointing 600 spectators. *The Plain Dealer* blamed the size of the crowd on Faulkner's poor drawing ability, and Ross blamed his loss on the fact that he had "a bad shoulder."

Ross was having better luck attracting fans on the outskirts of the Cleveland-Akron region where he had seldom made appearances in the past. A best-of-five match between Ross and Will Willie was concluded after just two falls, when Willie, who was being thoroughly outclassed by Ross, addressed the audience after the second intermission reached its end.

"Ross is the best all-round athlete in the world, and owing to an injured shoulder received in the recent Courtenay match, I am unable to finish the match, but I will deposit a hundred dollars in the Wayne County National Bank to meet Ross within sixty days at Cleveland for $500 a side," said Willie.

Surprisingly, Ross rejected Willie's offer on the grounds that he "had simply consented to meet Willie" because of the numerous challenges Willie had issued to him, and seeing that he had already proven that he was "the better man of the two," he would not accede to Willie's request for a rematch.

A few months later, Ross actually did face Willie again, and the evening ended with what *The Cleveland Leader* described as a disgraceful attempt to swindle Ross out of money. According to the report, Willie's manager John Mowery garnished the portion of the proceeds that were owed to Ross, and the famous athlete left the building with nothing. Ross retained an attorney to contest the matter on his behalf while he returned to Cleveland.

Highland Games and Hippodromes

In the meantime, Ross' rematch with Faulker — a best-of-five catch-as-catch-can bout — once again failed to attract an appreciable crowd. The perceived failure of Ross' return wrestling engagements in Cleveland likely contributed to the next series of business decisions he chose to make, which only seemed to further damage his name.

When April came around, Ross debuted his "athletic combination" in the area between Washington, D.C. and Baltimore, Maryland, the one-time home of Ross' deceased wife. The debut of his group at the Kernan Theatre was described as "somewhat uninteresting," owing to the ways in which the event's participants were poorly matched.

Ross defeated his former boxing protege Mervine Thompson in a first-bout wrestling exhibition, and Ross followed this by besting Pat Conners in a best two-out-of-three bout in which "the Scotch giant" had his small opponent seriously overmatched.

From there, Thompson's display of his boxing prowess against Canadian middleweight Foster resulted in the embarrassment of the former, who *The Washington Post* classified as "more of a sluggard than a slugger" as the audience "hooted and laughed at the spiritless contest until the curtain fell on the third round."

Back in Cleveland, *The Plain Dealer*, which had once been most favorable in its treatment of Ross, conceded that Ross' tour of Washington and Baltimore had "a very fakey look." The logic employed to arrive at this observation wasn't disclosed, but it seems to have been at least partially rooted in the fact that Sorakichi and Faulkner — who had once been characterized as bitter rivals of Ross — were both participating in the tour and tournament, along with Ross and Thompson.

As the tour continued, its appraisal at the hands of the Virginia press grew progressively more brutal. Ross scheduled an afternoon of entertainment in the form of a mounted sword contest at Gymnasium Park, which drew a crowd so small that the event was cancelled altogether.

Highland Games and Hippodromes

The report from *The Norfolk-Virginian* detailed how Ross was prepared to battle Sergeant Walsh on a baseball field, but only 100 people paid money to attend the show, and the managers of the venue decided that the crowd was so small that it wasn't worth "the trouble of the exhibition."

Refunds were issued to the fans inside of the ballpark. However, no refunds were provided to the "200 colored boys and men" who had paid 10 cents apiece "to stand on a shed erected in a yard next to the baseball grounds." That money was paid to the owner of the shed, who rented out the standing-room-only space independently from what the owners of the ballpark were charging.

The reports from a separate event that occurred later in the evening were so negative that Ross probably wished that event had been cancelled as well.

"At night the same organization gave some sort of show at the Academy of Music before a small audience, which consisted of sparring matches between four young negro men of this city, a wrestling match between Duncan Ross and Captain Daly, and a sparring match between Mr. Richard Vizzard, of this place, and Mervine Thompson," said *The Virginia-Pilot*. "The performance was a fraud throughout, and those who were absent last evening are to be congratulated."

Licking his wounds from the dismal failure that had been his Mid-Atlantic athletic tour, Ross returned to presenting swordfighting demonstrations in areas of the country that weren't accustomed to such exhibitions, and in some cases he clearly didn't account for the volatility of the crowds he was seeking to entertain.

In Milwaukee, for example, Ross decided to present himself as the opponent of "August C. Schmidt" in a city loaded with first- and second-generation German immigrants. The fact that Schmidt was likely one of Ross' usual opponents competing under a pseudonym is immaterial; the fans in attendance certainly believed "Schmidt" to be German, and acted accordingly.

Highland Games and Hippodromes

"The sword contest for $100 between Duncan C. Ross and August C. Schmidt Thursday night was stopped by the police in the twenty-fourth round," stated a June edition of *The Beloit Daily Free Press*. "The audience was made up principally of Germans, and when the referee decided several points against Schmidt, which they thought should go to him, they raised a terrific howl and were about to storm the stage and fire the referee out when the police arrived. The contest was given to Ross."

While the crowds in Milwaukee may have been unstable, Ross continued his habit of displaying a similar lack of stability in his personal conduct away from the spotlight. During the same stay in Milwaukee, Ross was arrested on a charge of drunkenness. After depositing his bail, Ross returned and testified in the Milwaukee courtroom of Judge Mallory that he had $600 in his pockets at the time of his arrest, but only $300 was returned to him. Ross' case was ultimately dismissed due to a lack of evidence.

Even if the bulk of Ross' swordfights were now unable to supply him with audiences of significant size and interest, a Highland Games event always presented Ross with an ample crowd that would consent to watching his performances. By this time, Ross was keenly aware of how the platform provided by these well-attended Caledonian events could attract national attention for his grand business ventures if properly leveraged.

At the games of the Scranton Caledonian Club that summer, Ross submitted a performance that succeeded in providing him with the exact sort of publicity he needed to promote his various shows. In front of 10,000 fans at the Scranton driving park, Ross trotted out upon a "beautiful bay horse," while clad in armor that made him look "the embodiment of a crusader" to face "Sergeant Charles Walsh," who in this case may have been played by shotputter John McPherson.

Playing out in a manner almost identical to what McPherson would later describe, but without the ethnic brawl at the end, the bout between Ross and Walsh continued until

Ross "struck him with a lightning-like blow with his sword across the mask, knocking him like a log from his saddle." The crowd fell silent, for it "seemed as if a man had been slaughtered before their eyes."

"At length the judges ran to the rescue and dragged the cavalryman across the track and rested him against the boards," reported *The Boston Globe*, which picked up coverage of the event. "A doctor was called, and for a few minutes it was thought that Walsh was dead. An examination of his mask showed that Ross' sword had almost cut it in two across the skull. A broad red mark across the wounded man's pate showed where the heavy stroke fell."

When Walsh recovered, he struggled to renew the fight, but needed to be restrained by the police. Ross was awarded the imaginary prize money of $500, while the finish to the bout, described as "the most savage affair ever seen" in Scranton, Pennsylvania, was said to have "created a regular sensation."

The stir created by the "near death" of Walsh spurred interest for Ross' swordfights in new markets, including New Orleans, where *The Daily Picayune* found it odd that Duncan Ross the wrestler would be the one to bring competitive swordfighting to the city where he had famously wrestled Theobaud Bauer amidst concerns that the two were indulging in hippodroming. Interest in the November event was sufficient to attract 2,000 fans to the local baseball diamond to observe the first competitive broadsword bout in the city's history.

"A great many who came did not expect to see a battle for blood, but were actuated by curiosity to see the new sport," explained *The Daily Picayune*. "Whether the contest was genuine or not, it was all right as far as the observance of forms went, for each man had put up $150, and some of the bouts were as heated as if the armored swordsmen were fighting for life. Even as an exhibition the contest was interesting, as the sport requires that its exponents be expert horsemen and skilled swordsmen."

Highland Games and Hippodromes

If these events had any potential for success, they were dashed by Ross' insistence on repeating the captivating finish from his Scranton exhibition in every market, including the show held in New Orleans. Just as in Scranton, Ross unseated Sergeant Walsh from atop his horse, only for Walsh to recover and lunge furiously at Ross. The police interfered to prevent the injured Walsh from getting to Ross, while one of the officers grabbed Walsh around the neck and pulled him to the ground, until the swordsman could be "dragged off the field bloody and breathless by citizens."

The repetitious nature of the finishes, combined with the recognition that Sergeant Walsh would have to be immeasurably foolish to repeatedly cheat death and always return for more, effectively exposed the swordfights as predetermined charades and killed-off whatever potential Ross' broadsword exhibitions once had. When Ross attempted to take his competitions overseas in December, he found it even harder to stoke interest abroad.

"Duncan C. Ross took his hippodrome sword contests over to Cuba, but the people there, who are accustomed to witnessing bloody bull fights, wouldn't turn out to see Ross' sham contests," wrote *The Boston Globe*. "Now if Duncan had stipulated to fight a bull he might have drawn a crowd."

Elsewhere, after swindling the citizens of Utah, Duncan McMillan took his act to the Midwest, where he surfaced at the beginning of 1887 as one of the tallest and strongest men on the circuit. In Hurley, Wisconsin, he wrestled J.P. Donner at the Grand Central Theatre in February, and bullied Donner by pinning him five times in 50 minutes. McMillan had been required to pin Donner six times in one hour to win, but Donner simply conceded the final fall to McMillan.

The pair had a rematch the following week, with Donner vowing to do better, at least by a small degree, as he sought to prevent McMillan from throwing him five times in one hour.

Highland Games and Hippodromes

The match was held in a venue that was "full to overflowing," and the ending to the match filled the building with excitement after McMillan scored the fourth fall at the 57-minute mark.

"As this left McMillan with only three minutes in which to throw his opponent the fifth time, a keen interest was taken in the last round, and it was watched with the greatest anxiety," printed *The Gogebic Iron Tribune*. "The fifth fall was declared, however, at the end of two and one-half minutes."

The wrestling events that McMillan featured in while in Wisconsin were of the multipurpose variety, where all of the wrestlers at the shows were equally as likely to be asked to perform impressive athletic feats as they were to wrestle. Owing in large part to his training as a Highland Games athlete, McMillan stood out as an unrivaled powerhouse at venues like the Beloit Opera House, even when standing next to some of the best and most popular wrestlers on the continent.

"One of the best features of the evening was some heavy dumb-bell lifting by Jack Carkeek, Evan Lewis, and D.A. McMillan, the famous wrestlers," printed *The Weekly Argus* of Beloit. "Carkeek put up a 140 pound bell three times with one hand. Lewis followed, raising the weight as many times, but not as easily. Lewis evidently is not quite as strong as Carkeek, or else he does not understand the dumb-bell as well. But the gigantic, good-natured McMillan astonished the house by putting up the weight six times in succession with apparent ease. McMillan was probably the strongest, and certainly the most finely proportioned man on the stage."

An important detail to establish is that this appears to be the period of time when McMillan became the stalwart training partner and traveling companion of Evan "The Strangler" Lewis. The pair began to appear at wrestling events as a double feature, with Lewis advertised as the catch-as-catch-can wrestling champion of the world, and McMillan billed as the mixed-style world wrestling champion.

The difference here is that Lewis had earned acknowledgement as the lineal world heavyweight champion of catch-as-catch-can wrestling — at least as far as recognition in the United States was concerned — when he defeated Joe Acton, the man who conquered Edwin Bibby, at the Battery in Chicago in April. Conversely, McMillan, who served as Lewis' lone second for the title bout with Acton, did not have any major victories by which he could stake his claim to being a mixed-style champion.

Jack Carkeek

The two men were generally inseparable during that time. When Lewis arrived in Muskegon, Michigan in August 1887 to wrestle against W.E. Gibbs at the Clay Avenue Armory, he reportedly arrived in the company of "D.A. McMillan, of the Caledonian club," and the two stayed overnight in rooms at the Occidental Hotel. *The Muskegon Chronicle* added that they would be continuing onward to Milwaukee, Wisconsin to take part in the city's Caledonian Games.

When they didn't have formal wrestling competitions arranged against opponents who were cast as antagonistic to them, Lewis and McMillan would host informal exhibitions to demonstrate the various holds and locks of wrestling in a non-combative atmosphere. As coverage of at least one of the exhibitions clearly indicates — a show in Janesville, Wisconsin that barely drew a crowd of 100 people — the events were not always rousing successes, and the public wariness of fakery was offered as one of the reasons that the shows were not more popular.

"There was so small an audience present, the exhibition was cut short, and no exhibition of sparring was had," recounted *The Gazette* of Janesville. "During the evening, Charles Moth, a noted wrestler, stepped on the floor and offered a challenge, but it appeared too much like a 'hippodrome game,' and he left the mat amid the jeers of the small number of spectators. Had the athletes appeared in our city and advertised a genuine exhibition of these sports, banishing all semblance of the hippodrome, they would have drawn together a large audience, and received fair pay for their coming. Our people have not forgotten the Greek George affair."

The "Greek George affair" centered around a bout that took place in Janesville — affectionately known as "Bower City" — in September 1885 between Theodore "Greek" George and Andre Christol, on the second floor of the Wilson block on South River Street. The bout was originally intended to be a private affair held in front of newspaper reporters and a few sporting friends of the wrestlers.

Word leaked out to the public of the bout's location, along with the fact that the wrestlers had agreed to wrestle to a predetermined finish, and many people paid money at the door to gain admission to the room, which ultimately contained many more standing-room observers than it was intended to hold. The person accepting money at the door was Deacon Monroe, the lessee of the building, and since his monetary cut was based on attendance, he stood to personally benefit from admitting as many people as the building could hold.

Seeing what he believed to have been too many complimentary admissions, Christol at first refused to wrestle, and left the building, with Greek George hot on his heels attempting to bring him back. Monroe left with the money, but was coaxed into returning most of it by the irate ticket-purchasers who were now of the belief that no event would be happening.

Eventually, Christol and the Greek returned to the assigned venue and began to wrestle, but according to *The Gazette*, the action was so obviously fake that the affair reportedly became "so gauzy that even the smallest boy present yelled 'Rats,'" while the crowd "left in disgust." The match then ended abruptly with no winner declared.

Years after the event, a sportswriter at *The Gazette* mentioned in the publication's pages that for a while after the Greek George episode "anyone that mentioned wrestling to a Janesville man died a horrible death," but added that the men of the city seemed prepared to reopen their hearts to professional wrestlers, likely at their own financial peril.

"Bower City sports are once more becoming anxious for someone to pluck them," joked *The Gazette* writer. "They might try their hands at betting on whether waterworks, the millennium, or a new Milwaukee street pavement will get here first."

Unsurprisingly, the hippodroming activities of McMillan and Lewis were by no means limited to the professional wrestling genre of sports. In a story that would receive a fairly wide circulation, both men were involved in fixing an athletic contest in what was described as a disgraceful affair.

The event that spawned the furor was a shotputting contest arranged in Madison, which involved McMillan, identified as the "trainer of Evan Lewis, the strangler," and wrestler J.C. Murphy, who was actually champion shotputter John McPherson performing under a pseudonym. *The Saint Paul Globe* reported that the men were competing for "stakes ostensibly amounting to $1,000."

"The gang succeeded in roping into the scheme a wealthy old horse buyer of Green Bay, who was induced to back McMillan for $100 of the stake money," continued *The Globe*. "This morning it was given out to the sporting public that an event of no little importance would occur in the afternoon, and the populace bit immensely. At 4 o'clock this afternoon accordingly about 300 persons gathered at a designated place ready to bet their money."

When the throwing began, McPherson presented himself as an athlete who lacked polish in the realm of shotputting, "and made very bungling work." In the first round, McMillan outthrew McPherson 40 feet to 37 feet. Seeing that McPherson was not as strong as McMillan, the crowd eagerly wagered money on McMillan, "and they were not slow in finding takers on the part of the insiders."

In the second round, McMillan outthrew McPherson by an even wider margin, besting him with a toss of 43 feet to McPherson's comparatively meager 37 feet. This toss was followed by an extended intermission, during which the majority of the assembled betting audience wagered heavily on McMillan.

The momentum began to shift in the third round, as McPherson finally outthrew McMillan 40-and-a-half feet to 39 feet. A little more betting activity was conducted, but at this time the expendable betting money "had become nearly exhausted."

The fourth round exposed precisely the direction in which things were headed; McPherson launched the shot 45 feet, while McMillan failed to throw it even 39 feet. Then, in the fifth and final round, with the athletes tied at two victories a piece, McMillan fouled "either accidentally or purposely," while McPherson launched the ball nearly 49 feet, topping

McMillan's best mark of the contest by more than five feet, and his own original mark by more than 11 feet.

Evan "Strangler" Lewis

"The crowd indignantly shrunk away, branding the contest as a most disgraceful affair," said *The Globe*. "It is needless to say that no money changed hands between the principals, the only losers being the suckers from Green Bay and the public to the extent of $300 or more. The scheme was arranged, it is said, by Evan Lewis, and the rest of the crowd for the purpose of defrauding Madisonians out of a little boodle, and it is not likely that it will add anything to Lewis' popularity here, where he has before been held as a great pet."

Fortunately for McMillan at least, most news outlets reported his name as either R.D. McMillan or D.R. McMillan, granting him some space for deniability if a new acquaintance ever introduced the episode as a topic of conversation.

As damning and damaging as a hippodroming accusation could be, there are clear instances where the wrestlers would wield the term against each other, either for the sake of enhancing their own reputations, or as payback if they felt as if they had been slighted or misled by their brothers in the grappling profession.

Evidence of this includes McMillan's public statements against Charles Moth after what seems to have been a falling out between Moth and the Lewis-McMillan pair, as McMillan opened 1888 in Wisconsin by writing to *The Beloit Daily Free Press* to blame the failure of a match between himself and Moth to materialize on the latter's desire not to work an honest bout.

"The wrestling match arranged between Mr. Charles Moth and myself, which was to have taken place at the Riverside rink in Janesville, Friday, Jan. 27th, has gone up like gas in the air," wrote McMillan. "The reason for this is that Mr. Moth got scared out and is going to Detroit, Mich., to wrestle with someone in that city. Now, to give Mr. Moth something easier, I will agree to throw him five times in one hour at catch-as-catch-can, two points down, for from $100 to $500 a side. Now, if Mr. Moth wants to wrestle, as he claims, let him come to the front like a man and put up or shut up. All he wants to do is to wrestle a hippodrome match, and this is not the first time he has shown the white feather, as he left Evan Lewis in Milwaukee last fall."

Five months later, McMillan sent a letter about Moth from Milwaukee to the newspapers of Muskegon, Michigan, to issue a similar challenge. Stating that he would throw Moth "five times in one hour Greco-Roman, or ten times catch-as-catch-can," McMillan sweetened the pot by promising that a victorious Moth could keep *all* of the gate money, but if McMillan won he would "present the receipts to any charitable institution in town to be selected by a committee of three citizens."

"I do this to show the people here the way the town has been hippodromed," added McMillan. "I will wrestle Moth any time between the 1st and 15th of July, but I want him to put up a forfeit of $50, I doing the same, money to be refunded after the match, but in case either fails to appear, the other to take the forfeit."

It would appear that McMillan had no plans whatsoever to engage Moth in an actual bout, and sent the letter across state lines for the sole purpose of tainting the reputation of Moth in a city where he was actively working at the time.

To say that Duncan McMillan had landed in the right place at the right time would be an understatement, but it's unlikely that he knew how much his position at the side of Evan Lewis would ultimately benefit him. It wouldn't be long before McMillan was on his way to becoming one of the most influential men in the entire wrestling business.

11 – Five-Style Champion

While Duncan McMillan was charging Charles Moth with hippodroming in select Midwestern markets, his own reputation was being whitewashed in a most bizarre way by his old friend William Muldoon, who had recently joined the Parson Davies management team and wrestled McMillan to a draw.

Muldoon told *The St. Louis Post-Dispatch* the story of how he rolled into Chicago with the Hallen & Hart Variety Combination, encountered McMillan, Lewis, and Carkeek already present in the city, and agreed to wrestle with them.

"The first man that ran against me there was Lewis, 'the Strangler,'" began Muldoon. "I struggled and fought with him for fifteen minutes, and when I got through with him I had a black eye and a couple of loose teeth to show for my trouble. Well, that was the first night, and I thanked my stars when it was over with. But I hadn't looked for enough. The next night Duncan McMillan faced me, and the struggle with him was almost as tough as it was with 'the Strangler.' I didn't know what was coming next, but I felt kind of blue on general principles, and was not surprised, therefore, when the next night, Carkeek came up, and the match with him was as bad as the rest."

The "Greco-Roman champion" Muldoon further explained how the men were the catch-as-catch-can, mixed, and Cornish champions respectively, and he had not expected to "work like a Hercules right along," but then he was summoned for a meeting with Parson Davies, the leader of the combination, who managed the work of the Lewis-McMillan-Carkeek trio.

"The Parson saw me, and told me he was going to take a combination of wrestlers on the road," alleged Muldoon. "These three men had told him they could throw me, and suggested how nice it would be to bill them something like this: 'Evan Lewis, champion, etc., the man who threw Muldoon;' 'Jack Carkeek, champion, etc., the man who threw Muldoon;'

'Duncan McMillan, champion, etc., the man who threw Muldoon.'

"'Now,' said the Parson, 'I've got nothing against you, Bill, and I don't want to cause you any unnecessary trouble. Suppose you leave Hallen and Hart and double with me.' I told the Parson I would if he would agree to my propositions, which he did. And so I doubled with him. Carkeek and McMillan are a part of the show, but the wrestling is all on the square and they get only what they earn, which is a mighty good little pile, as you could see for yourself."

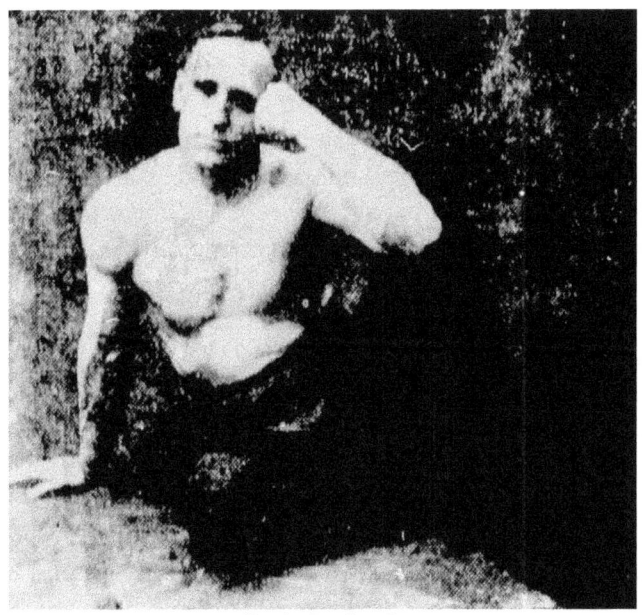

Jack Carkeek

The obvious irony is that it had been Muldoon who had done critical damage to the reputation of Donald Dinnie on the Pacific Coast by first alleging that Dinnie had been hippodroming in the Pacific Northwest with McMillan, and then admitting on his way out of town that the majority of his own bouts with Dinnie in the region had also been hippodromes.

As that news had either not penetrated the Midwestern media bubble, or had not stuck in the minds of readers, it was now Muldoon who was crediting McMillan and the rest of his new team with engaging in square mat work.

Muldoon's statement aside, it didn't take long for McMillan and Lewis to be forced to contend with their own fresh allegations of hippodroming. Under the headline of "A Hippodrome Spoiled," *The Inter Ocean* of Chicago informed its readers about the suspicious finish of a Cincinnati bout between McMillan and Lewis — well known in Chicago to have been the best of friends.

"It is suspected that the management intended the struggle to continue twenty minutes, and then, with a tremendous tour de force, end with a fall for no matter which," conjectured *The Inter Ocean*. "There was a tremendous show of energy on both sides for ten minutes and thirty seconds, each contestant barely failing several times to down the other. At the end of the ten-and-one-half minutes above specified, Referee Johnson tapped on the floor after the Strangler had made a herculean effort, and holding up his hand shouted: 'Fall for Lewis!'"

Lewis, McMillan and both of their seconds "illy concealed their disappointment" as the bout concluded in an unexpected fashion. Lewis was heard to remark to his second afterwards "I didn't claim a fall," but all of the men involved "hastened behind the scenes to laugh in spite of their chagrin."

In the pages of *The Cincinnati Enquirer*, it was said that "there were loud cries of hippodrome" from the crowd, although the writer from *The Enquirer* mentioned viewing nothing in the performances of the wrestlers to suggest any fakery, and even credited Lewis with wrestling as best he could even though he was sick.

What Lewis and McMillan had probably intended was reflected in a match they had just over a week later in St. Louis. At the city's Standard Theater, the terms of the bout were that Lewis would be required to defeat McMillan in under 15 minutes in order to claim victory, while McMillan could win the bout simply by remaining unpinned during that time. On top of that, McMillan could claim a $100 bonus if he actually managed to successfully pin Lewis.

McMillan only made one attempt to pin Lewis, by performing a headspin counter to a necklock, followed by a trip that brought one of Lewis' shoulders to the mat. McMillan was unable to force the other shoulder onto the ground, and when Lewis sprang to his feet, McMillan "abandoned the aggressive and adhered to the defensive policy only," right up until the mad scramble at the conclusion of the bout.

"The time limit was rapidly approaching, and it was clear that if Lewis was to throw his man he had better begin active work in a hurry," described *The St. Louis Post-Dispatch*. "This he did at last, and after two desperate attempts he succeeded in winning the match by throwing his man in one second after he had grappled with him. Muldoon, who acted as timekeeper, announced that the men had been wrestling 14 minutes and 59 seconds. The 'Strangler' had thus only one second to spare."

Off of the wrestling mat, McMillan continued his habit of participating in Highland Games in the Midwest, in part because they represented an opportunity for him to collect easy prize money, and also because such festivals continued to be one of the most effective ways for wrestlers like McMillan to promote themselves as real athletes, because they were, in fact, genuine Scottish-trained athletes.

At that June's Scottish Games of Janesville, McMillan brought Jack Carkeek with him and slaughtered the field, winning every throwing event by several feet — including the caber toss — before thoroughly impressing *The Gazette*'s writer with his prowess at the shot put.

"He 'put' the heavy stone — which happened to be a lump of cast iron about the size of a watermelon — out in the grass twenty-six feet and a half from where he stood, while the best that Carkeek could do was twenty-four feet and two inches," glowed *The Gazette*. "Then McMillan invested in 'puts' again, and sent what was christened with seeming irony 'the light stone' forty feet and eight inches. Carkeek followed him, but at a respectful distance, his throw being thirty-four feet."

In November, McMillan was still appearing regularly alongside Carkeek at wrestling events, but the matches apparently weren't attracting fans with the regularity that they had in earlier months. *The Beloit Daily Press* expressed that wrestling in general seemed to have lost its popularity, and laid the blame on the all too familiar culprit of hippodroming accusations.

"A couple of years ago wrestling matches attracted a great deal of attention, and contestants were sure to be well repaid, whereas now the sport arouses but little interest," said *The Daily Press*. "The secret of this withdrawal of public patronage is to be looked for in the great possibility of hippodroming that is open to the contestants and the too evident tendency in that direction shown in most of the recent matches. If on a square basis it affords one of the most interesting of all public athletic exhibitions, all professional wrestlers should seek to put the sport on a more reputable footing.

"And it is with wrestling like nearly every other sporting exercise — a game to catch enthusiastic suckers, either by gate money or bets. A famous runner once informed a *Free Press* reporter that 'not one in a hundred races were square.' It will be hard work for the sports to establish confidence in their matches even if they mean fair, and until square deals are certain, the less money people blow into shows, the less there will be of them."

Even with accusations of hippodroming nibbling at his heels, McMillan had treated Wisconsin's wrestling fans to several exciting displays on the mat, which established McMillan as a catch-as-catch-can wrestler nearly on par with Evan Lewis in the eyes of the region's fans.

This belief in McMillan's grappling superiority also worked to his detriment. In a best-of-five catch-as-catch-can contest held in early December 1888, McMillan dismantled Charley Parker en route to winning three straight falls. Because of this, the very next loss by McMillan prompted a wave of accusations that he was as guilty of match-fixing shenanigans as anyone.

In mid-December, McMillan entered a catch-as-catch-can bout with Tom Connors, and lost two straight falls in a best-of-three-falls match to lose the contest 2-0. To be fair, it wasn't merely the fact that McMillan lost that triggered a few raised eyebrows, but the way in which the loss was collected.

McMillan dropped the first fall to Connors at the West Side Turn Hall in nine minutes, and according to *The Chicago Tribune*, it happened in a way that gave watchers the impression that neither grappler realized a fall had been counted, as they continued to struggle after the bell. Then, very early in the second round, Connors "got a back crook," and pinned McMillan again, this time in only one minute.

It seemed odd that the mixed wrestling champion of the world, who'd had many dominant showings in the area, and who trained daily with the acknowledged catch-as-catch-can wrestling champion of the world, could be defeated so quickly and easily without offering much in the way of resistance.

The Cleveland Leader added that the "large crowd present" of 1,500 people expressed considerable surprise and displeasure at McMillan's poor showing.

The fallout from the bout saw McMillan's name mentioned in the context of match faking in *The Plain Dealer*, although the layout of the article — which opened by saying that McMillan was "a wonderful man" but that his recent bout with Tom Connors of Pittsburgh was "a bad fake and not worth notice" — makes it rather unclear what the writer's honest opinion of McMillan truly was.

"There are so many queer events in the wrestling line in these days that it is hard to pick out the good men," continued the article. "From Muldoon down the wrestlers are working on the sure thing plan, and the only square events are the handicap matches such as that next week between Parker and Ryan. This man McMillan is a better man than Lewis the strangler I am told."

Highland Games and Hippodromes

Upon making his return to the United States early in 1888, Duncan Ross turned to some of the Southern states that had been receptive to his wrestling exploits five years earlier. There were 1,000 fans in attendance for his bout with Greek George in Savannah, Georgia. It was a bout that was preceded by the once common and retroactively contemptible practice of permitting unskilled Black boys — in this case, four of them — to beat one another senseless for pocket change prior to the main event.

Ross won the match with George two rounds to one, prompting massive applause from the Scots in attendance who saw his victory over the Greek wrestler as a fount of ethnic pride. After the bout, George spoke to the press and protested that he had received a raw deal in the officiating, which had no doubt stemmed from "Ross' personal popularity in the city." If anything, he might have referenced the fact that Sergeant Walsh, despite dozens of near-death experiences at the hands of Ross, was still partial to him, and served as the referee for the match.

Ross' allure was apparently blunted in Atlanta. In a city with a population 50 percent greater than Savannah's, Ross attracted only 300 fans to watch his bout against John Muhler, another Greek grappler. The size of the crowd was even less impressive considering that the Ross-Muhler match was preceded by an entertaining boxing match between local fighters who repeatedly knocked each other to the mat and "brought blood from each other's noses."

Based upon the language employed by the sportswriter from *The Atlanta Constitution*, Ross' conditioning had improved since his last set of appearances on the carpet. No longer described as possessing a body adorned with excess flesh, Ross was described as "a brawny Scotchman" who was "as perfect a specimen of physical manhood as was ever seen in Atlanta."

With Greek George acting as Mulher's second, Ross tallied his second consecutive victory over a Greek opponent in "the Peach state."

Highland Games and Hippodromes

After leaving Georgia, Ross brought his swordfighting shenanigans to Texas, where he was eventually arrested in Galveston. More than one newspaper described the arrest as a byproduct of Ross having a falling out with his "fellow fakirs" — or con-artists — when he was charged with "swindling them out of their share of the gate receipts" they had earned for their participation in the broadsword exhibitions. He was further charged with threatening to kill his sparring partner "Captain Gaston," whose real name was provided to the court as "Muller."

Days later, *The Austin American Statesman* identified someone going by the name of Captain James C. Daly as being present for a wrestling match with Ross, "the well known Scotch-American athlete," after the kerfuffle over the distribution of swordfighting proceeds. The publication even brought up the disagreements between the two from when they "quarrelled over a division of gate receipts."

Assumedly, this would indicate that Ross and at least one of the traveling swordfighters in his troupe had patched things up well enough to continue doing business together; Ross won the match three falls to two. *The Mail* of Stockton, California caught wind of the event, and had some fun at Ross' expense while writing about the incident.

"Duncan C. Ross, the biggest hippodromer in the United States, but unquestionably a great athlete, has been fooling the Texans in Galveston by taking turns with his old antagonist and confederate, J.C. Daly of New York," printed *The Mail*. "Ross usually wins, but not too often to divest their successive contests from drawing gate money and catching suckers."

It was in this environment that McPherson's account of being personally cast by Ross as "Sergeant Charles Walsh" in Pennsylvania was released. Presumably, that would mean it was a different Sergeant Walsh that participated in the Ross' return trip to the Caledonian Club games in Scranton, which culminated in perhaps the most horrific conclusion to any of Ross' swordfighting endeavors.

Highland Games and Hippodromes

In front of 6,000 horrified onlookers at the Highland Games in Scranton — a turnout that was 40-percent smaller than that seen the prior summer — the acting Sergeant Walsh *killed* his own horse by running a spear straight through its body. The incident occurred during a series of special challenges that included multiple swordfights, and also a wrestling bout between Duncan Ross and Cumberland-style wrestler George Ross.

"The killing of Sergt. Walsh's horse on the field of sport was a shocking spectacle this afternoon," shared *The Buffalo Courier*. "Walsh was first to start off on the Indian pegging contest, and, in striking at the peg, his steel pointed spear stuck fast in the ground. His horse was on a gallop, struck the spear, dashed it forward, and then the animal impaled itself on the weapon, which entered near the right shoulder, and, passing through, came out through the back just behind the saddle. The rider's clothing was caught and torn by the spear, and he had a narrow escape from being pinned to the horse."

It reportedly took 20 men several minutes to pull the spear through the horse's body, while several ladies present at the scene fainted at the sight of the dead horse.

Ross' return to Canada in October of 1888 convinced everyone who beheld him that he was still an elite athlete, and arguably as good as he had ever been, although his best was not quite up to the standards of the up-and-coming crop of Highland athletes who devoted all of their training toward preparation for Caledonian power events.

In Nova Scotia, Ross agreed to duel John MacDougall head-to-head in a throwing competition. The writer assigned by *The Halifax Herald* began his summation of the article by saying that the people of Nova Scotia "love to encourage the games for which our good Scotch ancestors were so famous," and the fact that several hundred people braved inclement weather to witness the Highland throwing duel was "sufficient to show that the people of Pictou are in love with legitimate sports."

Highland Games and Hippodromes

Ross managed to throw the 16-pound-hammer a little more than 104 feet, which was one of his best lifetime throws in a legitimate competition. MacDougall immediately exceeded that throw with a 106-foot toss, but that attempt was ruled a foul, as were all of his others.

With the 12-pound hammer, MacDougall showed clear separation from Ross in terms of class, when he threw the implement 132 feet, prompting Ross to essentially give up when he could barely get the hammer to land within 10 feet of MacDougall's toss.

Following a brief intermission caused by rainfall, the two resumed their throwing match with the 22-pound hammer. MacDougall tossed his hammer a disappointing distance, at least for him, of nearly 88 feet, but Ross failed to throw the hammer a single time without fouling. Still, Ross was "well cheered" when he left the grounds.

Ross returned later that evening to wrestle an unknown opponent, who was later identified as Allan MacDonald. The crowd was said to be very sympathetic toward MacDonald, who was clearly overmatched when competing against Ross, and who was thrown five times in less than half an hour. The style of the wrestling was not disclosed.

"Much difficulty was experienced in securing a place to have the contest," added *The Herald*. "It was necessary to procure a license and a hall. Late in the day information came that the hall and license could be had for $7.50. The town hall being refused, the skating rink was secured and 350 people found their way through six inches of mud to witness the match and were satisfied with their trip. Although Ross was the victor, it cost him more sweat than anything he has undertaken this year. No doubt his opinion of Nova Scotia is increasing daily."

In areas of North America that Ross hadn't visited in years, he was still being cited as the exemplar of hippodroming. Following a bout between Tom Cannon and John Leon, which drew a disappointing crowd despite hard work from the wrestlers that convinced the writer from *The Courier Journal* to presume the action was real, the blame for the poor attendance was laid at the feet of an athlete who had been absent for half a decade.

"People in this city who remember Duncan C. Ross and men of his ilk fear a hippodrome when a wrestling match is announced, and this was responsible for the small attendance last night, but those who went to Liederkranz Hall were well rewarded by seeing a contest on its merits, every advantage seized and pressed and interesting from start to finish," insisted the writer.

Still, if you asked Ross — and a writer from *The Boston Herald* actually *did* ask Ross — the professional wrestling industry wasn't worth saving. While the prior grand analysis of the wrestling scene attributed to Ross could be dismissed as hearsay since it came through an unidentified third party, Ross was fully on the record in November 1888 when he was interviewed for an article entitled "End of the Wrestlers."

In 10 minutes' time, Ross dissected the careers of his wrestling peers and their present life circumstances. The net result was a sweeping lamentation about the state of the industry, the plights of the star wrestlers who participated in it, and a warning that pro wrestling was on its death bed, never to recover.

"All the old-time wrestlers are disappearing from public notice, and the worst of it is there are none others coming up to take their places," said Ross, before beginning a wrestler-by-wrestler evaluation of the greats of his era, which had really only lasted for six years as far as his participation in it was concerned.

According to Ross, Theo Bauer was keeping a saloon in San Francisco, had ballooned to 300 pounds, had "a paunch like a traditional alderman," and had saved "little for the rainy days that are sure to come."

John McMahon, who had once been "the greatest collar-and-elbow wrestler of his time," hadn't saved many dollars "of the thousands he had earned," having spent his money "on convivial enjoyment as fast as he got it." Had

McMahon's mother not passed away and left him a large tract of land to farm, Ross was convinced that McMahon would have been destitute.

In revisiting his engagements with Col. James McLaughlin, Ross practically confessed to swindling the people of Cleveland and Detroit by insisting that the pair had collectively pocketed nearly $12,000 in one night. Even taking the phony stakes money into account, this figure would have been impossible to attain.

At the event referenced by Ross, which was his March 24, 1884 bout with McLaughlin at the Euclid Opera House in Cleveland, floor seats sold for $3, balcony seats for $2, and gallery seats for $1 at a venue that seated about 1,500 prior to it burning down and eventually being rebuilt in 1893.

Even if *every* seat in the building had sold for $3, the maximum amount of money that could have been accepted at the box office was $4,500. In short, the only way Ross and McLaughlin earned in excess of $10,000 from that event is if they manipulated the betting to work in their financial favor.

"McLaughlin was one of the most popular men in Detroit — so popular that he could have been elected sheriff at one time if he would accept the nomination; but he declined because he wanted to open a saloon, in which enterprise he thought there was more money than in being sheriff," continued Ross. "Well, he sunk all he had in the saloon, and now he is a conductor on a passenger train running out of Minneapolis, Minn."

Ross moved on to William Muldoon, who had reportedly lost most of his money in "stock speculation," and still managed to maintain a nice ranch near Olean, New York. Unlike many of the others referenced, Muldoon was still active and "traveling with a combination of his own," but not making much money through the endeavor according to Ross.

With respect to Matsada Sorakichi, Ross divulged that the Japanese wrestler was being treated at a New York hospital for an arm injury that he had suffered while lifting weights. Ross added that the relations between Sorakichi and his

American wife were "pleasant," which was a marked improvement compared with how they had previously been.

In the estimation of Ross, the only wrestler other than himself with ample monetary resources to his name at that moment was Henry Dufur, who had saved his money, opened a tailoring business, and had been "a very careful man" with both his health and his finances. Ross guessed that Dufur must have been worth "a quarter of a million dollars," a staggering amount for the time, and equivalent to at least $7 million in 2020.

Finally getting around to speaking about himself, Ross averred that he owned a ranch in California and a place of business in Cleveland, and further assumed that he would one day "open a big roadhouse" where he would be "surrounded by horses, dogs, guns, rods, and reels."

In closing, Ross predicted "wrestling won't be popular much longer, because the old wrestlers are dying out and none others are coming up to take their places."

Staying true to his word that he would continue seeking out athletic contests as long as the offered money was adequate, Ross met Boston city contractor George Phillips at Beacon Park for a half-mile running duel. The result of the race was rather embarrassing for Ross, who lost to Phillips by three feet after a middle-distance run that lasted 2 minutes and 34 seconds.

With both men easily weighing more than 220 pounds — an indication that Ross' size had swelled once again — the reporter covering the race joked that it was "probably the greatest fat man's race ever seen in this city." Ross blamed the loss on a bad leg that had been "strained in a recent wrestling match," and he stumbled during the second half of the race and was unable to recover the lost distance.

The humiliating loss was reported by several news outlets all over the United States, but Ross' name still remained synonymous with all-around athleticism. His prowess in most athletic settings was unimpeachable, which helped him to compensate for the incessant hippodroming allegations that followed him everywhere he went.

As a case in point, Ross was referenced in an article by *The Wilkes-Barre Leader*, which credited him with being a champion at the sport of curling, and which then cited an edition of *The Scottish American Journal* that predicted curling would one day become "the most popular game in the world" by the mid-1900s as long as it could remain "free from gambling, betting, and other evils."

A fortuitous tragedy — professionally speaking — would provide Duncan McMillan with the perfect cover he needed to remain shielded from any flak that he was an impotent wrestler, albeit one who might hippodrome from time to time.

Throughout 1888, McMillan wrestled and defeated accomplished German gymnast and grappler Otto Wagner on several occasions, after which Wagner took a break from making any appearances on the mat. On February 2, 1889, it was reported that Wagner had died as a result of either injuries or severe exhaustion brought on during a bout with McMillan.

An article from *The Chicago Tribune* made a swift attempt to correct the narrative, confirming with Wagner's family that the departed grappler and multi-time National Turnfest champion had died due to an illness affecting his lungs, but McMillan's reputation as a potentially lethal grappler was elevated nonetheless.

That April, Duncan McMillan wrestled Evan Lewis at Turner Hall in St. Paul, Minnesota, as the men did their best to establish each other as the best in the world at their respective wrestling methods. In front of a building that "was not so well filled as might have been expected taking into consideration the prominence of the men," Lewis defeated McMillan in "one of the finest exhibitions of catch-as-catch-can wrestling ever seen in St. Paul."

Humorously, the referee of the match — former wrestler Harry Hotaling — made a preemptive announcement to the crowd immediately before the bout began "and emphasized that the match was a square one," likely raising suspicions to the contrary simply by offering that announcement.

Duncan McMillan promotional photo

"It was apparent in the first bout that McMillan was the cleverest man of the two," said *The St. Paul Globe*. "The first bout occupied one hour and fifty minutes, and lovers of square sport who never had a better opportunity of justifying their tastes in that direction tumbled to the fact that this hitherto deadly strangle hold was no use in this case, and that he must rely on his strength and science to win, aside from the trick which has downed so many men, and gained him his title. In this bout, McMillan repeatedly got a full nelson hold on Lewis, from which he has often broken away. On numerous occasions each man was on the point of obtaining a fall, and as frequently the advantage would be cleverly broken by the other."

McMillan won the first fall with his full nelson, but Lewis emerged for the second fall appearing "quite fresh," while McMillan seemed exhausted. Just two minutes into the second round, Lewis upended McMillan with a trip and evened the fall count. Afterwards, a great show was made by Lewis of insisting that they forgo the 20-minute intermission between rounds and commence with the third fall immediately, only for McMillan to insist upon taking the full 20-minute respite.

"The outcome of the match shows plainly that Lewis is superior to McMillan in endurance, while the latter can give the former points in science," continued *The Globe*. "McMillan had expended his resources in the first bout, and had but very little left in him for the remaining trials of strength. The third bout was won by Lewis in nine minutes, and the fourth in ten minutes by an overlock, which took McMillan's friends very much by surprise. Those who witnessed the match went home happy in the conviction that they had seen one of the most scientific, and as square a match as was ever seen under the stars and stripes. The four falls were made in exactly two hours and fourteen minutes."

The layout of this bout left no doubt in the minds of fans that Lewis was the superior catch-as-catch-can wrestler, and the owner of outstanding conditioning. On the other hand, McMillan's achievements in matches against competitors aside from Lewis further established that the talent gap between that duo and the majority of their opposition was vast, and especially when wrestling styles other than catch-as-catch-can were involved.

Back in Milwaukee, McMillan crushed Lucien Marc Christol in three straight Greco-Roman falls during a May event at the Milwaukee Garden, ending the evening's festivities in under 25 minutes of grappling time. The very next month,

Lewis very clearly returned the favor that McMillan had paid him during their catch-as-catch-can bout in St. Paul.

That night, McMillan dominated Lewis in a fashion reminiscent of how Lewis easily defeated him in their St. Paul match. McMillan extended Lewis to well over an hour in their opening catch-as-catch-can bout, with Lewis finally winning the round in one hour and 13 minutes. From then on, the match was all McMillan.

Duncan won the Greco-Roman round in 13 minutes. Then, when Lewis was disqualified during the round contested in side-hold, McMillan refused to accept the disqualification, and "insisted on wrestling to a proper fall, which he finally won in 7 minutes and 35 seconds." McMillan then capped the evening by winning the Cornish-style bout in just seven minutes.

The bout was advertised as a contest for the "five-style championship of the world," which was a championship that McMillan would insist on laying claim to for the remainder of his wrestling career. The major distinction between this championship and the sort of mixed-style championships to which men like Duncan Ross laid claim was that it necessitated the wrestling of five different wrestling styles during a single title bout, rather than the inconsistent mixture of two or more styles.

In just four years, Duncan McMillan had gone from being the junior partner in a hippodroming tandem with Donald Dinnie to being a world champion of sorts in a partnership with the premier attraction in the wrestling world.

It seemed like it would have taken an act of God to supplant McMillan as the most influential Scotsman in professional wrestling. Instead, it would simply take an intrusion from a Scottish-Canadian who was short of stature, but limitless in talent.

12 – The Little Scot

For Duncan Ross, 1889 began with his name still so thoroughly synonymous with hippodroming that even *The Plain Dealer*, which was once amongst the foremost cheerleaders of Ross and his various dealings, ran the report of a year-opening bout between Ross and Daly in Boston under the headline "Ross and Daly still faking."

Lost amidst the accusations of multi-front hippodroming is the fact that Ross was apparently quite adept with a blade in his hand, even if his clashes in battle armor were bogus. During a benefit event in Rutland, Vermont, Ross offered the audience a break from the rest of the entertainment, which consisted of a live band, a club-swinging demonstration, and a wrestling exhibition involving Henry Dufur.

Walking onto the stage with a sword in his hand, Ross sliced a potato in two while it rested on a boy's neck, and also cleaved a bar of lead in two while it was "suspended by slips of paper resting on sword points," along with other displays of his skill.

Finally, after years of hinting that he would follow Donald Dinnie to Australia, Ross finalized his plans to do exactly that. While counting down the days until his departure, Ross participated in a few more mounted horseback events, including some in the Pittsburgh region of Pennsylvania. A reporter from *The Pittsburgh Dispatch* described for readers how Ross paid him a visit while he was in town, and he identified the 34-year-old wrestler as "almost one of the old-timers." In reality, it had been just over a decade since Ross had emerged to issue public challenges to his athletic adversaries.

"Probably a better all-round athlete was never in this country," speculated the *Dispatch* reporter. "When I say this I am mindful of the existence of Donald Dinnie, but I have always maintained that Ross was a much superior all-round man than ever Dinnie was."

Highland Games and Hippodromes

The motivation behind Ross' next move would seemingly be to validate this opinion, through the outcomes of both sincere and insincere competitions.

From the moment Duncan Ross arrived in Australia, Donald Dinnie became firmly installed as the secondary player on a traveling combination under Ross' management. Early in their partnership, in January 1890, the pair competed at the Melbourne Athletic Club in a three-styles match that seemed oddly underpublicized given the notoriety of the wrestlers who were featured.

"For the catch-as-catch-can contest, the wrestling was of a modern character, Ross in the end gaining the fall rather easily," revealed *The Benalla Ensign*. "The Scotch style did not seem to suit Ross, and probably confident in winning the last turn too, he expressed his willingness to give in to Dinnie. This was not allowed, however, and after a good deal of strength had been wasted, the referee disqualified Ross and gave the fall to Dinnie — a rather barren honour, as events turned out, for the next trial in the Graeco-Roman style Ross had his adversary at his mercy and simply did as he liked. In two minutes or less after the beginning of the round, Dinnie was reeled onto his back. Ross therefore gained the match."

With wrestling trending in the direction that proficiency in styles other than Greco-Roman and catch-as-catch-can were beginning to matter less and less, the bout can be correctly interpreted in the modern vernacular as a "squash match" victory for Ross, who effortlessly defeated Dinnie in the two styles that mattered most, and gifted a disqualification win to the 53-year-old Dinnie in Scotch style without allowing Dinnie to benefit from appearing to be Ross' superior in the discipline.

The fact that Ross seemed to have swiftly acquired total control over the Australian wrestling scene, such that it was, in a remarkably short time was exemplified by a wrestling tournament held under the supervision of his company in April at Victoria Hall in Melbourne.

Highland Games and Hippodromes

Although "most of the well-known exponents of wrestling took part in the competition," as noted by *The Age*, Donald Dinnie was conspicuously absent, as was an "unknown" champion that had been advertised for the event.

With familiar names like Miller, Thomas, Conway, Perryman and Casten all making appearances on the card, Ross dominated the action, and defeated Miller in the finals to cement himself as the best wrestler in the colony. For some reason, the character of the wrestling didn't seem to sit well with the people in the audience, and the suspicions of hippodroming lingered.

"A good deal of dissatisfaction was expressed by the spectators at the manner in which the wrestling was conducted, and the opinion was freely expressed that some of the contests were not genuine trials of strength," contended *The Age*.

Ross' refusal to participate in a wrestling bout at the Highland Gathering of Goulburn on Anniversary Day resulted in Ross filing a fascinating lawsuit against the Highland Society and Burns Club. Given the presumption that Dinnie and Ross were in cahoots when it came to manipulating the results of wrestling matches, the information presented in the lawsuit becomes simpler to parse and contextualize.

Looking beyond its face value, the testimony recorded in *The Goulburn Evening Penny Post* in June 1890 probably preserves the extent to which Ross was willing to go to avoid having to face an uncooperative opponent at this stage of his career.

Ross approached the lawsuit demanding £150 from John McDonald of the Highland Society of Burns Club for "breach of agreement and prize money" from the Highland Games that Ross was contracted to compete in.

For the sake of posterity, it's worth mentioning that Ross "deposed that he was a Scotchman by birth, but lived in America for some years," which reinforces the idea that if indeed Ross was actually born in Turkey, a Scottish birth was his preferred origin story.

Highland Games and Hippodromes

From there, Ross attested that he only agreed to attend McDonald's event if he was guaranteed £100 for his appearance, along with compensation of £20 for his travel expenses, which was six times what McDonald initially offered to pay him. Furthermore, Ross testified that he demanded that the wrestling style of the tournament should be altered from Cumberland style to Scotch style, or else he would not participate in it.

When Ross arrived at the Highland gathering at Goulburn, he learned that the style to be wrestled remained Cumberland style, which was not in alignment with the agreement he had struck, but he was okay with it. What he was not okay with was the fact that he had been slated to wrestle Charles McHardy first, with Donald Dinnie receiving a bye to the finals.

Delving more deeply into the testimony, it was introduced during the trial that Ross had competed with Dinnie at other Highland events around Australia, but had only defeated Dinnie in the Scotch style in the technical sense that Dinnie had failed to throw Ross three times during the same fall. In other mixed style bouts against Dinnie, Ross had seemingly made it a point to lose the Scottish falls to Dinnie while winning all of the other falls.

To put it differently, if Ross and Dinnie were paired together in a Scotch-style wrestling bout, Ross didn't mind throwing the bout in Dinnie's favor, as Dinnie seemed intent on preserving his reputation for being undefeated in that style at all costs. Against anyone else, Ross seemed confident that he could surely defeat them in a true Scottish bout.

However, when the wrestling program of the Goulburn games went unchanged, Ross would be *forced* to wrestle a style at which he was far less proficient. Dinnie could have been compelled by agreement to lay down for Ross, but the requirement put it in place that Ross would first be required to get by McHardy in a bout that he could easily have lost created too much unnecessary risk of embarrassment with too little reward, since there was no prize money being awarded to the third place finisher in the wrestling tournament.

When McDonald took the stand, he confirmed that an agreement was struck to change the wrestling style from Cumberland to Scotch, and that Ross said that he was only interested in wrestling Donald Dinnie at the games. Conversely, McDonald denied that he had guaranteed Ross £100 and his travel expenses, but added that Ross could easily have earned £100 in prizes.

McDonald testified that Ross competed in only three events, and then proceeded to hound McDonald throughout the remainder of the day while requesting to be paid what he felt he was owed on the spot, and McDonald refused. In closing, McDonald added that Dinnie was guaranteed only £12 for his appearance, and was required to earn any additional money by winning prize money through his competitive efforts.

From there, sports adjudicator Solomon Meyer testified about the wrestling dispute, underscoring how Ross had only protested about the arrangement of the wrestling event after lots were drawn, Dinnie received the bye, and Ross was obligated to wrestle McHardy. Ross not only withdrew from the wrestling event altogether at that point, but also declined to compete in the competition on horseback — a contest that was apparently designed specifically with Ross' participation in mind — because Ross said "he would not chance being injured."

The judge ultimately returned a verdict in Ross' favor, and awarded him £100; McDonald announced his intention to appeal the decision.

Toward the end of 1890, Ross began to absorb a surprising number of losses in mixed-style wrestling events, which probably occurred because he was viewed as a prohibitive favorite by the betting public, and he took advantage of that perception by wagering heavily against himself through an intermediary to earn extra money.

Highland Games and Hippodromes

One example of this occurred at the Princess Theatre, where Ross abruptly dropped the fifth and final fall in a bout to Australian champion Harry Dunn after Dunn secured Ross "in his favorite Cumberland hold," which was followed by "the American champion going down almost immediately."

Rather than treating these events as indications that the level of skill in Ross' wrestling competitors was improving, the Australian press skewered Ross for his declining level of competence. *The Evening News of Sydney* judged Ross as "a conspicuous failure in Australia," while *The Maitland Mercury* rated Ross as "anything but a gorgeous success since his advent to Australia," remarking that he had been "defeated on several occasions at his own pet games."

"What a big hold Ross has on any kind of wrestling championship!" mocked *The Mercury*, providing a list of local boxers and wrestlers who "could tie [Ross] in more knots than he could ever undo."

The activities of the other members of the Scottish wrestling fraternity notwithstanding, the most pivotal event of 1890 in the wrestling world was easily the introduction of Daniel Stewart McLeod.

Details of McLeod's life prior to his arrival in San Francisco to wrestle for the Olympic Club would leak out slowly over the course of his career as he became more famous, and therefore, some of the details of his upbringing were surely massaged to maximize his appeal. As such, when McLeod's *Indianapolis News* biography informed fans that "McLeod was born in Scotland... and came to this country when he was an infant," it should be taken with a grain of salt; multiple records seem to confirm that he was born in Illinois on June 14, 1861.

What is definitely true is that McLeod's parents were immigrants of Scottish descent, who moved to the mining regions of Nanaimo, British Columbia, Canada, where Dan developed into a very powerful young man relative to his height, which maxed out at 5'6".

"Although greatest as a wrestler, McLeod is an all-around athlete, and is able to contribute to every part of an athletic entertainment, except boxing, in which he is not well trained," wrote *The News*. "The mining region where he lived was populated largely by native English and Scotch, who observed holidays with games and tourneys."

Illustration of young Dan McLeod

According to the lore surrounding McLeod, during one of these holiday tournaments, "an old Scotchman" saw him sitting alone and not participating in the sports or other entertainments. The elderly Scottish gentleman "viewed the boy's broad back and square-set figure, stout limbs and muscular neck," then "read the boy's athletic character" before asking McLeod if he would be willing to wrestle.

"He declined at first," continued *The News*. "He had seen many greenhorns go on the green sward to wrestle old-timers and receive punishment. When they told him it was a boy no better than himself, he decided to try it. So anxious was he to hold his antagonist on the ground when he threw him that he squeezed so hard that he broke two ribs of his antagonist. It was not long before he had to wrestle all the best men in Nanaimo."

Endeavoring to broaden his athletic horizons, McLeod traveled all the way to the Olympic Club in San Francisco, and after six months of instruction, he wrestled and defeated 12 different opponents during the club's amateur tournament to win the trophy and the title of club champion.

A portion of McLeod's development as an amateur wrestler was captured in the pages of San Francisco's established newspapers. In April 1889, McLeod wrestled W.J. Kenealey for the heavyweight championship of the Olympic Club — contested then at a weight of 168 pounds — with the "perfect Hercules" McLeod gaining his two falls in just over four minutes of combined activity.

Wrestling aside, the Highland influence on McLeod was identifiable through his mastery of the 12-pound hammer at the Olympic Club's athletic exhibition at the Haight Street grounds. McLeod hurled the hammer 105 feet 7 inches, breaking the Pacific Coast amateur record by more than five feet.

Evidently, McLeod accepted some form of a monetary reward for his participation or placement in either a wrestling or athletic event along the way; the papers are not clear as to which one it was. What *is* clear is by the end of April, McLeod was officially "charged with professionalism," and had to plead his case before the committee of the Pacific Coast Amateur Association.

In the pages of *The San Francisco Call*, McLeod admitted to having broken the laws of amateurism, but pleaded that he had only transgressed the law "through ignorance." One month later, *The Examiner* reported that McLeod's amateur standing remained "under a cloud," but that the charges he faced were not so severe that reinstatement was unlikely.

Clearly, McLeod was not particularly distressed by whatever ruling the committee ultimately handed down, as he had his first openly professional wrestling bouts against Jack Perrie, Peter Schumacher, E.W. Johnson, and M. Woodburn that very fall after traveling home to Nanaimo. Then he opted to return to San Francisco to fully commit himself to a career as a professional wrestler.

The March 20, 1890 edition of *The Victoria Daily Times* of British Columbia identified Dan S. McLeod as one of 10 passengers who sailed to San Francisco aboard the Walla Walla. Yet, this act of departure was far from the first action McLeod ever performed that merited mention in his hometown newspaper.

Seemingly every move taken by the young McLeod, including the casual arrivals and departures of both McLeod and his trainer J. Gallagher, was covered by *The Nanaimo Daily News*. This included a discussion about how much money local backers from Nanaimo were willing to bet on their young prodigy when they traveled to support him at his matches in the provincial capital.

Also evident in the press coverage was the fact that McLeod's competitive spirit was very much aligned with that of Duncan Ross. *The Daily Times* reported of McLeod dominating a walking match after completing 32 miles and 10 laps by the time the seven-man contest concluded, besting the second-place competitor by nearly seven full miles.

Preparing to leave Nanaimo yet again, McLeod was treated to a massive banquet in his honor, at which he was presented with a gold watch by mayor Mark Bate. McLeod's subsequent arrival in San Francisco was quickly followed by a complaint to *The San Francisco Report* that he was being unfairly denied a match with local resident, former world champion, and wrestling trainer at the California Athletic Club, Englishman Joe Acton. The complaint was reprinted in its entirety in *The Nanaimo Daily News*. Ironically, it included accusations that Acton and several other local wrestlers were hippodromers.

To the Sporting Editor Daily Report —

Dear Sir: The report has reached me that prominent members of the California Athletic Club accuse me of being a faker and pretend that it would be infra dig for the so-called champion, Joe Acton, to engage in a contest with me. Considering that the California Athletic Club has no money at stake in the contest, I have vainly endeavored to force upon Acton by posting my own money on the result and publicly challenging him to a contest. I do not think their objection founded on logical reasoning, unless it be that they suspect their own champion of being a faker. Judging by the recent exposure in regards to "greased wrestlers," perhaps their doubts are well founded.

As for myself, I have never faked, nor have I ever been thrown. If I desired to make money in that dishonest way, I could easily do it, as Quinn, the Jap, and nearly the whole fraternity have made proposals to that effect to me. These people will not wrestle me on my merits, because they know I can throw them, and it looks as if Acton were afraid to risk any money on the result of a square issue. The fact of the matter is, without assuming any other virtue than the desire to make money, I would be a fool to fake, for I have no fear of Acton or any of the men he has ever competed with. Feeling this confidence in myself and being ready at all times to back it up with my own money, I think it unfair and ungenerous on the part of men who pride themselves on their love of fair play, and who have wittingly or unwittingly paid a good deal of money to undoubted fakers, to borrow for me and stigmatize me with an appellation I do not deserve, and which they cannot prove by an actual test with their own champion, or any wrestler on earth.

Dan S. McLeod, Olympic Club, San Francisco, May 16th, 1890

McLeod had apparently landed in the right place at the right time. *The Call* reported the following month that all indicators pointed to "a wrestling boom" that would "replace pugilism" in the San Francisco Bay area. Even as a rookie, McLeod was identified as one of the key figures behind that boom, along with the aforementioned Acton, the only wrestler on the West Coast who carried the prestige of being a former world champion of what was rapidly becoming the only wrestling style that truly mattered.

Parson Davies

In the report, Acton was characterized as aching to face whatever wrestling star that Midwestern promoter Parson Davies would be willing to bring westward to face him, and that individual turned out to be none other than the man recognized as either the American or world champion — depending on what part of the country he was wrestling in — "The Strangler" Evan Lewis.

It was cautioned by the local papers that McLeod "had better acquire a reputation" if he wanted to wrestle Acton, since the former American champion had better things to do "than to enter upon a contest with every common scrub that presumed to challenge him." Apparently, McLeod took this to heart, and challenged Lewis directly in what amounted to a trial that would allow McLeod to prove his worth. In effect, Lewis would be given 15 minutes to pin McLeod's shoulders to the mat, and all McLeod needed to do in order to prove his mettle was to hold the world champion at bay until the time expired.

"McLeod intimated to some of his friends that he thought he would try to withstand Lewis for fifteen minutes, because, if he did, those who belittled his ability and professed belief in his inferiority to Acton might consent to a match for a purse worthy of consideration," shared *The Nanaimo Daily News*.

That August, Lewis and Davies had arranged for the world champion to provide San Franciscoans with nightly exhibitions at the Orpheum Theatre, which was conveniently positioned almost directly across the street from the Olympic Club, and when it was announced in the streets that "Lewis the Strangler" would try to defeat "McLeod the Scotch Champion" in 15 minutes or less, apparently the members of both the Scottish Thistle Club and the Olympic Club "turned out en masse" to view the proceedings.

When Dan stepped out to face Lewis, who outweighed him by more than 30 pounds, one of the spectators was said to have remarked "Look at the little fellow; he has no chance." The crowd then watched, mouths agape, as McLeod warded off every attack from Lewis for the full 15 minutes. In the end Lewis was described as appearing "completely exhausted," while McLeod "was fit for business still."

"During the struggle, every time that McLeod broke a lock or spun out of Lewis' hold the audience went frantic with delight, and as the referee stepped forward and declared him the winner, Nanaimo itself could not have raised such a pandemonium," added *The Daily News*. "Long after the audience had dispersed, the streets resounded with the cheers of the Olympian, and indeed every face on the street seemed radiant with satisfaction. McLeod is the hero of the hour and the newspapers vie with each other for complimenting him."

In roughly the same amount of time that it would have taken Lewis — himself the son of a Welsh immigrant father — to walk from the Orpheum Theatre to San Francisco's famed Fisherman's Wharf, he had made a star out of McLeod and minted him as a hero amongst the local Scottish residents.

By late August, the entire United States had been made acutely aware of the fact that McLeod had become the professional wrestling champion of San Francisco's celebrated Olympic Club, albeit definitely not in a manner McLeod would have wished for that news to be disseminated.

Syndicated reports across the U.S. carried the results of the rematch between McLeod and Lewis that had been held under the stipulation that Lewis was required to throw McLeod three times in an hour in order to earn the victory. McLeod held out longer than in the first bout before he was pinned, but after first pinning the little Scot in 29 minutes, the Welsh world champion scored the second pin in a mere three minutes, and then took only 11 minutes further to net his three pins well within the required time frame.

Lost in the nationwide syndicated reports is what Lewis admitted to *The San Francisco Examiner* immediately after the bout, and what the 3,000 spectators inside the Orpheum Theater witnessed firsthand: McLeod had actually pinned Lewis *twice* while the men were down on the mat, but only Lewis' pinfalls counted toward the result. In essence, the crowd had watched "the Little Scot" pin the world champion, and *The Chronicle* assured its readers that McLeod "will lose no prestige because of the defeat."

Like Dinnie, Ross, and to a lesser extent McMillan, the preponderance of McLeod's allure in San Francisco and throughout his career was owed to the athletic gifts he displayed in Highland competitions, specifically the remarkable strength and speed he wielded relative to his size. Equally true is the fact that McLeod's tenure at the Olympic Club overlapped with that of a fighter who would become one of the most important boxing figures of that era.

For one of the defining bouts at that stage of his career, McLeod was accompanied to his match at Irving Hall against Irishman Tom McInerney by none other than his Olympic Club teammate, James J. Corbett. The future boxing legend and motion picture star was undefeated in 22 fights, and only two years shy of becoming the world heavyweight champion. He was also the man who would finally dethrone John L. Sullivan, which was an event that Duncan Ross had been eagerly hoping would come to pass.

If his bouts against Evan Lewis had permitted McLeod to display his skill against the best catch-as-catch-can wrestler alive, then his skirmish with McInerney would serve as the ultimate testament to McLeod's grit and toughness. McLeod's durability was tested throughout a match that would last three hours and 47 minutes, and which *The San Francisco Chronicle* confirmed to be one of the longest falls on record. Granted, that time included both the intermissions between falls, and the delay caused by a rather lengthy interruption that transpired in the middle of the exhausting match.

About 45 minutes into the bout, McInerney applied a stranglehold to McLeod as Evan Lewis — who served as McInerney's second — looked on approvingly. McLeod reversed the hold, only for McInerney to counter it with an ankle lock. Then McLeod cried out in pain and loosed his arm from around McInerney's neck as referee Ratto rushed in to speak with both men. After a few seconds of deliberating, Ratto turned to the crowd and announced that McLeod had earned the fall because McInerney had attempted to break McLeod's leg.

"Then there was pandemonium," reported *The Chronicle*. "Lewis, Parson Davies, McInerney, and all their supporters protested vigorously, while the Olympians howled themselves hoarse. Ratto announced his decision, and then McInerney stepped forward and said he had McLeod by the leg, and the latter howled to him to let go. He refused unless McLeod would give him the fall, 'and,' said the Irishman, 'he said, I give you the fall, and I let go.'"

This announcement started a riot, and the stage was swarmed by angry spectators. Whether the anger of the crowd altered the final plans for the bout's climax is unknown, but the crowd was calmed when James Corbett stepped forward "and announced that McLeod would wrestle it out."

From there, the men "banged each other around until the boards creaked," and McLeod was cautioned several times for kicking McInerney in the neck. Finally, McLeod scored the first fall of the bout after two hours and 36 minutes when he clamped a half nelson onto McInerney and rolled him onto his back.

After a rest of 15 minutes, the men resumed their work, and it only took another five minutes for McLeod to repeat the feat and pin McInerney with another half nelson. As the crowd went wild, McInerney "charged wildly around the crowd looking for the referee" with his fists clinched, but he was grabbed by Lewis and forced back to his dressing room. When McLeod was examined after the match, it was "discovered that the third finger on McLeod's left hand was broken and the little finger on his right hand dislocated."

As the year drew to a close, it was reported in Nanaimo that local boy McLeod had met an opponent that he couldn't subdue. Joking that McLeod had "met his fate at last" and "received a square fall," *The Nanaimo Daily News* explained how the grappler had "succumbed to the charms of Miss Cameron, a popular young lady of San Francisco," and had married her on the 12th of December.

Once McLeod arrived in Nanaimo for the Christmas holiday, he made a beeline for the office of *The Daily News* and denied the report of his nuptials, attributing it to "a joke sprung by some of his friends in San Francisco."

Highland Games and Hippodromes

Over the course of just one year, Daniel McLeod had become a household name in San Francisco and had skyrocketed to success as the hottest young commodity in the wrestling business. On the other side of the world, his Scottish predecessors would find their fortunes trending sharply in the opposite direction.

Highland Games and Hippodromes

13 – The Consummate Idiots

Far across the Pacific Ocean from where Dan McLeod was impressing wrestling fans in San Francisco, Duncan Ross opened 1891 with a Caledonian Games victory in New Zealand. Much was made of the win, and Caledonian Society president W. Dawson presented Ross with a championship medal bearing the inscription "Wrestling Championship of New Zealand, Won by Duncan C. Ross (and £14), Caledonian Games, Dunedin, January 1891."

"By reference to our report of the contest, it will be seen that Ross won the championship with a score of 12 points, viz, 1st in Cornish and Devonshire and 1st in catch-as-catch-can, Caledonian rules," said *The Otago Daily Times*. "Ross did not compete in the Border style. It may be mentioned that Ross' military feats were greatly appreciated, and that the Governor, before leaving the sports on the first day, complimented him on his performance, especially for the skill with which he carried off every peg consecutively in the Indian tent-pegging display."

To win his bouts, it seems that Ross fairly defeated a field consisting of seven additional wrestlers, none of whom seemed to have any name recognition. In spite of Ross' penchant for hippodroming whenever it was convenient, a fair assessment of his grappling abilities would definitely place him in the upper echelon of athletes during his era, even if he wasn't amongst the most elite of all practiced wrestlers.

At the time, the total population of New Zealand was under 700,000 residents, and the games appear to have taken place in Dunedin, which had a total population of fewer than 50,000, including its surrounding boroughs. When taking into consideration the fact that the turnout for the games was also low due to inclement weather, it becomes perfectly reasonable to believe that Ross could have justly won this wrestling event.

The demonstrations of swordsmanship and horseback riding by Ross at the games created interest in how he had developed his skills in those pursuits. This led to Ross being queried about the military background of his youth with increasing regularity.

"I was born in Glasgow, in March, 1856," Ross told *The Lyttelton Times*, shaving a full year from his age if he was quoted accurately. "My father was in the Royal Engineers. I joined the Scots Greys in 1868, and soldiered with them between four and five years. I was very young, but I became rough-riding sergeant before I left. I began my career as an athlete in the regiment. They hold what are called Balaklava sports on every anniversary of the Battle of Balaklava. I was champion of the Greys in 1871, and won the championship of the Aldershot garrison in 1873. After I left the Greys I went to the United States, where I joined the 2nd Ohio Volunteer Cavalry, in which I hold a commission now. Swordfighting on horseback is my forte. It is a sport not practised in England, and is pretty rough work."

In fairness, swordfighting on horseback — at least the version in which both combatants wore full suits of armor and insisted that their combat was authentic — was not a sport that was commonly practiced in the United States until Ross attempted to popularize it, and it hadn't exactly been a raging success. Still, Ross maintained that he had defeated skilled cavalry officers who had served with many militaries, including the "English, American, French, German, Italian, Spanish, and Mexican armies."

"I have never been beaten yet," Ross added, selectively omitting his defeats to Captain Jennings in San Francisco, including his loss of the Donahue Diamond Medal and the "world swordfighting championship."

The touring of Dinnie and Ross in tandem continued well into 1891, but by this point Ross had abandoned any pretense that he was attempting to remain in the sound physical condition that had long been part of the bedrock of his reputation. *The Referee* of Sydney bluntly opined that Ross "looked too fat," whereas Dinnie, "The grand old Scotch athlete," now in his mid-50s, appeared to be "as he usually does, in good trim."

At this juncture, the well-worn act between decaying champions had deteriorated into a question of whether a "fat" Ross or an "old" Dinnie was better positioned to win a wrestling bout. As usual, the answer to that question could have been answered by identifying the person holding the purse strings.

In the summer, Dinnie and Ross engaged in a head-to-head wrestling contest at the Olympic Club in Sydney, for which they served as the principal attraction, with no other athletic contests offered as a sideshow to their tussle. The description of the bout serves as a detailed encapsulation of how Ross was able to keep Dinnie satisfied while the latter was still clearly in a position of servitude to Ross, and required the younger Scotsman to help him earn a living.

In the opening Greco-Roman struggle, Dinnie threw Ross to the ground six times, but was never able to force Ross onto his shoulders to complete a pinfall. In effect, Ross waited for Dinnie to tire himself out before suddenly seizing him and hurling him clean onto his back "where he held him completely powerless." Ross was presented with a bouquet of flowers during the 10-minute intermission, and then the bout continued.

Unsurprisingly, Dinnie easily won the Scotch-style bout by tossing Ross to the ground and keeping him tightly clasped there for the required 30 seconds. This held true to the pattern of Scottish wrestling being the only style that Dinnie was concerned about upholding his reputation in.

From there, Ross overcame Dinnie in the catch-as-catch-can fall to win the event, and the advertised purse of £100. *The Evening News of Sydney* characterized Ross' victory as "a complete surprise to everybody," not due to a lack of ability, but attributable to the fact that Ross was not in visibly good shape.

For the sake of balance, a direct comparison between the two athletes may have been partly to blame for this perception. Ross weighed 204 pounds in comparison to Dinnie's 184 pounds, and Ross weighed much closer to 230 pounds during several of his bouts in North America prior to his temporary relocation to Australia. In other words, Ross was grappling well beneath his peak weight, and only appeared unhealthy in relation to Dinnie.

It was evident by the end of 1891 that the partnership of Dinnie and Ross had fully outlived its welcome in Australia. One of their final collaborations was recorded as being "only moderately attended," and if the reporting by *The Singleton Argus* is to be believed, neither man appeared particularly enthralled by the prospects of remaining in Australia either.

"Certainly what little exhibition there was of the two stalwart champions' prowess was good — some of it very good; but the performers evinced an evident desire not to exert themselves a whit more than they could possibly help, and were nearly half the time behind the scenes praying that the performance was over, while a stray wizard and some amateur boxers were induced to ascend the platform and amused the audience," detailed *The Argus*.

The writer from *The Argus* praised Dinnie's handling of 50-pound weights, which included demonstrations in which Dinnie suspended the weights from his individual fingers. Similarly, Ross' displays of swordsmanship were likewise applauded. However, the wrestling match between the two presented "very little that was either new or exciting," and the show-closing boxing match between two unknown young fighters "was about the most interesting and amusing thing in the programme."

After this "scant and disappointing performance," Dinnie and Ross reportedly engaged in execrable behavior at their hotel, resulting in the pair hastily departing from the town on the 1:00 a.m. train headed for Tamworth.

"Some dispute arose about the forfeiture of a £1 deposit paid on behalf of Ross, by his agent, for a £10 match with a local athlete. Ross withdrew from the match on the rather transparent plea that he would not compete against a 'colored man,'" added *The Argus*.

Ross summarily refused to settle the hotel bill unless his deposit money was refunded, but the landlord refused, at which point Ross harshly insulted the landlord.

"During the dialogue which ensued, the host told the undesirable disputants to 'make room,' and forthwith had their luggage bundled out of his bus on the street," illustrated *The Argus*. "One of the irate champions then fired off a choice assortment of sonorous expletives of various 'hues,' and 'made night hideous' indeed for those unwilling listeners in the vicinity who had been rudely awakened from the midnight slumbers by his unchaste, voluble explosions."

November 1891 would serve as perhaps the truest indication that Dinnie was losing his touch at the wrestling style that he had naturally been the most proficient in, as well as his novelty with the Scottish-descended people of Australia. That month, he participated in the annual sports gathering of the Australian Scottish Association at the Breakfast Creek Sports Ground, which only 300 spectators attended as more than half a dozen events fell through due to lack of athlete participation.

On that day, Dinnie clearly and officially lost a Scottish-style wrestling contest at a Caledonian games event for the first time on record, with the loss being registered at the hands of a competitor named McGuire, "a sturdy young Irishman of Herculean dimensions."

Dinnie was also closely pressed in the strength events during the same festival by James McCook, another Irishman, but it was clearly the loss in the wrestling event that Dinnie found the most bothersome… *so* bothersome, in fact, that Dinnie attempted to get the ruling officially expunged.

A few days later, *The Brisbane Telegraph* reported that Dinnie convened a special meeting of the Australian Scottish Association's general committee, and made his appeal to the chair of the organization, J. Begbie, that the result of the wrestling event should be overturned. The grounds by which Dinnie hoped to have his loss stricken from the record books went unstated, but "it was unanimously decided to uphold the winner," meaning that the blemish on Dinnie's Scottish-style wrestling record would remain.

That same month, it was revealed how Ross had parted ways with Dinnie and ventured onto Thursday Island, which sits north of the northernmost portion of Queensland. It was there that Ross performed a weightlifting exhibition and challenged anyone from the audience to match his feats. A "Rotumab darkey" described as being no taller than 5'8" joined Ross on stage and "equalled Duncan in all of his lifting feats."

Pressing onward, Ross arrived in Batavia in the Dutch East Indies — which would be rechristened Jakarta when Indonesia gained independence — and found himself in a spot of trouble after opening to a house that paid £120 for admission.

"A local swordsman gave him three prods and received only two in return, so was declared winner of 250 guilders prize hung up by Ross," elaborated *The Patea County Mail*. "A wrestler came on the scene, but Duncan could not put him down, so the Dutch audience became enraged and rushed the stage. About 300 infuriated Hollanders attacked him with sticks when he retreated outside and gave them the slip, leaving them belting at each other in the darkness."

Unless he wrestled under an undisclosed alias — which is actually more likely than not given his confirmed activities later on — Duncan McMillan kept a fairly low profile for the better part of two years before he reemerged in the San Francisco Bay area where his career had its origin. There was no wrestling during this visit; McMillan won the 56-pound stone toss at the Caledonian Club picnic, and then immediately left for Montana.

It could be said that Montana is the place where wrestling promoters thoroughly embraced McMillan's Scottish identity, on the basis of both his ethnicity and his prolific participation in Scottish athletics.

As had been his custom in several of the towns he visited during his career, McMillan made it a point to compete in multiple Highland Games upon making his entry to

Highland Games and Hippodromes

Montana. First he dominated the Caledonian Club games at Deer Lodge. Then he was advertised to appear at the annual games of the Scottish American Society of Anaconda, and the town of 4,000 residents was introduced to McMillan in a manner that had usually been reserved for the world's most famous Scottish athlete and his North American equivalent.

"It is generally thought that McMillan has only one superior in the world at putting the shot or hammer, and he is the great Donald Dinnie, the Scotch champion, and 'Mac' is consequently confident of winning," stated *The Anaconda Standard*, preparing its readers for the private showdown during the games between McMillan and strongman Joe Sheehy. "He at first offered to give Sheehy one foot with the shot and five feet with the hammer, but the latter refused to accept these odds, saying that if he couldn't win even up, he didn't want to win at all."

Instead of a private duel between the two men, the contest was an open challenge, with McMillan sweeping the throwing events rather easily, by at least 10 feet each, and also impressing everyone with his skill at tossing the caber.

After wowing his fellow Scots in Anaconda, McMillan made his Montana wrestling debut in Butte. Described as "the sturdy Scotchman," McMillan brutalized Gus Hardy by winning five consecutive catch-as-catch-can falls in 24 minutes. The wager had been whether or not McMillan could succeed in pinning Hardy five times within an hour, and McMillan accomplished the feat in less than half that time.

If his goal had been to manipulate the flow of the betting prior to the next bout of this variety, McMillan had the people of Butte right where he wanted them. Approximately 300 people entered the Butte City Hall building to watch McMillan score falls in 12 minutes, 13 minutes, and nearly 14 minutes, with the third fall ending after Pete Schumacher was hurled through the air and "struck the floor with terrific force, and was partially stunned by the shock."

"It was thought that the fall would partially disable Pete, but he came up for the fourth hitch as strong as ever," observed *The Standard*. "The men were on the floor nearly all the time in the hitch, and Schumacher got away from a half Nelson half a dozen times. After 11 ½ minutes of the hardest kind of wrestling, McMillan put Pete's shoulders down with a roll and half Nelson."

Accordingly, this left McMillan with just over nine minutes to win the bout. Yet, at a point where Schumacher should have been thoroughly exhausted from 50 minutes of defending himself and failing, he mustered up the resilience to ward off McMillan's attacks until the remaining time expired. Keeping the tension at a high level throughout the contest, McMillan "had Schumacher's shoulder within three inches of the floor" as the final second ticked away, leading *The Standard*'s sportswriter to assume that McMillan "might have got him down in 10 seconds more."

From there, McMillan was prepared to wage war with Cornish wrestling champion Jack King, and officially defend his five-styles wrestling championship for the first time in years. McMillan was alternatingly described as being a "Scotch athlete," and also "the champion Scotch athlete of the world," which could have served as references to both his ethnicity or his particular preference in athletic contests.

To drive home the latter point, *The Standard* presented a timeline of McMillan's career beginning with a tournament that had allegedly taken place in San Francisco in May 1883. At this fictitious event, McMillan lost a Scottish backhold bout to Donald Dinnie, but bested Dinnie using the collar-and-elbow method before he then "easily defeated" Duncan Ross.

Of course, no sequence of matches resembling this ever occurred. The wrestling and all other strength events held at San Francisco's Caledonian Club picnic in May 1883 were dominated by Dinnie, and McMillan did not participate in the wrestling. During that same time, Ross was on the other side of the country in Rochester, New York wrestling against Henry Dufur.

This effort by *The Standard* was plainly intended to make McMillan the inheritor of the legacies of Dinnie and Ross as the new Scottish standard-bearer of both wrestling and athletics, with the combination of both being necessary to vault McMillan to such a lofty position.

McMillan's rivalry with King, which began at the Athletic Club pavilion in Butte, billed as "the greatest battle between giants," would ultimately live in infamy, but no one would have known it at the time. Both men tipped the scales at 196 pounds, and after first making a show of disagreeing about who would officiate the world title match between them, they settled in to present the packed facility with "an exhibition of wrestling such as few people present had ever witnessed."

McMillan began the evening by relying on a grapevine with a front lock to win an unusually long sidehold bout that lasted an hour and five minutes. King then selected his specialty of Cornish wrestling for the next fall, and it was believed that he would dominate. Again, the fall lasted an unnaturally long time, which was attributed to McMillan's masterful defense.

"McMillan was on the defensive all the time, and this fact coupled with his long reach and marvelous agility made King's task a most difficult one," explained *The Standard*. "Time and time again did he try to get his deadly strangle hold, but McMillan slipped out of his grasp as often as he tried it. King had McMillan up in the air a half a dozen times, but as soon as he lifted him from the floor, a pair of long legs were wrapped around him and he could not get him down."

Given the next choice of style, McMillan selected catch-as-catch-can — the method in which he had famously captured a fall from the style's world champion Evan Lewis after battling him for an hour. The smart money would clearly have been wagered on McMillan, which is why the audience was reportedly stunned when King pinned McMillan with a half nelson and a hammerlock in 27 minutes.

Due to the preposterously long lengths of the first two falls, it was now 1:30 a.m., and it was agreed that the men would reconvene to finish the bout two days later, when the Greco-Roman and collar-and-elbow styles would determine who ultimately won the world championship of five-styles wrestling. Neither man was a reputed savant at either of the grappling methods, and the continuation of the match would carry massive intrigue since McMillan, the defending champion, would be down two falls to one at the time of the continuation.

Fortunately for the fans who attended on night one, they would not be charged for readmission if they presented their ticket stubs for the return engagement.

With his back seemingly against the wall, McMillan won the collar-and-elbow bout to level the fall count, and when the men returned to the mat for the final round of Greco-Roman wrestling after the 20-minute intermission, "the spectators crowded around the ring in a frenzy of excitement and yelled themselves hoarse over the clever work of both men."

"This was generally considered to be the prettiest exhibition of the lot," opined *The Standard*. "For half an hour the men twisted themselves into every conceivable shape and rolled around over the carpet with one first and then the other on top. King got a half-nelson on McMillan, but it was no good, and a few minutes later Jack cleverly got away from a similar hold by first bridging and then turning completely over on his head. After that, both got away from some dangerous holds in good style. McMillan finally got King on his side and slowly forced him down with a far-arm and half-nelson until his shoulders touched the floor, winning the final fall and the match."

The spectacle of the McMillan-King bout was celebrated at the time, but very soon rumors began to trickle through the streets of Butte that the bout had been the product of collaboration between the grapplers. This led *The Standard* to defend McMillan and King against "the consummate idiots in Butte," who "lose no opportunity to inflict upon innocent and unsuspecting people a lot of silly twaddle."

"With the latter class of fellows, everything is a fake," accused *The Standard*. "The Corbett-Sullivan fight was a fake and they knew just how it was going to turn out, although they called the big fellow up to half past 10 on the night of the fight. Then they displayed their great shrewdness by changing their tune. According to their theory, there never has been a square match of any kind in Butte, and the McMillan-King contest was the last in the list of fakes.

"These are the chumps who think that one point down constitutes a fall and don't know Greco-Roman from Cornish wrestling. The only way to satisfy such fellows is to put a couple of men in the ring with axes and guarantee that one of the men shall be killed or the spectators will get their money back at the door, and even then, if one of the men should be killed, they would swear that they got the double cross and that it was fixed for the other man to win."

The Standard ended its relentless attack on the "few numbskulls" who had the nerve to question the sincerity of the McMillan-King match by offering a concession that would come to typify wrestling fandom a century later.

"But even admitting for the sake of argument that the McMillan-King match was a job — which it was *not* — the fact remains that it was the prettiest and most scientific exhibition of wrestling that has ever been seen in Butte," insisted *The Standard*. "Both men worked hard and earnestly for over six hours and a half on two nights, and if anyone imagines that they would have prolonged it so long if it had been a fake is simply an unadulterated and unmitigated fool."

In essence, the crux of the argument was that the wrestling fans who paid to see McMillan and King wrestle were entitled to hold no grievances against a fake match because its entertainment value was unquestioned. Moreover, the length of the bout somehow served as assurance of its authenticity, as if the men couldn't have accounted for this in their efforts to deceive.

Tacked onto the end of the article was a statement of assurance that the complainers would still be "the first to buy tickets for the next event, as well as the first to commence growling as soon as it is over."

Highland Games and Hippodromes

Departing from Butte, McMillan was far less successful in the future ghost town of Granite, Montana, where he wrestled against "Michigan's best man " Gus Stoll at the Miner's Union Hall. Stoll won the first fall in 40 minutes, and McMillan won the remaining three, but the attendance of the match portended the ultimate fate of the town. No more than 30 people paid to watch McMillan wrestle Stoll, and it was estimated that only $30 was collected in gate receipts.

McMillan returned to Butte to close out 1892, and resumed his rivalry with King with a bout at the Comique, which McMillan won three falls to two. The aftermath of the match would land both men in "a whole lot of trouble," although the initial report from *The Helena Independent* downplayed the severity of the incident, and innocuously reported the detail that "a couple of thousand dollars changed hands on the outcome."

The next day, it came to light that King's backer John Jacobs believed he had been swindled out of $1,270, and then loaded his pistol and set out to find the two wrestlers who perpetrated the scam. Fortunately for the pair, King and McMillan had skipped town, but Jacobs still sent messages to all of the surrounding towns urging the authorities to arrest both grapplers on charges of embezzlement.

"This afternoon a message was received from Marshal Galvin of Helena stating that he had the men and asking if a warrant had been issued for them," stated *The Standard*. "Jacobs then went before Judge Colman and swore out a warrant against McMillan and King, charging them with cheating."

The arrest warrant alleged that the men "did wilfully and unlawfully, feloniously, knowingly, and designedly falsely pretend and represent to John Jacobs that they, the said defendants, were to wrestle in a fair and honorable manner, and that if said John Jacobs would advance his money on such a wrestling match that the same would be conducted fairly and impartially, and the same would be decided upon its merits, and thereby, and by reason thereof, said John Jacobs was induced to and did advance the sum of $1,270, whereas in truth

Highland Games and Hippodromes

and in fact as said defendants then and there well knew, that said wrestling match was not fairly conducted, and was not decided upon its merits, and thereby and by reason of said misrepresentation, said John Jacobs was defrauded out of $1,270, and said false representations were made by said defendants with the intent to defraud the said Jacobs thereof."

Even with an official legal complaint leveled against the wrestlers, and with arrest warrants sworn out against them, *The Standard* still sided with the wrestlers, adding that "Mr. Jacobs will have all his trouble for nothing," because "the fact that McMillan is able to easily defeat King on the square will make it very difficult to prove that there was any fake about it."

King and McMillan jointly retained attorney C.B. Nolan as counsel, and when questioned by *The Independent*, Nolan claimed to know of no provision of law that would cover the case "*even* if the charge were true." The detail was included that McMillan had produced a telegram from world wrestling champion Evan Lewis requesting his assistance in Wisconsin to help prepare Lewis for a tournament in New Orleans.

Both men were ultimately released, and *The Standard* capped its coverage of the entire ordeal a few days later by printing that "the Scotch wrestler who will be well remembered by Butte people is in Ridgeway, Wis., training Evan Lewis for his match with Ernest Roeber." Despite the best efforts of John Jacobs, McMillan had escaped Montana with his freedom and his life.

The telegram sent from Lewis to the authorities in Butte was true, in as much as the presence of McMillan in Lewis' camp *was* truly desired. When Lewis arrived in New Orleans to battle Roeber, McMillan was there acting as Lewis' spokesperson before the New Orleans press, and if he was originally meant to be there in an ornamental capacity, McMillan now handled much of the media attention for Lewis, whose wife Hattie had passed away one month earlier from Bright's disease.

"D.A. McMillan, the trainer of Evan Lewis, is a fine looking man and is himself no slouch at wrestling," elaborated

Highland Games and Hippodromes

The New Orleans Times-Democrat, as it identified the traveling companions of the catch-as-catch-can champion. "The training quarters of the wrestler are located at Ridgeway, about thirty-five miles east of Madison, Wis., where Lewis was born. The death of the athlete's wife, McMillan states, caused serious interruption in the six weeks' work which Lewis put in, and the mental worry deprived him of much time which would otherwise have been put to good advantage."

Ernest Roeber

    Lewis defeated the Greco-Roman specialist Roeber rather easily in a catch-as-catch-can bout, and he and McMillan together collected the winner's end of the purse at the New Orleans Olympic Club the morning after the bout, while Lewis reviewed the many congratulatory wires that were sent to him from supporters back in Wisconsin.

Highland Games and Hippodromes

As evidence that events occurring in other states were often ignored if they were inconvenient to promoters, both Duncan McMillan and Jack King returned to Minnesota in March, and both claimed to be in possession of the world championship of five-styles wrestling. All of this was stated in spite of McMillan having defeated King multiple times in five-styles title bouts in Montana.

While *The Saint Paul Globe* explained how McMillan was disputing King's claim to the throne, apparently McMillan never took the simple step of revealing that he had beaten King just two months earlier in matches for that same championship, and that King had no reasonable claim to McMillan's rightful title.

From a business standpoint, the decision to ignore the events that had taken place in Montana was probably for the best; reporters looking into the particulars of the McMillan-King matches in Montana would undoubtedly have unearthed details of the scandals that followed.

The match between King and McMillan in St. Paul was a catch-as-catch-can bout won by King, which elevated King in the eyes of Minnesotans while still leaving the question of the five-style championship in doubt. It was a matter that would go unsettled, as McMillan disappeared again, only to emerge a few years later, conspicuously close to one of the next great legends of professional wrestling.

It appeared in the early stages of 1891 that Dan McLeod would establish himsef as a fixture atop the wrestling world by the year's end, as a victory by McLeod over Joe Acton would signify a seismic shift in the balance of power on the Pacific Coast. Instead, an injury to Acton delayed the anticipated changing-of-the-guard match for an entire year, while McLeod contented himself with accepting lesser bouts in order to earn a living.

Late in 1891 while McLeod was back in Nanaimo, he agreed to engage in a hammer throwing contest for money against W. Dunbar. Again, McLeod would be disappointed, because Dunbar "refused to enter the contest under Pacific

Coast rules," and insisted that if the bout was to come off at all, "it must be under Caledonian rules." This was apparently perplexing to McLeod, who said that he would gladly throw the hammer under any rules Dunbar proposed.

If McLeod's series of matches against Evan Lewis and his stablemate Tom McInerney had been the most important sequence of bouts in McLeod's short career prior to March 1892, then the night that McLeod finally lured Joe Acton onto the mat exceeded their collective significance in just one evening. As *The Nanaimo Daily News* aptly phrased it, Acton had been "an acknowledged champion of the catch-as-catch-can style of wrestling" for many years, and was "well entitled to the sobriquet of the 'little demon.'"

The 39-year-old Acton was said to be the heaviest he had ever been in his career at 170 pounds, but could "train down no finer," potentially due to limitations caused by his injury. Across the mat, the 23-year-old McLeod stood at a lean and muscular 162 pounds.

"Both men appeared to be in good condition, though Acton showed a little too much fat, and a boil that looked like a miniature volcano was conspicuous on McLeod's right knee," assessed *The Daily News*. "Acton's round body was in peculiar contrast to the broader one of McLeod, and the latter's finely formed legs seemed to give him a great advantage. The difference in weight was not otherwise apparent."

McLeod labored in vain for nearly 50 minutes to maintain any sort of hold on Acton, and "the crowd laughed at his attempts," but just as the laughter had reached its peak, McLeod reversed Acton's attempt at an arm roll, countered with a waist roll, and forced Acton's shoulders to the mat. When the fall was announced, "a volley of cheers rose from Olympic Club, Scotch and Canadian throats."

The action resumed, and Acton became more aggressive while trying for half nelsons, and hammerlocks. He finally grasped McLeod in "a dangerous bar lock" that McLeod soon twisted out of. Suddenly, McLeod gave Acton a quick arm roll that landed the Englishman's shoulders on the mat, and the spectators thought McLeod had won his second fall. Referee Cook saw things differently and urged the wrestlers to continue.

Joe Acton

"McLeod seemed maddened and made a vicious rush at Acton, and in less than two minutes had him down again on his back with an arm roll and slowly but surely forced him flat on his back just as the clock showed that twenty-three minutes had elapsed," concluded *The Daily News*. "The match was won, and McLeod had established a reputation that will entitle him to claim equal ranking with almost any living wrestler."

From there, *The Daily News* devoted an unusual amount of space to delving into the quantity of money that was wagered on the long-awaited McLeod-Acton bout at multiple local venues that took action on the fight, along with valuable guidance as to how the live betting odds shifted once the action on the mat was underway.

Specifically, it was claimed that $13,000 was staked at Corbett's, $4,000 was wagered at the Wigwam, and another $3,500 was bet at the gambling parlor at 411 ½ California Street. Before the match began, the pools sold at 10 to 7 in favor of Acton, and then "the Olympic Club members and northern men handed over heavy sacks to the pool sellers" until the betting became even. Once McLeod scored the first fall, the betting odds swung to 10 to 4 in favor of McLeod.

Through his victory over Acton, McLeod claimed the title of world middleweight champion of catch-as-catch-can-wrestling, and had symbolically acquired Acton's position as the best "little man" in wrestling. The glory of this moment would make the actions he took next all the more stupefying to those who viewed him as pro wrestling's ultimate straight-shooter.

14 – Character and Conduct

Now that Dan McLeod had surely made an international name for himself by defeating Joe Acton, it seems antithetical to his objectives that his next noteworthy stunts would stem from activities that he had hoped would remain a secret, but that's precisely what happened, and it would be the first in a series of events that would ironically serve McLeod well in retroactive arguments about who was the best real wrestler of his era.

As *The Modesto Bee* reported in April 1892, a stranger by the name of "Stuart" accepted the open challenge of wrestler Maurice Loventhal of Modesto. The stranger had undertaken to throw the undefeated Loventhal three times in one hour, which was a feat that those who had previously seen Loventhal in action believed to be impossible.

Stuart quickly got to work "handling Loventhal as a cat would toy with a mouse," and the undefeated wrestler "was soon winded and groggy under Stuart's pumping tactics," and literally fainted after the second fall was awarded to Stuart.

"There were cries of foul and accusations that the stranger had struck him, or 'back heeled' the lad on the neck," reported *The Bee*. "Then it was that Lou Comins and others seemed to discover in a flash that their local darling of the arena had 'fallen up against' the champion middleweight of the world — Daniel Stuart McLeod, who recently threw Joe Acton. McLeod maintained that his name was Stuart, but did not deny that it was also McLeod. The money was given to the world's champion."

Rightfully so, many of the betting men in the audience thought it was unfair that "the king wrestler of the United States," Daniel Stewart/Stuart McLeod, would "hunt tender game in the rural hills," arguing that "it was like unto a lion dressing in sheep's clothing and eating up the dear little lambs, tail and all."

Later events would increase the likelihood that this account was truthful. McLeod could have earned more money from gate receipts by arranging a bout with another top draw, but those events took time and publicity to arrange. In the meantime, McLeod could continue to earn money as "Stuart" by wagering on himself as an unknown underdog — or a ringer — and then raking in the whole pot.

Illustration of Dan McLeod with his signature mustache

It wouldn't be long before McLeod was found guilty of performing the same stunt in other countries. When McLeod disappeared from San Francisco, a mysterious American wrestler by the name of "Dan Stewart" appeared in Australia and began to terrorize the local wrestlers, including an easy two-falls takedown of Australian champion Jack Perryman in under 26 minutes.

"A Sydney sporting paper came to Robinson by the Monowai yesterday and it contained a portrait of Stewart, who is none other than D.S. McLeod, the sturdy young Scotchman who beat Peter Schumacher in such a manner as to make his admirers sick, and afterwards had such a tussle with 'Little Demon' Acton," printed *The Examiner*. "The wood cut in the paper received by Robinson is not very clear to features, but there is no mistaking McLeod in the outlines."

The Examiner included that "Stewart" had been "suspected of being a ringer," but since he had "retained enough of his name," he had avoided the heavy penalties that could be imposed in Australia for "misrepresentation in the land of square sport."

"When McLeod left here after the fiasco with Parson Davies' pair, McInerney and Strangler Lewis, it was whispered that he was off on a scouting expedition, and that he was well provided with money to back himself wherever he might land by a local manager, who also hails from the land o'cakes," added *The Examiner*.

Also considered to be evidence of McLeod's identity was the fact that he had signed a challenge "to toss the heavy hammers against all comers, this being a sport at which he is in the champion class."

Before he returned home to the United States, McLeod ultimately did make good on a proposal that he would show off his prowess in hammer throwing. McLeod entered a hammer-throwing contest with Dugald Cameron of Melbourne and defeated him by throwing the 22-pound hammer 80 feet, the 16-pound hammer 99 feet, and the 12-pound hammer 118 feet, all in standing throws. He then participated at the Highland Games in Dunedin, New Zealand, and registered a throw of 103 feet with the 16-pound hammer.

Free from his dealings with Donald Dinnie, Duncan Ross had partnered up with Tom Cannon by early 1892, and the two brought a wrestling show into Calcutta, India.

Highland Games and Hippodromes

American newspapers cut Ross absolutely no slack in reporting on his overseas exploits. *The Nashville Banner* introduced the topic of Ross and Cannon in India by reminding readers that the pair had "worked America for years as hippodrome wrestlers."

Despite looking as though they were anatomically superior to their Indian opponents — Cannon reportedly entered the ring "looking like Achilles" — if the results of the bouts they engaged in were real wrestling challenges, then it appears as if Cannon and Ross bit off more than they could chew, or at least grossly underestimated the skills of Indian wrestlers.

"On receiving the signal, according to the account of an Anglo-Indian spectator of the struggle, the opponents came immediately to close quarters, and the native, by a dexterous movement, succeeded in throwing Cannon on his knees," relayed *The Banner*. "The latter appeared to be unable to obtain a grip of his opponent, and the match, although protracted to nearly ten minutes by Cannon's defense, was practically decided during the first few seconds. Finally, in spite of his adversary's stubborn resistance, Karim Bux, according to this account, secured the throw with a movement which exhibited not only his great physical strength, but bore testimony to his science and skill as a wrestler."

The news that Ross also suffered a defeat at the hands of Bux was received via mail by *The Sporting Judge of Melbourne* several months later. The same missive included news of the outcome of a mid-April match between Ross and Gulam Khadir Kalifa, an Indian wrestler who had defeated both Cannon and Bux during prior in-ring appearances. Kalifa was described as "thirty years of age" with a chest measurement of more than 50 inches, and supported by "the biggest thighs and loins" of any man the writer had ever seen.

The mailing confirmed that the bout was a mixed-styles contest, immediately placing all previous bouts involving Ross and Cannon in India beneath the shadow of presumed hippodroming, even if they weren't mixed-style bouts. Then again, it's conceivable that Ross introduced Kalifa to the concept of a mixed-style and taught him how to "do business" in a way that would generate interest in future matches and maximize gate revenue.

In this instance, the Ross-Kalifa match attracted 3,000 fans to the Bangalore Maidan, and the bout was over in a brief three falls. In the eyes of the spectators, it must have been perceived that Ross pulled off a monstrous upset by defeating Kalifa two falls to one when the Indian grappler refused to wrestle the final fall in the Cumberland style, thereby conceding the match to Ross.

It went unreported how many of the spectators were British military personnel or their family members, or what level of betting on the bout was taking place out in the open.

In between these events, Ross traveled to England, where he appeared as the American wrestling champion to face English champion George Steadman in a unification bout for the world championship of mixed-styles wrestling. Ross lost the bout, which had the net result of enabling Steadman to lay claim to being the mixed-styles wrestling champion of the world in his native country.

Final results aside, the execution of the bout and the explanations provided for its pattern of outcomes underscores the selective inconsistency of mixed-style encounters. Ross won the catch-as-catch-can bout and the Greco-Roman match, but lost the collar-and-elbow match to Steadman, when in past contests this had usually been one of Ross' specialties.

Far more surprising was the fact that Ross finished the match by losing rounds conducted in the Scotch and Cumberland styles, with *The Victoria Times* maintaining that Ross was not accustomed to either style, even though Scotch style had often been specified as one of his strengths.

The title bout in England between Ross and Steadman had occasioned surprisingly little publicity for a world title match. Be that as it may, the far more interesting setting for a Duncan Ross wrestling match would be any location on Scottish soil.

Highland Games and Hippodromes

Ross' name had been mentioned by the Scottish press for years, with his initial hammer-throwing victory over Dinnie drawing significant interest from the nation's newspapers. Whenever he was discussed in relation to athletic endeavors that were deemed to be newsworthy in the land he claimed as his birthplace, including at least one swordfighting exhibition against a "German" opponent, Ross was commonly recognized as a Scotsman.

This highlights the extent to which Scottish expatriates and their offspring would still receive the courtesy of being acknowledged as Scottish in the late 19th century — at least when they were seen to be doing something of value in service of the expatriate Scottish community.

Ross made his long-awaited debut on Scottish soil in November 1892 in the Grand National Halls of Glasgow. *The Glasgow Weekly Herald* quickly pointed out that Ross was "a native of Glasgow, born of Ross-shire parents," which placed the origin of his family line squarely in the Scottish Highlands.

The paper also compared Ross most favorably with Tom Cannon of Lancashire. While the Englishman was described as being older and heavier than Ross, and in possession of "tremendous bodily power," Ross was touted as "a perfect type of athlete," owing to his extensive background in athletics and swordsmanship to complement his wrestling prowess.

Strangely, it was said that Ross had "lately returned to his native city after an absence of 16 years" before issuing an open challenge that Cannon accepted, as if the two hadn't been touring India together earlier in the year. Whether or not Ross made a strip to Scotland in 1876 is indeterminable, but the fact that he and Cannon went through the motions of having Ross issue the open challenge for Cannon to accept is surprising when the collaboration of the two men in India was reported by the Glasgow papers just a few months prior.

Since Ross had theoretically lost his unification bout with George Steadman in England without any rematches taking place, presumably the world championship of mixed

Highland Games and Hippodromes

wrestling that Ross claimed to hold upon entering Scotland was a wholly new invention.

Winning the toss, Ross selected Scotch-style for the opening fall and won his first-ever round of wrestling in Scotland in only three-and-a-half minutes. This elicited "great excitement" from the crowd. Unfortunately for those who wanted to see a Scottish sports icon from the other side of the Atlantic achieve an outright victory, Ross lost the Greco-Roman and catch-as-catch-can rounds one right after the other.

Tom Cannon

"The referee then decided that Cannon had won the championship, but Ross' party took exception to the decision, declaring that the articles of agreement stipulated three clear falls," stated the description. "The men at the finish were pretty much exhausted, for the work had been very severe and trying. As a scientific display by two heavy men, it has never been excelled in Glasgow."

Of all the reasons for which the result of a world championship wrestling match would be tainted by controversy, the referee arbitrarily deciding that two falls were sufficient to win a best-of-five-falls match without any further wrestling occurring has to be one of the most anomalous.

Somewhere along the way, the representation of Ross' military service that he made to a reporter in Melbourne was circulated through the newspapers of the United Kingdom, prompting Sergeant-major Masterson, who served with the Scots Greys during a period that overlapped with Ross' stated term of service, to contact the press and assert that "no such boy entered by troop."

Embarrassed, outraged, and "apparently much annoyed by the contradiction," Ross promptly sought out reporters during his time in Glasgow and presented them with documents proving his service record with the Scots Greys.

"[Ross] enlisted in the 2nd Dragoons (Scots Greys), while in Aberdeen, on the 23rd November, 1870, when eighteen years of age, and put in two years' boys' service previous to his more formal enlistment," began the lengthy report. "He was in C troop, and his regimental number was 1,128. He went with his regiment from Longford to Dublin, and previous to embarking for Scotland was seven days at the Royal Barracks there. For a whole twelve months Ross was stationed at Piershill Barracks (Jock's Lodge), Edinburgh, and while in the Scottish capital won all the principal prizes for athletic excellence at the Balaclava anniversary day sports. Hamilton was Ross' next station, and from there he was removed to Aldershot, having charge of the advance guard of the Remounts. This march of 530 miles occupied thirty-three days.

"In Aldershot, he was quartered in the North Camp, was afterwards chosen one of an escort of twenty-one, acting as non-commissioned officer of this escort to the Shah of Persia, Lieutenant McLintock-Bunbury being in command. He was afterwards ordered to Exeter, from which place he went to Dartmoor Downs, where he acted as orderly to Sir Charles Stevely, general commanding the district.

"Having been in the Scots Greys as from 23rd November, 1870, to March, 1874, he purchased his discharge, his father paying the amount ($28), and at which time he was a corporal. Ross holds his discharge, dated 'Horse Guards, March 5, 1874,' and showing that he was corporal at that date. This discharge further bears the following certificate: — 'Character and conduct very good; in possession of one good conduct badge and first-class certificate of education.'"

Ross' documents apparently settled the matter of his military service record in his favor. All the same, his disappointing outings in sports events that were both real and preplanned had the net effect of blunting the impression made upon Scottish athletic fans who had welcomed back a national hero who had been loaned to the former colonies across the Atlantic.

When Dan McLeod finally made landfall back in San Francisco in March 1893, *The San Francisco Examiner* declared his trip to have been a rousing success, since he had returned with "a comfortable sack of sovereigns to show for his year of absence," and was ready to meet any wrestler weighing between 170 and 175 pounds.

It was assumed that McLeod's priority would be to get back on the wrestling mats of San Francisco as quickly as possible — especially as Joe Acton incessantly hassled him in the press about a rematch — but as 1893 progressed, McLeod seemed to be far more focused on maximizing his potential as a Highland Games athlete.

At the 27th gathering of the San Francisco Caledonian Club at Shell Mound in May, McLeod finished first in the caber tossing event, likely benefitting from his low center of gravity in spite of his overall lack of size. In the remainder of the putting and hurling events, he was less successful than his Scottish pro wrestling predecessors had been, although he seemed to make up for it by being the most natural wrestler of the group.

McLeod finished second in throwing the light hammer, being edged out by Thomas Caroll, and also fourth at putting the stone. He also participated in amusing events that the likes of Donald Dinnie and Duncan Ross would have considered beneath their participation, like the members-only relay race, and the three-legged race with partners.

The following month, summer arrived, and McLeod was in Sacramento to compete in the throwing events of the annual Caledonian Games of that city. He won the light hammer toss, and finished second in both the caber toss and the putting of the light stone.

In July, McLeod was back at Shell Mound for the Scottish Thistle Club's rendition of the Highland Games. As usual, McLeod was a standout at the throwing events, hurling the heavy hammer nearly 90 feet and the light hammer more than 111 feet to win both events, and he also finished as the runner-up in the caber toss, throwing it more than 38 feet, and losing to Tom Carroll by less than a foot.

Two months later, McLeod attended an Order of the Scottish Clans event at Scottish Hall, organized by Clan Fraser, and participated in a wrestling exhibition. This served as a prelude to his showing at the Admission Day Highland Games festival, under the auspices of the Order of the Scottish Clans, which once again took place at Shell Mound.

McLeod was drafted onto the OSC team to compete against the rival team of Caledonia, and he won the heavy hammer throw, the caber toss, and cruised to an easy victory in the wrestling tournament. He was also the runner-up in the 12-pound hammer throw, the light hammer throw, and surprisingly, the pole vault.

McLeod's Caledonian games output throughout the year is a sure sign that he was deeply connected to the Scottish community and felt a strong affinity for the culture that was prevalent amongst the second-generation Scots. His appeal to his culture would also come into play during his wrestling exploits that year.

While McLeod answered Joe Acton's challenges in the press by teasing the former champion that he had already defeated him on his own turf, and that it was only fair that Acton now travel to British Columbia for the rematch, most of McLeod's wrestling matches in 1893 flaunted his supremacy over wrestlers who were doubtlessly beneath him.

Thanks to McLeod's incredible displays of skill and power in both amateur wrestling matches and professional wrestling bouts — *some* of which may actually have been completely real — it was simply not believable to think that a grappler who had easily handled Joe Acton and stood toe-to-toe with Evan Lewis and his crew could suddenly be challenged by local wrestlers of inferior stature. As such, most of McLeod's San Francisco bouts in 1893 centered around how long his opponents could survive on the mat with him.

Seconded by Thomas Carroll, the only hammer-thrower in the state who could keep pace with him at Caledonian events, McLeod entered a bout with Jess Clark at the Olympic Club needing to throw his adversary five times in one hour in order to claim victory.

"There were combinations, leg holds, hammer-locks, and spinnings without number for the first 28 minutes, when a combination hold in which McLeod executed a neat half-Nelson with his foot landed Clark fairly and squarely on his shoulders," reported *The Call*.

Judging from the fact that it took nearly half the allotted time for McLeod to pin Clark even once, there were justifiably "many predictions that McLeod could not throw him four more times in the remaining thirty-two minutes." Certainly, those placing mid-match wagers on the bout took this into consideration, but the only provision for rest in the match was that it was up to McLeod to decide if he wanted to halt the action in between falls while the clock continued to tick, and he opted to continue wrestling, and even went so far as to deny Clark his request for a drink of water.

"The other falls followed in close succession," continued *The Call*. "In a minute and a half, [Clark] was shoulders down again, the result of a half-Nelson, which was evidently a surprise to him. The third was in one minute, also from a half-Nelson. The fourth was more of a struggle, though it ended in ninety seconds. McLeod had his opponent nearly down with a half-Nelson, but could not complete the coup. He showed his agility by gradually reversing to the opposite half-Nelson, when Clark succumbed."

Just two minutes later, McLeod tallied his fifth fall over Clark, completing the trick of capturing four falls in six-and-a-half minutes after taking 28 minutes to capture the first. The timing of a match with an ending this fishy was bewildering. Just two days earlier, *The Call* published an article about a recent match between A. Lean and William Haberley at the Olympic Club that raised quite a few eyebrows over its perceived fakery, and which was under investigation.

"In the Stockton and O'Farrell Street poolrooms some betting was done on the result, but a majority of the money wagered was bet on the time each bout would last," divulged *The Call*. "Among the bettors was a medium-sized man who wore a heavy black mustache and a Roman nose. He was foreign to the fraternity of gamblers that frequent the gambling quarters, and as he displayed considerable cash and manifested a desire to take all bets offered 'on time' he was therefore an object of attraction.

"His knowledge of the time each bout would occupy was phenomenal, as was subsequently proven when the poolsellers cashed the winning tickets. He bet that Haberley would be thrown in the first bout inside of 15 seconds; that Lean would lose the second fall inside of 30 seconds, and that Haberley would win the third fall within 35 minutes. His guesses were exceptionally clever, and, as a result, he scooped the poolrooms."

In light of this flagrant evidence of hippodroming, *The Call* placed its faith in McLeod as being the one wrestler that readers could be assured had "always wrestled on the square," precisely because of his activities outside of the U.S., and primarily in Australia, where he crashed wrestling events under a fake name and cleaned up.

Thanks to his showing with Clark, McLeod's matches in San Francisco would join the others in being viewed through a lens of skepticism that would only grow thicker with time.

That August, McLeod was spotted assisting his Olympic Club teammate James J. Corbett — by then the world heavyweight champion of boxing — as he trained for his forthcoming January 1894 fight with Charley Mitchell. While this training was ongoing, McLeod had already committed to participate in an eight-man international wrestling tournament scheduled for the middle of September, with McLeod listed as the grappler representing Scotland.

The most enticing aspect of the tournament was the prospect of a rematch between McLeod and Joe Acton. The two men had been kept separate from one another for more than a year, and Acton, who had been attempting to bait McLeod into a confrontation through the newspapers almost the entire time, had been afforded several months to train free of any injuries that might have otherwise handicapped his performance.

As expected, Acton and McLeod easily dispensed with their preliminary opponents on the way to their long-awaited showdown at Odd Fellows Hall. The final match would be a multi-night contest, with one round contested on night one, and two rounds held on night two if the loser of the night-one bout was able to win the first fall on the second night.

The Chronicle reminded readers — as if they weren't already acutely aware — that Acton had been taunting McLeod in print for a year, and had been "anxious to once again meet the descendant of old Scotland on the padded mat."

The single-fall match on the first night lasted only 20 minutes, and Acton very nearly pinned McLeod with a chancery. The near-fall only seemed to inject the Scotsman with a surge of adrenaline. As they rose from the mat and Acton rushed in, McLeod grabbed Acton around the neck, inserted his leg between Acton's legs, and "threw him on the mat, shoulders down, and quick as lightning fell on his prostrate antagonist." The pinfall victory for McLeod "came as unexpectedly as a thunderclap from a clear sky."

If Acton's supporters expected him to rally on the second night of the climactic tournament battle and win at least one fall from McLeod, they were sorely mistaken. McLeod quickly ensnared Acton in a half nelson and crotch hold, and promptly flattened his shoulders to the mat to win the final bout of the tournament in just seven minutes.

With Acton vanquished and silenced beyond all doubt, McLeod returned to the business of bullying the rest of his local opponents, and continuing to do so in ways that would spark doubt as to the authenticity of the matches' outcomes.

On December 1, McLeod wrestled Vincent White in Oakland under the familiar stipulation that McLeod would need to defeat White five times within an hour in order to claim victory. Ironically, *The Examiner* stated prior to the bout that the frequent gamblers of Oakland "felt comparatively certain that there was no collusion" due to the rivalry that was said to exist between both men.

Half an hour crept by without McLeod scoring any falls on his opponent, who "had evidently schooled himself in acting on the defensive." Finally, after 36 long minutes, McLeod fastened a hammerlock on White's right arm leaving him with no choice but to "allow himself to be flatted out" or "have his right arm wrenched off at the shoulder." White chose the former, and was pinned. Still, those who wagered against the five falls being won by McLeod were surely feeling as if they'd made safe bets.

However, White was now moving very gingerly, and "made but a feeble resistance" when McLeod hauled him back to the mat, caught him in a half nelson and armhold, and rolled him onto his shoulders and off of the mat. When they returned to the center of the mat, White found himself trapped in a hammerlock once again, and not only allowed himself to be pinned, but then quit the match altogether, automatically surrendering all three of the remaining falls to McLeod by default.

McLeod's apparent luck at winning matches that required him to rack up falls at an unfathomable rate had not escaped notice. By the end of the month, many of the Bay's perennial gamblers seemed far less excited about wagering money on his matches.

"When it was announced that Sebastian Miller, the 'strong man,' and Dan McLeod, the wrestler, would wrestle at the Orpheum, the knowing ones shook their heads and said it was a fixed thing," reported *The Chronicle*. "Nevertheless, the hall was crowded to the outer doors last night, and standing room was at a premium. The repeated assertions of those interested in making the match, too, helped to dissipate the suspicions of an exhibition wrestling match, and many of those who paid their way into the Orpheum went to see business."

This is when *The Chronicle*'s sportswriter revealed his foreknowledge as to how the McLeod-Miller bout "was fixed and not fixed," as McLeod accused Miller of having visited him in advance and saying "I want to make some money."

"And so it was agreed that McLeod should permit himself to be thrown after a proper period of wrestling," continued *The Chronicle*. "Then it was decided by the canny Scotsman that he would do his best to throw Miller. This was kept very quiet, and probably not a half-dozen people on the stage last night were aware of the agreement between the two men and the resolution of McLeod."

In theory, this would mean that McLeod *had* agreed to concede the Greco-Roman fall to Miller before they advanced to the catch-as-catch-can fall, since there were only two rounds scheduled, and the bout seemed designed to ensure that it would end in a draw.

"Two to 1 that McLeod would win were the odds offered," added *The Chronicle*. "No big bets were made, and though the bookmakers used their lungs freely, 10 to 5 was the limit in the house. One hundred dollars was the largest sum offered yesterday."

Presumably, McLeod's reluctance to lay down for Miller and the Scotsman's sustained aggression during an opening round that he had supposedly agreed to lose would explain why Miller grew "more and more astonished" as the round wore on, and subsequently attempted to injure McLeod by throwing him hard all over the mat.

"McLeod got on his feet, and with a vicious 'Why don't you wrestle?' tried to get the big man's waist," continued *The Chronicle*. "The 'one hour and a half' was called. Miller made the remark that he was willing to take a rubdown for fifteen minutes. McLeod's only reply was a dash at his adversary and a ringing slap on his bare shoulders, which got the Dutchman mad. 'Mein head!' he cried, pointing to his head, while the audience laughed."

When McLeod won a pinfall soon after with a full nelson, "applause shook the house" while Miller "walked disconsolately off the stage." After the 10-minute rest, McLeod wasted no more time, and crushed Miller quickly to end the match.

Taking McLeod's version of events at face value, he had simply outed and double-crossed a hippodromer. Far more likely is that he had reneged on an agreement, and was placing Miller in a position where the big German could either admit to what McLeod was alleging, or insist that the bout was entirely on its merits, in which case he would be conceding that he had been defeated cleanly in fair combat by a much smaller man.

If it was indeed a betrayal on the part of McLeod, it would explain the complaint McLeod lodged with *The Call* in March 1894, grumbling that since his match with Sebastian Miller at the Orpheum, McLeod had "found it hard to induce any of the crack athletes of the East to meet him at his favorite game, catch-as-catch-can wrestling."

Highland Games and Hippodromes

McLeod eventually secured Tom McMahon, the wrestling instructor of the Detroit Athletic Club, to venture out to California for a match with him that month. *The Chronicle* informed the public that the local gambling pools were offering 10-to-6 odds in favor of McLeod, with "very little money in sight even at those odds."

Those who bet confidently in favor of McLeod — and especially those who wagered that McLeod would win the opening fall in an ordinary length of time — were no doubt stunned when McMahon surprised the local hero "by a few fancy moves" and secured a bar hold on him, thereby winning the first fall in only one-and-a-half minutes.

"The result surprised the friends of McLeod, who looked dumfounded and could not understand how any man could possibly down the Scot in such quick order," said *The Call*.

McLeod came back to win the second fall in 27 minutes, and during the intermission prior to the final fall, Alcazar Theater was interrupted by the presence of poolseller Harry Corbett, who entered the room and yelled to everyone present "I'll bet $10 to $2 that McLeod will win the match!"

"Some interested spectator, who was evidently disturbed by the intruders' remarks, informed the uncouth-looking individual that he was out of place and that the potato market was located somewhere on Clay Street near the city front," illustrated *The Call*. "The reply had evidently the desired effect, as the alleged poolseller was silenced as quickly as a clam by a sudden departure of the tide."

Succeeding in making his supporters atypically nervous with his first-round defeat, McLeod rallied back to win the final fall from McMahon with a half nelson transitioned into a reverse nelson and bar hold.

"The Little Scot" was about to show the wrestling world that his ambitions were far greater than the state of California could contain. His eventual relocation to the Midwest would coincide with a sudden change in allegiances by "The Big Scot" Duncan McMillan, which would ultimately see the world heavyweight championship fall into a different set of Celtic hands.

15 – Forgotten His Cunning

Approximately 5,000 miles away from where Dan McLeod had been dueling with Tom McMahon, Duncan Ross had remained in Scotland in the early part of 1893 and continued to appear in as many wrestling matches as he could string together. That April, Ross wrestled colossal Highlander Sandy McFee, with the bet being that Ross could throw McFee four times in a single hour. As a monster standing 6'8" and weighing 280 pounds, McFee presented an imposing challenge, and the coverage of the event makes it clear that betting was conducted on the scene.

"Ross succeeded in throwing McFee three times in 52 minutes, and when the time had expired, Ross failed to win the fourth bout, and the Highlander and his friends won not only the stakes, but several big wagers of $10 to $100," relayed *The Brooklyn Citizen*. "It requires a wrestler of the first water to throw any ordinary wrestler of the same height and avoirdupois four times in one hour."

Even this "loss" by Ross was engineered to make him appear competent to defeat a much larger opponent, even if he failed to log the requisite number of falls to achieve victory per the terms of the match. However, losing a Highland athletic contest would go much further in effectively tarnishing the reputation of Ross, and against George H. Johnstone of Aberdeen, Ross participated in an athletic match that "resulted disastrously so far as he is concerned."

Figuratively speaking, the throwing duel was a bloodbath. Ross lost the heavy hammer throw 88 feet to 83 feet, the light hammer toss 116 feet to 104 feet, and the 56-pound weight throw 27 feet to 24 feet. Ross refused to compete in the stone-putting contest, and he was only able to complete the tossing of the caber once in comparison to Johnstone's five successful tosses.

In fact, the only event Ross didn't lose to Johnstone outright, which was the wrestling match, bore all the signs of hippodroming. Johnstone won the Cumberland bout, Ross won the Scotch-style bout, and the event was then declared a draw with no tiebreaker round.

When Ross returned to North America, he remained quiet for sufficient time that the press grew curious about his activities and interests, since he had spent a solid decade loudly promoting events somewhere on the globe. *The Montreal Gazette* revealed that Ross had been running a sawmill near St. Faustin in Quebec, but hinted of a return to action by Ross if he had not "forgotten his cunning."

In October, Ross reemerged to challenge catch-as-catch-can world champion Evan Lewis at The Grotto, a Chicago establishment on Michigan Avenue near Madison Street, while Ross was still claiming to be the mixed-style champion of the world. *The Daily Picayune* of New Orleans categorically dismissed any such claims by Ross as ludicrous.

"The story of the match between Evan Lewis and Duncan Ross for the wrestling championship of the world would make any follower of sport laugh himself into a fit," said *The Picayune*. "Just what right Ross has to claim the championship of the world is a mystery to all well-posted men of a sporting turn of mind. Besides any match in which the 'all-round' athlete would take part would be looked upon with a certain suspicion, just why, I cannot explain, except that the community that patronizes sports has a wonderful lack of faith in Ross.

"Outside of the fact that Ross would not make a good drawing card, I think that he would have as much chance of winning from the great 'Strangler' as a snowball would in the 'demnition bow-wows.'"

Media mistrust notwithstanding, that November, Lewis and Ross engaged in a multi-night series of shows that offered every appearance of being an coordinated series of events intended to squeeze every last dime out of the betting people of Chicago.

On the first night, Lewis won the Greco-Roman bout in only two minutes, and immediately after the catch-as-catch-can round started, Lewis "got a strangle hold and about all possible points in about ten seconds." The result of this fall was ultimately thrown out due to Lewis' insistence on using a stranglehold, so Ross was able to survive a further six minutes before Lewis finally won that fall. Ross won only the Cumberland style, and the wrestling on night one concluded after only 11 minutes of total wrestling.

At the next event, Ross would be seen to deliberately injure the arm of Lewis in the early going, and then took advantage of the injury by taking the lead in the total fall count heading into the final night of the series.

Unfathomably, the series was designed to conclude after 16 total falls had been registered. The even number of rounds made it impossible for the Lewis-Ross series to achieve the usual conclusion where a win or a loss for either wrestler hinged on the result of one last round; it could end only in a win for one of the wrestlers, or as a tie.

Ross and Lewis concocted a creative ending to account for this problem after Lewis announced before the bout that he would destroy Ross "and would not take any pains to spare his opponent's feelings." Lewis backed up his proclamation by winning the opening Greco-Roman fall to tie the score at seven victories each with only two rounds remaining. This meant that the winner of the following catch-as-catch-can fall effectively guaranteed that the worst outcome they could face would be a draw.

"When the catch-as-catch-can was announced, [Lewis] went at Ross like an infuriated bull," described *The Evening Bee*. "In a short time he had secured the hammerlock, and slowly but surely began to twist Ross' arm over above his head, causing the latter the most excruciating agony. Ross groaned from pain, but said nothing to indicate that he wanted to give up the fall.

"Referee Siller, therefore, remained silent, while Lewis, with brutal slowness, lowered his man's shoulders to the floor. At the call of the fall Ross sharply criticized Referee Siller for not having given the decision before, but all the athletes who witnessed the encounter, including Ross' second, admitted that

Siller could not do otherwise than he did. Ross was so badly injured that he refused to go into the third bout, and thereby sacrificed the prize to Lewis."

Following his bout with Jack King in St. Paul, Lewis' friend Duncan McMillan kept a low profile, or at least participated in events that flew beneath the radar of the major media. When he did emerge, it was at an April 1894 event hosted by the athletic association of Sioux City, Iowa, and the proceedings were coincidentally tainted by rumors of hippodroming that didn't directly implicate McMillan.

Fighter Joe Sheehy was set to face Jack Davies in an advertised boxing event, but those who gathered to watch the match "liberally 'cussed' the management for enticing them to pay their good money for the worst kind of hippodrome."

A dispute occurred behind the scenes over the weights of the gloves used in the fights, and the chief of police — referred to as "Chief Young" — evaluated the appointed gloves backstage and ruled that it would be too easy for an unskilled fighter to deliver a knockout blow with them. On the spot, he made a ruling that every fight contested by fighters wearing those gloves would be limited to a single round.

"When the chief announced that only one round would be permitted, (promoter) George Lyon literally 'hit the ceiling,'" observed *The Sioux City Journal*. "It was unexpected, he said, and out of all reason that the chief should thoroughly enjoy the minor slugging matches between lightweights and then stop a friendly bout between heavyweights. In vain he pleaded and begged, but the chief stood 'pat' on his reputation which he had to sustain and also to protect the bondsmen of both himself and Sheriff Davenport."

Sheehy apparently did not want to appear before the crowd for even one round, "as the audience would think the fight was a fake," and his chances of presenting any future fights of greater length would be ruined. Conversely, his opponent, Davies, wished to go on with the fight to demonstrate that he was willing to box under any circumstances.

Highland Games and Hippodromes

While this mess was being sorted out, McMillan entered the ring for a wrestling match. His scheduled opponent, James Gallatin, "evidently scented trouble in the air" because of the events playing out behind the curtain "and failed to put in an appearance."

Instead, Joe Sheehy, who had been afraid that his participation in a one-round boxing match would give the appearance of a hippodrome, volunteered to take Gallatin's place, and *won* the opening-round sidehold match against the five-styles world champion. This was followed by a 10-minute catch-as-catch-can round that ended when Sheehy simply threw in the towel because he was afraid of tiring himself out before his boxing match.

At 11:00 a.m., Sheehy and Davies entered the ring, and when their fight commenced, the two boxers "pranced around the ring for three minutes without an effective blow being struck with the big pillows."

"At the end of the round, Chief Young, according to the programme, called Referee Lyon aside and told him the contest could not continue," added *The Journal*. "The announcement was made from the stage, and the spectators hissed, 'Give us our money,' 'Rats,' 'Fake,' and similar expressions were heard as the sporty individuals hustled out of the theater."

When it was all said and done, *The Journal* reported that McMillan came by their offices to issue a challenge for Sheehy to compete with him in contests ranging from pole vaulting to sprinting and caber tossing, which Sheehy apparently declined.

Ostensibly, McMillan remained in the area a little while longer to try his hand at the promotion of boxing events. On the night of a scheduled fight between Jack Davies and James Burns in Covington, Iowa, McMillan reportedly crossed the river at 9:00 a.m. "to prepare the ring and make the other preparations" only to return with a report that Alderman Heath, the proprietor of a hotel in Covington, "had sworn out a warrant for the arrest of Davies and Burns."

Highland Games and Hippodromes

The warrant was purported to have been in the hands of the local marshal, who was to serve it to the two men as soon as their boat arrived. No explanation was offered as to what arrestable offense the two fighters had committed.

In June 1894 it became crystal clear what McMillan's foremost motivation for staying in Iowa had been. As the month opened, the Sioux City newspapers announced that McMillan had agreed to wrestle "Farmer" Martin Burns — the ascendant star in all of professional wrestling alongside Dan McLeod — in a catch-as-catch-can bout.

The Sioux City Journal printed long bios of both men, which included McMillan's claim to five-style supremacy of the wrestling world, but omitted the fact that he had most famously proclaimed that title while operating as the partner and trainer of Evan Lewis, who was still the reigning champion of catch-as-catch-can wrestling. This omission was especially conspicuous due to the fact that Lewis was mentioned no less than *three times* in McMillan biography.

McMillan and Burns met at the Peavey Grand Opera House on June 28, with each man billed as the champion of his respective state. In this instance, McMillan, who was born and raised in Canada, was said to represent California, the location where he had done the bulk of his foundational work in wrestling.

"Both men looked well and professed to be satisfied with the results of their training," observed *The Journal*. "McMillan, who stands 6 feet 2 inches tall, loomed up over the Iowa man like a giant, and at first it looked as if Burns was outclassed. The spectators held to this opinion throughout the first bout, but the tide soon turned. Both men displayed strength and agility, but if Burns' advantage can be located it was in his superior trickiness and staying qualities."

Aside from the size difference between the two wrestlers, with Burns being both four inches shorter and 25 pounds lighter than McMillan, the reason it appeared as if Burns was outclassed by his Scottish adversary was because the catch-as-catch-can bout was contested almost identically to the bout between McMillan and Evan Lewis, except that the events in Iowa unfolded far more quickly.

"Farmer" Martin Burns

McMillan trapped Burns in a full nelson that the Iowan fought against for some time before finally being pinned in 22 minutes. The pinfall victory had very clearly been earned by McMillan, but the Iowa crowd was decidedly behind Burns, and hissed the decision.

Visibly exhausted by the first fall, McMillan requested a 15-minute break, but Burns made a show of wanting to resume wrestling immediately, and the referee agreed to a slightly reduced resting session of 12-and-a-half minutes.

The second fall appeared to be playing out similarly to the first, except that Burns managed to break out of McMillan's full nelson, avoided a subsequent pinning attempt, and then pinned McMillan with a takedown and a half nelson in 30 minutes.

Once Burns had seized the momentum, he won the next two falls in 20 minutes and 25 minutes respectively, and was rewarded with "deafening cheers." Burns and McMillan walked to the center of the mat and shook hands to a second round of applause before disappearing behind the curtain.

In front of *The Journal*'s reporter, McMillan conceded that he had been beaten fairly, and that his defeat could be attributed to the Farmer's superior conditioning. Burns was likewise complimentary of McMillan, calling him a "hard man to handle," but added that the tussle "was not as long and hard as he anticipated."

At the very instant that McMillan and Burns had been getting acquainted with one another, it was being reported by *The San Francisco Chronicle* that Dan McLeod was aching for an opportunity to wrestle any of three different men, two of which McMillan had now been closely linked to.

"His recent successes have emboldened his backers, who are now negotiating for a match with either 'Farmer' Burns, Wimmer, or Evan Lewis," said *The Chronicle*. "Wimmer will probably be given the first chance, as McLeod is anxious to defeat every prominent wrestler in the country before tackling such a formidable opponent as Evan Lewis, the acknowledged champion of America. McLeod is a formidable man of his weight, and his admirers in this city think that he can give Lewis the greatest match of his life, notwithstanding the fact that he would have to give away so much in weight."

The next time Burns and McMillan were spotted together, onlookers never would have guessed that they'd been at one another's throats just a few weeks earlier. At the Fourth of July picnic at Riverside Park, attended by 8,000 residents of the Sioux City region, Burns issued an open challenge to anyone present who wished to go to the mat with him, and when none of the ordinary citizens stepped forward to face him, he agreed to wrestle in exhibitions with seven different athletes who were present at the park, including McMillan.

"McMillan was the only one that made the exhibition look very much like a wrestling match, though Burns would play with the others from three to ten minutes each," said *The Journal*. "Burns and McMillan gave two friendly bouts, each winning one, and gave very pretty exhibitions of the head spin, the bridge, the half and full Nelson holds, the crotch and arm hold, the shoulder hold, etc."

The display at the picnic gave every indication that a friendship and partnership was blooming between the two commanding grapplers. Further confirmation of the alliance can be inferred from the ways in which both men immediately moved to downplay the significance of Burns' win over McMillan.

"Duncan A. McMillan, who was recently defeated by Farmer Burns in this city, had been doctoring for two weeks before the match," revealed *The Journal* in mid-July. "He went in five pounds under his best weight, and was in no condition to wrestle such a man as Burns. McMillan said last Wednesday that he had lost eight pounds since the contest, on the 27th of June. The big Californian looked to be in poor health, and ate scarcely anything. Farmer Burns also said that Mac was out of condition. From this it may be seen that McMillan's recent showing is no measure of his true ability at catch-as-catch-can wrestling."

Analyzing these statements rationally, Burns had defeated a man who outweighed him by 25 pounds on the night of their match, and was essentially negating the validity of his victory over the much larger man, partially on the grounds that the man *should* have outweighed him by even more.

McMillan — claiming to hail from Butte City, Montana of all places — made a brief visit to Bay City, Michigan along with "his backer" F.A. Smith toward the end of October, and if

Highland Games and Hippodromes

they didn't participate in a hippodrome, the report of *The Bay City Times* provides every indication that the fans in attendance perceived it as such.

"They arranged a wrestling match with Tom Cannon, of Buffalo, at $100 a side," stated *The Times*. "The match came off last night before about 40 men and boys for a shake purse of $12.50. After the contest was over, the Montana sports gave a fine exhibition of sprinting between the opera house and hotel, followed by a mob armed with superannuated eggs. The Montana heavyweight is a well known Bay City wrestler, and Tom Cannon, of Buffalo, comes from Grand Rapids."

The report circulated all over Michigan, likely ruining whatever plans McMillan might have had about setting up a base of operations in the Great Lakes State. Instead, McMillan returned to Iowa to participate in further wrestling exhibitions with Farmer Burns, whose rapidly increasing fame seemed to be expanding the map around Iowa and Illinois in which wrestlers could successfully ply their trade.

Back in San Francisco, Dan McLeod lost a match with Tom McMahon at the outset of 1894 according to the stipulation that the Scot was required to throw McMahon three times in one hour in order to be the victor. The timing of the falls followed the customary cadence of such bouts, with McLeod winning two falls in about 25 minutes each, leaving him with only seven minutes after a brief rest to attempt to secure the final fall, which he was unable to do.

Far more compelling than the action of the bout is the fact that referee John P. Casey spoke to the audience before the match began and "announced that all bets on the match were declared off." Casey's rationale was that "it was understood that the poolsellers had secured the good will of one of the wrestlers," and that Casey had declared the bets off "to prevent any chance of hippodroming."

Casey neglected to mention exactly which of the two wrestlers had been accused of cozying up to the local poolsellers.

Highland Games and Hippodromes

Certainly, dropping a stipulation match to McMahon did nothing to reduce McLeod's standing on the Pacific Coast, and the results of his next marquee matchup would see his reputation double. That was when distinguished Greco-Roman wrestler Charles Moth arrived in San Francisco in June after challenging McLeod for months, and they finally met on the mat for a mixed-style wrestling match at the Alcazar Theatre.

Moth won the choice of styles for the first round and naturally selected Greco-Roman. Twenty minutes into the affair, Moth caught McLeod in a full nelson and "nearly twisted McLeod's head off his shoulders." From there, he drove McLeod's face toward the canvas mat, then forcefully halted his smaller opponent's bridging efforts "by lifting McLeod up and dashing him upon the floor." With both men down, Moth switched to a half nelson, threw his entire weight on top of McLeod, and held him there just long enough to be awarded the fall.

McLeod roared out of the gate at the start of the post-intermission catch-as-catch-can round. He tripped Moth all over the mat, and hounded him incessantly until he finally caught the German in a reverse nelson hold.

"At Greco-Roman, [Moth] could have escaped from this easily, but at catch-as-catch-can, McLeod, being allowed the use of his legs, pinned one of Moth's arms to the floor with his knees while he worked on the other," explained *The Chronicle*. "Moth struggled gamely, but finally collapsed. The time of this bout was eight minutes."

Having won the second fall in a shorter time than it took Moth to win the first, McLeod was offered his choice of styles for the final round and obviously selected catch-as-catch-can. The match was a repeat of the second fall, as Moth fell to the floor, McLeod "pounced on the prostrate German," grabbed him in "[McLeod's] favorite reverse Nelson hold," and pinned him for a six-minute victory.

The Examiner's coverage of the bout included a note that McLeod was a 2-to-1 betting favorite "when the men shook hands for the first bout," suggesting that Moth's round-one win may have caused the odds to fluctuate as the action progressed.

Charles Moth (left) and Dan McLeod

In the press, Moth justifiably credited McLeod only with being the recipient of good fortune, and asserted that he would have defeated McLeod easily if the third fall of the bout had been in Moth's specialty of Greco-Roman. In order to silence Moth for all eternity, McLeod agreed to a return bout with the unfathomable stipulation that he would defeat the Greco-Roman expert three times in one hour using only the Greco-Roman wrestling style, or otherwise Moth would be ruled the winner.

It's difficult to think of another scenario from this era where the path to victory for one wrestler over another appeared so daunting, but the two men met at the Alcazar

Theatre one week later with McLeod facing a challenge that seemed impossible.

The Examiner remarked of how the betting pools reflected this belief, as for the first time in quite a while, McLeod was a solid underdog. On the day of the rematch, Moth "sold for $100 in the pools against $70 for McLeod's chances."

Just a few minutes into the match, McLeod rolled backwards while maintaining a grip on Moth's right arm, forcing Moth onto his back. McLeod then straightened up and secured an armlock on Moth, who "realized that he was mastered" as McLeod stunned the fans in attendance by besting Moth at his own style in just under five minutes.

The second fall took considerably longer, because Moth got behind McLeod, drove him to the mat, and rode him for more than 20 minutes. Just when it seemed like McLeod would be stuck there for the remainder of the contest, he suddenly "reversed positions with Moth and secured a half-Nelson." Just like that, Moth had been pinned again, and McLeod had only taken 32 minutes to notch his first two falls.

Only one minute of resting time followed, after which McLeod "jumped around like a kitten for a minute," and then grabbed Moth in another half nelson. The thoroughly overwhelmed Moth "made little resistance," and McLeod took the pinfall victory to complete his annihilation of Moth in his own style in just 33 minutes and 52 seconds.

After this resounding victory in a bout that he entered as an unquestioned underdog, McLeod appeared emboldened during subsequent interviews, and began to issue very vocal challenges to Evan Lewis, Ed Atherton, and Farmer Burns, all of whom were comfortably 2,000 miles away at the very least.

Ostensibly owing to the fact that he heard no replies from the other top-ranked heavyweights in the U.S., McLeod simply began referring to himself as "the catch-as-catch-can champion of the world" in the fall, and expressed his intent to "pack his little grip and start for the East," where he expected

Highland Games and Hippodromes

"to cause some consternation in the ranks of the wrestling contingent there."

"Dan's reason for determining upon this course is the falling through of his latest effort to get on a match with Atherton, the New York gladiator, whom 'Strangler' Lewis and the rest of them declined to meet," said *The Chronicle*. "The local athlete's backers wrote to Atherton, offering him a match at catch weights for any amount he desired to put up. His reply has been received and it is on a par with those received from other wrestlers. He, too, is not overanxious for a hugging contest with the doughty little Scot."

Wrestling successes aside, McLeod also enjoyed quite a fruitful year at the Highland Games competitions contested in California, although his presence seems to have sparked annoyance amongst at least a few of the other contestants at some of these events, who seemed to perceive the participation of a professional athlete as unfair.

"On Friday last, [McLeod] bundled up a few things and started for the City by the Slough, and on the following day he was the observed of all observers when he contested against all comers in the open events and won twelve first prizes out of thirteen events he had contested for," reported *The Call*. "It is hardly necessary to remark that there were Scotch athletes present from Sacramento, Marysville, Stockton, and many other cities who looked upon Daniel as being an interloper, and who wished him in any place but Stockton, which latter city is hot enough at times to please the most fastidious taste. McLeod won over $100 by his little voyage up the Sacramento River."

It would appear that the era typified by a reverence of Donald Dinnie in the United States — at least the spirit of it — was over. Either that, or the phenomenon of North American Highland Games competitors gladly resigning themselves to lower placements simply for the privilege of sharing the field with a star was not transferable to the younger generation.

Highland Games and Hippodromes

In reality, McLeod was not on the level of Dinnie, or even Ross, as an overpowering force in Caledonian athletics. Still, his performances would still rank him in the upper echelon of most competitions held during the 1890s. At the Caledonian Club gathering at Shell Mound, he finished third in both of the hammer throwing events, and won the caber toss outright against at least two other competitors. This is in sharp contrast to when Dinnie had difficulty finding a North American man to even convincingly lift a caber next to him 20 years prior.

In September, McLeod improved his placements at the throwing events when he competed at the fourth annual games of the Order of the Scottish Clans, winning both the heavy and light hammer throws.

True to his word, McLeod relocated to the Midwest in the spring of 1895, although the news publications with insight into the wrestler's origin reported the move as less of a relocation and more of the return of McLeod to his childhood home. *The Daily Times* of Davenport, Iowa was quick to point out that McLeod "nominally hails from San Francisco," but was in fact "a native of Illinois" who had been seen visiting his relatives in Morrison, which sits only 12 miles from the Iowa border.

Family reunions may have been an added enticement for McLeod to make his Midwestern move, but from a business standpoint, his purpose in displacing himself from his West Coast haunt was to stalk Farmer Burns and Evan Lewis. Arriving in Chicago in the middle of March 1895, McLeod expressed his disappointment to *The Inter Ocean* that Burns and Lewis had already committed to wrestling one another for the accepted world championship in April, but promised to leave them alone until they finished their business with each other.

In the meantime, McLeod would satisfy himself by offering Midwestern audiences a taste of the abilities that had made him a legend to wrestling fans in the San Francisco Bay area. As an inbound competitor with a national reputation, McLeod was afforded plenty of respect in the way he was promoted. In Marion, Indiana, he was announced as "the champion heavyweight wrestler of the world" without any amendments or qualifications to the title.

For his debut match in Indiana, McLeod arrived in the company of his manager C.J. Blake for a bout with local champion Harvey Parker after spending the afternoon touring the Canton glass works and meeting the residents of the city. In observing McLeod during these moments, *The Marion Leader* described him as "one of the finest proportioned men who ever participated in a sporting event in this city."

McLeod's match that evening was another classic case in which he, as a short-statured Scotsman generously listed at 5'6", was tasked with pinning his taller but far lighter opponent four times in an hour in order to be deemed the winner.

As usual, McLeod was dominant, and racked up four victories over Parker in under 28 minutes before finalizing his travel arrangements to witness the Burns-Lewis match in Chicago the next night.

McMillan was prominent in his proximity to both Burns and Lewis during the weeks and months that preceded their title showdown in Chicago. Burns and McMillan made preparations for a wrestling exhibition at the opera house of Dixon, Illinois to open 1895, and the editor of *The Dixon Telegraph* seemed more concerned about the character of the entertainment being brought to the town rather than whether or not the competition would be real.

"We have been assured that this entertainment will be conducted in an unobjectionable manner, and while personally we do not regard the sports of the Roman arena as the highest style of entertainment for our nineteenth century civilization, if these can be conducted in an unobjectionable manner, they will certainly be attractive to many," printed *The Telegraph*.

In Dixon, Burns and McMillan both issued open challenges to the attendees that they could not be thrown in 15 minutes' time in either of their specialties. Anyone who survived 15 minutes on the mat with either wrestler without being defeated would be given $50, although it could be deduced that McMillan was far more generous as he presented the opportunity for men to face him in any style at all, while Burns would accept challenges only in catch-as-catch-can.

Incidentally, it was included in the challenge that Burns fancied himself as "a rival of the great (Eugen) Sandow," and was willing to give any man $25 if they succeeded in choking him despite the prodigious thickness of his neck. The choking challenge was apparently going to be "conducted in such a manner as not to offend the most fastidious."

With all due respect to Burns, who weighed about 165 pounds at a height of 5'10", and who was very well developed relative to the average man of the era, he would have been by no means perceived to be a physical rival of Eugen Sandow by anyone who appraised their proportions firsthand. By all accounts, Sandow carried around approximately 190 pounds of lean muscle at a height of 5'5", and is universally eulogized as the "father of modern bodybuilding" a full century after his death in 1925.

As Evan Lewis and Farmer Burn readied themselves for a world-title showdown and Dan McLeod loomed in the background, it seemed like it would be a few short months before McLeod would have his long-awaited title opportunity. Sadly, he was about to get a multi-year master class in the politics of professional wrestling.

16 – A Pity 'Tis True

As the spring of 1895 unfolded, that's when Duncan McMillan seemed to play an underrated role — if not an untraceable role — in one of the most consequential coronations in professional wrestling history. The development of events began when McMillan and Evan Lewis faced each other in Iowa, with the two men advertised as "very bitter against each other" after Burns defeated J.C. Comstock to earn a shot at Lewis' championship.

In a throwback to their bout in St. Paul years earlier, McMillan captured a single catch-as-catch-can round from Lewis in Decorah, Iowa, but fell in four falls to the man to whom he had been inextricably linked for the better part of the latter three years. Before the bout, it was written that McMillan's "friends in Decorah" would certainly lose a lot of money on the result if McMillan lost.

By this time, the major bout in Chicago between Lewis and Burns for the catch-as-catch-can championship of the world had already been agreed to, and some newspapers viewed Lewis' mastery of McMillan as an indication that "The Strangler" was still unbeatable.

"Everything seems to fall before Evan, and we should not be surprised to hear of him being challenged by a cyclone some day, as that seems to be the only thing left in this country that has not been stretched on the mat by him," stated *The Chronicle* of Dodgeville, Wisconsin.

While this was being printed in Wisconsin, preparations were being finalized in Chicago for the major April 22 catch-as-catch-can showdown between Lewis and Burns. During the pre-match weigh-in, Lewis shocked the press by arriving in such poor shape that he would be described in print as being "fat as a prize pig." According to reports, Lewis weighed 200 pounds at the time of the fight; he clearly looked every inch of a man that was wrestling at 20 pounds above his customary weight.

The title match played out in a way that plainly protected the reputations of both grapplers. Lewis won the first fall in 15 minutes, lost the second in 25 minutes, and then captured the third in 22 minutes. Had it been a best-of-three-falls affair, Lewis would have been the victor. With two more falls to go, the superiorly conditioned Burns roared back to even the fall count at two apiece by winning the fourth fall in one minute, setting the stage for a historic final round.

"Burns, after three minute's hugging, worked loose, and then went at Lewis like a cyclone," described *The Neligh Leader*. "He had Lewis with one shoulder on the floor, trying to drop Lewis on his back. He twice had Lewis with his head to the floor and his feet in the air. The second time he dropped quickly, and in a twinkling had Lewis half turned with a hammer lock. The champion struggled like a wild man, but it did him no good. Burns turned him slowly, inch by inch, and finally downed him, amid deafening yells from the 3,000 spectators."

As an indication of just how intertwined Duncan McMillan had been with the world championship picture through his professional dealings with both the new and former champions, when McMillan had a match of his own against Gideon Perry the following night in Chicago at the Olympic Theater, *The Inter Ocean* described McMillan as "the wrestling partner of Evan Lewis." Evidently, in the eyes of some members of the Chicago media, the flip of McMillan from the camp of Lewis to Burns had failed to register.

Only one announcement was made following the title change; Parson Davies issued a challenge to the new world champion "on behalf of D.C. McLeod, the Scotchman."

Before and after issuing his challenge to Farmer Burns, McLeod enjoyed a slew of victories over easy opponents, and only faced one opponent during his inaugural Midwestern tour who was perceived as a true challenge: Greco-Roman specialist Charles Wittmer. The two competed against each other in a mixed-styles bout in Indianapolis that June, and Wittmer secured the advantage by winning the toss for the choice in styles. Quickly capitalizing on this by selecting Greco-Roman as the opening style, Wittmer won the first round in just over 15 minutes.

When the style switched to catch-as-catch-can for the next round, McLeod "showed wonderful celerity" in swarming Wittmer and pinning his shoulders to the mat in only six minutes. McLeod then won the toss for the final style, and only needed another six minutes to end the match.

The St. Louis Globe-Democrat reminded its readers that Wittmer enjoyed a 35-pound weight advantage over McLeod, but McLeod possessed "remarkable agility" that "told against weight," and was fearless despite his size. That same fearlessness in the face of what would ordinarily have been dispiriting odds was proposed as the reason why Farmer Burns refused to face McLeod despite the little Scot's incessant challenges.

"I want to wrestle Burns, and I will agree to any time between now and December 20," McLeod promised *The Inter Ocean* after months of his challenges had gone unheeded. "He claims to have unlimited backing, at least for others, and there should be little trouble for him to raise enough to get the match on. I do not want to wait until I am gray-haired, and if Burns does not cover my forfeit in five days, it will be taken down, and the world will accept this as a virtual acknowledgement from Burns that he fears and will not wrestle with me."

Burns submitted a one-sentence response to *The Inter Ocean*, freely agreeing with McLeod's assessment of the situation: "I would rather wrestle [Evan] Lewis a dozen times than McLeod once."

Simultaneous to this report, *The Inter Ocean* offered an origin for McLeod that differed starkly from those that were usually provided for him. It alleged that McLeod "was born in the highlands of Scotland twenty-nine years ago," and that he arrived on the North American continent "when yet an infant in arms" to spend his childhood in Pictou, Nova Scotia before relocating to Carroll and Whiteside counties in Illinois.

Highland Games and Hippodromes

While this proposed pattern of migration likely followed the movements of McLeod's parents, evidence disputing an Illinois birth for McLeod has been difficult to come by.

For anyone who had studied the strategy through which Duncan McMillan first became established as a five-style wrestling threat when allied with Evan Lewis, they would have to watch as a nearly identical scenario played out when a catch-as-catch-can world title bout was signed between Farmer Burns and his versatile partner and rival McMillan. The match was booked for Des Moines during the first week of June, in what was clearly intended to be a home-state victory lap for newly crowned champion Burns.

The Daily Tribune of Des Moines elaborated on the abstemious lifestyle of the world champion, who had "never used tobacco and liquor in any form," whose beverage of choice was "cold water," and who consumed nothing other than "health- and strength-giving foods."

Concurrently, *The Tribune* granted McMillan a European birth ahead of the highest-profile bout of his career, claiming that he was "born in Scotland" on May 22, 1864 before immediately driving the point home even further and adding that he was also "of Scotch parentage." It also provided a long list of opponents that McMillan had defeated, taking great care to add Donald Dinnie to the list, and to include that Dinnie was "the champion of Scotland" at the time.

Burns won his match with McMillan in Des Moines, and then defeated him again in Davenport later that same week. Nevertheless, from the perspective of McMillan, he was clearly making deposits that were going to pay off in a massive way. One week after confirming the fortitude of Burns as the catch-as-catch-can world champion in Iowa, McMillan agreed to defend *his* mixed-styles world championship against Burns in St. Paul, Minnesota.

Arriving in St. Paul, Burns presented his opinion on why interest in wrestling had declined in previous years, and why the business was now beginning to show signs of life. He attributed the diminished fan interest to an absence of "celebrated wrestlers," and a shortage of athletes who had been able to capture the imagination of the public.

"I think the future of wrestling is much more encouraging than it has been for some time," Burns told *The Minneapolis Times*. "There has not been as much activity among this class of athletes for several years, but already it is beginning to revive. Wrestling is the cleanest of all athletic professional sports. It is very rarely that you hear of a man being injured or his usefulness impaired in any way, while it gives him opportunity to show his physical prowess to the fullest extent. I expect a revival of wrestling within the coming two years."

In Chicago, the sentiment that Burns and McMillan were harbingers of professional wrestling's resurgence was being echoed in the pages of *The Inter Ocean*. The paper assured its readers that "lovers of the vigorous art of wrestling" who "sigh for the good old Battery D days when wrestling was the rage" would have been satisfied by the displays of Burns and McMillan, who gave "an excellent exhibition" reminiscent of the era of "Muldoon, Acton, Christol, Sorakichi... and other heroes of the mat."

The Minneapolis Times described "the mob at Athletic Park in Minneapolis" on the night of the Burns-McMillan mixed-style championship match as overwhelming in relation to the comparatively small crowds that had filled the baseball grounds to watch actual baseball games. As far as the match that was presented to the enthusiastic fans was concerned, *The Times* described it as a "beautiful contest," before adding the dubious detail that it possessed "the rare merit of being wholly on the square."

"Furthermore, it was a contest from the beginning to end, and there was not a moment when the contestants were not at work," observed *The Times*. "No monkey work or even a suggestion of shirking was noticed. Throughout the two hours of wrestling, both men worked hard and in earnest, and the man who was not satisfied with the show given him for his money would certainly be hard to please."

Highland Games and Hippodromes

With all due respect to the sportswriters of *The Times*, the bout was obviously orchestrated to present McMillan as superior to Burns as an all-around wrestler. In the opening sidehold bout, McMillan crushed Burns in eight minutes. In the catch-as-catch-can round that followed, the world champion of the style *barely* won in 33 minutes after narrowly avoiding being pinned by McMillan on several occasions.

Duncan McMillan shows off his strength

McMillan rebounded from this and breezed through Burns in only six minutes to secure the Cumberland fall, and then Burns pulled off an upset by winning a hard-fought

Highland Games and Hippodromes

Greco-Roman scuffle — the style closest in resemblance to catch-as-catch-can — in 19 minutes. This left only the collar-and-elbow round remaining to decide the world championship.

"Burns seemed to recognize the superiority of his opponent at this style and remained on the defensive," continued *The Times*. "McMillan threw him around savagely for a few minutes and then allowed him to rest a short period. Beginning again, he did not waste much time, but went to work with a will to end the struggle, which he did in a short time. He got Burns upon his hip and threw him down with a thud that could be heard all over the grounds, winning the bout in 15 minutes and 50 seconds."

By bullying the new catch-as-catch-can champion of the world in every style of the five-styles match that did not resemble Burns' specialty, and also by making the catch-as-catch-can bout highly competitive, McMillan staked a tangible claim to the title of being the world's most well-rounded wrestler, if not its *true* best.

The Times added up the times of the falls, verified that McMillan won his three bouts in 30 minutes while Burns had required 50 minutes to win two rounds, and concluded that Burns was "evidently not the equal of McMillan at mixed-styles."

The San Francisco Chronicle took note when Burns and McMillan took their act westward, and reported of it in relation to McLeod's withdrawal of the $500 he had posted with *The Times-Herald* in Chicago two months earlier in pursuit of a match with Burns. McLeod was reportedly "disgusted at Burns' failure to come to an agreement."

"[Burns] promised to cover a part of the forfeit before he left Chicago, but did not do so, and is now in the Northwest, playing in variety theaters with Duncan McMillan," poked *The Chronicle*. "McLeod will be in Chicago the week after next."

While Burns and McMillan were busy raising each other's stock, McLeod remained primarily in Indianapolis where he continued to be promoted as the world heavyweight champion of catch-as-catch-can wrestling. Yet, when he was forced to return home to California without securing the bout with Farmer Burns that he had so desperately sought, he effectively renounced any past claims he had made to world title status, and then insisted that Burns needed to wrestle him "or drop the affix 'champion' in signing his name and decorating his billing."

"Burns must wrestle me, and if I am successful with him, I will take on Lewis eight weeks later for as much money as the 'Strangler' can raise," McLeod informed *The Inter Ocean*. "If I took on Lewis now and won, I would be as far removed from the championship then as I am now. Burns is champion. I aspire to that title, and after I get it, Lewis, or anyone else who wants a chance at the title can have it."

As the holder of the most respected wrestling championship in North America, Burns — who was himself the son of two Irish immigrants — now had one of the two best Scotsmen in the business at his side, and the other hot on his heels.

While McLeod and McMillan were at the center of the key happenings in professional wrestling in 1895, the press seemed to regard the 40-year-old Duncan Ross as a has-been who was waiting to be put out to pasture. More provocative, however, is the fact that Ross' ethnic identity as Scottish now seemed to be treated with less importance than a tendentious national identity that some publications seemed intent on imposing upon him based on his reported birthplace.

"Duncan C. Ross was once the greatest leg and arm wrestler in the sporting world, but wrestlers have learned the tricks of the handsome Turk, and now they almost do unto him as he used to do unto them," said *The Pittsburgh Press*. "Ross at one time thought no more of twisting an arm out of place during a wrestling match than a cat would of killing a rat. Lately, however, Sir Duncan hasn't been as 'bad' as he used to be. Some nights ago in Bradford, England, Tom Cannon, who was here in March, 1885, wrestling the Britisher, Joe Acton, met and defeated Ross, winning almost as he pleased.

Highland Games and Hippodromes

"Although Ross has seen his best day as a wrestler, he's one of the most interesting characters on the sporting stage, having traveled the world over one or two times. Duncan C. Ross was born in Scentil, Turkey, in 1855, and stands over six feet high, weighing in the neighborhood of 200 pounds. He is tremendously strong, and a perfect gladiator to look upon. He was, and rightly so, too, conceded to be the most vicious of all modern athletes, and in his heyday probably maimed more than a half dozen men in the sporting business. But he's a 'beaut' in more sense than one, for all of that."

The losing streak of Ross "The Turk" would continue, and the fact that Ross seemed to lose with such ease implies that the matches were either authentic, or he had lost some of his leverage in ensuring that his star shone the brightest.

The Cincinnati Enquirer reported in March how Ross was destroyed by Greco-Roman specialist Charley Wittmer at the People's Theater, with Wittmer finding Ross to be "in no condition" and "very easy to handle." Wittmer was said to be in training for a bout with Dan McLeod, and quickly disposed of Ross with three flying falls followed by a full nelson that culminated in a pinfall.

In the middle of the summer, Ross also met Ernest Roeber for a match on the roof of the Police Gazette Building, and was crushed in one minute and 52 seconds. Subsequent to this slaughter, *The New York World* declared that "Ross' pretensions to championship honors have recently acquired an unwarranted boldness."

The next month, Ross faced Roeber again in a match at the Winter Circus of Philadelphia for a bout that a local sportswriter referred to as "one of those brazen fakes which have soured the people of this city on traveling professional wrestlers." The writer described the fraud as being easy to spot, as "Ross merely laid down to Roeber when he got too tired or lazy to work" during the Greco-Roman portion of the proceedings.

"The first fall took three minutes and two seconds, and the second four minutes and forty-eight seconds," explained the writer. "The crowd began hooting and groaning, and whistled the 'dead march' in derision. After fifteen minutes of this, the contestants were given two minutes to rest. The manager of the show dismissed the men from the ring after saying they agreed to call it a draw."

To be fair, *The Philadelphia Inquirer* countered the claims of the rival reporter by contending that the Winter Circus contest was "strictly on the level, despite the assertion to the contrary by a local sportswriter." Nonetheless, the refusal by *The Inquirer* to declare the match a sham rested upon the reputation of Roeber, who was "well known in this city" and against whom "suspicions of engaging in 'fake' matches" had never been cast. The publication neglected to mention how Ross had been one of the premier targets of such accusations for more than a decade.

In September, *The Chicago Tribune* published an editorial mourning the decline of professional wrestling, and in doing so, positioned a familiar Scotsman as a culprit behind its demise, while pinning a portion of the hope for the restoration of the sport upon another.

"A few years ago wrestling was one of the most popular of sports, and a meeting between two noted exponents of the art was certain to attract large crowds," began *The Tribune*. "But, like others, the wrestlers have themselves killed the goose that laid the golden eggs, and have by their crooked work and hippodrome tactics disgusted the public. I used to think that Evan Lewis was a square wrestler, and I even hesitated to believe that there was anything wrong in the match in which he was last winter defeated by Farmer Burns. I have since changed my opinion, however, and have now the best of reasons for believing that match was about as crooked as any that Duncan C. Ross, that prince of hippodromers, ever indulged in."

The writer of the editorial based his assumption of Lewis' misdeeds on the fact that Burns was rumored to not even have received a penny's worth of payment for his win, "having to be content with the prestige that a so-called victory over Lewis gave him." The writer then referred to a source who illustrated for him how Lewis was "hired to wrestle and throw the match by three professional gamblers," and that Lewis had used that money to purchase a new home on a farm in Ridgewood, Wisconsin.

"This being the case, it is not difficult to see why Farmer Burns has thus far refused to be drawn into a match with (Dan) McLeod, who is believed by good judges to rank next to Lewis as a wrestler of the first class," added the writer. "McLeod is after a reputation, and as he cannot be cajoled into laying down for Burns, the latter does not care for any of his game, preferring to make hay while the sun shines out of the reputation as a champion that he now enjoys. I am sorry to have my delusions regarding the honesty of Lewis shattered. I did believe that there was one square wrestler in the world. Now I confess I have my doubts on the subject and grave doubts too they are. A pity 'tis true."

That same month, a public family altercation betrayed the fact that not all was well within the Ross household, along with the fact that Ross' penchant for significantly younger women had remained intact a full decade after his scandal with Eva Hurlburt had played out in the San Francisco press.

The New York Evening World conveyed the embarrassing story of how "Duncan Claverhouses Ross," whose weight had ballooned to 250 pounds according to the report, had his new wife Mamie Ross, who was 24 years old and weighed 110 pounds, arrested for assault.

"Policeman McQuade of the Old Slip station, was meditatively pacing his lonely post in deserted lower Broadway at 10 o'clock last night when loud cries for the 'watch' made him quicken his pace towards Fulton street," began *The Evening World*'s account. "There he found 'Mousie' belaboring the mighty Scotch athlete and his 15-year-old son, Charles C. Ross, tall and athletic, too, with her silk umbrella."

It was Duncan Ross who had been yelling for the officer and demanded that his wife be "immediately arrested" for the assault upon his son, and McQuade obliged him. The intoxicated Mamie Ross was taken directly to the Oak street station where she languished until she could be brought to court "to answer the heinous charge of brutal assault upon her husband and his son by his first wife."

The younger Ross, who was reported in other publications to have been 17 years old rather than 15, had apparently been home from school and preparing to enter the U.S. Naval Academy.

The Evening World reporter described the diminutive Mamie Ross as "under five feet in height" with "hair of raven hue" and "big black eyes that sparkle like diamonds." She was bedecked in "a black and white check gown, with black moire silk yoke and big sleeves." At that stage of the evening, the gown was "spotted and soiled."

"Oh, my life with Duncan Ross has been miserable," she cried. "He does not treat me well, as you see. If he can afford this sort of thing, I can't. We were married in England two years ago when he arrived there at the close of his triumphal tour around the world."

A short time later, Ross entered the room to confront his wife, and he was described as a "towering form" clad in "a double-breasted cutaway suit of black cheviot," carrying "a big white sombrero in his right hand," and the jewelled symbol of "an extremely exclusive and highly expensive secret society" dangled in front of his waistcoat. He announced to the assembled reporters that he was "engaged just now in the Cuban rebellion" before turning to address his wife.

"You'd better keep your mouth shut!" He threatened. "You've made yourself notorious enough now. It isn't you; it's *me* that's injured by this racket. I've got some friends in New York and elsewhere, and this will hurt me with them. You keep still!"

"Oh you have!" she replied, mockingly. "Here is the great and only Duncan Ross, whose boast is that he was never beaten, and he complains that I beat him! How grand is the spectacle!"

Highland Games and Hippodromes

Ross responded by threatening to ship his wife back to England, to which she reminded him that she had been a famous bareback rider in England before marrying him, and that he had wasted all of her money "on liquor and gambling."

When the couple finally appeared in court, Mamie Ross testified on the record that her husband was the person who had attacked her with the umbrella first, and that she had merely pulled it away from him and struck him back in self defense. Judge Wentworth asked her to simply return to the courthouse if Ross ever assaulted her again so that the court could issue a warrant for his arrest.

Ross and his wife turned to leave, but upon reaching the corridor outside the courtroom, Ross wheeled around and shouted threats at Judge Wentworth on the basis that he had essentially sided with Mamie in the matter and presumed it to be true that Ross had abused her in public.

The Evening World concluded its coverage of the matter with a prediction that Mamie Ross' bareback-riding persona of "Viola Rivers" would soon be reappearing in England, because she professed to be leaving Ross immediately.

In *The New York Sun*'s coverage of the incident, Ross' wife added the claim that he was in possession of $3,000 of her money, and she wanted it returned to her.

Early in 1896, a massive exposé in *The Inter Ocean* revealed the lengths to which Farmer Burns, with Duncan McMillan as his accomplice, had stooped to hippodrome the people of Minneapolis. The bulk of the accusations made against Burns stemmed from his "latest successful attempt at confidencing a confiding public" in Graceville, Minnesota, which he "burned up" alongside McMillan, who had been working under the alias "H.F. Rundell."

Posters featuring the images of Farmer Burns and Eugen Sandow had been plastered all over Graceville for weeks prior to the event. McMillan had allegedly arrived in the town two weeks ahead of Burns, where no one knew who he was. To initiate the deception, McMillan, operating under his alias of Rundell, gathered together the betting men of Graceville and convinced them that he was a competent wrestler "and announced that he would challenge Burns."

Burns obliged and accepted the challenge of Rundell, and when the world champion arrived in Graceville, Burns and McMillan retreated to hotels and training facilities at opposite ends of town, and made a tremendous show of pretending they had no familiarity with one another.

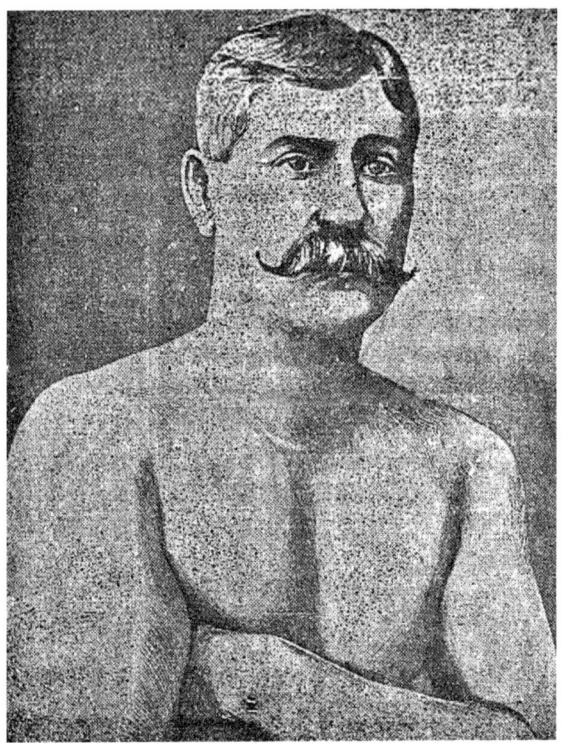

"H.F. Rundell," AKA Duncan McMillan

"It was with the greatest difficulty that the rivals were kept apart when they met on Main Street," stated *The Inter Ocean*. "They snarled at each other, sent emissaries to meet emissaries and wager large wads of money on their chances, and kept the columns of the local weekly aflame with derisive taunts and charges of cowardice. All the while, the good people of Graceville were figuratively breaking their necks to get at those $1, $2, and $3 seats."

"Mr. Rundell" was observed to place no money on the final result of the match, except that he would win the first fall, and that he would also gain a fair fall in less time than Burns would. On the night of the bout, everyone of significance in the town of Graceville made an appearance, including the village board, the justice of the peace, the county road commissioner, the town clerk, the sheriff, and the marshal.

The match played out as though Rundell had a peerless sense of clairvoyance. He won the first fall with a hammerlock and body hold "amid the wildest sort of uproar," and by doing so "won the money that the dense ones of Graceville had laid to the contrary."

"Then 'Farmer' Burns won two falls straight," continued *The Inter Ocean*. "The last one was won in less than five minutes, and the Graceville sports who had Burns for the quickest fall felt their money was secure. It was — for just ten minutes. Immediately after the rest which followed the second fall that Burns had won, the men went at each other, and in three and one-half minutes Burns found that an impending financial crisis made it imperative for three points of his wrestling anatomy to touch the mattress."

Because Burns so rapidly succumbed to the force exerted against him in the fourth round, "Mr. Rundell again pocketed the gold of Graceville sports." From there, Burns waited "just long enough to 'cinch' the quick-fall money for 'Rundell'" before finally winning the match and retaining his world championship.

Other newspapers presented an alternative introduction to the report to heap additional shame onto Burns. They implied that Dan McLeod had been doing his level best to secure a legitimate world championship match with Burns, while Burns and McMillan had been resorting to "wrestling tricks" and "skinning suckers with fake matches" in small towns where they could fly beneath the radar.

Highland Games and Hippodromes

The fact is that McMillan did not always work in cahoots with Burns when making appearances under the Rundell name. Prior to the Graceville scandal, McMillan wrestled as "H.F. Rundell, a Montana heavyweight" at the Spooner Opera House of Morris, Minnesota in early December 1895.

On that night, McMillan had accepted a challenge that he could not defeat five different amateur wrestlers in less than an hour. In spite of these plans, only four men materialized to go against "Rundell," resulting in the further stipulation that the man who held out the longest against McMillan during their initial tussle would be granted the honor of facing him again in the fifth round if he lasted that long.

Of the four "amateurs" slated to meet Rundell, one of them — Charles Uhl — was a trained, professional wrestler who was well known in some parts of the country, although apparently not in Morris. As such, two things should come as no surprise. First, that McMillan was able to manhandle three wrestlers who were probably untrained, beating one of them in as little as 23 seconds, and second, that Uhl lasted 10 minutes during his initial run at Rundell.

The fact that Uhl wrestled first, and that McMillan dragged one of the remaining opponents to nine minutes and 46 seconds worth of wrestling automatically raises suspicions that there wasn't a side bet placed with respect to who would qualify to wrestle Rundell in the final round of the night.

By securing the opportunity to wrestle Rundell in two of the five falls, including the last fall, Uhl was able to guarantee that the bout went to its desired conclusion by cooperating with Rundell in the final round, which lasted for 17 minutes until it arrived at its inevitable conclusion with a Rundell victory.

It was then that Rundell faced the other professional wrestler working that night: the referee for the five-bout challenge, lightweight champion of the Northwest James Powers. The wager on the table was that McMillan would be able to defeat the smaller Powers in less than 15 minutes.

"Rundell worked the hardest he ever did, but he was scientifically met at every point and trick by the slippery lightweight, which afforded no end of amusement and applause from the audience," recounted *The Morris Tribune*. "As the time drew near the cheers came faster, and when time was called at the end of fifteen minutes with Rundell not having floored Powers, the audience simply went wild. The two men were surrounded by their many friends, who extended congratulations in their efforts to subdue their opponents."

Perhaps because their scheme to bilk the gamblers of unsuspecting small towns out of thousands of dollars was exposed, McMillan and Burns parted ways for a time. Still, despite the controversy, McMillan continued to work his way through the Dakotas in the late winter and early spring of 1896, under the names of both "H.F. Rundell" and "C.F. Howard."

In Fargo, "Rundell" defeated J.F. Schoenborn of Butte by capturing seven falls from him in under an hour, while Schoenborn "acted on the defensive through the match, making no effort to throw his heavier opponent," according to *The Fargo Forum*. Then in Wahpeton, Rundell defeated Frank S. Lewis four times in under 50 minutes, but then withdrew from the match, "his left wrist being lame," certainly disappointing those who accepted the bet that Rundell would defeat Lewis five times in under one hour.

As the winter of 1896 neared, either McMillan was uncharacteristically willing to reveal his true identity to the inhabitants of the Dakotas, or he had been found out. Either way, no one seemed to care about the deception very much, as it was very casually mentioned that McMillan had wrestled in Fargo earlier that year under the name Rundell, "and at the Forks under the name of Howard."

With his real name out in the open, McMillan continued to work under his pseudonyms all the while alongside Uhl and Schoenborn in the various towns around the Dakotas.

Temporarily removed from his position at the side of Farmer Burns, McMillan had proved that he could still hippodrome with the best of them. Within a year, he would be back at the side of Farmer Burns, and just in time for the most meaningful coronation of a Scottish wrestler to date.

Highland Games and Hippodromes

17 – Looking for Easy Game

When a title match against Farmer Burns failed to manifest itself, Dan McLeod made it a point to spend 1896 targeting the rest of the grapplers who were often mentioned in the same breath as himself and the Farmer. This effort commenced in January with back-to-back matches against Ed Atherton and Strangler Lewis.

In Cleveland, McLeod lost the first round to Atherton in 21 minutes, but *The Plain Dealer*'s coverage of the bout treated Atherton's victory like it was a fluke, and clarified that Atherton "did not at any time look like a winner." McLeod won the latter two falls in 32 minutes to leave Cleveland with a clear-cut victory over one of the most respected names in wrestling.

The Cleveland Leader echoed the sentiments of its competitor, stating that "it looked as though McLeod ought to throw Atherton with little or no trouble," but also attached the consideration that McLeod was heavier than Atherton, "and therefore the better wrestler" because "there is nothing that tells the tale quicker than weight."

The long-awaited rematch between McLeod and Evan Lewis was burdened by a stipulation that led to an unsatisfying ending. The two elite wrestlers with title aspirations were only scheduled to wrestle for 15 minutes at Miner's Eighth Avenue Theater in New York City, and Lewis was the only wrestler incentivized to attempt any pinfalls.

"The conditions of the bout were that Lewis was to receive $100 if McLeod was thrown in fifteen minutes, or $25 for his labor if he could not throw him within that time," stated the syndicated report. "After fifteen minutes of intense excitement the bout was declared a draw, and the audience went into a furor of cheers and exclamations over the result."

Just days after Lewis and McLeod had their draw in New York, the sports section of *The Buffalo Express* published an anonymously sourced account about a double-cross that

McLeod attempted either with or against a man named "Mahon" in the town of Ingersoll, Ontario, near London.

According to the report, McLeod attempted his old trick of "masquerading under an alias," and wrestled Mahon in a two-hour bout that ended in a draw. According to *The Express*, this was all a ruse to convince Mahon that the two men were evenly matched. Therefore, when McLeod addressed the audience at the end of the bout and proposed that he would return in a few evenings to pin Mahon five times in an hour, the crowd thought he had gone loony.

This was only one aspect of the deception. Behind the scenes, McLeod's manager had supposedly presented Mahon with a story about how he was being mistreated by his client, and desired to get even. Instead of signing a contract requiring McLeod to pin Mahon five times in one hour, he affixed his signature to a contract that required McLeod to pin Mahon five times in just 15 minutes.

"All the time, McLeod knows that he is capable of throwing the Canadian 15 times in 15 minutes, and the match is like finding money for him," said *The Express*. "By and by, he pretends to get on the fact that the time in the articles has been changed, and to square his manager makes a great bluff, but of course the articles are signed and he will take a chance anyway."

According to the story, McLeod's true identity was outed before the match occurred, and the double-cross never took place. While this story is extremely far-fetched, there is a more likely scenario submerged within the more fantastical version of events.

The far likelier scenario is that McLeod wrestled under a pseudonym with the knowledge and cooperation of Mahon — or whatever his true name was — in order to con the bettors of the small town into wagering big money against McLeod so that he and his team could rake in the whole pot.

As the top contender to the world heavyweight championship, McLeod would have suffered untold reputational damage if he was extended to a two-hour time-

Highland Games and Hippodromes

limit draw with a small-time opponent. Beyond that, if he executed the same pattern of matches under his real name against an opponent without a stellar reputation, it would have been one of the most obvious hippodromes on record. No one would believe that a wrestler could struggle for two hours to score a pin on an opponent, and then pin that same opponent five times in 15 minutes — or even one hour — during the very next outing.

In short, the story told by *The Express* at least advances the idea that McLeod was engaged in a hippodroming hustle that could elude detection as long as he remained outside of the large markets where he could be recognized, and at the time, that consisted of nearly the entire eastern half of the North American continent.

As far as the media coverage of dignified wrestling was concerned, McLeod's reputation was only continuing to blossom. *The Chicago Times-Herald* advised Farmer Burns that he needed "to do some bona fide wrestling or quit the business," and was apparently under the impression that Burns had already forfeited the world championship to McLeod by refusing to make a match with him for so long.

Burns' reluctance to face McLeod, combined with McLeod's growing reputation for being a ferocious, sawed-off Hercules, led *The Buffalo Express* to surmise that McLeod had pressed Evan Lewis for a championship match so aggressively that the Strangler "was compelled to make a match with Burns and allow himself to be thrown, knowing that Burns would avoid a meeting with McLeod by hook or by crook."

Soon thereafter, McLeod was officially promoted as the world heavyweight champion for his matches in portions of Ohio, as if he was annexing territory from Burns one city at a time. Curiously, McLeod brought Ed Atherton along with him to these events in Ohio, and the two were advertised as part of the same promotional package, in a manner akin to Burns and McMillan.

One month later, in April 1896, *The Express* explained how McLeod's touring combination with Atherton had been dissolved, and that Atherton had returned home to Rochester and proceeded to "make cracks" about McLeod's wrestling ability not being as good as advertised.

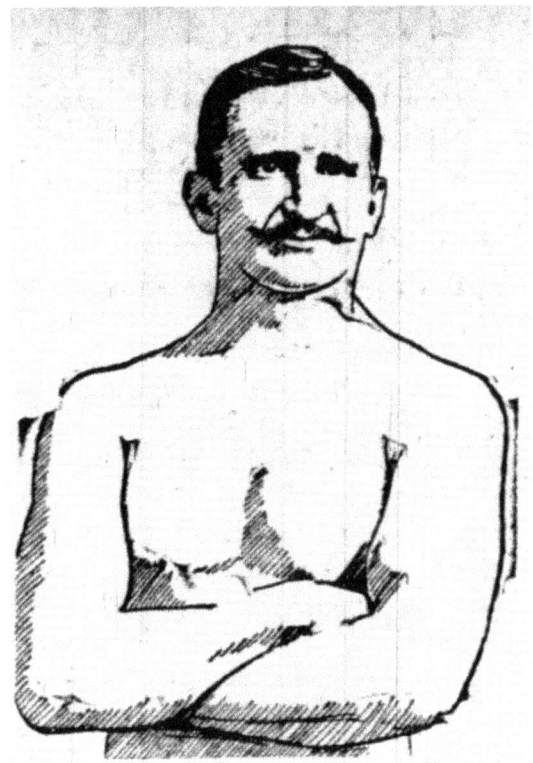

Ed Atherton

As a test to see if this was true, and to acquire evidence to wield against Atherton, McLeod attested that he sent J.H. McCormick and Harvey Parker under cover to make a match with Atherton, who signed the contract, but then "smelt a rat and demanded the name of the opponent."

"He's an unknown," said Harvey Parker, who signed the articles for the unknown.

"I'll wrestle any man at the weight, but I won't wrestle Dan McLeod," stipulated Atherton.

Highland Games and Hippodromes

This apparently pleased McLeod, who was now satisfied that Atherton respected his skills. Nevertheless, news of this incident supposedly received enough diffusion through Rochester that the wrestling fans in the area were "at a loss to account for Atherton's showing 'backdown,'" and McLeod was said to carry with him a copy of the agreement that Atherton signed before he chickened out and declined to wrestle him.

Temporarily done with Atherton, McLeod returned to Cleveland in May to wrestle against up-and-coming wrestling star Tom Jenkins, who was quickly becoming the king of wrestling in his home state of Ohio. Positioned as a star on the level of Burns and McLeod, Jenkins had installed himself as the leading wrestler in the valuable network established by Duncan Ross that extended from Cleveland to Rochester.

Tasked with defeating Jenkins twice in one hour in order to claim victory, the advertised world champion McLeod did more than anyone preceding him to accelerate the rise of Jenkins by failing to pin him a single time during their tangle at the Star Theater.

Two weeks later, McLeod, who had supposedly trained himself down to 158 pounds, returned to Rochester to wrestle his former associate Ed Atherton for the latter's claim on the middleweight championship for the world. McLeod was described to have looked "somewhat weakened by coming to weight, but his superiority was plainly evident."

"It took [McLeod] 28 minutes and 20 seconds to get the first fall, and the intermission was fifteen minutes in length," printed *The Elmira Gazette and Free Press*. "It was the work of 12 minutes and 27 seconds to gain another fall, and during that time Atherton was on the defensive all the while."

"A great deal of money" reportedly changed hands as a consequence of McLeod's straight-falls victory for the world middleweight championship, which therefore gave him loose claims to world titles in two different weight divisions.

Proving that he had not left his penchant for Caledonian competition back in San Francisco, McLeod made an appearance at the August Scottish games in Kenmore, New

Highland Games and Hippodromes

York. McLeod was not a regular competitor at the games, but was invited to observe them as a spectator by his friends John Slocum and Peter Forrestel.

Still, McLeod was very much in shape for such an event. His workout had been previously described by *The Rochester Democrat and Chronicle* as a daily regimen of weight training, medicine ball throws, wrestling, and running, which meant that his strength, power, and conditioning were always adequately maintained even when he wasn't actively training for Highland events specifically.

The Buffalo Express made it clear, in very colorful terms, that McLeod "had not gone to make a hog-killing with the innocents," but he still wished to compete in some events, and was disappointed to learn that he could not compete in the throwing contests because they were closed to non-members of the St. Andrew's Scottish Society.

Demonstrating his personal fondness for wagering money, McLeod approached Alex Collie, the winner of the shot put event, and bet him $10 on the spot that he would be able to better his mark by a full 10 feet as soon as the competition ended. Fortunately for the wallet of either McLeod or Collie, the officials in charge of the event cleared the shot-putting zone before an agreement could be reached.

At the hammer throwing event, McLeod was unable to resist inserting himself into the action when he saw that the winning light hammer toss of Duncan McDonald landed far short of McLeod's average efforts, so he appealed to the officials to give him a chance to display his power.

"The officials of the grounds consented to an exhibition, and the sturdy little Scot bared himself for the effort," illustrated *The Express*. "Then came the first surprise for the spectators. McLeod is a small man, about five feet six inches high, but the sight of his powerful chest, 47 inches span, paralyzed the assemblage. Twice around his head the light hammer flew, and then away it started on an aerial flight."

McLeod's casual toss with the light hammer landed 110 feet away, bettering the official winning mark of the day by

Highland Games and Hippodromes

nearly 40 feet. Following this display, there were "many requests for an introduction to McLeod," and in a situation that was said to be "not unusual among a crowd of Scotchmen," McLeod was introduced to more than one person at the event who was also named "Dan McLeod."

Two weeks after this Highland Games event in Kenmore, McLeod defeated Atherton in yet another Rochester wrestling match, except this one had a controversial finish. As McLeod had promised to defeat Atherton three times in an hour to win the match, it appeared as if he might not succeed since it took him more than 30 minutes to win the first fall. The tone of the match suddenly shifted when it was announced that Atherton had vomited in his dressing room during the intermission.

When the bout resumed, Atherton didn't look nearly as vibrant as he had in the first round, and after losing the second round in less than 10 minutes, it was reported that Atherton had vomited once again, and had withdrawn from the match, conceding the final fall to McLeod.

Two weeks later, *The Express* reported that the Atherton-McLeod bout had concluded in a double-cross, although it couldn't decide exactly who had been cheated.

"There are very persistent stories circulating in certain local resorts to the effect that this match was arranged to be a hippodrome, despite the apparent bitterness between the two men," said *The Express*. "There was no money up on the side or at least only a small amount, for there was $50 a side up, and it was alleged to be arranged that McLeod was to allow Atherton to win, 'to hold him up,' in the parlance of the knights of the mat. There was only a small house at the match, and it is difficult to see where the money that would have rewarded the wrestlers was to come from, unless in side bets, with the unsuspecting."

The Express contended that there should have been "lots of Atherton money in sight," yet on the night of the match "McLeod money went begging," which was a situation that was rather difficult to explain in light of the belief by the insiders that Atherton was slated to win the match.

"Even some of those who thought they were on the inside are at a loss to understand who has been double-crossed in this match," a prominent local gambler explained to an *Express* correspondent. "That someone was double-crossed must be a fact, when it is known that McLeod was understood to believe that he would lose instead of winning the match.

"There are two solutions to the problem. One is that McLeod and Atherton stood in on the deal and that while the report was spread that McLeod was to win, inside money went the other way all the time. The other solution is that the men agreed to have Atherton win the match, McLeod to throw him twice in an hour, and then fail to get the third fall in the prescribed time, but that Atherton, seeing a chance to get even with his rival, had his friends gobble all the McLeod money and then put it out of the power of McLeod to carry out his part of the agreement by failing to stay on the mat and compelling a decision in the other man's favor. I am inclined to the first solution, owing to the fact that there was little demand for the McLeod money on the night of the match, everyone seeming to fancy the stranger."

For the remainder of the year, McLeod toured the Midwest accepting and winning bouts in which he was the evident favorite, but complaining at times that the wrestling business seemed to be "in a pretty bad way," because there was "little interest in the sport just now." McLeod offered this opinion to a reporter from *The Kentucky Post* after being spotted at the Palace Hotel in Cincinnati wearing a button in support of Republican presidential candidate William McKinley.

One of the reasons for this perceived downturn in the popularity of wrestling, aside from the constant suspicion of hippodromes, was the fact that there had been a lack of interaction between the wrestlers believed to have been the best, with the lion's share of the public blame for this quagmire was laid at the feet of Farmer Burns.

Highland Games and Hippodromes

In October, *The Chicago Chronicle* agreed that Burns "has not had a serious match since he defeated Evan Lewis for the championship of catch-as-catch can." In response, Burns admitted that he was "looking for easy game," and confessed that he thought McLeod would be a very difficult opponent to defeat. All the same, the accused champion agreed that he would wrestle McLeod somewhere close to his own home in Iowa, and insisted that he wouldn't even think about wrestling a championship match in Chicago "because expenses would be too large and receipts too small."

This admission was enough incentive for even more Midwestern sportswriters to condemn Burns and throw their support behind McLeod. *The Cincinnati Enquirer* outright declared McLeod to be "by all rights and usages, the champion catch-as-catch-can wrestler of the world," and justified the claim by saying that when "an alleged champion like Burns… tacks on a condition that he will wrestle no place except his own town, he deserves to forfeit."

After publicly dominating and "making a plaything" of Ed Atherton yet again in late January 1897, McLeod's claim to being the *real* world heavyweight champion received even more backing when *The Inter Ocean* of Chicago printed an illustration of McLeod and captioned him as "Heavy-weight catch-as-catch-can champion of the world, by reason of Martin Burns' evasion of a match." *The Inter Ocean* also included a dig at the manner in which Burns acquired the title, saying that Burns only "won" the world heavyweight championship due to "a lay-down" by Evan Lewis.

As if on schedule, Duncan McMillan reemerged in the spring of 1897 in his familiar haunts, touching off what could retroactively be considered a rather bizarre sequence of events that would persist throughout the year. The first step along the way would see McMillan reunited with his former partner Evan Lewis, who was continuing to capitalize on his celebrity and wrestle around the Midwest even though he was no longer the world's catch-as-catch-can champion.

Highland Games and Hippodromes

At the Beloit Opera House, McMillan joined with the city's well-known trainer Johnny Kline to supervise a series of wrestling exhibitions, with McMillan also serving as the timekeeper. Once the preliminary bouts were concluded, McMillan offered a bag-punching exhibition, demonstrating such impressive skill at the endeavor that "his exhibition drew forth applause."

The show ended with a very brief exhibition of catch-as-catch-can wrestling between McMillan and Lewis, which McMillan lost in consecutive falls of eight and seven minutes.

Just days later, McMillan was back in Davenport, Iowa standing next to Farmer Burns — the conqueror of Lewis — as the two appeared before the press and "the well-known Hercules of the mat" promised to personally train Burns for his long-awaited match with Dan McLeod.

"Burns is in fine form and will at once proceed to get in still better condition by a thorough and systematic course of training," assured *The Davenport Times*. "The champion recognizes the fact that McLeod is a wiry man on the carpet and does not hesitate to say that the forthcoming match will be a spirited one from start to finish. At the same time, he has the most unbounded confidence in his own prowess and proposed to put up one of the finest contests of his life. It is certain that the match will be one of the best exhibitions of the kind ever seen in this country, and all indications point to an immense attendance."

A *Times* reporter was even invited to visit the training quarters of Burns at Armory Hall and observed Burns and McMillan training on the mat for half an hour where "they fought with muscles of iron and nerves of steel for the master one of the other." Burns was said to have broken every hold that McMillan could secure upon him, "and with great apparent ease resisted every effort of his big Scotch trainer to put him on his shoulders."

The training room was described as twenty feet square, with a skylight, with hot and cold baths and a shower in adjacent rooms. There was also a room with a punching bag, a pulling machine, a workout mat and a set of six-pound dumbbells.

Farmer Burns displays his grappling prowess

"The Farmer uses the pulling machine for wrist development as well as the development of his brachial muscles," added *The Times*. "After working this appliance, which is simple, the Scott County boy punched the bag for a while until he knocked a hole in it and let the wind out when he was compelled to stop. He then invited the reporter to put on his gloves, but the scribe believed still in his facial beauty and desired to preserve it for still a while longer. Another onlooker put on the mitts, but stopped only two of the Farmer's drives when he asked for a truce.

"Then followed bridge work. That is, the Farmer and his trainer would be down flat on their back and gradually draw their heels and head together under them, forming a bridge, which looks like the letter D resting upon its flat or left side in an inverted position. In this position the head rests upon the floor and the muscles of the neck are largely benefitted. While occupying this ticklish position the Scott county boy kept up a running fire of conversation, continuing the same while actually in the act of turning a handspring or a head spring without any interruption whatever. The Farmer is cool and clear-headed and studies every move of his opponent. He has complete control of every muscle and evidenced this to the satisfaction of the reporter."

In the mornings, Burns and McMillan went for 12-mile runs along Locust Street, and maintained a seven-minute mile pace throughout the training period before returning to the gym for dedicated strength work and mat work. Afterwards, Burns was "rubbed down by the Scotchman," and then given a shower, followed by a hot bath and a cold bath.

In parting, Burns said that he expected a hard match from McLeod, as he considered "McLeod, Evan Lewis, and Tom Jenkins the best wrestlers in the world."

After several years of wrangling, the match between McLeod and Burns finally took place on May 6, 1897, at the Turner Opera House in Davenport, Iowa.

"The audience that gathered to greet these gladiators was worthy of the fame of these two noted men," opined *The Davenport Daily Republican*. "As early as 7 o-clock the auditorium began to fill, and from that time until the last seat was filled, a constant stream of humanity kept pouring through the doors. The gallery was packed, all the boxes filled, 275 chairs on the stand and the lower floor comfortably filled. A fair estimate of the attendance would be to say that more than 2,000 were present."

McLeod walked onto the stage first, greeted by "a generous share of applause" from what was undeniably a very Burns-friendly crowd. Audience members who had not seen McLeod in person before were surprised by his "enormous chest and arms," which were supported by a pair of legs "which seemed fully in keeping with his upper body."

Then Burns strolled out and took his place on the right of the stage "amid a perfect ovation." *The Daily Republican* reporter noted that Burns was obviously taller and slimmer than his challenger, but his muscles stood out "like whip cords."

In the opening round, McLeod looked every bit like a man capable of becoming the new world heavyweight champion, and after several minutes of leg work, McLeod expertly transitioned into a half nelson and a cross lock that Burns was unable to break free from. After years of waiting for the opportunity, McLeod had taken the first fall of his world-title match with Burns after 27 minutes, and "amid loud cheering" from the Iowa crowd.

Just as reliably as the half nelson had worked for McLeod, it was equally as lethal for Burns. Thirteen minutes into the second round, Burns ensnared McLeod with the same hold, and "with the power seemingly of a giant," yanked McLeod to the floor as the Scotsman was "struggling against fate like mad," and pinned him to even the match.

The third fall of the bout was defined by a pindrop silence that was uncharacteristic of wrestling matches, as the audience "plainly showed its anxiety, not a word being murmured in the vast assemblage as the gladiators grappled."

"Then came the final tackle," wrote *The Daily Republican*. "McLeod made it, and as the wrestlers grappled for the hold, men in the audience forgot to breathe, realizing that the end was near, and as the 'Farmer' went to the floor with the Illinoisan lying fair and square on his back, the audience went wild with enthusiasm and applause. It was all over, and 'Farmer' Burns, 'the husky Iowa boy,' was again victorious in a world's championship wrestle."

Observably bleeding from his cheek, Burns was quickly "hustled into his dressing room" where he was stitched up. Meanwhile, McLeod blamed his loss on poor officiating by referee Ed Westaway, and *The Daily Republican* added a final note that "nearly $3,000" had likely been gambled on the Turner Opera House premises during the match.

Highland Games and Hippodromes

While *The Daily Republican* chose to refer to McLeod as an Illinoisan in its coverage, either due to McLeod's boyhood ties to Illinois or the fact that he was so strongly backed by supporters in Chicago, *The Daily Times* preferred to describe McLeod as a Californian in its coverage.

The Daily Times also lavished an unusual amount of praise upon "the big Scotchman" Duncan McMillan for his role in organizing the Burns-McLeod match, although it somewhat belittlingly mischaracterized the relationship between McMillan and Burns as teacher-student by referring to Burns as "his pupil."

"[McMillan] has put in considerable extra time in connection with the match, and the smoothness with which it passed off, so far as caring for the crowd was concerned, was largely due to his well laid plans," commended *The Times*. "He has had much experience in large events of this nature and therefore proceeded with his work in a methodical way. The stage seats and the press quarters, which were constructed under his supervision, were admirable coigns of vantage and commanded an excellent view of the gladiatorial combat.

"Mr. McMillan planned well, and in staging an affair of this kind as well as arranging all the accessories, his work here shows that he is a past master of the art. It is universally conceded that there was not a flaw in the arrangements for the contest and the way they were carried out is a sufficient indication that Davenport can put on metropolitan airs when occasion demands."

With the McLeod bout behind them, Burns and McMillan proceeded with their exhibitions before preparing to meet the other wrestler who was rapidly rising in the ranks, Tom Jenkins, who continued to fill the void along Lake Erie left vacant by Duncan Ross.

Beginning with Jenkins, a pattern would seemingly develop of McMillan functioning as Burns' underboss, with worthy challengers to Burns' catch-as-catch-can championship first being required to prove their worthiness by defeating

Burns' trainer, who was the world champion of five-styles wrestling in his own right.

Tom Jenkins

Against Jenkins in August, McMillan essentially allowed himself to be obliterated, losing the first fall in nine minutes, the second in 13 minutes, and the third in 10 minutes, without ever appearing to present Jenkins with any sort of respectable threat. He was even highly complimentary of Jenkins, who told *The Cleveland Press* after the fight that McMillan was "a good wrestler," but one who had already "seen his best days."

"This man Jenkins needn't hesitate about going after any wrestler in the world. He's a wonder," McMillan told *The Press* after being swept three falls to zero. McMillan paid

Jenkins the further compliment in heralding him to be "the coming champion of the world," and even added that Jenkins wasn't even appreciated in his hometown of Cleveland "as much as a yellow dog would be."

McMillan revisited his role as championship gatekeeper when he wrestled Daniel McLeod again in September, forcing McLeod to re-establish his candidacy for a future title rematch against Burns.

"'Farmer' Burns, who has 'wrestled 5,000 matches and only lost seven,' rode in a smoking-car from Omaha to Indianapolis, and reached this city just in time to accept the job of referee of the bouts between Dan McLeod and Duncan McMillan at the Grand last night," printed *The Indianapolis News*. "The audience never saw a better wrestling match, and 'Farmer' admitted that it stood on a par with the best he had seen. McMillan weighed 190 pounds, while McLeod weighed 162. McLeod made up for the difference by his remarkable skill and strength. He had a comparatively easy victory."

McLeod fittingly objected to the installation of Burns as the referee for the match, but Burns vowed before the crowd that he would call the match "square," and would declare a fall "when he saw the shoulder blades touch."

Burns was apparently true to his word and remained impartial; McLeod defeated McMillan three falls to one in the battle between the top active Scotsmen in North America.

"Both wrestlers made the usual 'speeches,'" added *The News*. "Burns declared his readiness to meet McLeod in any city in the world except Chicago. Al Roberts was on the stage, but made no effort to challenge either of the big fellows. It is probable a match between Burns and McLeod will be arranged."

Indeed, a rematch between Burns and McLeod was arranged. After McLeod had the entirety of the summer to stew in his regret over losing his title match with Burns, and had then defeated Burns' trainer and consistent co-headliner, McLeod was awarded his rematch at the Grand Opera House of Indianapolis, in a city that had always been predisposed to favor him. Accordingly, the writer from *The Indianapolis Journal*, upon first spying both wrestlers, described McLeod as being aesthetically superior to Burns in almost every way.

"[McLeod] was three pounds lighter than Burns, but appeared to be in better condition, and he presented a better appearance as an athlete," gushed the writer. "His muscles are hard and larger than would be expected upon a man of his weight. Burns is two or three inches taller, but his limbs are almost perfectly straight and there is not the muscular development to which the other man can lay claim."

After 10 minutes in which McLeod was unable to make much progress with his pursuit of a hammerlock, he released the hold and forced Burns to the mat by pulling his legs out from beneath him. McLeod then held the world champion "in a cramped and straining position" with a half nelson and crotch hold for two minutes before he was finally able to get both of Burns' shoulders onto the mat and log the first pinfall of the match.

Burns was able to win the second round by using McLeod's characteristic aggression against him. When McLeod seized Burns' left arm and attempted to work it into a hammerlock position by "running around on his knees in front of Burns," the Farmer instead grabbed McLeod's right arm in a hammerlock of his own, and used it to flatten McLeod in 37 minutes to even the tally.

The third round was a hard struggle, during which McLeod "threw his antagonist about the stage like a dummy." After Burns was thoroughly worn out, McLeod grabbed him in a half nelson, and then pinned Burns with a plain body hold after 17 minutes to finally win the true world championship.

In the dressing room after the bout, the newly minted world champion Dan McLeod stood quietly next to his backer George McKay, who informed the press that McLeod "was willing to meet any wrestler, at any time, and for any amount of money."

Speaking of money, *The Journal* also informed the public that McLeod was the betting favorite at 10-to-8 odds going into the match, although some of the bets were taken at 2 to 1. Furthermore, *The Journal* also reported of a rumor that circulated during the afternoon of the bout that the affair was "fixed as wrestling matches usually are." Moreover, the prediction that was disseminated through the rumor turned out to be uncannily accurate.

"The rumor not only had the result of the match as it was, but went so far as to say that McLeod was to win the first and third bouts, and that the second bout was to be the longest, to give the people a 'run for their money,'" said *The Journal*. "Along with this rumor floated the report that a prominent betting man had $4,000 on McLeod, of which $2,000 was money belonging to Burns. The match had not the appearance of being other than a hard contest for victory between the two wrestlers."

Rumors of hippodroming notwithstanding, the undersized Dan McLeod had struck a monumental blow for Scottish immigrants by capturing the most important wrestling championship on the North American continent.

More to the point, McLeod's acquisition of the championship capped a solid decade in which the world title traveled from the son of Welsh immigrants to the son of Irish immigrants, and then to the son of Scottish immigrants. Observing this pattern, it would have been reasonable to say that the road to the world heavyweight wrestling championship ran through the Celtic nations.

As meritorious as the occasion was, its significance to the general public was about to be severely cheapened. Within a year, the unforeseen invasion of the North American pro wrestling circuit by a "terrible" set of adversaries would be so disruptive that it would cause almost everyone to rethink McLeod's standing in the wrestling business, and his right to call himself a world champion.

Highland Games and Hippodromes

18 – The Terrible Turk

After Dan McLeod relieved Farmer Burns of the world heavyweight championship, Duncan McMillan closed out 1897 with an October bout against Frank Gehle in Piqua, Ohio, two falls to one in a catch-as-catch-can contest before heading off for a fall tour of Wisconsin. This turned out to be one of the locations that McMillan's reputation apparently preceded him, as multiple Wisconsin newspapers printed what amounted to a warning about McMillan's presence, and cautioned wrestling fans that he had "been in many queer matches" and had "not yet forgotten how to fix things to suit himself."

With Farmer Burns now separated from any claim to a world championship, *The Davenport Daily Times* — Burns' home state newspaper — insisted that Burns was still the *real* world champion based on the premise that Burns' strong suit was his remarkable endurance. Accounting for that, McLeod's refusal to face Burns in a best-of-five contest had thereby negated Burns' natural advantage.

It would be on this basis that Tom Jenkins would begin claiming to be the rightful world heavyweight champion in January 1898 when he defeated Burns in Cleveland by winning three straight falls while surrendering none, to effectively sweep Burns completely out of the world title conversation.

In the meantime, a serious wild card had landed in North America, and was tossed directly into the championship mix. The 300-pound Yusuf Ismail, commonly referred to as "The Terrible Turk," arrived in North America early in 1898. As a representative of the Ottoman Empire, Ismail projected size and strength that was far superior to any of the North American wrestlers active during the time.

Also, as a Muslim Turk from a nation that was perceived as an incessant threat to the Western world, Ismail effectively laid the blueprint for menacing foreign bad guys — or "heels" — in the wrestling world, without truly doing anything other than being himself.

Highland Games and Hippodromes

When Ismail began to issue challenges to opponents in mixed-style bouts, McLeod readily agreed to accommodate the Turk, who made himself an even greater attraction when he was seen to have injured Ernest Roeber in front of 9,000 extremely hostile fans — some of whom reportedly yelled "Lynch the Turk!" — at Madison Square Garden in New York City.

Yusuf Ismail

No match between McLeod and Ismail ever materialized, but Ismail was part of a sequence of events that confounded professional wrestling historians for decades. On May 5, 1898, Ismail defeated Tom Jenkins in front of the latter's hometown audience in Cleveland, handing Jenkins the first undeniable loss of his career.

Highland Games and Hippodromes

By virtue of this victory, Ismail inherited Jenkins' highly disputed claim to the catch-as-catch-can championship of the world, even though Dan McLeod was generally regarded as the world heavyweight champion everywhere other than the Lake Erie corridor that Jenkins controlled.

The situation grew even murkier when Ismail defeated Evan Lewis in front of 10,000 fans in New York City for what was advertised as a mixed-style world championship match, but which was *not* contested for a world championship with a traceable lineage. However, the massive publicity connected to the bout led many people reading sports pages around the U.S. to conclude that Yusuf Ismail truly was the undisputed world champion of all styles — including catch-as-catch-can — heading into the summer of 1898.

That's when an unfathomable tragedy occurred. Early in the morning, on July 4, 1898, the French ocean liner La Bourgogne collided with the British ship Cromartyshire 60 miles from Sable Island, east of Nova Scotia in the Atlantic Ocean. Only 165 of La Bourgogne's 725 passengers were rescued, and Yusuf Ismail was among the missing.

In the wake of Ismail's death, some members of the press became exceedingly vicious once the tale circulated that Ismail could have saved himself had he not insisted on attempting to swim while retaining possession of a leather belt around his waist that contained "gold coins to the amount of $8,500." One editorial in particular, from *The Enterprise* of La Farge, Wisconsin, devoted an uncomfortable amount of space to interrogating the deceased Turk's weight and dining habits.

"Yusuf was not a nice man with whom to dine, for he had his own ideas as to table deportment," offered *The Enterprise*. "The ideas revolved mainly about his fingers, and he was ambidextrous as far as feeding himself was concerned. If Yusuf had been a centipede he would have been happy, because he probably could have fed himself faster. He ate 20 meals a day. Three things worried him always, his hunger, his lack of four hands, and his money belt.

"These are some of the characteristics of the strange, powerful man who went down with La Bourgogne. Add to these an irascible temper and you have Ismail Yusuf, Turk, wrestler, glutton, miser, dead man."

The loss of North American professional wrestling's preeminent box office attraction was a minor casualty in light of the catastrophe, but the sudden disappearance of Ismail undeniably made it more difficult for many people to apprehend who the rightful world heavyweight champion of catch-as-catch-can wrestling truly was.

Make no mistake about it: In July 1898, Dan McLeod was *still* the lineal world heavyweight champion as recognized on U.S. soil, and pretty much everywhere else aside from the minds of Tom Jenkins and his supporters.

Despite this, McLeod was uncharacteristically quiet for nearly the entire remainder of 1898 following some victories over lower-tier opponents in the month of April. Then, Turkish wrestler Abdul Halil Adali — whose name was soon simplified to "Hali Adali" — arrived in New York City to fill the void left vacant by the death of Ismail, which only confused matters even more.

With his height and weight often inflated to dimensions of 6'6" and 300 pounds, Adali was quickly positioned as the focal point of the wrestling world. In November 1898, he crushed Tom Jenkins at Madison Square Garden, more or less replicating the victory over Jenkins that his predecessor Yusuf had enjoyed, albeit in a grander venue.

This act effectively garnered Adali some semblance of unofficial acknowledgement as the interim world heavyweight champion. While McLeod remained out of sight, Farmer Burns offered the statement that he would decline any sort of match with Adali, justifying his position with the reasoning that if Jenkins was no match for the Turk, then certainly neither was he.

Elsewhere, with catch-as-catch-can wrestling becoming the leading style of wrestling, Duncan McMillan had considerable difficulty attracting respectable audiences to attend his mixed-style bouts. That, plus the simple fact that McMillan was not as well known as some of his peers, may have played a role in the small turnout of fans for his bouts in Wisconsin, along with the fact that Wisconsinites had been forewarned specifically about attending McMillan's bouts.

An event headlined by McMillan and W.M. Clark in Wausau, Wisconsin "was not largely attended," but the match still proceeded as scheduled. McMillan took the first and third falls due to his superior "wind and bull strength," and he concluded the action when he "shoved Clark's shoulders to the floor with a bridge."

"D.A. McMillan is probably the most scientific wrestler in the world," glowed *The Wausau Record*. "Endowed with extraordinary strength, he has made a thorough study of the game, and can make the contest extremely doubtful with any man who may go on the mat with him, not barring Evan Lewis, 'Farmer' Burns, or Dan McLeod."

Acknowledging that the professional wrestling world was experiencing a resurgence, another article was published in May 1898 about the downfall of pro wrestling that preceded the recent rise, and it blamed Duncan Ross specifically for the problem. *The Morning Star* of Sandusky declared that wrestling had been one of the greatest sports in the United States, but that it had "retrograded" to such an extent that it was unlikely to ever return to its past zenith.

"Fake matches and hippodromes conducted by dishonest persons for the purpose of wheeling dollars from unsuspecting patrons of the sport and swindling betters on the results have well-nigh killed the wrestling game, which outright should be one of the noblest sports of them all," affirmed *The Morning Star*. "Of all the faking of the wrestling man, Duncan C. Ross stood out prominently. He was to wrestling what Tom Sharkey and Wyatt Earp are to boxing."

First praising Ross for legitimately being the best athlete in the United States during his prime, and then thoroughly overinflating the praise by adding that Ross was "as good a wrestler in his day as ever stepped on the mat," the editorial said that Ross was tempted by friends and followers to throw matches. In short, *The Morning Star* pinned the entirety of the sport's retreat in popularity on Ross, declaring that with Ross's downfall "came the downfall of professional wrestling."

"He made money, and soon of course had many imitators, who sought to grow rapidly wealthy through wrestling 'hippodromes.' But the public soon got 'next' to the game, and wrestling of all kinds for a long time was done for," continued the editorial. "But for a little while back a revival has set in. Ross, though still on earth, is not so much in clover, and is growing old. New aspirants for championship honors have come to the front and quite a galaxy of stars are now helping to revive interest in wrestling."

Doubtlessly, the article can be blamed for mistakenly crediting Ross with wielding entirely too much power and influence, not to mention the fact that it ascribed far stronger wrestling ability to Ross than he actually possessed by implying that the only way Ross could possibly have lost a bout was if he had intentionally thrown it.

Over and above that, the article represents a rare case in which Ross was unfairly blamed for the effects of his hippodroming, if only because he was cited as the sole cause for the downfall of wrestling, as if there weren't clear-cut and admitted examples of hippodroming by other top-tier stars of the profession.

Among the wrestlers *The Morning Star* urged fans to invest hope in were Evan Lewis, Ed Atherton, Farmer Burns, Tom Jenkins, and Dan McLeod.

Unbelievably, Ross was still not quite finished wrestling in high-profile settings. As Hali Adali continued his reign as the second of the "Terrible Turks," Ross was brought in to challenge the successor to the title of the top foreign threat in the history of North American wrestling.

The two men met at the Empire Theater of Indianapolis in December 1898, and *The Indianapolis Journal* focused the early portion of its article to detailing what Adali was alleged to eat on a daily basis.

Highland Games and Hippodromes

"It is said that Mr. H. Adali only eats two or three porterhouse steaks, and four or five dozen eggs, and eight or nine bushels of potatoes, and two or three barrels of bread at one meal," opened *The Journal*, as it worked its way to the punchline. "This must be a mistake. Adali can surely eat a whole beef, and a whole potato patch, and a whole bakeshop, bakers and all, at one sitting, and then go out and drink a brewery to wash the meal down.

Hali Adali

"He is so big that he keeps getting bigger the longer you look at him. If a man would come suddenly upon him after a night with the boys, and Adali had his working clothes on, or, rather, didn't have any clothes on to speak of, which is his working attire, that man would never, never drink again. To see him when you are sober is enough to make you see things in the dark for a week to come. Wrestling with him must be something like trying to push over the Statehouse."

Continuing, the paper added that Ross was the first grappler to be introduced and "showed up in fine form" at a weight of 250 pounds. Either this was a mistake, since other reporters had described Ross as "fat" whenever he weighed more than 220 pounds, or this was simply stated in relation to the appearance of Adali, who weighed more than 300 pounds and "dwarfed" Ross by comparison. The very sight of Adali was said to arouse curious interest, "as if he were a big fat beef trotted out for inspection."

The actual match was an easy victory for Adali, as Ross could do absolutely nothing with him during the first fall, and his attempts to yank the Turk around had "about the same effect as if he had pulled at a big oak tree."

"The Turk jumped away and brought Ross to his hands and knees. In a minute the Turk had a hammerlock hold and it seemed as if he had the fall, but Ross made a very clear twist and broke loose," described *The Journal*. "Then ensued some smooth work on Ross' part, in which he got away from some apparently hopeless grips, but soon the Turk had a half-Nelson and pinned him to the mat. Time, four minutes."

It could be generously said that Ross "won" the second fall quickly, which was contested in what was described as Ross' "own style"— collar-and-elbow wrestling in a special harness. The terms of the bout dictated that a fall could be awarded if the hold of a man upon his opponent was broken. Seen to be taking advantage of Adali's implied ignorance of the style, Ross threw the Turk over his shoulder, causing Adali to release his hold and thereby concede a fall to Ross in a minute and a half.

If the second round had been crafted with the intention of allowing Ross to technically claim a form of victory over the invincible Turk, the third round appeared to have been formulated to provide Adali with a brutal response. In short order, Adali bested Ross three additional times — while still only being awarded one further fall — to put the icing on an overpowering win.

"The first time was with a half Nelson, and Adamson patted the Turk on the back to signify that the bout was his, but the audience yelled that it wasn't a fall and the men kept on," explained *The Journal*. "Ross wriggled out and the Turk secured a crotch hold in which he pressed Ross' shoulders to the mat fairly, but still Adamson seemed desirous of giving the crowd their money's worth, and Adali had to go after Ross once more.

"This time he brought him over with a hammerlock, followed by a half Nelson and then laid down on him and simply rubbed him into the mat. When the Turk secured the first down on Ross in the third bout, and seemed willing to throw in a few more downs for good measure, Cologne Fennessy, who was standing in the wings, said: 'Well, this match is the Turks' no matter who gets the rest of this bout.'"

The second round against Ross was deemed to be the first fall Adali had ever surrendered during his tour of the United States, while his manager went the further step of saying it was the first fall Adali had ever surrendered in his career. Of course, Ross neglected to include the detail that the fall he captured on Adali had been due to a hold break during a collar-and-elbow bout, and would falsely imply that he had successfully pinned the Turk to the mat during subsequent attempts at self promotion.

While Ross had been seeking another run as a top attraction, Duncan McMillan spent 1898 expanding his capacity as an all-purpose promoter of athletic events. In Ironwood, Michigan, on the border shared between that state's Upper Peninsula and Wisconsin, McMillan even promoted a sprinting event between local men named Dooley and Hogan.

As usual, many wagers were made on the event, and the announcement that the race was stated to be for $200 a side "created some suspicion among the sports," while a "rather small crowd" actually paid admission to watch the two men sprint 100 yards in a one-on-one contest. The event was won rather easily by Dooley.

"Hogan's poor showing is claimed by many to account for rumors of faking," said *The Ironwood News-Record*. "Dooley's performance during the Houghton tournament won for him hosts of friends throughout the county, who would deeply regret that he should engage in any crooked work."

The paper concluded the article by adding that Hogan was "said to have been backed by D.A. McMillan, the well-known promoter of honest sports," which is quite humorous given that a statewide warning about McMillan's promotional dishonesty had been distributed throughout Wisconsin, the border of which was one mile from Ironwood.

In December, McMillan welcomed the long-absent Dan McLeod back to the mat in St. Paul, Minnesota, and made it crystal clear that the lineal world heavyweight champion was capable of bullying wrestlers who were far larger and stronger than he was due to McLeod's unparalleled skills, and also due to his superior conditioning.

When the men stepped to the center of the stage to shake hands, the writer from *The Saint Paul Globe* observed that McMillan "seemed to be out of condition," if only because "his flesh looked soft and his actions were slow," while every muscle in McLeod's body was visible.

McMillan's lack of aesthetic beauty may have been a reflection of how much more time he had been devoting to promotional efforts in lieu of training for wrestling contests. Regardless, the size disparity between the two men was still immense, and the match reestablished McLeod as an inexorable force on the mat.

McLeod won the first two falls over the much larger McMillan in around 30 minutes, which made P.A. Eagan's announcement of a future bout during the break — in which McLeod would throw accomplished wrestler Hjalmar Lundin 10 times in one hour or forfeit everything if Lundin threw him even once — seem like a bet worth taking. Then the third fall began.

Highland Games and Hippodromes

"McMillan again got McLeod in a grapevine and hammerlock, but McLeod slipped away, and the next moment he sent McMillan to the floor and was working to get a hammerlock on him," recorded *The Globe*. "McMillan had a back hold for a moment, but it was of no avail, and McLeod played again for a hammerlock. McMillan now breathed hard and seemed thoroughly exhausted, and in a few minutes McLeod forced him slowly but surely down until Referee Whitmore declared that both shoulders were squarely on the floor, and announced McLeod the winner, in 19:50."

McMillan's only statement after the bout was that he had been beaten fairly and had nothing to complain about, while McLeod expressed that he was "ready to meet any wrestler of his own weight and class, catch-as-catch-can, at any time for any amount of money."

In theory, as the heavyweight champion of the world, McLeod's "own weight and class" would have been unlimited, as heavyweight wrestlers usually didn't place weight restrictions on their opposition. In light of the fact that McLeod had just completed a match in which he was the lighter wrestler, he seemed to be imposing a self-demotion on himself, and signifying a move down in weight class.

If this is an accurate interpretation of what McLeod was attempting to convey, it is more likely than not that Hali Adali's presence on the wrestling scene had something to do with it. Nearly every time the newspaper assessed McLeod's chances at competing with Adali, the idea of a McLeod victory over "Terrible Turk No. 2" was dismissed as ludicrous in light of the height and weight differential between the men.

"What a great fall there will be, my countrymen, when Dan McLeod, the famous athlete and Scotch wrestler, meets the burly Turk No. 2 in a wrestling engagement," joked the editorial page of *The New Orleans Picayune*. "McLeod doesn't carry enough guns to match with the man from the sultan's section of the world, and he should fight shy of bouts with men so much larger than himself. The Scot has the science while the Turk has the weight and strength, and that the latter will tell in the end almost goes without saying."

That McLeod was silently conceding away his claim to the heavyweight championship in some way when making such statements is supported by the press coverage of his eventual meeting with Adali at the St. Paul Athletic Club on the final day of January 1899. *The St. Paul Globe* outright confirmed that McLeod "objects strongly to being classed as a middleweight," even though the terms of the bout itself were rather disrespectful in light of the fact that McLeod was *still* the lineal world heavyweight champion.

The terms of the bout were such that Adali was asked to pin McLeod twice in order to claim victory, while all McLeod needed to do was avoid being pinned for one hour. *The Duluth News* only acknowledged that McLeod was "the champion catch-as-catch-can wrestler *of America*," and referenced the difference of nearly 100 pounds in weight and eight inches in height between the two men.

The betting odds reflected the recognition of the perceived mismatch by the Minnesota gambling community; odds started at 3 to 1 on Adali, "but McLeod's friends were so numerous that the odds dropped to 2 to 1."

It would seem like this was a vote of confidence in McLeod, but given the terms of the bout, it serves as evidence that a greater than expected number of gamblers believed McLeod could ward Adali off adequately enough to avoid being pinned twice, *not* that he would mount any worthwhile offense of his own.

Those who wagered on McLeod went home very happy that evening. Yes, McLeod was pinned in 27 minutes and 16 seconds, but in the second round he managed to remain outside of Adali's reach for the majority of the time.

"The crowd went wild as the referee called time while the men were in a terrific struggle on the mat," illustrated *The Duluth News Tribune*. "The Turk either did not hear the time called or lost his temper, for he gave McLeod a terrific fling against the ropes. Dan jumped up and made a pass at Adali, but the referee and the seconds ran between them and trouble was averted."

To underscore just how much of a mismatch the bout had been presented as, McLeod was lauded for being "the first man who ever succeeded in getting on the Turk's back" even though he failed to gain any advantage beyond that. He was also praised as the best wrestler in the world "outside of the Turk."

Within a month, even though most other publications continued to acknowledge McLeod as the catch-as-catch-can champion of America, *The St. Paul Globe* would downgrade McLeod all the way to "local champion" when discussing the results of the Adali match.

The Globe also added the further vital detail that Duncan McMillan served as McLeod's second during the bout. This would become an interesting element of the bout to reflect on for two reasons. First, because McMillan has seconded three consecutive world champions, and second, because a managerial relationship between Duncan McMillan, Farmer Burns, and Hali Adali may already have been formalized.

The situation surrounding McLeod's status as the world heavyweight champion grew even murkier as the year progressed. In April, a rematch clearly advertised as being "for the championship of the world and $1,000 a side" was signed between McLeod and Burns in St. Paul.

Curiously, while the newspapers maintained that the winner of the match "would be entitled to claim the championship title," most of the media covering the event appeared to go out of their way *not* to identify who the reigning champion was, with *The Davenport Times* making a casual reference to the fact that McLeod had won the most recent title bout between the men, but that the series of matches between them was tied at one apiece.

The description of the bout recorded by *The St. Paul Globe* fails to make any sort of reference to a title being on the line at all during the match, and the bulk of the emphasis was placed on the match's unsatisfying conclusion. McLeod won the first fall in 32 minutes, Burn evened the score in one hour and five minutes, and then confusion reigned.

"Neither contestant went to the mat in the third bout, which commenced at 11:55, both men remaining on their feet throughout its twenty minutes' duration before mutually agreeing to quit," explained *The Globe*. "Burns appeared as fresh as when the match started, but McLeod seemed to have in some degree felt the fatigue. Part of the undetermined bout was pretty from a spectator's standpoint, as the men executed some lively tactics. Once they stopped and smiled at each other, and Burns said something to the referee. This was about 12:10. After ten minutes more they again backed away from each other and both interchanged a few words with Capt. Whitmore, then left the platform, while a shout of 'Fake' went up from all parts of the big hall."

There was lingering controversy over the gate money collected for the third Burns-McLeod match, which seemed to stem from a misunderstanding of what was to happen in the event of a draw vis-à-vis the specific *Police Gazette* rules that governed the match. According to a St. Paul sporting authority, the wrestlers were entitled to 66 percent of the gate receipts no matter how the match ended; the only matter that should have been in question was how that money was distributed between the wrestlers.

Reading between the lines, the greater issue seemed to have been the matter of what happened once the clock struck midnight, which was theoretically the only way in which the bout could have been declared a draw.

"The men could quit at midnight, and the rules, while meaning that they should continue the next day, may be construed as you wish, and if they wanted to agree to a draw the next day they could do so. If they could agree to a draw the next day they could agree to a draw after midnight," elaborated the anonymous sporting authority.

Inserted into the coverage, but likely the matter at the very heart of the issue, was the question of how the decision to rule the bout a draw would have influenced the betting. The only way the match could have reasonably concluded in a draw would have been for the pair to wrestle past midnight, and then agree to a draw by mutual consent.

Had the bout been ruled a "no-contest," all bets would have been off. However, since the official result had been a draw, those who had gambled on the least likely result would have cleaned up financially, while any wager placed on a win or a loss for either fighter would have been deemed a losing bet.

Pragmatically speaking, it's difficult to fathom why two of professional wrestling's biggest stars, locked in a struggle for the heavyweight championship of the world, would consent to a draw with the score knotted and only one round remaining. However, by doing so, both men could have made a financial killing that night if they happened to place third-party wagers that the bout would end in a draw.

In all probability, this is precisely what happened, as the two grapplers ensured that they wrestled safely past the early morning deadline. Therefore, the match would be logged as having officially concluded past midnight according to anybody's pocketwatch.

Ironically, this rather obvious hippodrome between Burns and McLeod was nostalgically previewed in *The Globe* as an event that "recalls the olden days when legitimate sport was at its highest in St. Paul, and when crowds came hundreds of miles to witness any contest of note which came off in this city."

As for the lineal world championship that the two men were officially wrestling for, the shadow of Adali over the wrestling business was so oppressive that even the press in Burns' own home state could scarcely feign interest. *The Davenport Democrat* used quotation marks to mock the idea that the bout was "for the championship of the world," and opined that the match was being called a title contest "in happy obliviousness to the fact that there are terrible Turks and others with whom neither of them would stand a ghost of a show."

Highland Games and Hippodromes

Outside of the wrestling spotlight, McLeod apparently spent his time in Minnesota volunteering his might in service to the community. In May 1899, *The Minneapolis Times* disclosed that McLeod was discovered working as a member of the firefighting team that responded to a blaze at the C.B. Lyon & Bros. paint store at 172 E. 5th Street in St. Paul.

"Several firemen narrowly escaped injury while ascending a ladder to the third floor," said *The Globe*. "One of their number was nearly to the top of the ladder when he dropped an ax. The heavy implement whirled down between the others, but fortunately did not strike anyone. Some of the spectators at the fire who noticed a rather short, heavily built individual in the salvage corps uniform recognized Dan McLeod, the wrestler, in a new guise. McLeod makes the runs with the salvage corps when he is about headquarters and works like a beaver with the other members. He throws a tarpaulin over threatened merchandise as easily as a dining room maid spreads a table cloth."

When the year had opened, Duncan McMillan had been one of the most often-referenced grapplers when discussions were had about who could unseat Hali Adali from his unofficial claim to being wrestling's true world champion. This was owed to McMillan's scarcity as a true heavyweight in an era where most of the large professional wrestlers weighed 190 pounds or less, and was not a rational extrapolation based on McMillan's match results, considering how easily McMillan had been mastered by men like Jenkins and McLeod.

"Duncan McMillan, the champion mixed style wrestler of the world, arrived in the city from St. Paul last evening and is stopping at the St. Louis (hotel)," reported *The Duluth News-Tribune*. "McMillan is a giant. He is 6 feet 2 inches in height and will strip for his contest with Hjalmar Lundin at the Lyceum Theater tomorrow night at 205 pounds. Mac is a big rawboned Scotchman and looks strong enough to crush even the famous Turk with whom he will wrestle shortly."

Still claiming to be "the champion mixed wrestler of the world," McMillan lost to Lundin by failing to defeat him three times in one hour, after which McMillan delivered a speech that was highly complimentary of his opponent.

Hjalmar Lundin

"That man Lundin is the making of a champion," McMillan began, in his efforts to establish Lundin as a fixture in the area. "He does not know much about the business yet — that is, he is a little raw — but, with proper training, there is a man that will beat the world. I have wrestled a good many matches in my time, but tonight for the first time I met a man whose arm I could not turn. I tried for a hammerlock all through the match, but I could not get it. Lundin's strength is wonderful, and he will in time be a wonderful wrestler."

Highland Games and Hippodromes

Claims that McMillan would be an ideal opponent for Adali notwithstanding, his first newsworthy interaction with Adali was when McMillan served in the atypical role of Dan McLeod's second for their Market Hall match in St. Paul. From then on, McMillan was a ubiquitous presence in Adali's orbit.

The very next month, in Duluth, McMillan teamed up with Hjalmar Lundin to wrestle Adali in front of a crowd of 3,000 people. The terms of the bout were that Adali would need to pin each of the men twice in 90 minutes, and he accomplished his task so quickly that the time limit of the bout was never a factor.

Lundin was pinned in falls of eight minutes and 11 minutes, while McMillan only did slightly better, lasting 13 minutes and 17 minutes in each of his falls. As a further indication of Adali's sweeping dominance during the era, a huge deal was made in the press about McMillan managing to successfully take Adali's back twice, and becoming the first man to ever apply a half nelson to Adali in the heat of battle.

In March, McMillan was able to claim some small semblance of a victory over the Turk when he teamed with D.B. McIntyre to wrestle Adali in front of 3,000 St. Paulians. Adali was tasked with defeating "the two Macs" four times — twice each — in one hour. After Adali won three falls in 35 minutes, McMillan valiantly held off the Turk for the remaining 25 minutes.

After the match, McMillan sat for a lengthy interview with *The Duluth News Tribune*. During the discussion, he insisted that Adali was "the greatest wrestler he ever saw," that anyone who had failed to see the Turk wrestle would never be able to appreciate how wonderful he was on the mat, and that the additional weight he had piled on since his bout with McLeod made him that much more invincible.

"He now weighs 272 pounds stripped, and what is harder on us more ordinary mortals in the wrestling business is that the Turk has learned American methods of wrestling on the mat since he wrestled McLeod, and a man has a harder time with him than did McLeod," swore McMillan. "I have the honor to say, however, that I am the second man he has ever met that has gotten behind him, and the first to put him on the defensive. I can say, also, that I made Mr. Turk tired enough so that he was glad of the opportunity to waste a few of his precious minutes in resting on the mat."

McMillan also added that the Turk was "a surprisingly fast man," who acted "like a cat watching a mouse," and was "just about as nimble to seize his prey." Throughout the remainder of the year, McMillan was served up as Adali's prey on several occasions. This included a May handicap-match loss to Adali with McMillan and Jack Carkeek teaming together, and a June straight-falls loss to Adali in a one-on-one bout. His "victories" over Adali occurred in bouts where he extended the Turk past whatever time limit was imposed on the match, and when Adali was involved, the time limit had to be a very short one in order for him to lose a match according to such stipulations.

By this time, it was undeniable that Adali had fallen beneath the managerial control of McMillan and Farmer Burns, and their partnership would ultimately conclude with one of the most famous flameouts in pro wrestling history.

19 – The Ringer

While Dan McLeod was keeping a relatively low profile, and certainly not flaunting the championship status that he had earned by every right, Tom Jenkins was reestablishing himself as the American champion as recognized within the Lake Erie corridor between Rochester, New York and Cleveland, Ohio.

The match that Jenkins had arranged to restore his claim to championship honors was against the same Ed Atherton that McLeod had annihilated in every match the two had ever had. In justifying Jenkins' claim to supremacy and championship laurels, *The Buffalo Review* leaned on the notion that Jenkins was "the only man whom Yusuf had much difficulty in throwing," and that Jenkins had a three-hour draw with Adali on his record.

Both of these points were lies, with the latter being the most condemnable. Jenkins had a victory in Pittsburgh, Pennsylvania over a wrestler branded as "The Turk," but it was definitely not Adali, who was busy wrestling Duncan McMillan in North Dakota that same day. The identity of the Turk involved in that match seemed to be kept intentionally ambiguous, as at least a few news outlets misidentified the anonymous Turk as Adali.

In his lone encounter with Adali, Jenkins was defeated easily. Moreover, the same article alleged that Jenkins had "whipped" Dan McLeod, among other wrestlers, when his only bout with McLeod to date had been a victory by virtue of McLeod's failure to pin him before the bout's time limit elapsed.

As for McLeod, he continued to wrestle sporadically for the remainder of 1899, but even into the next century, the labels used to describe the stature of his championship varied widely. In several regions, McLeod was still referred to as the American heavyweight champion, but he was often tabbed as the holder of the world championship of a lower weight division.

Highland Games and Hippodromes

On the occasion of McLeod's first trip to England in December 1899, he was said to be bringing the "lightweight wrestling championship" with him when he debuted in Stalybridge on the outskirts of Manchester. Days later, *The South Omaha Tribune* rightly acknowledged him as the "champion heavyweight of the world," but then in February, *The Sheboygan Telegram* identified McLeod as the "champion middleweight wrestler" when he dismantled the rather out-of-shape local strongman Harry Muldoon by pinning him four times in one hour.

"To a man who didn't know anything about the game, it looked, when the men stripped, like a safe bet of a pint of extra dry against a buckwheat pancake that Muldoon could eat up his opponent without experiencing a very bad case of indigestion," joked *The Telegram*. "After they had been wrestling a few minutes, however, Muldoon must have come to the conclusion that 'Mac' had been living on a diet of hair snakes all his life, for the latter slipped around like a greased eel in a basin of Mrs. Winslow's soothing syrup. At the expiration of 10 minutes and 15 seconds there was a dull thud like a fat girl falling into a feather bed, and Muldoon was on his back. The four falls were taken in 10:15, 13:15, 10:14, and 8:15. As McLeod had agreed to throw Muldoon four times in an hour, it will be seen that he had time to burn."

Far more important to the British Isles than Dan McLeod's debut was when Donald Dinnie made his long awaited return to Scotland after a sustained absence of 17 years in January 1899. *The Aberdeen Express* referred to the moment as "a landmark in the history of Scottish athletics."

"It is not to be expected that Donald, with his sixty-one years, should be the man he once was; but his figure, though not as bulky as of yore, is still well knit and upright," observed *The Express*. "His accent still proclaims him the Scotchman, and especially the Aberdeenshire Scotchman, and he referred with pride to the fact that he had shown his patriotism by upholding the honor of Scotland in many an athletic competition in every quarter of the globe."

Dinnie spent the bulk of the prior five years in Australia, often competing in athletic contests, but also managing the developing career of his son, Edward Dinnie, who was progressing into a formidable physical specimen in his own right. Very seldom did Dinnie participate in any wrestling bouts, but he still occasionally took to the stage to wrestle, including multiple bouts in New Zealand.

In the summer of 1896, with Dinnie rapidly approaching his 60th year of life, he was trotted out in New Zealand to face both T. Tuohy and J.W. Sutherland — a pair of wrestlers in their mid-20s — at the Agricultural Hall in Auckland. The best-of-five-falls contest was wrestled exclusively in Greco-Roman style.

Dinnie had already surpassed the average life expectancy in the Western world during that era by more than a decade, but he was still regarded as "the champion," and *The Auckland Weekly News* reported that Dinnie still resembled "a mass of muscle" who was far leaner and fitter-looking than the much younger Tuohy.

With Tuohy and Sutherland trading places between each fall, Dinnie won the first two falls in under 20 minutes. He then lost a seven-minute fall to Tuohy, meaning that the rapidly tiring Dinnie would need to pin Sutherland in the fourth fall or be forced to face a rested Tuohy in the deciding fall after struggling through yet another losing round.

Dinnie appeared to win the fall in six minutes, only for the referee to disqualify Dinnie for using a stranglehold. Dinnie protested, and Sutherland surprisingly echoed Dinnie's appeal by conceding that he had *not* been strangled by the Scottish legend.

"It was agreed to wrestle the fall over again," continued *The Weekly News*. "The men set to work in earnest, and the clever way in which Sutherland wriggled from his opponent's powerful grasp was a treat to witness, and the enthusiasm displayed by the audience was great. At last Dinnie got on that severe hold, the hammerlock; and Sutherland's second seeing he could not clear himself, gave Dinnie the fall. The referee then declared the fourth fall and match in favor of Dinnie."

To those paying close attention, it would have seemed, as if by magic, that Dinnie's skills at Greco-Roman wrestling, not to mention his endurance, had dramatically improved with age to such a degree that he could outlast a pair of skilled 20-year-old opponents who were advertised as having at least 100 victories under their respective belts.

Dinnie made his announcement that he would leave Australia and return to Scotland in 1898, following a brief stay in South Africa where he had been tasked with promoting Highland events. The members of the Highland Society and Burns Club of Sydney endeavored to arrange a special sendoff for him, although it was mentioned in *The Referee of Sydney* that Dinnie was hoping to have one final wrestling match of significance before he left.

Now years removed from the most damning of the hippodroming accusations that dogged him, and also the allegations that his athletic competitions were rigged in his favor, Dinnie was regarded more favorably by the Aussie press, and it was said that "few men have done more in the way of advertising their country than has this brawny Celt for his native heather-clad hills."

Unfortunately for Dinnie, his last-ditch effort to organize a final match apparently fell through, and after penning a final goodbye to the Australian sportswriters, he voyaged to South Africa along with his friend Sutherland as a travel companion, who it would soon be realized was there for the express purpose of losing wrestling matches to Dinnie.

In Cape Town, Dinnie was immediately put to work as a guest of the South African Sports Society. *The Cape Times* described how the 61-year-old Dinnie treated the South African Scots to an iconic representation of his Highland sports excellence when he appeared in Highland dress with "his breast literally covered with gold and silver medals."

The Times also attributed feats to Dinnie that were clear exaggerations. It was described how Dinnie "succeeded in tossing the caber fairly over" in two or three attempts, which was "no mean feat for a man of his age, especially when it is taken into consideration that the piece of timber 'tossed' weighed over 400 lbs and was 18 feet long." A regulation caber of 18 feet usually weighs less than 180 pounds, which means that the writer was likely doubling the stated weight of the caber for effect.

In a scene that would be imitated by wrestlers of Scottish descent for generations to come, "three pipers played the famous Donald Dinnie into the ring," at which point he defeated his companion Sutherland two falls to one in what *The Times* confusingly described as both a Cumberland and catch-as-catch-can contest. The match concluded when Dinnie "grassed his agile opponent with a buttock stroke in the third fall."

For his Scottish homecoming, Dinnie was seemingly resigned to the fact that he might spoil the memories of his prior deeds as a strongman by hoisting weights that were less impressive than his countrymen were accustomed to seeing. Instead, Dinnie replicated a swordsmanship routine that was remarkably reminiscent of the sort performed by Duncan Ross. He sliced a potato in two as it rested on the nape of his son's neck, then cleaved a bar of lead in two as it hung lightly suspended on two pieces of thin paper.

Dinnie's demonstration with the blade preceded the Scotland debut of his son, Alf Dinnie, in weightlifting. The younger Dinnie emulated his father by raising a 140-pound dumbbell into the air using only one arm, then replicated the feat with a 160-pound dumbbell.

The elder Dinnie demonstrated that he was still in excellent shape by performing alternating shoulder raises with two 57-pound weights, and then he offered a statement to *The Aberdeen Journal*, boasting about the prowess he still professed to wield as a competitive wrestler.

"In Scotch wrestling he maintains he has never been defeated, and he expressed his confidence in being able to beat Muldoon and other champions of the 'catch-as-catch-can' and

Greco-Roman styles of wrestling if he had the opportunity of putting his experiences now to the test," printed *The Journal.*

In light of this statement, Dinnie was plainly ignoring the official loss in Scottish-style wrestling that he had suffered while in Australia years earlier, and also drastically overstating his skills at Greco-Roman and catch-as-catch-can wrestling, which had always been the grappling styles in which he was least adept.

Whatever shining prospects there had been for Dinnie's long-awaited return to the United Kingdom — and to Scotland in particular — the luster faded rather rapidly. In June, Dinnie's dumbbells were confiscated as a condition of a lawsuit brought against him by his own son, Edwin Dinnie.

The details of the lawsuit, presented in Aberdeen Sheriff Court, were that Edwin Dinnie signed a contract in December 1898 to work as an employee of his father for the sum of £3 a week, and had paid a further £12 simply to travel to South Africa to join his father's company of traveling performers based on the promise that his father would reimburse him. According to Edwin, he was never reimbursed for his travel expenses, and was then wrongfully terminated by his father at a time when the elder Dinnie still owed him £9 in salary.

"On 27th January last, defender wrongously dismissed pursuer from his employment as a member of his company of performers, in breach of the engagement for twelve months," recorded *The Aberdeen Journal.* "Pursuer is ready to implement his part of the engagement, and he holds that defender is owing him £39 as damages for wrongous dismissal, and three months' salary at the rate of £3 per week. In lieu of notice, the whole amounting to £60.

In answering to the complaint of his son, Donald Dinnie insisted that Edwin was paid all of the money he was owed. As if the embarrassment of being sued by his own son hadn't been sufficient, it was recorded during the proceedings that Dinnie's confiscated weights, which had been seized based on their presumed financial value, were collectively only worth about 15 shillings — or three-quarters of a pound — for the value of their iron.

Furthermore, Dinnie's representative — Mr. Wilson — admitted on the record that he didn't think Dinnie would even have been able to scrape together £5 if requested, "as his entertainments had not been a success."

In January 1900, Duncan McMillan began his first of what would eventually be many attempts to promote professional wrestling bouts in the Pacific Northwest. The move would have seemed somewhat perplexing on multiple fronts to anyone who had been able to evaluate the entire breadth of McMillan's career. They would have first taken into account his embarrassment at being caught hippodroming there with Donald Dinnie, and then found it odd that he was there as the promoter for Hali Adali, the Turkish wrestler whom he had just spent a year getting manhandled by.

At the time of the initial announcement, McMillan was described as "the famous wrestler" who was looking to bring a giant wrestler from the Dakotas out to Washington to match size with Adali.

"I want to see a man who can give the Turk a good time, and I am of the opinion that I can get him in Spokane in a week or so," McMillan told *The Spokane Chronicle*. "I have had my eye on him for some time and am sure that if he is near his former home he will come. I wrote to the man last week and will receive an answer shortly."

The man in question was Matt A. Simmer, a wrestler who McMillan swore he had seen lift "2,200 pounds dead weight with his hands, and 4,200 with harness." No matter what McMillan might have meant by the use of the word "lift" in this instance, he was citing preposterous numbers that were at least four times greater than the known world records for squatting and deadlifting in 1900.

Simmer was a strongman of German descent who had acquired a bit of wrestling experience in the Midwest over the prior two years, but he would not be accompanying McMillan out to the Pacific Northwest at this time. Instead, McMillan returned to being a frequent victim of Adali, and continued to lose to the giant Turk in handicap matches, except on occasions when Adali actually refereed McMillan's bouts, as he did in the Scot's win over Louis Cannon at Spokane's International Theater.

On March 1, McMillan debuted the "bear lock" in Washington to defeat Cannon in the fifth round of their best-of-five contest, which was held in front of a crowd that was so "ridiculously small" that the wrestlers "would have been justified in refusing to go on."

"The bear lock has never before been used in Seattle in a professional match, although someone may have caught it in practice by accident without knowing what it was," stated *The Seattle Post-Intelligencer*. "Hali Adali, the champion of champions, brought it with him from Turkey, and as he says, when a heavy man gets it on one who is lighter, it is all up with him."

In applying the bear lock, McMillan hooked both of his legs around Cannon's body, "well up under the arms, and then locked them." He then twisted Cannon over, "compelling him to bridge." Without laying a hand on Cannon during the entire exchange, McMillan was able to use the hold to force Cannon's legs to the mat, and the move was "a revelation to old followers of wrestling."

New wrestling techniques aside, the lack of fans willing to attend wrestling events in Seattle was a clear problem, and the staff of *The Post-Intelligencer* laid the blame for the "lost interest" in the sport of wrestling at the feet of another high-profile wrestler from the era, Charles Moth, who toured with a man "who passed himself off as a brother of 'Strangler' Lewis" and "killed the game" in both Seattle and Tacoma.

Even in reminding Seattle residents of Moth's fakery, the newspaper still heaped praise upon the wrestlers touring Washington at the time, as if they were the real deal. This applied twofold to McMillan, who was lauded as "the ideal of scientific wrestlers" who operated smoothly on the mat "with his brain, hands, legs, and body," and with whom "every move is beautifully timed."

Highland Games and Hippodromes

During this tour, McMillan was praised as a strongman who was forged in the mold of Donald Dinnie, advertising himself as the "champion all-around wrestler and athlete of the world," although unlike Dinnie it is difficult to find any athletic contests that McMillan dominated against world-class opponents. In his head-to-head throwing trials against Dinnie and Ross, McMillan routinely threw well short of their marks.

Speaking of such events, McMillan had been conspicuously absent from major Highland Games festivals for years, but made a point of competing in the 24th annual picnic of the Sacramento Caledonian Club in June 1900. At this event, the advertised special attraction was a wrestling match between McMillan and Adali, but on the day of the games, Tom Carroll also participated.

The results of the games may be an indication that age and a lack of commitment to training for Scottish sports was beginning to creep up on McMillan. The thousands of attendees watched as McMillan failed to win a single event. He finished third behind Tom Carroll and P.A. McIntyre in the heavy hammer throw, second behind Tom Carroll in putting the heavy stone, and second behind Carroll in throwing the 56-pound weight.

The outcome of the wrestling event also begs the question of whether or not the action on that day was authentic. *The San Francisco Call* reported how both McMillan and Carroll "managed to keep the Turkish wrestler at work for four minutes each before he downed them," which either means that McMillan, as a Scot, willfully allowed a Turkish competitor to decimate him at a Scottish-themed athletic event, or the gap between his skills and those of Adali during genuine wrestling contests was wider than their outcomes from ordinary wrestling shows would indicate.

After the Caledonian Club event was over, McMillan remained in California, promoting Adali and offering $1.00 per minute to any man who could stand up to him, including the trained wrestlers who were advertised to wrestle against him.

Farmer Burns also joined the tour, and apparently accepted a demotion of his championship in Adali's presence.

In Salt Lake City, advertisements for appearances by the world title trio labeled Adali as "the world's champion catch-as-catch-can and Greco-Roman wrestler," McMillan as "the world's mixed champion wrestler," and Burns as "the 160-pound champion of the world."

Also thrown into the mix was Jim Ryan of California, "the 187-pound champion of the world," and the smaller men all lined up at the Salt Palace to be demolished by the Turk. In order, Adali pinned Ryan in eight minutes, Burns in 13 minutes, and McMillan in 12 minutes. Per the stipulations of the matches, each man was awarded with a dollar amount from Adali equivalent to the number of minutes he survived.

The nature of the relationship between Burns, McMillan and Adali, and how it came to exist, was revealed in the pages of *The Sioux City Journal* and *The Davenport Democrat* once Burns and McMillan returned to Iowa from the Pacific Northwest, with Adali nowhere to be found. It was then explained that Adali had at some point left the management of Lou Houseman of Chicago, having snuck into Canada to hide until his contract expired, and then deciding to write to Burns "to come west and show with him."

"The Turk and the others parted in Denver the other day because, as Burns says, the big fellow got too proud to wear his Turkish clothes anymore, which destroyed his value as a drawing card," explained *The Democrat*.

The story told by *The Salt Lake Tribune* was probably far more accurate, and also quite different. First, Adali lost a match to a 168-pound man "who positively refused to let Hali throw him in 15 minutes, as per agreement." However, the bigger issue was Adali's falling out with Duncan McMillan, who *The Tribune* conclusively identified as Adali's manager.

"Mac claims that Hali owed him $25 and refused to pay it," said *The Tribune*. "A row ensued and Hali called the McMillan-Adali syndicate a thing of the past. McMillan accordingly swore out an attachment in a justice's court in Denver. The constable at first refused to serve the attachment, alleging as an excuse that he did not yearn to have Adali practice new strangle holds on him, but McMillan offered to go along and help the constable serve the writ, and annexed Hali's trunks, shoes, and fez. Hali, it seems, will have to come in with $25 or lose his fixtures."

Back with Burns in the Midwest without the 300-pound Turk beside him who he had just been advertising as the *real* world heavyweight champion of catch-as-catch-can wrestling, McMillan accompanied "The Farmer" to Nebraska, where they treated a small audience at the Kerr Opera House in Hastings to a casual demonstration of the five different styles of wrestling to which McMillan claimed to be an expert.

Far more entertaining than the explanations of the wrestling styles was the inducement Burns provided in favor of clean living. At the beginning of his speech, Burns "scored the cigarette smoker unmercifully" and claimed to know of 3,000 young men "who had quit cigarette smoking as a result of his efforts."

"I am thirty-nine years old, yet I never drink liquor, smoke or chew tobacco or swear, and I never drank a cup of tea or coffee in my life," Burns continued to preach. "The American boy nowadays is no good. He wants to smoke cigarettes, part his hair in the middle, wear a high stand-up collar around his little slim neck, and let the old man do all the work to earn money to send him to college. Make the boy do some work and it will do him good and make a man of him."

Continuing with his rebuke of sluggards, Burns added that light wrestling was the best kind of exercise available to anyone, and that every municipality in America should supply a gym where young men could receive instruction in the art of grappling.

Infinitely more important than Farmer Burns preaching an abstemious lifestyle, or even the separation of Adali from the managerial tandem of McMillan and Burns, was the first public encounter on the mat between McMillan and the newest member of the Burns' wrestling stable, Frank Gotch. The powerful 22-year-old heavyweight from Iowa had grown in popularity very rapidly in the first half of 1900, and McMillan did nothing to slow his momentum. The men met on the mat in Iowa, and the result was quite shocking.

The terms of the bout were that the world's champion of mixed wrestling, McMillan, was required to defeat Gotch three times in an hour, or he would forfeit the match. Under ordinary circumstances, fans would expect to see Gotch on the defensive throughout the bout, with McMillan winning at least two falls in the first 50 minutes. A mad scramble would punctuate the final stanza, at which time McMillan may or may not have captured the winning pinfall.

In Humboldt, a packed opera house watched as McMillan won the first fall from Gotch in 30 minutes, and then *lost* a fall to Gotch only 14 minutes later, which immediately halted the match, with Gotch being awarded the victory.

The momentum of Gotch only grew throughout September when he captured a fall from Burns during a 2-1 loss to him, and then made it to the finals of a tournament in Des Moines. During the tournament, Gotch first defeated Ernest Roeber and Ole Shellenberger, Burns defeated McMillan two falls to one, and then Burns and Gotch wrestled to a draw, which apparently awarded the tournament victory to Gotch per the terms of the contest.

Frank Gotch

Frank Gotch had seemingly emerged out of the blue to infiltrate one of the most established and successful wrestling partnerships in the United States, and had effectively taken Hali Adali's place as the fresh attraction within the trio.

Highland Games and Hippodromes

The story of how Frank Gotch was first motivated to become a professional wrestler would reach near mythical proportions in later years when Gotch ultimately became a household name. If factually true, the spark of inspiration was provided by none other than Dan McLeod in either 1897, 1898, or 1899, depending on which account from Gotch is accurate, during a chance meeting in the area between Livermore and Lu Verne, Iowa, at a picnic hosted by the Modern Woodmen.

The challenge in pinning down the precise date of the encounter stems from the fact that Gotch told several versions of the story to different newspapers starting in 1904, and extending into 1905.

While the crucial details of the meeting itself are essentially identical, Gotch's lack of consistency on the date — he said it took place "six years ago" in 1904, and alternatingly six and eight years ago in 1905 — has made it difficult to isolate the year. However, in a few tellings of the tale, Gotch repeated the assertion that the picnic was a July 4th celebration of U.S. independence.

Judging from the range of dates offered, it is probable that at the time of the first contact between the two grapplers, Gotch was about 19 or 20 years old, and McLeod may very well have been the reigning world heavyweight champion. Gotch reflected upon the event fondly, referring to it as "the first real wrestling match I ever had."

"There were all kinds of athletic games, and one of the men entered against me in the shot put and several other similar events was a well-built chap whom the crowd knew only as 'Dan,'" Gotch told *The Cincinnati Enquirer*. "I put it all over him in the 50-yard run and made him look like 30 cents at throwing the hammer, so to get even he proposed a wrestling match. Being young and ambitious and thinking in a cinch, I could not let that chance get away from me and accepted without a moment's hesitation. Someone furnished me with an old pair of trunks and I asked where the match was to come off. Dan took the trouble to make the reply in front of a big crowd of people and selected the middle of the main street of the town.

"We stripped off our clothes and went right out there on the cobble stones and wrestled like a couple of Turks. Head spins and all sorts of things that you see in a wrestling match in a big hall were indulged in and the crowd nearly went wild with excitement. Just imagine what shape we were in when the bout ended by Dan putting my shoulders to the mat after an hour and 45 minutes of wrestling on these hard stones. I was defeated, but not disgraced, as they say, and after shaking hands with my opponent, wished him well. No one knew who he was or where he came from, but by posing as a member of the Woodmen he managed to enter all the athletic events. Just as he was to step on the train, he handed me a card familiar to every big wrestler in America. It read: Dan McLeod, 'Champion Catch-as-Catch-Can Wrestler of the World.'"

For the sake of balance, this was *not* the only version of the story told by Gotch, but it is the one that makes him look the best. In an alternate telling of the tale by Gotch to *The Quad City Times* of Davenport — a newspaper from within the state where the events were said to have actually occurred — Gotch presented himself far less flatteringly with respect to how he fared against McLeod, who was competing under the guise of a furniture dealer by the name of "Reynolds."

"Well, in the course of the day's sport Reynolds beat me in almost everything except the high jump and the 100-yard dash and the team tug of war, in which Humboldt beat Lu Verne," said Gotch. "He won the discus throw, the hammer throw, the shot put, etc., and in every case I ran him a close second. It was really a contest between the two of us, with nobody else in the meet who compared at all. The crowd got very much excited, and every event was fiercely contested. I was straining every nerve to win, for it galled me to be beaten out by anybody."

With all due respect to Gotch and his prior telling of the events of the Modern Woodmen picnic, *this* account of the event makes more sense, given McLeod's eliteness at hammer throwing and other hurling events, and his lack of specialization in sprinting and leaping.

"Our fellows got suspicious that Reynolds was not a bona fide Woodman, for some reason or other, so they tested him, and the rascal had forgotten every sign," laughed Gotch. "Well, you know, I was a big country boy sore as a boil, and I wanted to fight it out right then and there. It was with difficulty that they could keep me from pitching into McLeod, alias Reynolds."

Learning that Gotch was a skilled amateur wrestler, McLeod proposed that the two should wrestle for nothing other than pride, although Gotch insisted that if McLeod had offered a contest for money, the Iowa farmboy would have been able to find many people present who would have been willing to back him due to his local reputation as a wrestler.

Gotch repeated his claim that the men proceeded to wrestle on cinders for well over two hours, with McLeod winning both falls. In this version, McLeod did not reveal his identity to Gotch directly, but Gotch learned of it later, and did not personally meet McLeod for another five years.

In yet an account of the incident delivered even later, in 1907, Gotch claimed that McLeod personally stopped by the Gotch family home weeks later and handed his business card to Gotch's father to give him during dinner. In still another version, Gotch would claim to have been tipped off in advance that "the Ringer" at the picnic was McLeod, and that he won $50 by winning a fall against him.

Given the frequency with which McLeod was around Burns and McMillan during the period between 1897 and 1900, it is not only possible, but even *probable* that McLeod helped to recruit Gotch into the Burns and McMillan camp. In several accounts of his discovery offered by Gotch in 1910 and beyond, he heavily implied that McLeod helped to make the direct connection between himself and Burns.

Speaking of McLeod, he opened 1900 in Fond du Lac against Kara Hasam, one of the lesser Turks, and bested him in three straight falls. As defeating a Turk had become a mark of distinction, and there weren't enough Turks to go around, additional Turks were either imported or created through the use of costumes.

Cartoon of a promoter fantasizing about managing a Turk

By all indications, the man known as Kara Hasam was an Armenian who would have been more accurately referred to as an "Osmanli" or "Ottoman," but not as a "Turk," since that label was usually reserved for the ruling class of the Ottoman Empire who were ethnically Turkish. This detail came to light in court when Hasam was required to speak through his

Armenian translator — Jacob Markarian — after he was arrested for allegedly robbing his own business manager, "Mr. Charlson," of $50.

"The Turk hadn't a cent, but Attorney Herbert Swett was touched by the man's pitiful condition and took his case," explained *The Sheboygan Telegram*. "Charlson stated that he hired the Turk and Markarian at a salary of $15 a week each, and that the Turk was also to have $25 every time he wrestled. He said that the Turk and the interpreter had that morning, after receiving $36, taken him down and robbed him of $50. He therefore prayed the court to get him his roll back and send his two wicked assaulters to the local bastille."

When asked to comment on the matter, McLeod's words revealed his role as the coordinator of the affair, in as much as he was responsible for doling out the money to his opponent's business manager before or after the match. The world champion admitted that he "made a mistake in handing Charlson any money at all."

"What I ought to have done is to have given the count to that poor devil of a Turk," said McLeod. "He needs the money, and I ought to have seen that he wasn't skinned out of it."

With the most imposing of the Turks effectively eliminated, Dan McLeod was about to have his significance on the North American wrestling seen hastily restored. Along with this sudden return to relevance would come a rather public return to hippodroming activity that would inevitably cause McLeod's status as a free citizen to hang in the balance.

Highland Games and Hippodromes

20 – On a Charge of Swindling

Throughout 1900, Dan McLeod had made a habit out of wrestling as the world middleweight champion, which was perhaps due to a mutual agreement with Duncan McMillan and Farmer Burns that McLeod would cede the upper weight division to their Turkish protege who they had taken great pains to advertise as the heavyweight titleholder.

Accordingly, McLeod routinely bested Fred Beell in middleweight title defenses without Beell putting up much of a challenge. However, the permanent relocation of Hali Adali from the U.S. to Europe led to an almost comical excuse being offered as to why McLeod could no longer wrestle in the lower weight divisions.

"McLeod now tips the scales at over 170 pounds and cannot in the future hope to reduce his weight to 158 pounds and win against Beell or [Ed] Adamson," said *The News* of Marshfield, Wisconsin. "Under these circumstances, McLeod is practically out of the middleweight class, and the championship which he has long held falls to Fred Beell. He is now ready to defend the title against all comers."

By October, it was disclosed by *The Buffalo Express* that McLeod was once again hippodroming through Canada. This time, the site was Niagara Falls, and since *The Express* had been getting into the habit of minimizing McLeod's achievements for the sake of propping up Tom Jenkins as either the *real* American heavyweight champion or world heavyweight champion, it spun a narrative about how McLeod, operating incognito, had unintentionally confessed that Jenkins was the one wrestler that he would rather not have to compete against.

According to the story of *The Express*, McLeod — in his identity as little-known wrestler C.H. Gridley — was in the midst of manhandling Farmer Davis of Springbrook at the Lyceum when he was recognized and approached by James E. Kinney, "a friend of Tom Jenkins."

"Say, Gridley, if you want a match, I've got an unknown near Buffalo, weight about 160, maybe a little more

338

or a little less," Kinney claimed to have said while introducing himself to McLeod. "I'll post the forfeit for him now."

According to Kinney — who can't be regarded as a very reliable source under the circumstances — McLeod replied by saying "I'll wrestle any man in America, bar one: Tom Jenkins."

The Express immediately wrapped up the tale by implying that if McLeod, "the best man on the mat," opted to bar someone, it was clear that whomever McLeod desired to bar — in this case, Tom Jenkins — must be the *true* champion of wrestling.

If McLeod wasn't already sitting at the top of the all-time list of wrestling stars from his era who attempted to soak up wagered cash through surreptitious practices, the events that took place in the spring of 1901 certainly place him in the upper echelon of such rankings.

The enormous Paul Pons of France, standing 6'5" and weighing 260 pounds, was advertised as a successor to the departed Hali Adali as the most imposing foreign giant touring North America. In March, Pons was booked to wrestle at Montreal's Sohmer Park in front of 7,000 spectators against a tiny 5'6" Canadian named George Little, who was *actually* Dan McLeod competing under an alias.

Judging from the result and its aftermath, McLeod double-crossed and embarrassed Pons in some form or fashion during a Greco-Roman bout in which Pons had been tasked with pinning McLeod five times in an hour to claim victory. Pons failed to register a single pinfall against McLeod, who nearly pinned the much larger Pons during the final five minutes of the bout.

At least some semblance of the truth would be exposed in May, when McLeod was taken into custody in Hamilton, Ontario alongside "Gid" Perry of Brussels, and then shipped off to Montreal "on a charge of swindling." *The Ottawa Journal* reported that the two had been accused of playing a "coon game" in several places around Canada.

"Regarding the Montreal case, it is alleged that the pair put up a job on another fellow by letting him win $400 on one of their matches and then doing him up for $2,650 by giving him 'the double cross' on another match," printed *The Journal*. "They have worked the same game in Buffalo and Hamilton."

Having fun with the arrest, *The Buffalo Times* joked that McLeod's "swindling" activity explained why he was able to stay in Buffalo's Iroquois Hotel and "live like a prince" while he lodged there.

"The man who dallies with the 'sure thing' game deserves to be bitten, and the Montreal 'come on' who dropped a small fortune on the recent Pons-McLeod match got just what was coming to him," declared *The Times*. "He isn't entitled to an atom of sympathy no matter whether the affair was crooked or not. He was told that it was 'framed' and bet his money with the intention of skinning the other fellow. Instead he got stung himself and it served him just right. The game is an old one and the fact that it can still be played only goes to prove the old adage that there's a sucker born every minute."

At the time the article was published, McLeod was still locked tightly in a Montreal jail cell, and *The Times* added that McLeod's decision to hide his identity would not help his case.

"Gid Perry, McLeod's Montreal manager, is also a prisoner, and the police are trying to make him tell how 'come on' Thompson's $2,650 was invested in the match," continued *The Times*. "If he does, it will go hard with McLeod, for there is quite a little public sentiment against him in Montreal. The French end of the population furnished the larger portion of the crowd, which saw McLeod defeat Pons, the French champion, and to a man almost what little money they bet was up on their compatriot. Consequently, Thompson's affirmation that the match was fixed has left them in an ugly frame of mind."

A report on the scandal by the Associated Press — in an article titled "Scotch wrestler accused of defrauding

Thompson out of $2,650" — delved into the matter even further.

"Thompson alleges that he gave the money to Perry to bet on Pons, who lost the match, but claims to have evidence that Perry did not bet a cent and also fixed the match to make it appear that Pons had really lost," reported the AP.

Paul Pons (left) and Dan McLeod

The article inserted the detail that the Montreal wrestling game had "received a severe jolt" as a result of McLeod's actions. However, it then proffered a defense of McLeod, as it seemed that "McLeod evidently wrestled as well as he could or else the huge Frenchman would surely have won."

According to the AP's reasoning, even if McLeod had lied about his identity, his wrestling was "on the level," and Pons was justifiably embarrassed, as the French giant "didn't throw the little Scotchman once," and "took the next steamer back to home and mother."

During the trial, Thompson explained that he felt compelled to wager his money on Pons because he was told by Gid Perry that Pons was likely to beat McLeod, and McLeod personally told Thompson that he "thought the big man would tire him out."

McLeod was discharged by the Montreal court due to a lack of evidence against him, since he was visibly seen to have wrestled his best and won. Upon recrossing the border into Buffalo, McLeod told *The Buffalo Times* that the international publicity the story had received "had hurt him seriously."

In retrospect, the only real question is whether or not Paul Pons was in on McLeod's act, and the rational evidence points to this not being the case. Granted, Pons was regularly accused of hippodromes in his own right, including in a bout with Ernest Roeber in New York one month before his match with McLeod, and then later that same month in a bout with Nouroulah, the latest of the Terrible Turks.

What makes the McLeod bout distinct is how thorough the embarrassment of Pons was. The match could have been structured in a way that enabled Pons to appear competitive. Instead, the 5'6" McLeod shut Pons out completely, and the Frenchman never wrestled in the province of Quebec — home to the largest first-world French-speaking population in the Americas — again in his life.

If there's any truth to what McLeod told *The Buffalo Express* during a later interview, it may be possible to extrapolate McLeod's feelings for Pons from his stated sentiments about all of the "Turks" who were involved in wrestling. When asked about continuing to wrestle against Turks, McLeod said that he "believes in boycotting those elephants," and added that they "hurt wrestling" in terms of the quality of the overall business.

Judging from this answer, McLeod seemed to have a broader resentment for wrestlers who were more size and sizzle than substance, in which case he may very well have harbored the same animosity for Pons.

During what was apparently an extended stay in Buffalo, McLeod practically moonlighted as a columnist telling stories about — of all things — the exploits of Duncan Ross in Australia. This is surprising because the two men had never before been officially linked together in the press.

Aside from their shared association with the Scottish Thistle Club in San Francisco, through which the two men were several years removed from each other, there was nothing to superficially connect the two men other than shared Scottish ethnicity, a fondness for tossing large objects, and the fact that they both knew Duncan McMillan.

Despite their improbable connection, McLeod seemed to have intimate knowledge of every colorful act Ross had ever partaken in during his time in Australia.

"There is one of the most unique cards in the athletic world," McLeod said of Ross, in perhaps the first public acknowledgement that he even knew who Ross was. "He was a great athlete in his day, and he has had more ups and downs than anyone else I know of. Ross is a good-hearted fellow, but a regular wild Indian when on a spree. He had some experiences in Australia that were exciting as well as laughable. The people of the Antipodes, especially the police, will never forget Ross, and knowing the circumstances, one cannot blame them."

McLeod then told the tale of how a drunken Ross had supposedly donned the armor that he customarily wore during his swordfighting exhibitions, and "rode his horse on a mad gallop" through the parks and streets of Melbourne. When approached by police, the inebriated Ross simply drew his sword from its sheath and held it aloft as if intent on slaughtering them.

"He shouted to the police: 'Stand back there; the first mother's son that comes within reach of me, I'll cleave him in two!'" said McLeod. "And he continued on the mad gallop up and down the green, swinging the sword and slashing away at some imaginary foeman."

The policemen retreated and called for reinforcements, and the horse gradually slowed down as it began to tire. Eventually, an Irish police officer who Ross recognized was able to talk him off of the horse, and Ross was taken into custody and brought down to the courthouse. Ross was soon bailed out of jail.

In a later edition of *The Courier*, McLeod told another story about how Ross — once again under the influence of alcohol — barged into the wrong house in Sydney thinking that it was an inn. Plated and placed on the dining room table sat roast mutton, mashed potatoes, and asparagus, and a "matronly looking woman" and two little boys sat at the table's far end.

"Ross tossed his hat onto a sofa, and bowing graciously to the lady, he threw himself into a chair with the remark: 'Just in time, ma'am. Just in time. And you couldn't have suited us better if we had sent our order in advance,'" laughed McLeod.

The woman "uttered a series of piercing screams," and her husband rushed into the room and asked Ross why he was trespassing in their home. Still not realizing that he had invaded a private residence, Ross said he was happy to pay in advance, but the man insisted that Ross leave his home at once.

"The infuriated head of the house ran for a stick that stood in a corner of the room," McLeod continued. "Ross, now realizing that he was in for trouble, deliberately reached across the table and grabbed up the leg of mutton by the shank. He retreated towards the kitchen as the man came bounding towards him with blazing eyes, and cane uplifted. Ross brandished the leg of mutton as though it were a huge club."

While the men thrusted and parried with canes and cuts of meat, the woman and her two sons ran off to summon the police. According to McLeod, this incident served as a direct precursor to Ross' ultimate departure from Australia, as

Duncan saw fit to lay low in Melbourne for a few weeks before exiting the country.

After years of insisting that Tom Jenkins was the true American heavyweight champion of catch-as-catch-can wrestling and minimizing any claims that McLeod had to the title — even though McLeod's claim was inarguably the respected lineal claim everywhere outside of Tom Jenkins' stronghold — the press in Cleveland and Buffalo finally acknowledged McLeod's reign just long enough for Jenkins to officially end it.

Tom Jenkins

Even so, the pro-Jenkins publications never wavered from their assertion that Jenkins had been a legitimate champion prior to his November 1901 bout with McLeod, dubbing Jenkins "the undisputed champion of America" and that Jenkins had "made good" on his prior claims to being the champion.

The crowd at Cleveland's Central Armory was estimated to have been at least 4,800, with some guesses ranging as high as 6,000. *The Courier*'s writer observed that there were several sporting men amongst them; the odds had been 10 to 8 on Jenkins earlier in the day, but jumped to 2 to 1 in Jenkins favor by the time the men reached the mat.

At well over 200 pounds, Jenkins "looked a giant alongside the stocky McLeod" and "appeared 30 pounds heavier" than the true defending champion. Yet, McLeod displayed his power despite the size difference. Twenty-six minutes into the bout, McLeod "got behind the giant," lifted Jenkins up, and smashed him to the mat "with tremendous force for a flat fall, all fours down."

This fall shocked Jenkins' hometown fans who had seldom seen him manhandled by anyone who didn't swear allegiance to the Ottoman Empire. It was also the first official fall registered in any match between McLeod and Jenkins, and by pinning Jenkins a single time, McLeod had already fared better against him than Farmer Burns.

Jenkins won the final two falls in slightly over 40 minutes to finally win the lineal world heavyweight championship, or the American heavyweight championship as it was referred to on that evening.

Interestingly, no one raised the same objections about Jenkins' victory over McLeod that had been used as grounds to justify Jenkins' original title claim three years earlier. Specifically, Jenkins claimed to have been the real champion because he had defeated Farmer Burns in a best-of-five match rather than a best-of-three. Now that Jenkins had won the lineal title in a best-of-three bout, he apparently had no grievances about the format.

For the fourth straight time, the world heavyweight championship had passed into Celtic hands. Jenkins was the son of Welsh immigrants, and the Celtic stranglehold on the lineal world championship recognized in North America continued into its 14th consecutive year.

All things considered, the press coverage of McLeod's loss was quite complimentary of the dethroned champion. The syndicated account of the match that was widely circulated explained that "the great little Scot was nowise disgraced," and that Jenkins' only advantages were in size and strength, because he was "not a match for McLeod in skill."

Stinging from the defeat of their hometown hero, *The Vancouver Province* first reestablished that McLeod had been, in fact, the catch-as-catch-can champion of the world when he took to the mat with Jenkins in Cleveland, and then reminisced about the events that led McLeod to enter the wrestling profession.

"Dan S. McLeod is a British Columbian and wrestled the first match of his life in Nanaimo," recollected *The Province*. "He was working as a boy in the coal mines over there and early showed his strength in the Caledonian games and sports picnics and the like. It was in putting the shot, throwing the hammer, and tossing the caber that he first came into prominence. After taking up wrestling, though he knew really nothing of the art of the game, he quickly became the best man in the district."

It would have been a fitting epitaph to McLeod's world title candidacy to credit the Highland Games of McLeod's youth for helping him ascend to the status of world heavyweight wrestling champion, but McLeod was not yet finished with Jenkins or the world title.

After dominating Ed Atherton early in December at Buffalo's Convention Hall and pinning him five times in one hour, McLeod announced that he was ready for a rematch with Jenkins. However, the path to a world championship rematch would be a lengthy one.

While Dan McLeod had been preoccupied with matters related to Paul Pons and Tom Jenkins, Duncan McMillan had made a triumphant return to his home province of Ontario. This was news worth celebrating in his home town of Cornwall, the seat of Stormont, Dundas, and Glengarry counties.

The Freeholder of Cornwall began its introduction with a commentary about how outside of Stormont and Glengarry "every Scotchman from this section seems to be referred to as a Glengarrian" before sharing an excerpt from *The Toronto Star* about how Duncan McMillan, "brother of Dan McMillan of Harrison's Corners," fared in his bout with Joe Lynn.

The Star referred to McMillan as "the Glengarry giant," and if there was any truth to the weight listed for him by the paper, he had swelled to an enormous size of 232 pounds, far more of which was body fat than in previous years. Regardless of his growing dimensions and what it may have meant for his health, McMillan had little difficulty with Lynn, as "the big Glengarrian" won three straight falls to make good on his return.

Sadly, McMillan was prohibited from showcasing his grappling prowess in front of his friends and relatives in Cornwall. Once McMillan had finalized his plans to meet Hjalmar Lundin of Sweden in Cornwall on May 15, a town by-law was discovered that prohibited wrestling matches from taking place in Cornwall.

"This is to be regretted, as Mr. McMillan has won a name for himself abroad, and the people amongst whom he spent his boyhood days would like to have an opportunity to see him display his strength and skill and maintain the reputation he has made in other places on his native heath," complained *The Cornwall Standard*. "We can see no reason for objecting to a properly conducted wrestling match. As Mr. McMillan said when he appeared before the Town Council on Wednesday night, there is more that is objectionable in lacrosse and football than in scientific wrestling."

Instead of Cornwall, McMillan and Lundin tussled at McLean's Hall in South Finch, a community about 20 miles north of Cornwall in the township of North Stormont. *The Ottawa Citizen* lionized the local hero as a "son of Scotia," ensuring its readers that the past-his-prime McMillan would have won the bout legitimately despite the "unfortunate accident" that sent the two wrestlers plummeting four feet from the platform onto the floor and into a row of spectators.

"The Scotchman was on top, and Lundin landed on the front row of the seats, dislocating his shoulder," described *The Citizen*. "He was unable to continue and asked for five minutes in which to recover and fix up the injury. This McMillan refused to consent to, and the match was awarded to McMillan. McMillan had the better of the bout and would in all probability have won it had the accident not occurred."

The closing statement of the report declared the match to have been "on its merits," which was "contrary to the general rule." Evidently, at this early point in the 20th century, at least in some communities, it was believed to be more likely than not that wrestling bouts were coordinated affairs.

As perhaps the king of coordinating such affairs, Duncan Ross found it increasingly more difficult to maintain his attractiveness as a draw as the 20th century opened. His act was either well worn, or fans were simply no longer interested in watching a wrestler who had been in circulation for the better part of 20 years, and had spent many of those years fending off widespread accusations of being a phony.

In Elmira, New York, *The Gazette and Free Press* described a November scene at the city's Washington Street Opera House, where Ross was slated to compete against "The Syracuse Hercules" Professor Adam Miller in a best-of-five match. When it was time to start the show, there were only three people sitting in the reserved seats of the lower level, "and about forty boys in 'peanut heaven'" in the upper deck.

Miller stepped onto the stage and announced, "Gentlemen — I came here this evening to wrestle Duncan C. Ross, but there being such a small attendance, I cannot see my way out, so step to the box office and get your money."

In February 1902, Ross suffered perhaps his most humiliating defeat in a bout that was more likely than not to have been genuine. In Old Town, Maine, Ross had been performing in exhibitions while offering 25 cents per minute to all comers if he failed to defeat them. According to *The Herald of Yonkers*, a New York City publication, this was not an offer Ross had any business extending to anyone, as he was "far from his old-time form, being out of training, fat, and considerably the worse for wear."

Highland Games and Hippodromes

An untrained local known as "Big Muskrat" from the Penobscot Indian Island Reservation took Ross up on his offer, and arrived accompanied by his fellow tribesmen clad in buckskin trousers and moccasins.

"At the call of time the Indian was on his adversary with a tigerlike spring, and came near securing a fall in the first ten seconds," described *The Herald*. "The contest was a terrible one, and, while Ross had the advantage in weight, height, and skill, the quickness of the Indian and his ability to wriggle out of holds and locks saved him many a fall, while he succeeded in getting Ross on the points three times. Although only a fractional part of a second, the referee called them falls and awarded the bout to the Indian. The decision was questioned, but the referee was obdurate."

The Boston Post also picked up on the humiliating episode. The paper expressed surprise that Ross was wrestling at all, condemned him as "one of the oldest of the old timers," claimed that everyone "thought he had called it all off," and scoffed at the notion that he fancied himself to still be "a world beater."

The following month in Bangor, Maine, an embarrassing scenario of a different kind played itself out at the local opera house, and *The Daily News* of Bangor dismissed it as "one of the greatest fakes of the season."

"Capt. Duncan Ross was to have met Ed Seguin in a wrestling and boxing match, and also to give an exhibition of feats of swordsmanship," began *The Daily News*. "Seguin was not even in town, and Ross had imbibed so much of the ardent that he was in no condition to give an exhibition of any kind. After a few exhibitions of boxing between small boys belonging in town, Ross came upon the stage and wrestled with Leon Thomas of Mapleton, and was thrown twice. This ended the 'athletic exhibition.'"

Duncan McMillan and Dan McLeod were back to working with one another by the spring of 1902. In Buffalo, the burgeoning partnership between the two Scotsmen was revealed in an article titled "McMillan is training Dan

McLeod," and supported by the subtitle "Gigantic wrestler from the pacific coast working secretly with the great little Scot."

This coach-trainee relationship had reportedly been formed to help McLeod prepare to wrestle against English champion Jim Parr in Hamilton, Ontario, but *The Buffalo Courier* included quotes suggesting that the relationship between the two men went way back, and even alluded to McMillan's identity as a "Scottish-American" as providing a basis for the alliance that was rooted in ethnic pride.

"I have known Dan since he came out as a wrestler; I want to say to you that I have never seen him so strong and fast as he is at present," said McMillan. "I really believe he can throw any white man in the world from three to five times an hour, and I firmly believe that he will do the trick to Parr in much less than the hour."

For the record, the qualification that McLeod could only throw "any white man" represented a common hedge of the time, which made allowances for wrestlers primarily from the Ottoman Empire and India, who were scarcely considered human as a consequence of their exceptional size and strength.

The training services seemingly worked both ways. Two weeks after McLeod's victory over Parr, when McMillan was preparing to take his own shot at Parr in a mixed-styles bout, *The Hamilton Spectator* printed that McLeod would be training McMillan for his opportunity at the Englishman.

McMillan lost the bout, but retained his claim on five-styles championship status as only three styles were wrestled in the bout.

Realistically, the relationship between McMillan and McLeod was whatever it needed to be in the setting and circumstances the two Scotsmen found themselves wrestling in. When both men soon migrated eastward to Waterbury, Connecticut, they faced each other as adversaries with nothing divulged of their prior relationship or training partnership from just a few months earlier.

Highland Games and Hippodromes

In a bout with a result that McMillan would never acknowledge until the day he died, McLeod defeated him in a five-styles wrestling match "for the American championship held by McMillan" in Waterbury by winning the catch-as-catch-can, sidehold, and Cornish falls, while McMillan won the Greco-Roman and collar-and-elbow rounds. Ostensibly, McLeod entered the match at a weight of 168 pounds and surmounted a 50-pound weight difference in order to beat the 218-pound McMillan in his signature match.

As almost a tacit acknowledgement of this defeat, McMillan downgraded his championship claim. By the time he wrestled and defeated M.J. Dwyer in a five-styles match in Scranton, Pennsylvania that December, he was only bold enough to boast of being the "champion of Milwaukee."

McMillan stated after his victory over Dwyer that he would next challenge "Daniel McLeod, champion of the world," who he had "wrestled to a tie match several years ago." McMillan seemed to be conceding that McLeod was the five-styles champion of wrestling while also selectively omitting his loss to McLeod from two months earlier.

McLeod and Tom Jenkins wouldn't meet on the mat again until the summer of 1902. That June, McLeod spent a great deal of time in Cleveland training at the Star Theater with "The Cuban Wonder" Clarence Bouldin — an undersized wrestler and future world middleweight champion who was secretly half-Black. Afterwards, McLeod and Jenkins met in a non-title bout in which Jenkins endeavored to defeat McLeod twice in an hour and a half, but was able to gain only one fall after nearly a full hour of wrestling.

On July 4, 1902, McLeod and Jenkins had a rematch at Cleveland's League Park, and Jenkins took two consecutive falls from McLeod in well under an hour to retain his championship. It would later be seen that this bout was merely a ruse intended to lure the overconfident gambling community of Cleveland and Buffalo into an eventual trap.

Paying close attention to the way money was being wagered on the fight, *The Akron Beacon-Journal* reported that

Jenkins was a betting favorite at 2 to 1, "but there was little betting on the final result." Instead, the majority of the wagers being placed were even-money bets that McLeod would get a fall. Truly, this was the only logical way to capitalize on the most gullible gamblers of Cleveland, since the city was too wild about Jenkins to ever wager against him outright.

Of course, publications like *The Buffalo Enquirer* viewed the bout as being emblematic of Jenkins' growing dominance, and underscored that Jenkins was now the real champion of America and champion of the world, "barring the gigantic and hardly human Turks."

"This will forever dispose of McLeod as an aspirant for championship honors, at least until Jenkins retires from the mat," the paper proudly proclaimed.

As sure of this statement as wrestling fans in Cleveland and Buffalo may have been, elsewhere in the country, McLeod was nigh unbeatable. As the year progressed, McLeod bullied the rest of his opponents, regardless of their weight. In Massachusetts, he crushed heavyweight Hjalmar Lundin in three straight falls. Then McLeod followed that up by defending his world middleweight championship — a title he still selectively laid claim to in parts of the United States — by winning three consecutive falls over Ed Atherton.

This activity was restorative to the reputation of McLeod and served as a prelude to one of the most controversial finishes in the early history of professional wrestling in North America.

Finally facing Jenkins on what could best be described as the neutral ground of Mechanic's Hall in Worcester, Massachusetts, McLeod recaptured the world heavyweight championship from an "injured" Jenkins in front of 1,100 fans. The bout is best remembered for its theatricality, as Jenkins — who complained of "blood poisoning" in his left leg — took to the mat with his leg wrapped in leather, "and with a strip of steel extending from his knee to his ankle."

"The case was fastened with brass buckles, whose pins were bent in the third bout of the match," reported *The Boston*

Globe. "The pins began to dig into the flesh, and after 20 minutes, Jenkins could stand the pain no longer. Jenkins told McLeod he was willing to go on, or quit and have the match called a draw. McLeod insisted on continuing, but Harry Pollok, Jenkins' manager, refused to let his man wrestle, fearing he would injure his leg permanently."

Two-time world heavyweight champion Dan McLeod

McLeod was then awarded the title of world heavyweight champion for a second time, as the crowd "showed its disapproval of the abrupt ending by hissing."

Perusal of the Cleveland media's reaction to Jenkins' title loss reveals that the result of the Worcester match probably had less to do with the gambling activity in

Massachusetts than it did with reviving box office interest in Jenkins back in Ohio, where fans had "begun to look at the Newburg man as being almost invincible"... which had been financially ruinous.

"In truth it had become a fact that the local wrestling enthusiasts failed to attend the bouts in which Jenkins was a participant, being of the belief that Tom's opponent would be defeated," conceded *The Plain Dealer*. "When he met McInerney at the Gray's Armory ten days ago, there were only about 1,000 persons present, but it is no exaggeration to say that after 10 o'clock that evening the *Plain Dealer* received at least 300 telephone calls asking the time of the falls. The fact that they did not ask 'who won' shows the confidence reposed in the former champion."

As a consequence of the amorphous way in which McLeod was defined after capturing the world heavyweight championship from Farmer Burns, his recovery of the title from Jenkins was almost required to validate his original championship reign.

The lone caveat to that claim is that the manner in which McLeod reacquired his world championship was easily the most unorthodox in the title's lineage. It marked the first time that the premier wrestling championship in North America adorned a wrestler who was seen as being inferior to the wrestler he had taken it from during the very match in which he captured it.

Soon, it wouldn't matter whether Dan McLeod or Tom Jenkins was the better wrestler of the duo. The fact is McLeod's eye for wrestling talent had been transcendant, and his recruit from years earlier would prove to be so pivotal to the wrestling industry that within a few years he would render almost everything that preceded him as inconsequential.

21 – The Hottest of Them All

Following his re-coronation at the expense of Tom Jenkins, Dan McLeod traveled to New York City, and as 1903 began, he provided a quote about his tainted world title victory to *The New York Sun*.

"It has been my ambition all along to beat Jenkins and at least I have succeeded," offered McLeod. "I knew right along that I was his master, and those who witnessed the bout will agree that I won on my merits. I see Jenkins says that he quit because his leg was injured, and that he was afraid of blood poisoning. Well, that may look feasible to some, but the general public will not swallow that gag.

"Jenkins, to all appearances, was fit, and in good trim when the bout started. The way he started negotiations for the first fall proves that he was strong and out to down me. But I was well supplied with strength, too, and gave back as good as I received. I am not afraid of Jenkins nor any man breathing. I will meet him again any time. He gave me a chance to retrieve myself, and I will give him another chance, too."

Meanwhile, a crestfallen Jenkins provided an apologetic statement to the people of Cleveland through the Associated Press. After beginning his apology by saying that he had no desire "to belittle McLeod's showing," the dethroned Jenkins proceeded to do exactly that.

"I was in no condition to go on with McLeod. I am no quitter, and never as yet disappointed an audience," said Jenkins. "My forfeit was up, and rather than abandon the bout at the last moment, I consented to go on. In my bout with Jim Parr, the English champion, at Buffalo last week, I received an ugly kick on the shin of my left leg. A bruise resulted, and the color from the trunks which I wore ran into my blood and I was threatened with blood poisoning.

"Although I suffered intense pain, I met Bothner for a full hour. During that affair the bruise grew worse, and despite the warning of my physician I agreed to take McLeod on. In my contest with McLeod, the twisting, turning and rubbing against the bruise aggravated matters to such an extent that I thought my leg would come off from sheer pain. After 20 minutes' work in the third fall I gave up, not because I was not game, but because I didn't care to jeopardize my life. I have beaten McLeod on several occasions, and do not wish to be considered as having a streak of yellow in me. It was an unfortunate ending to what looked like a sure victory for me. If McLeod will meet me again I will agree to make a match for the best part of $5,000 a side as soon as my wounds heal."

The Rochester Democrat and Chronicle, attempting to assess the matter neutrally, reminded readers that just six years ago there was no wrestler in the country that "ranked with the Scot," but that Jenkins had handled his opponents with such ease that he was "tacitly given the title" that belonged to McLeod before cementing his hold on the championship through an actual victory over him.

"[Jenkins'] defeat in the last two falls was entirely unexpected to those who had watched his brilliant work in the first bout," observed *The Democrat and Chronicle*. "Subsequent to the match, McLeod declared that he had really thrown Jenkins — falls which were overlooked by the referee — and he added that while it was practically impossible to defeat Jenkins in Cleveland, he would take care of him the first time he got him outside of Forest City. And he did. McLeod is not the man to stand still now that he is at the top. He will keep on wrestling. There is little reason to believe that Jenkins will be denied an early return match, and McLeod, while in Buffalo the other night, declared he stood ready to meet Parr and expected the match would be made shortly."

A landmark reunion occurred during McLeod's second reign with America's top wrestling title. During another stay by McLeod in Buffalo, he was reunited with his former Olympic Club training partner James J. Corbett, who had lost his world heavyweight boxing championship to Bob Fitzsimmons in 1897 after a four-and-a-half-year reign, and who was now enjoying a short retirement from the ring that would not be his last.

The men reunited in front of reporters at the Iroquois Hotel, and reminisced about the days when Corbett seconded McLeod during his San Francisco wrestling bouts, and especially his bout against Evan Lewis' associate Tom McInerney, which resulted in a near riot.

"There's the hottest of them all on the mat, the best wrestler, and it seems remarkable how quick he picked things up," Corbett remarked to the gaggle of reporters about McLeod after the Scot was temporarily summoned away. "He was green first in the good old days out there, and for a time in the gymnasium I tossed him about, but I soon had to stop that, and so did better wrestlers. And McLeod is wrestling better than them all after all these years!"

The reference to McInerney was not merely for the sake of dredging up old memories. That same month, McLeod returned to Cleveland, the home of his arch-rival Jenkins, to defend his newly restored championship against McInerney at Gray's Armory, more than a dozen years after their first meeting nearly 2,500 miles away.

"It was not a one-sided affair by any means, and the conqueror of Jenkins had to work hard to win the deciding fall," stated *The Cleveland Leader*. "For a time it looked as though the Scotchman's claim to the championship would be short-lived, but he proved himself to be the hard man of yore, and when the contest was over McInerney was hardly able to leave the ring."

McLeod lost a rare fall to a wrestler not named Burns or Jenkins when he dropped the first round to McInerney, but came back and definitively won the final two falls to retain his championship.

In one respect, McLeod definitely managed to upstage Jenkins in his own city. *The Leader* reported how "every seat was taken" at Gray's Armory that night, resulting in a crowd that was "the largest that ever attended a match in this city." *The Plain Dealer* backed this observation with facts by confirming that there were more than 3,000 fans present at the Armory to watch McLeod battle McInerney, while Jenkins had struggled to attract even 1,000 attendees to his most recent matches.

The April return bout between Jenkins and McLeod was held at the 65th Regiment Arsenal in Buffalo, and McLeod managed to hold out for one hour and 17 minutes in the first fall before Jenkins eluded his grasp and pinned him to the mat. Fourteen minutes after the action resumed, Jenkins pinned McLeod once again after "smashing [McLeod's] bridge with his two hundred pounds flat to the mat."

For one of the first times in his career, McLeod was evidently the less fit grappler on the mat. McLeod's normally chiseled frame was uncharacteristically soft, "his flesh being somewhat flabby despite the hard training and weight reduction," in the words of *The Cleveland Leader*.

Again, the press sought to draft McLeod's epitaph, insisting that Jenkins had permanently banished McLeod from the upper echelon of heavyweight title contenders. They would be forced to revisit this opinion in four short months when McLeod and Jenkins reunited in Ontario.

Refusing to defend his title against McLeod again until the Scot earned the right to compete for it, Jenkins instead endeavored to face McLeod in a handicap match, wherein Jenkins would be required to defeat McLeod twice in one hour or be declared the loser. Aside from this, McLeod could bring a halt to the contest early by pinning Jenkins only once.

In front of as many as 1,300 Hamiltonians, the least likely ending to the bout miraculously played out, as McLeod was aggressive throughout the majority of the match, which his friends in the audience thought was a "fatal error" in his strategy. At first it seemed as if they were correct in their assumption, as Jenkins earned the first fall of the match in less than 16 minutes.

It goes without saying that the betting at this juncture would have leaned heavily toward Jenkins winning the match outright, since he still had 44 minutes remaining to apply the winning fall to McLeod. Yet, when the action resumed,

McLeod was the clear aggressor, and "went at his big opponent like a demon and quickly forced him to the mat."

"The Clevelander twisted, squirmed and bridged in his efforts to get away, but failed," recounted *The Hamilton Spectator*. "For fully a minute he struggled in vain. McLeod finally placed one knee on the champion's neck and then threw his whole weight onto his chest, breaking his bridge and forcing his shoulders to the mat. Jenkins was all out when he got up and staggered to his corner. The audience became wildly enthusiastic and cheered the game little Scot to the echo."

"I have no excuses to offer," Jenkins told the crowd after McLeod hastened back to his dressing room. "I took a long chance in giving McLeod such a handicap, and there's no use complaining now."

McLeod's sudden recovery to pin Jenkins was startling to anyone who either wagered that Jenkins would win the match, or that McLeod would win by extending the bout to its time limit.

When the men wrestled two months later at Old City Hall in Pittsburgh, in an event touted as the "effort to introduce professional wrestling into Pittsburgh," and "the first time in the history of Pittsburgh that a world's championship in wrestling was decided here," it was a financial disaster.

On the night of the match, no more than 400 fans showed up to Old City Hall to watch the men tussle for the world championship. Jenkins won the first round in 18 minutes with a half nelson and arm lock, and then McLeod flattened Jenkins with a three-quarter nelson in only five-and-a-half minutes. Eight minutes later, Jenkins won the final round and the entire match with another half nelson and arm hold.

Days later, the low attendance for the bout was blamed on the distrust of the public that what they were watching was feigned action, combined with the fact that the feud between Jenkins and McLeod, which had now continued for the better part of two years, had run its course.

The Buffalo Times skewered the pair's Pittsburgh bout, calling it "an alleged wrestling match," and saying that it was "pretty nearly time that the chestnut bell was rung on this pair," citing an expression from the era that was used to signal when a joke had become stale and had lost its humor.

"These so-called matches between these two men are merely exhibitions, and as such lack interest and novelty," accused *The Times*. "How long a gullible public will stand for them is a question hard to solve, as some unidentified philosopher ages ago gave utterance to a great truism when he declared 'A sucker is born every minute.' Promoters of honest sport will serve the public and themselves a good turn by refusing to put this pair on in the future."

Ignoring the request that they should pack it in, McLeod and Jenkins still had one more high-profile bout left in them. In December 1903, they met in New York City's Madison Square Garden in front of 3,000 fans — a figure only one-third of that drawn by the Terrible Turks at that same venue during their brief era of box office dominance.

In an effort to regain his lost championship just before the year reached its end, McLeod was apparently willing to pull out all the stops. After dragging Jenkins to the mat in the opening round, McLeod applied a full nelson to his opponent, and then made the unusual transition to a stranglehold that mirrored the tactics of his old foe Evan Lewis.

"Jenkins struggled desperately to keep the slowly advancing sinewy member from approaching the throat, for he realized that its pressure meant the strangle, and, with the already secure crotch lock, an almost certain fall," reported *The New York News*. "But the arm steadily crept up, and just as steadily McLeod crept over the receding form. A final shove brought McLeod's wrist across Jenkins' windpipe, and he ceased breathing. McLeod felt the great chest under his suddenly stop heaving, and threw all his weight on Jenkins."

McLeod was awarded the first fall after nine minutes and 52 seconds, but he would not be able to capitalize on his early success. Jenkins won the second fall in 22 minutes with a "roll and bar lock," and then exploited McLeod's loss of balance when the Scot attempted to apply a hammerlock, and rolled him up for the final fall after another 10 minutes and 39 seconds.

Incidentally, *The New York News* featured several details about McLeod's origin in its coverage, including his background as a Highland Games competitor. However, it also added the detail that he had paid a year of tuition to Joe Acton, "at that time the professional instructor of wrestling for the Olympic Amateur Athletic Club." The paper then stated that McLeod had turned against Acton, challenged him, and then "won from him in one of the famous matches in the sport."

In actuality, Acton had been employed as a wrestling instructor for the California Athletic Club of San Francisco, a rival organization of the Olympic Club to which McLeod had never directly been associated. Be that as it may, it can't be ruled out that McLeod received some direct instruction in the art of working a professional wrestling match from Acton.

Evidently, the McLeod-Jenkins series had run its course, as their matches drew rather poorly relative to the crowd sizes that other matchups had been able to attract at the same venues. At the conclusion of the series, McLeod was on the outside looking in with respect to the world heavyweight championship. The elevation of the next world title contender would displace McLeod even further from title contention, while simultaneously adding to his legend and legacy.

While McLeod and Jenkins had been feuding over the world heavyweight championship, Farmer Burns prepared to face Frank Gotch in yet another of a series of passing-of-the-torch matches, and he took the time to reflect on his career to *The Tacoma Daily News*. Clearly doing his part to position Gotch as the biggest star of the next era, Burns described his protege as "the fastest big man of his size" that he had ever seen in the sport, and tacked on that Dan McLeod shared his opinion that Gotch had "a better chance of securing the championship of America than any other man."

Burns also spoke very favorably of his old associate Duncan McMillan, who "in his day was good at five styles of wrestling" and "could defeat me in those kinds of wrestling, while I could beat him at catch-as-catch-can."

At the time these words were uttered, McMillan had already made the decision to permanently resettle in the Pacific Northwest, and allowed his activities as a trainer and promoter to move to the forefront. Now thousands of miles from where he had lost his five-styles title to McLeod, he nominally reclaimed the championship for the sake of boosting his reputation in the new area he had chosen to call home.

"McMillan is a native of Hamilton, and though he has been a professional athlete for many years, in all-round wrestling he is top of the heap yet," declared *The Vancouver Daily Province* as it introduced McMillan to wrestling fans in Dan McLeod's home province. "McMillan is also famous as a champion in Caledonian games, and has two or three trunks full of medals which he carried away at St. Andrew's Day celebrations."

McMillan may have changed his base of operations and his primary role in the wrestling business, but capitalizing on the greed of sportsmen still remained one of his obvious priorities. In Whatcom, Washington, the result of a Gotch bout that McMillan promoted was projected to "bring an end to the wrestling carnival that has prevailed here for several months" on account of the money that was lost by the local gamblers.

Gotch faced John Berg that night, the "champion of the Northwest" who had gone undefeated in all of his prior bouts in the area. Because of his unblemished record, Berg's Swedish friends reportedly "backed him to the limit." Even after Gotch won the first fall, *The Tacoma Daily Ledger* observed that Berg's supporters "were still betting on him, getting odds heavier," only to be devastated when Gotch immediately took the second fall and ended the encounter. *The Ledger* estimated that pro-Gotch bettors left with "$6,000 in good coin of the local sports."

When the 25-year-old Gotch very abruptly replaced McLeod as Tom Jenkins' primary rival, and almost as quickly won the world heavyweight championship from him at a

McMillan show in Bellingham, Washington, it marked the return of the world title to its familiar home in the camp of Burns and McMillan, and also cued the start of a new era in professional wrestling.

Farmer Burns (left) and Frank Gotch

At the same time, the ascension of Gotch — the son of German immigrants — ended the Celtic immigrant monopoly over North America's top title that had extended to nearly 17 consecutive years.

Concomitant to this, Gotch's coronation transformed the tale of his first encounter with the disguised Daniel

Highland Games and Hippodromes

McLeod from an interesting anecdote into a crucial piece of professional wrestling lore.

One of Gotch's first orders of business as the new world heavyweight champion of catch-as-catch-can was to tour the Pacific Northwest and headline the events promoted by McMillan. Gotch further proclaimed himself to be the one true world heavyweight champion, and feigned umbrage at McMillan's audacious claim to be "the best five-style wrestler in the world."

"Mr. McMillan has claimed for some time that he is the champion five-style wrestler of the world, and it seems no one has disputed it, but I do now, and post my money to that effect," said Gotch. "I will name six styles of wrestling, and he can pick any five he wishes. The six styles are Greco-Roman, collar-and-elbow, either in jackets or harness; side holds, Cumberland, Cornish, and catch-as-catch-can. I will make this match for any part of $1,000."

The Gotch-McMillan five-styles bout would be delayed, but the effects of Gotch's popularity were already evident. When their tour hit Montana in May, *The Montana Daily Record* reported how the Gotch-Jenkins title bout in Washington had performed even better financially as a pure box office attraction than the bout between Jenkins and McLeod that was held in New York City's Madison Square Garden.

While these signs of wrestling's resurgence had been underway, Duncan Ross had continued to struggle along. October 1903 brought about perhaps the greatest in a multi-year string of embarrassments for Ross, as *The Transcript* of North Adams, Massachusetts was on hand to cover the opening of Ross' school of physical culture at the city's G.A.R. Hall.

Still claiming to be the world champion of mixed wrestling, at least for the sake of promoting his own school, Ross opened the ceremony with a display of his swordsmanship, and then offered the Canns — a pair of brothers who attended his school's grand opening — 50 cents for every minute that they could avoid being pinned by him. Wilfred Cann stepped forward to face Ross first, and the scene that ensued was thoroughly humiliating.

"A.T. Lacey of Adams was chosen referee and Captain Ross started in on his contract. Cann never before demonstrated his agility and ability to escape from tight places so satisfactorily as he did last night," reported *The Transcript*. "Although about 80 pounds lighter than his big opponent, there were only two instances when he narrowly escaped a fall, both times Ross having a half Nelson. For about six minutes Cann succeeded at one time in remaining behind his big opponent, industriously and dexterously avoiding all efforts to break his hold around Ross' waist. Cann was heartily cheered when Ross, at the end of 30 minutes announced that he was sorry that he could not throw Cann, 'But he squirms and flops around and is too quick for me,' he said."

Failing to pin even one of the Canns, Ross was forced to fork over $15 to Wilfred Cann and then declined to face the younger Cann brother. This scene likely caused those who gathered in the hope of attending Ross' school to wonder exactly what there was of value about wrestling that Ross was actually qualified to teach them.

In March 1904, Ross' name was invoked during a discussion as to whether or not the armory in Manchester, Connecticut would be permitted to hold a wrestling event. The local Pierce Athletic Club requested to hold an amateur wrestling show there, but wrestling events had been categorically banned in the city due to a volatile situation that followed a particularly chaotic show.

"The building is owned by several men in town and is managed by F.E. Watkins, and it was rumored after the night that Duncan Ross was escorted to the police station by Chief Sheridan and followed by a howling mob that the armory would not be again rented for such events," informed *The Waterbury Democrat*. "This rumor has been verified by the refusal of Mr. Watkins to rent it to the Pierce Club. When the committee reported this to the meeting of the club, it was decided best by the members to drop all connection with wrestling matches."

Coincidentally, this public reminder about the bedlam left in Ross' wake and its lingering consequences ran alongside a separate article about the popular suggestion of adding a points system to wrestling bouts. The intention was to shorten the lengths of matches to keep them standardized, and prevent them from lasting too long.

As the 1904 Olympic Games would mark the first time freestyle wrestling was contested, the incorporation of a points system became a critical device for drawing clearer lines of separation between amateur and professional wrestling contests, enabling both combat forms to evolve along different paths.

Still touring New England in May, Ross held a wrestling show at the armory in Burlington, Vermont in front of "about fifty local sports" while advertising himself as "the only man that ever threw the Terrible Turk," and challenging all comers to face him. Apparently, there was nothing about the conduct or disposition of the nearly 50-year-old Ross that would have convinced anyone present that he had ever been a championship-caliber athlete, let alone a world-class wrestler.

"How much of a wrestler he may be when in good condition cannot be judged from the exhibition of Saturday night, for at that time he staggered about the room, telling in disjointed sentences what he could do, and challenging any of those present to go to the mat with him," reported *The Free Press* of Burlington. "As this call met with no response, Eugene Ladue of Syracuse, who is travelling with Mr. Ross, wrestled with him. The supposed champion Ross weighs about 250 pounds, and Mr. Ladue scarcely more than one-half that amount, but the little fellow had but little difficulty in taking two falls out of his gigantic adversary in less than ten minutes' time."

It's unknown whether the loss to his assistant was pre-planned in order to maximize revenue from wagers, or if a drunken Ross truly instructed Ladue to defeat him if he was able, believing that he couldn't possibly do so. In either case, a convincing loss by Ross to an assistant half his size did little to polish an image that was becoming more tarnished with each passing week.

Ross' exhibition in the Vermont town of Barre the following month made matters even worse. In the middle of a bout with Robert Ewen at the Barre Opera House, Ross turned his back to his opponent, walked to his corner, and refused to complete the match after complaining that Ewen had attempted to strangle him twice and had not been cautioned by the referee.

Referee Jerry Donahue explained to the press afterwards that Ewen's arm had been "around the back of Ross' neck, but not on his throat," and that he requested Ross to return to the mat three times before stepping to the center of the stage and declaring the bout to have been won by Ewen.

"There were about 250 people present and they set up a terrible din when the decision was announced," observed the sportswriter from *The Daily Times* of Barre. "Cries of 'fake' and 'squealer' were heard and many people rushed the stage."

The next day, Ross visited the office of *The Daily Times* and ranted to the sports editor that he had "never run up against such a dirty, cowardly pack of thieves and robbers" as he had in Barre, Vermont, and that included his travels "all over Europe, China, Japan, and the United States." The furious Ross added that he "forgot more wrestling every day than his opponent ever knew or ever would know," and then threatened to bring legal action against "the pack" that had troubled him in Barre.

The Daily Times followed this up soon thereafter with a pronouncement that "the sports of Barre" had simply been "the latest to be inveigled into spending their money to see a wrestling match conducted by that wreck of a once powerful athlete, Duncan C. Ross."

"They are indignant because the match was a fizzle, although all of the affairs which Ross has conducted in

Highland Games and Hippodromes

Vermont of late have ended in about the same way," added the paper. "There was a time once when immense crowds of people in New York and other large cities paid high prices to see this man in action, but he fell a victim to the allurements which are constantly in the way of men of his kind, and now is merely picking up an existence in small towns on the strength of his past reputation. But there are very few more dollars waiting for him in Vermont evidently."

Many miles away, Dan McLeod was lured back to the Pacific Northwest for an extended homecoming in British Columbia. Perhaps not so coincidentally, the move coincided with Duncan McMillan's promotional efforts in the region, and the prospect of a future world championship match between Frank Gotch and Dan McLeod on the little Scot's home turf was dangled in front of wrestling fans for several months.

The men finally presented the long-awaited match to between 2,000 and 4,000 Vancouverites in August 1904 at Brockton Point. The event was held under the clear management of McMillan, who stepped before the crowd to introduce the referee, and signalled for the entry of the combatants.

The sportsmen of Vancouver were highly active throughout the match, with Gotch's supporters "offering two to one on their man," while "plenty of McLeod money was to be had," and "several thousand dollars changed hands at the ringside on Saturday afternoon."

Thirty-one minutes into the bout, McLeod trapped Gotch in a half nelson and crotch hold, turned Gotch onto his back, and then "threw himself on the visitor's chest." Gotch attempted to bridge out of it, but the strength of his neck waned beneath McLeod's weight, and McLeod was awarded the first fall of the bout. The grand stand at Brockton Point "shook with applause," as "hats went in the air and voices cracked." The B.C. residents cheered their hometown hero for scoring a first-round pinfall against the reigning world heavyweight champion, and the gambling men at ringside made a few rapid recalculations to the offered odds.

Highland Games and Hippodromes

"After the first fall, which went to McLeod, betting was still free at even money, and even when Gotch won the second fall, many of the visitor's supporters considered even money still good enough, though some went back at two to one, and a few figured the correct odds as ten to eight on Gotch," observed the writer from *The Vancouver Daily World*.

Dan McLeod with his signature cross-armed pose

Once Gotch recovered to level the bout at one fall apiece 23 minutes into the second round, he appeared to display conditioning superior to that of his older Scottish opponent. Inevitably, Gotch took McLeod down, caught him in a scissor hold and a half nelson, and pinned McLeod "amid roars of applause and the fluttering of $100 bills and big gold pieces."

Two weeks later, a report began to circulate that McLeod and Gotch had been hippodroming during their match at Brockton Point, which McLeod vehemently denied, and implied that he would visit violence upon the originator of the rumor.

"What might have been arranged between the men possibly, no one knows but themselves," reported the sports editor of *The Vancouver Province*. "This much, however, the sporting editor of this paper can say: McLeod's story that he did not see Gotch after the last match at Brockton Point is true."

The Province then accounted for the whereabouts of both men after the event, specifically that McLeod was occupied with a bath while Gotch was catching the train out of town.

"It is only fair to both men to state these facts," continued *The Province*. "All sorts of rumors have been going around, as they always do, and *The Province* has heard as many of them as anyone else. What has happened since, or what might happen, cannot, of course, be known, but any tale of the men coming together immediately after the match and making new arrangements may be set down as absolutely false."

Apparently, no one bothered to ask whether or not McMillan — the organizer of the bout between his protege, Gotch, and his fellow Scotsman who had aided in the recruitment of that protege, McLeod — had visited with both men either before or after the bout.

It wouldn't be until August 1905, in another bout that McMillan would deny to have taken place, that Frank Gotch effectively ended any claims McMillan may have had to any sort of world championship status when he defeated him in three consecutive falls in a five-styles match. Gotch took the opening catch-as-catch-can round in 19 minutes, the Greco-Roman bout in nine minutes, and the Cornish fall in just over four minutes.

Highland Games and Hippodromes

The people of Butte were said to be "not surprised at the outcome of the match," as the 51-year-old McMillan — who was claiming to be 43 — was crushed by the 27-year-old superstar whose wrestling career McMillan had helped to launch.

While not a true championship unification bout, the match served to definitively mark the end of an era, as catch-as-catch-can became the only wrestling style of importance as far as pro wrestling was concerned, and the differences in interpretation between the "amateur" and "professional" methods of that style would only grow more pronounced as time passed.

Incidentally, right before that match, Gotch issued derogatory comments about a new grappling style sweeping the nation known as jiu jitsu. The world heavyweight wrestling champion categorically dismissed it as "a fad" that was essentially worthless against other styles of combat.

"They have not a hold which is not known to our wrestlers, but the first rule of wrestling is that nothing unfair is allowed, hence in wrestling we do not break fingers, gouge out eyes or choke a person," proclaimed Gotch. "As for killing a man, if called upon some evening to protect yourself, would you not rather get up the next morning with the knowledge that you had protected yourself without doing so than to know that you had?

"A person versed in jiu jitsu may be able to practice it all right on an inexperienced person, but the experienced wrestler and boxer can guard against jiu jitsu. To make jiu jitsu effective you must first get close to your opponent and secure a hold, and this hold the wrestler can prevent your securing. A wrestler or boxer can break an arm or leg easily enough, but disdains to do so. Wrestling is more civilized than jiu jitsu. Wrestling is a sport. Jiu jitsu is too dangerous for that, being essentially a method of offense or defense without the redeeming features of wrestling or boxing."

Within a few years, Gotch would win what would become universally recognized as the truest of world heavyweight wrestling championships when he defeated strongman and wrestler George Hackenschmidt in Chicago to claim the honor.

This victory would elevate Gotch to American folk-hero status, while also erasing from consideration the fact that the "American championship" that Gotch had previously owned was once almost universally regarded as a world championship in its own right on North American soil.

Along with this erasure of a world-title lineage also came a general disregard for much of what preceded Gotch's rise, with the influence of the Scots who aided his ascent fading from memory rather than ascending into legend. As such, the era of professional wrestling that was flavored with a steady dose of both Highland Games and hippodromes was also forgotten, as the period of the Highland Clearances passed, and was followed by the widespread immersion of Scots into a homogenized North American identity.

Epilogue

As a man who had made the bulk of his lifetime income by winning prizes in athletic competitions, it was improbable that Donald Dinnie would simply fade away and disappear from Caledonian festivals altogether, at least not immediately. Even in his 70s, Dinnie was still endeavoring to arrange any sort of contest that would allow him to impress a crowd, even if they could no longer marvel at his prowess in an absolute sense, but were instead wowed by Dinnie's strength in consideration of his advancing age.

Ahead of the 1907 Highland Games of Clydebank, which sits to the northwest of Glasgow, Dinnie said he was willing to wager £25 that no other person 60 years of age or over would be able to outwrestle or outthrow him, thereby offering a handicap of up to 11 years.

For the record, Dinnie's throwing challenge was accepted by Mr. Gray of Glasgow, "but Donald proved himself still a capable exponent of the hammer, winning easily." He went on to repeat the challenge at other games, with his offers seldom accepted, and when Dinnie *was* taken up on his offer, it was nearly always the offer to throw the hammer alongside him, as few dared to wrestle against him.

Perhaps it's just as well that no one took Dinnie up on his wrestling challenge considering the lengths that he had not only gone to in efforts to expunge the loss in Scottish-style wrestling that he suffered in Australia, but also the lengths he would ultimately go to in order to defend his legacy from public criticism, including his competence as a wrestler.

In October 1908, Dinnie filed a lawsuit in an Edinburgh court, suing the Moray and Nairn Newspaper Company for £500. In the lawsuit, Dinnie alleged that the news publisher had made slanderous statements against him when they committed the unthinkable offense of suggesting that he wasn't as superb of an athlete as he had been advertised to be.

"In their issue of '*Northern Scot and Moray* and *Nairn Express*' of Saturday, August 31, 1907, the defendants published a letter signed 'Athletic Correspondent,' which contained the following statement: 'As a matter of fact, Dinnie was only a third-class wrestler and hammer-thrower when at his best, the only feat he was first-class at being the caber,'" reported *The Liverpool Echo*. "It was also alleged that he had no records.

"These and other statements which were made, the plaintiff says, were untrue and slanderous, and were published maliciously. They were intended to represent, and did represent, he says, that his reputation as a first-class athlete was without foundation, and that he held no records as a professional athlete. He further avers that it was represented that he was unable to attain distinction in hammer-throwing unless he had a particular hammer, which enabled him to take an unfair advantage of the other competitors, and that he was accordingly guilty of dishonest practices in hammer-throwing competitions in which he engaged."

As the criteria for determining the skillfulness of a person in one discipline or another are often skewed by the reference point that is chosen for comparison, it would be completely unfair to dismiss Dinnie as a third-rate wrestler in an absolute sense. However, in comparison to other professional wrestlers who received years of advanced training and polish in the finer points of the catch-and-catch-can and Greco-Roman disciplines, it does not appear that Dinnie should be included in their number.

Yet, if we eliminate the pretense that most professional wrestling shows were making no efforts to actually determine who the best wrestler truly was, and were instead constructed for the sole purpose of attracting money, and priming the audience to fork over even more money for future appearances, Dinnie's name recognition as perhaps the most well-rounded athlete in the world at one point in time made him a reliable and potent draw for many years, and in several nations.

On the other hand, the accusation that Dinnie was a third-rate hammer thrower is flatly wrong; the permitted technique of hammer throwing on the world stage evolved over time to permit hammer throwers to rotate their bodies several times before releasing the hammer into the air.

The accepted technique permitted at Highland Games remains the half turn that was allowed in the 19th century when Dinnie was at the peak of his powers, except that even Highland throwers later evolved the technique to permit the practice of spinning the hammer several times overhead before turning to hurl it.

These modifications aside, it is undeniable that Dinnie was a world-class hurler of heavy weights in his day, and a holder of several records.

It was reported around this time in a syndicated piece that Dinnie had won over $125,000 in his career, but had the misfortune of having his considerable savings wiped out by "the great bank failure" that occurred in Australia late in the 19th century, with the bulk of these losses occurring in 1893.

With all due respect to Dinnie, the preponderance of the evidence denotes that he endured ongoing hardship in his efforts to earn a living in Australia. Over the course of Dinnie's professional travels, there were no signs that he came into possession of the resources needed to invest handsomely. Furthermore, in January 1893 — well before the majority of the Australian banks began to flatline — stories of Dinnie's financial struggles were all over the Australian newspapers.

"All over the world Dinnie has traveled, and now past his prime finds himself not so well supplied with worldly gear as he should be to make life at all worth living," disclosed *The Sportsman*, as 1893 opened. "His friends have therefore decided to give him a monster benefit at the Hibernian Hall next Thursday. All admirers of probably the world's most famous all-round Scottish athlete should be present."

Considering the available evidence, it would seem that the Australian banking crisis was used as a cover story to explain how Dinnie had lost a fortune that he had never truly amassed.

In 1913, Dinnie's life challenges were laid bare before the entire world. *The Philadelphia Inquirer*, doing its part to

Highland Games and Hippodromes

spread the heartbreaking news, revealed how Dinnie, "at one time champion and all-round athlete of the world, is now, at the age of seventy-six, living in poverty in Croydon."

The publication praised Dinnie for being able to live for 50 years on the money he had acquired through competitions, but since the elderly athlete had exhausted all of his resources, a fund was being raised to keep him in comfort for the remainder of his life.

The paper credited Dinnie with winning "the American *Police Gazette* mixed wrestling championship" along with "the Melbourne tournament, when he wrestled in seven styles." Seemingly, both of these conferred achievements were references to his exploits in Australia, where he defeated William Miller in a seven-styles bout to win Australia's version of the world championship, but there is no record of him winning the faux version of the *Police Gazette* diamond belt in Australia, as he lost the bout for that version of the championship to Tom Cannon.

When Donald Dinnie passed away in April 1916 at the age of 79, the newswire stated in its description of Dinnie that he was "regarded by many as the greatest athlete Scotland ever produced."

"As far back as 60 years ago, no Highland gathering was complete without the presence of the stalwart son of Aberdeenshire," pitched in *The Springfield Union*. "In later years, when the stalwart frame became less supple, Donald could be found at each of the principal games at Haddo, Stirling, Pitlochry, and Inverness, ready to do his bit and to conquer. At such gatherings, the big burly frame in kilts, with rows upon rows of medals upon the tunic which surmounted it, was inseparable from the elite, for Donald was a proud man; proud of his achievements and proud of the fear which in younger days he had forced upon men."

Sadly, the expected efforts of newspeople to be laudatory of Dinnie to a superfluous degree following his passing led to accomplishments being attributed to him that were wholly unsupported by fact. This was abundantly true when it came time to support his pro wrestling exploits.

"It was in 1882, when in his 45th year, that he won the *Police Gazette* Champion Medal for mixed wrestling in the United States," reported *The Buffalo Times*. "The bouts took place in Plainfield, N.J. in five different styles, and Dinnie threw all the best men of the day, including Captain Daly and Duncan C. Ross. He was 48 years old when he won in six styles out of seven at the Melbourne tournament."

In the first instance, the writer was plainly misremembering the details of the athletic contest that saw Dinnie and Ross compete as teammates against Thomas Lynch and James Daly in an athletic contest that included no wrestling to speak of. Likewise, the "Melbourne tournament" was actually a single mixed-styles bout in which Dinnie defeated the reigning champion William Miller, and held the title for only two weeks before losing it to Clarence Whistler.

Duncan Ross reportedly arrived in Baltimore in January 1917 after he had been erroneously reported dead. With the ownership of Ross' property on West Lexington Street in dispute — presumably property that he had inherited from the estate of his first wife — Ross surprised his relatives by appearing on the scene to "put an end to the mourning for him," and then decided to remain in Baltimore from then on.

Settling into his new home, Ross led a relatively quiet existence by managing a shop on Pennsylvania Avenue, and was referenced in the local press in July 1919 for the bizarre reason that an exhausted carrier-pigeon bearing the notation "G-7073, July 17" under its wing was discovered in his yard.

This occurrence provided Ross with one final opportunity to show expertise of an atypical sort, as he represented himself as an expert in the behaviors of carrier pigeons, and claimed that he would keep the bird in his possession until he had deciphered the meaning of the note.

Two months later, Duncan Ross passed away in Baltimore, Maryland on September 8, 1919. According to the report of his death that ran in *The Baltimore Sun*, Ross was "found dead in the rear of his little curio shop at 1811 ½ Pennsylvania Avenue, shortly after 9 o'clock." Despite Ross having been married at least twice and siring multiple children, he lived alone in his shop, and "there was no one with him when he passed into the great beyond."

Illustration summarizing Duncan Ross' career

"Persons in the neighborhood failed to see him in his shop this morning and thought he might be ill," stated *The Sun*. "They told Patrolman Hitzelberger, of the Northwestern district, who works the post on which he lived, and failing to get any response to his knock, the policeman broke open the door. He found the body of the old soldier lying on a cot. His features were calm and he apparently died peacefully."

Highland Games and Hippodromes

Ross' neighbors had been so concerned about his health that they called the police to check on him one week earlier. The policeman who arrived on the scene to check on Ross found him "sitting in his accustomed chair," and when asked how he was feeling, Ross replied that he was "getting along all right," and would be in good health within a few days.

Ross' body was interred at Loudon Park Cemetery.

Following, Ross' death, he was celebrated as an all-around sports hero of the highest magnitude. Mentions of his achievements included nostalgia-drenched accounts of his wrestling and swordfighting bouts, without any allusion to the fact that Ross had been repeatedly pilloried as the personification of fakery for his exploits in both forms of sports-entertainment. Moreover, his contests with Sergeant Walsh were characterized as a "great feature at the Caledonian games in the North," without mention of the traumatizing incident that resulted in the gruesome death of a horse.

"He could run and jump, put the shot, and toss the caber, which is one of the most difficult as well as dangerous feats listed among sports," gushed *The Norfolk Ledger*. "The caber is something like a wooden telegraph pole, a regular tree stripped of its bark. The athlete raises it, balances it on his hand, and then tosses it with the same motion used in putting the shot.

"It takes a strong man to toss the caber and only a wonderful athlete can tip it, that is, toss it from him so that the butt will hit the ground first and the end of the pole, or tree, strike the ground farthest from the tosser. In other words, to tip the caber the end must fall away from, and not toward, the man who is tossing it. Ross was one of the few who could tip the caber, and the strength and skill required to do this may be imagined when it is recorded that more than one giant has been permanently injured through a dislocated spine sustained when engaged in the sport."

Several years after his retirement, Duncan McMillan would admit to a portion of his hippodroming shenanigans, but only under the veil of insisting that he was always the only one in on whether or not he threw his matches.

McMillan claimed to have been working in Texas under the name of "Turner," and defeated the "big Scotchman" Tom Shields three falls to one by concealing his true identity. Afterwards, McMillan apparently hit up the town of Temple, Texas, and answered the open challenge made by another wrestler while going under the name "Anderson."

"Dunc got a seat in the gallery and finally got a chance," began *The Freeholder*. "The town was wild and money was pretty free. One man recognized McMillan. He placed a big wad of money on him, spreading it around in small bets. Dunc knew this and he also bet $1,000 of his own money, through his friend. The funny part was that he really believed that if he won and got away with the money, he stood a good chance of being killed, the town was so wild.

"So again, he could not afford to win too easily. His opponent was somewhat of a cheese — for Dunc — and he let him get the first fall. This was taking an awful chance, as the match was two in three. But Dunc had to win by the smallest possible margin, and even after losing a fall, had to almost lose another dozen times. He threw the travelling man and again had to come near being thrown several times. Finally, he threw his opponent again, and after he got his money waited in a quiet place for a train that left at 4 o'clock in the morning."

The November 1928 death of Duncan McMillan was amongst the most underpublicized and inauspicious passings of a prominent wrestling figure ever recorded. Time had stripped most people of their memories of McMillan, and a Vancouver street car did the rest, as a two-day delay in the identification process moved what would likely have been a front-page story to page eight of *The Bellingham Herald*.

"Wrestling enthusiasts in the city will regret to know that it was Duncan McMillan, the old-time champion grappler, who was killed by a street car on Thursday at the corner of Georgia and Denman streets," revealed *The Herald*. "The remains are at present lying at Centre and Hanna's undertaking parlor awaiting burial, but the date of the funeral has not yet been set. Efforts are being made to trace whether McMillan has any living relatives, and in the event of none being found, he will be buried by the city."

Dan McLeod passed away in his sleep at his Temecula, California home on June 20, 1958. He had lived to reach the ripe old age of 97. At the time of his passing, McLeod was the oldest member of the Old Time Athletes' Association of Los Angeles, after having spent many years teaching wrestling in the area.

Composite photo and illustration of an older Dan McLeod

At the time of his death, McLeod was living at 2920 W. Adams Street in La Crescenta, California. He had been claiming California as his home state for 74 years by this time, and Los Angeles as his home region for 35. Both of his parents were listed as being born in Scotland, and his mother's surname was provided as Mackay.

Highlighted in the report of his death in *The Los Angeles Times* were McLeod's several years as the wrestling instructor of the Los Angeles Athletic Club. More than five decades after the story of his discovery and defeat of Frank Gotch had first circulated, his victory over Gotch remained the bedrock of his reputation, and was included in even the briefest syndicated mentions of his death.

"The Late Hugh Nichols, a wrestler himself and a student of wrestling, argued often and long that pound for pound Dan McLeod was not only the greatest wrestler the world had ever known — and in the days when it was a serious sport and *not* a hippodrome entertainment feature — but also one of its greatest athletes. In addition to his wrestling, Dan McLeod was an international track and field star for a decade and a half, from 1885 to 1900.

While it was a slight exaggeration to refer to McLeod as a former international track and field "star," he was undeniably capable of displaying power in throwing events that was worthy of respect in his day. More to the point, the reference to McLeod's all-around athletic prowess was emblematic of the era he belonged to, and his departure from the mortal plane marked its symbolic end.

McLeod was the last man standing from a period in which men of Scottish blood built reputations based on world-class athletic prowess, and wielded it as a prerequisite for entry into the semi-legitimate sport of professional wrestling that was beginning to develop on North American soil.

The fact that the Caledonian quartet of Donald Dinnie, Duncan Ross, Duncan McMillan, and Dan McLeod were all athletes of an elite class transferred credibility to everything they did as wrestlers, even if much of what they were involved in was clearly feigned combat upon closer inspection.

Through both direct or indirect actions, these men, who wore their Scottish identities openly and proudly, helped to establish the foundation of what professional wrestling and

Highland Games and Hippodromes

sports entertainment would ultimately become, as their fingerprints are all over the evolution of wrestling as both sport and entertainment, from the growth of promotional territories and the development of its biggest stars to the legacies of its most prestigious championships.

In the years that followed, the presentation of Scottish performers became more theatrical, based far less on the sporting traditions of the Highlanders, and far more on outward acts performed with kilts and bagpipes. Still, the legacies of these men — several of whose families were casualties of the Highland Clearances — still echo into the present, not only when Scottish grapplers appear for battle at the drone of a bagpipe, dressed in kilts and flashing claymore blades, but in the very continuation of an industry they helped to forge more than a century ago.

Highland Games and Hippodromes

AFTERWORD

One could be forgiven for dismissing the efforts of Donald Dinnie, Duncan C. Ross and other athletes of the Highland Games circuit who were accused of 'hippodroming' their wrestling matches, but this would be a disservice to the truth. Even if some of their own truths were built on lies or, at the very least, stirred by a shrewd manipulation of a media and infrastructure that was far less sophisticated, communicative and accessible as it is today.

It would be grossly underplaying their athletic skills, personal and career achievements to label such early practitioners of mixed-style grappling as a mere parcel of rogues. These individuals made indelible contributions to the modern era of professional wrestling, by pioneering its craft during its formative years. Even if it is to be accepted that their athletic endeavours were not always legitimate 'tussles', this would be turning a blind eye to their mastery of promotion and, in some cases self-promotion, that became a critical part of professional wrestling presentation which remains to this day.

Indeed, these enduring figures are among the founding fathers of the sport. But it is not just professional wrestling that has parallels to the influence of the pioneering Scots depicted in this book by revered author and historian Ian Douglass.

The modern-day interest in mixed martial arts is partly due to the intrigue presented by the first Ultimate Fighting Championship event in 1993. Based around a notion to determine which fighting style was the most dominant, the initial tournament pitted entrants from various disciplines, including boxing, grappling and other hand-to-hand combat sports in an effort to exploit the curiosity of its viewing audience. But that concept was not really a fresh one at the time, even if it was marketed as such and did spur a later interest in a hybrid fighting style. In actuality, it was retreading the ground of the mixed-wrestling style attractions of a previous time, as depicted in the matches between folk wrestlers in the nineteenth century.

Within that era, the United States of America had gradually become a cultural hotbed of grappling action so the American Heavyweight Wrestling Championship was created to serve as the first major accolade in the sport. Its lineage began in 1881 when England's Edwin Bibby defeated Duncan C. Ross in a catch-as-catch-can bout in New York City. It would later be held by Scots catch great Dan McLeod, as well as two sons of Welsh-born immigrants, Evan 'Strangler' Lewis and Tom Jenkins, forging a Celtic influence on the title which lasted for almost a quarter of a century. It was titlist Jenkin's subsequent loss on 4th May 1905 to 'The Russian Lion' Georg Hackenschmidt which spurred American recognition of Hackenschmidt's claim to the World Heavyweight Championship, an honour which the Estonian strongman had held since January the previous year.

As a Celtic dialect had permeated into the global wrestling landscape, there was a clear audience appetite for its type of sporting spectacle within the nation of Scotland. People across the country demanded the finest grappling action, which had grown beyond the traditions of the Highland Games.

On 28th October 1905, legions of spectators would converge in Glasgow's Ibrox Park to witness Scots star Alex Munro face Hackenschmidt for the World Heavyweight Championship. Munro was an established draw who had already faced American champion Tom Jenkins seventeen months prior to his World title challenge at the same venue. With the Munro-Hackenschmidt bout being held on the same afternoon as the main soccer fixtures, the attendance of local football matches suffered. Contemporary reports estimated an attendance ranging wildly from 10,000 to 30,000 spectators, but a median number is more likely and this remains as Scotland's biggest ever wrestling crowd. Whilst the evolving sport and its newly formed championship had proved to be a success, this drew the ire of the soccer establishment. The decision makers behind Britain's most popular team sport petitioned to block a repeat of this type of concurrent promoting of grappling and soccer, but one thing became clear: the presentation of professional wrestling had firmly captured the public's imagination on both sides of the Atlantic. Regardless of who carried the World title, the claimant's standing would always attract controversy, particularly by promoters who were unable to secure booking dates within the champion's diet. Nevertheless, the establishment of a singular World Heavyweight Champion was a key part of an increasingly organised attempt to create a tangible semblance of validity for the industry's most revered name talent.

While the creation of a touring World titleholder had added intrigue and spectacle, professional wrestling's transition from a pure form of sport into an entertainment form was irreversible. But this did not derail its appeal, as professional wrestling became part of the cultural zeitgeist. The exhibition bout legacy of Donald Dinnie and his string of successors had continued into a new age, or rather, a new century.

The term 'hippodroming' would later be superseded by the premise of professional wrestling bouts being 'worked' by its practitioners. But to protect the business, most of these in-ring prospects would have to be skilled in legitimate, or rather, 'shoot' forms of wrestling. This was a safeguarding measure that was used to ensure that anyone entering the ring would have to earn the trust of their peers before they could progress. Those within the inner circle feared that an exposure of professional wrestling's predetermined outcomes would be catastrophic for its audience appeal. It was essential that the wrestlers preserved an aura of toughness, so the presentation of real combat was never questioned. Like every art form, this also evolved.

The nineteenth century exploits of larger-than-life athletes such as Donald Dinnie and Duncan C. Ross had illustrated an audience desire for supermen to face off in public competition, but by the twentieth century, the focus of wrestling promotion became increasingly fixated on the personalities and temperament of these individuals, sketching out a line of conflict between good and evil. The era of star making had been pioneered, and promoters across the world would seek to exploit the drawing value of names that sometimes took years to establish. Predetermined results were essential to ensure the most marketable talent could continue to attract a lucrative return at the box office. At least, until the powers-that-be determined that it was time for a new act to supplant the established draw.

Scotland has had its fair share of drawing acts since the pioneering efforts of Dinnie, Ross and Munro. Some of the names may have faded from public consciousness over the years, but heavyweight stars such as George Clark and 'Wild' Ian Campbell ruled rings on both sides of the Atlantic in their respective eras. Former Games competitor Jim Anderson transitioned into professional wrestling as a powerhouse cruiserweight, and his exploits even took him into Asia during a career which spanned from the early 1930s to the late 1950s. Middleweight talents also achieved glory in Scotland and beyond its realm. Charles 'Chic' Purvey was a star of the 1960s domestic scene, while Clayton Thomson helped advance the fine art of mat wrestling through his tours of Japan in the 1970s, and Frank 'Chic' Cullen earned great respect in Canada a decade later. Groundbreaking female wrestler Rusty Blair was a World titleholder who toured several continents and fought for gender equality before headlining the first-ever women's main event at The Royal Albert Hall, London in 1987. But it was in the bustling lightweight category where Scotland's talent was most revered. A division which boasted names such as Tony Lawrence, Andy Anderson, and Jim McKenzie, it was also the domain of Scotland's most legendary professional wrestler, George Kidd.

Kidd's style was as far removed from the rigid grappling of Scottish Backhold or other legitimate forms of wrestling that one could imagine. Mastering a unique dialect of intricate chain wrestling that appeared seamlessly fluid to captivated audiences, George became a sensation in his home country. A level of cooperation from his opponent was essential to craft this artistry, but it mattered not to the public, many of whom considered Kidd to be the finest performer of his generation. His work was highly kinetic and his ability to craft such an illusion earned him the nickname 'The Houdini of the Mat'. George's drawing capacity was evident in tours of France and Spain, and his reputation spread even further, only adding credibility to him being anointed as the World Lightweight Champion in 1949.

Almost a century after the exploits of Dinnie and Ross, the influence of the Highland Games continued to permeate into professional wrestling as its popularity rocketed following the advent of television. Practitioners of Scottish Backhold or Cumberland and Westmorland styles of grappling such as Jim 'Willie' Bell, Andy Robin, Bill Ross, and Duncan Faichney all made a transition from the Games fields to the squared circle during the Sixties boom. In the case of Andy Robin, he first tasted in-ring stardom in North America while touring with a festival troupe which exhibited a variety of ethnic sports. After returning to his homeland, Robin arguably became the nation's most beloved wrestler, a reputation boosted by a unique association with his adopted grizzly bear Hercules (which shared a home with Andy and his wife Maggie).

Each of these stars emerged as local favourites while the system in which they operated had developed a strong British character. The United Kingdom had become a hub for an identifiable style of wrestling, often associated with its national coverage on the television network ITV. For over thirty years, it broadcast professional wrestling bouts, including a weekly fixture each Saturday afternoon as part of a block of variety sports programming called *World of Sport*. The matches featured on ITV are representative of a bygone era, but its showcased talent often attained plaudits for the believability of their craft. In part, this was due to a framework that supported this – but was yet another construct to convince the public that the product they were watching was real.

Highland Games and Hippodromes

For generations in the aftermath of the Second World War, bouts in British rings were settled under a strict ruleset devised by a committee led by Admiral-Lord Mountevans. The Mountevans commission set a structure for matches being fought under multiple falls within a set series of rounds, either within rigid weight categories or 'catchweight' contests between wrestlers from different classes. These rules were widely implemented with an aim to preserve the 'legitimacy' of the sport, amidst press and public claims it was all simply theatre and each match was a 'fix'. By the 1990s, the Scottish domestic professional wrestling industry had all but collapsed, due to changing audience tastes and a slew of external factors. But it gradually grew back under a new generation of dreamers, who were able to help rebuild the circuit and kickstarted the 'BritWres' revival of the twenty-first century.

The BritWres boom represented a major reboot of professional wrestling across the breadth of the United Kingdom. The traditional Mountevans rules were wholly discarded, as promoters nationwide adopted the structure of American style wrestling which had become increasingly popular via imported television programming and resultant live event tours. While the Scots had helped influence the dawn of the American professional wrestling industry, it was evident that the route of influence had since reversed.

By the new millennium, Scottish professional wrestling shows had changed to appeal to a modern fanbase and create a more sustainable industry. In the decades since, most cities within Scotland have an established local promotion as well as a reputable professional wrestling school. It is now possible for young hopefuls to enter and grow in the industry and be totally unhindered by geography.

While the fortunes of Scotland's wrestling circuit survived through crests and troughs in popularity, there is a renewed presence of Scottish identity on the international stage. Since his American debut with World Wrestling Entertainment in 2007, Ayr wrestler Drew Galloway has risen to claim multiple World championships within several major promotions and has been a featured act on countless historic cards. Billed as Drew McIntyre, the most famous of these appearances being his WWE Heavyweight title victory over Brock Lesnar at *WrestleMania* in 2020. He also headlined WWE's inaugural internationally-broadcast Scottish supercard, *Clash at the Castle*, which drew the largest gate revenue in his home nation's history.

Today, a new breed of Scottish talents, including Joe Hendry, Grado, Nikki Cross, Piper Niven and many others are forging their own path, as a lineage that once had its origins in the Highland Games enters a new age of evolution. The performers of today have more opportunity for expression and can now celebrate their skills as esteemed performers. Their appeal goes beyond the outcome of matches with predetermined outcomes. They can thrive in a unique art form that proudly combines storytelling with athleticism and can incorporate a multitude of other physical, mental, and verbal talents.

Moreover, the public perception of professional wrestling has changed, as it remains a major part of pop culture. The community within the industry is seldom faced with sneering attitudes towards any accusations of 'hippodroming' activities – those days are passed now. And in the past they must remain.

In an industry which has become increasingly diverse and connected with improved infrastructure, the Scots can still rise now, and become champions again.

Bradley Craig
Founder of The Professional Wrestling Hall of Fame for Scotland

Highland Games and Hippodromes

EDITOR'S NOTE

Legal sports betting has become ordinary in a way that would have sounded absurd not long ago: not merely tolerated, but heavily marketed as some sort of civic, GDP-boosting pastime, wrapped in the language of harmless fun and "engagement." In that environment, the oldest problem in modern sport returns to the center of the conversation: what happens when the outcome is known, shaped, or quietly negotiated before the public ever sees it? Match manipulation is the logical endpoint of a system that invites people to treat competition as a financial instrument.

Professional wrestling, of course, lives under a different legal and cultural label. It is the one combat "sport" that admits the essential truth: prearranged outcomes can make performances even more compelling than unscripted ones as long as spectators are kept in the dark about how the stories will be finished. That honesty is often treated as a quaint exception, useful for jokes about "sports entertainment" and "fake fighting," but irrelevant to the serious history of sport. Ian Douglass's *Highland Games and Hippodromes* makes that dismissal impossible, and not simply because it is packed with neglected facts. It is impossible because Douglass demonstrates, repeatedly and with receipts, that the boundary between legitimate sport and arranged spectacle was not a twentieth-century development. It was already visible — named, debated, and exploited — decades earlier than most historians of wrestling (who are almost invariably concerned with post-1950 and especially post-1984 goings-on) are willing to concede.

Highland Games and Hippodromes

Douglass also does something else, and it may matter even more for the long-term shape of wrestling history: he ties the lineal heavyweight championship — pro wrestling's most fought-over claim to legitimacy — to a specific immigrant ethnic identity. From the beginning, the book insists that "Scottishness" in North America has been both deeply desired and oddly easy to adopt, a ready-made badge that can be purchased, worn, and performed. Douglass notes that Scottish identity can function as "a very convenient guise for North Americans to slip into when the situation benefits them." Anyone who has watched a wrestling entrance built from bagpipes, tartan, and borrowed accent (or any combination thereof) can recognize the point immediately.

Yet the book refuses to leave Scottishness as mere branding. In the foreword, hulking current WWE superstar Drew McIntyre describes the familiar feeling of being treated as an outsider in an American business, then encountering this manuscript and realizing that "Scottish immigrants who were quite proud of their heritage shaped the foundation of the professional wrestling business."

McIntyre's reaction is a reminder that wrestling's ethnic "gimmicks" did not emerge from nowhere. Rather, they grew from older networks of community institutions, competitions, and audiences that already understood Highland athleticism as proof of character. When those institutions collided with the money and temptations of the late nineteenth-century sports world, the result was the early pro wrestling industry in recognizable form.

The most important corrective Douglass offers is also the simplest to state: these Scottish performers were not marginal "color" in someone else's story. Instead, they were central actors at a formative moment, and their careers braided together the two forces that shaped wrestling's future — ethnic identity and contested legitimacy — long before promoters learned to sell those forces with posters and catchphrases. By the end of the book, Douglass can say, without reaching, that Dan McLeod "was the last man standing from a period in which men of Scottish blood built reputations based on world-class athletic prowess, and wielded it as a prerequisite for entry into the semi-legitimate sport of professional wrestling."

He names the cohort plainly: "the Caledonian quartet of Donald Dinnie, Duncan Ross, Duncan McMillan, and Dan McLeod," elite athletes whose credibility "transferred" to everything they did on the mat, "even if much of what they were involved in was clearly feigned combat upon closer inspection." That sentence conveys the book's governing principle. Veteran historian Douglass is not writing a morality play in which purity is lost and innocence betrayed, but instead describing an environment where legitimacy was a resource earned through real athletic achievement, then spent in staged contests that could make more money than honest ones. He also describes, with his trademark degree of specificity, how that spending happened.

Consider McLeod's rise, which Douglass reconstructs as both athletic narrative and coming-to-America story. In San Francisco, after McLeod's celebrated victory, a paper exults: "McLeod is the hero of the hour and the newspapers vie with each other for complimenting him." Douglass notes that Evan Lewis, himself the son of a Welsh immigrant father, "had made a star out of McLeod and minted him as a hero amongst the local Scottish residents."

Just as revealing is Douglass's attention to rules, stipulations, and the quiet manipulations that allowed reputations to survive defeats. After a rematch with Lewis, syndicated reports said McLeod had lost, but Douglass foregrounds what the crowd actually saw: "McLeod had actually pinned Lewis twice while the men were down on the mat, but only Lewis' pinfalls counted toward the result." The *Chronicle* reassures readers that McLeod "will lose no prestige because of the defeat." In other words, the machinery for protecting a star — through stipulations, selective accounting, and narrative management — was already in place.

The championship story is where Douglass's work will prove most enduring. Wrestling fans love lineage talk, and wrestling promoters have always loved abusing it. Douglass treats the lineal heavyweight championship as both a concrete thread and a contested claim, and he demonstrates how often it passed through Celtic hands, with McLeod positioned as a kind of "North Star" in that inheritance. When McLeod captures what Douglass calls "the true world championship," Douglass writes that it "struck a monumental blow for Scottish immigrants," and that, in this period, "the road to the world heavyweight wrestling championship ran through the Celtic nations."

Douglass traces the line forward to Tom Jenkins, "the son of Welsh immigrants," and notes that "for the fourth straight time, the world heavyweight championship had passed into Celtic hands," continuing "into its 14th consecutive year." When Frank Gotch defeats Jenkins in 1905, Douglass is able to recognize its overlooked significance: Gotch's victory ends "a Celtic monopoly over the lineal world title that had lasted 17 years." Gotch then becomes an American folk hero, and folklore, especially pro wrestling folklore, has a habit of simplifying history into a single "face of the industry" (you know them all: Gotch, Jim Londos, Lou Thesz, Gorgeous George, Buddy Rogers, and so on) . Douglass argues that Gotch's ascent "erased from consideration" the earlier understanding that Gotch's "American championship" had once been "almost universally regarded as a world championship."

Along with that erasure came "a general disregard for much of what preceded Gotch's rise, with the influence of the Scots...fading from memory rather than ascending into legend." That is a historiographical claim worth taking seriously. Wrestling history, like history in general, is not merely lost, but overwritten by the winners, then reprinted by the next generation as if it were some kind of neutral record.

The second major contribution of *Highland Games and Hippodromes* should prove even more disruptive to the standard narrative: Douglass convincingly moves the origins of widespread worked wrestling, and (more importantly) of documented public suspicion about worked wrestling, back into the 1880s, and he does by quoting blunt contemporary language from primary sources.

Histories of "the fix" in pro wrestling often treat the 1910s and 1920s as the decisive period, a time when the sport's competitive veneer finally cracked and a handful of rogue geniuses you could make more with a "work" than a "shoot." Douglass shows that the veneer was already cracked, and that many smart journalists were writing as if the cracks were obvious to any attentive adult (in retrospect, how could it not be?). What changes, across the decades, is not whether the public suspected fakery, but how openly the press described the mechanisms, and how frequently the business reinvented itself to keep bettors and paying customers from walking away.

One document Douglass highlights reads like a modern *60 Minutes* whistleblower transcript, except it ran in Louisville in the nineteenth century. In 1883, *The Courier-Journal* publishes "a piercing exposé on the practice of hippodroming," focusing on professional wrestling as it grew in popularity. The paper interviews an anonymous wrestler, cautious about betraying "the wrestling fraternity," and then prints an explanation that should permanently end any claim that early fans had no vocabulary for "worked" matches.

The source states flatly that "nearly all the wrestlers" were involved, while adding, almost as a consolation, "I am glad to say that a few of them are square." Even more important is the explanation of how a working system becomes a business system. The wrestler describes how a respected competitor can be punished financially for being too legitimate — "He could then get no one to wrestle him, and, consequently, could not make any more money" — and how that economic pressure produces collusion: first "draws," then more elaborate arrangements. The anonymous wrestler explains that "the custom of wrestling mixed matches was gotten up…for this purpose," since a man could "win at that style, and allow himself to be thrown in the other styles," keeping his reputation intact.

Highland Games and Hippodromes

Douglass is right to call this wonderful piece "something akin to a Rosetta Stone," given that it reveals how "sport" and "spectacle" were not opposites, but business partners. The exposé also makes the betting context explicit. Wrestlers extend matches to heighten suspense, target places where people can be "easily gulled," and stage fake public feuds through the press so audiences believe the men are "bitter enemies." As someone who has extensively covered sports betting's modern growth for a variety of publications, I can attest that a small but not insignificant part of its business model depends on persuading outsiders that what insiders already know is untrue.

In other sources Douglass assembles, the language becomes even harsher. A writer warns San Francisco readers to "guard their hearts and wallets" because "in nine cases out of ten, such affairs are what are known as 'hippodromes,' or…'put-up-jobs.'" Donald Dinnie, in that account, is dismissed as "nothing better than a showman's fat woman…or any other catch-penny curiosity," and the writer concludes there would be "no very serious injury to the community" if "the whole gang were safely laid by the heels" in jail.

Douglass's point is that, by the 1880s, many people were already describing the wrestling business as a con built for gate money and bets. At times, the press treats hippodroming as an open secret, reported with the casualness of a train schedule. A reporter spots Dinnie and McMillan at a depot and says they are heading to Denver "to hippodrome at the Scotch games."

Nor were such suspicions limited to the biggest cities. Douglass includes the story of Janesville, Wisconsin, where memory of a fixed match becomes local folklore. The *Gazette of Janesville* complains that an exhibition "appeared too much like a 'hippodrome game,'" and warns that "Our people have not forgotten the Greek George affair." Here's what that "affair" was: in 1885, word leaked that the wrestlers "had agreed to wrestle to a predetermined finish," people paid at the door, and the action became "so gauzy that even the smallest boy present yelled 'Rats,'" while the crowd "left in disgust." Years later, the paper jokes that locals are once again "anxious for someone to pluck them."

In one of my favorite passages, Douglass quotes *The Globe* on a fixed athletic contest arranged "for the purpose of defrauding…out of a little boodle," adding that "the only losers" were "the suckers" and the public, to the tune of "$300 or more." The fix, the "work," is less about entertainment and more about identifying the marks who can be exploited.

And when the fix goes wrong, the reporting should remind us modern readers of the various John Stossel-style "exposures" of the business from the early 1980s that were, in actuality, being written and rewritten over the course of pro wrestling's long history. Under the headline "A Hippodrome Spoiled," *The Inter Ocean* describes a Cincinnati bout between McMillan and Lewis, "well known…to have been the best of friends," and speculates that management planned for twenty minutes before the scripted finish. A referee calls "Fall for Lewis!" at an unexpected moment; afterward Lewis is heard saying, "I didn't claim a fall," and the men "hastened behind the scenes to laugh."

Betting appears throughout these episodes. During the Burns–McLeod match at Davenport's Turner Opera House, a paper notes that "nearly $3,000" had likely been gambled on the premises. Douglass includes a rumor from the same era that could have been written about any rigged sport: "A prominent betting man says that McLeod and Burns had $4,000 in some bank…$2,000 of which belonged to Burns. The match was fixed as wrestling matches usually are."

Douglass' analysis of a later Burns–McLeod draw shows how rules disputes and officiating controversies can function as cover for gambling schemes. He explains that, with a draw officially declared, "those who had gambled on the least likely result would have cleaned up financially," while wagers on either man would lose. Douglass then notes the obvious incentive: "both men could have made a financial killing" if they had placed third-party bets on the draw. He concludes,

"In all probability, this is precisely what happened." Match results cannot be separated from the money surrounding them, and the nineteenth-century press understood that just as well if not better than our modern press does.

Modern sports leagues invest heavily in "integrity" language, in part because legalized wagering has changed the optics of competition. In the late nineteenth century, there was no such public relations machine to soothe bettors. There were only newspapers, outraged ticket buyers, and promoters hustling to the next town before reputations collapsed. Douglass' book functions as a compelling case study in how betting markets pressure competitions toward manipulation, and how audiences respond when they feel fleeced.

Douglass also shows how the business paid a price for its own cynicism. A Chicago editorial laments that wrestlers "killed the goose that laid the golden eggs" through "crooked work and hippodrome tactics," and refers to Duncan Ross as "that prince of hippodromers." Another report notes that people who remembered Ross and "men of his ilk fear a hippodrome when a wrestling match is announced," reducing attendance even when a contest might be legitimate. The industry's long-term problem wasn't so much one-off fixes (they're everywhere in athletics) as that the audience learned to assume the fix and withhold their money accordingly.

That brings me back to the Scottish through-line that gives this book its structure and argument. Douglass refuses to treat these Caledonian athletes as either saints or frauds. He shows how the prestige of Highland Games competition (involving real throws, real speed, and real strength) created a kind of cultural credit. That credit could be redeemed in wrestling matches that were sometimes legitimate struggles and sometimes "hippodromes," and the same tough man could move between those categories depending on the town, the purse, and the gamblers in the crowd. Douglass quotes one economic assessment of Dinnie: the value of Dinnie's name was too large to risk on authentic losses, and "any wrestling contest that included Dinnie would need to be a hippodrome" to prevent a "reputation-lessening loss." That is the clearest description I have yet seen of how star protection worked before the language of "booking" (much less booking with the assistance of AI, as the WWE is apparently now beginning to do!) ever existed.

The final achievement of *Highland Games and Hippodromes* is the way it makes these mechanisms legible without draining the period of its strangeness. Douglass reconstructs in precise detail how ethnic clubs, theaters, opera houses, and sports pages turned individual athletes into top-dollar traveling properties. He shows how championships and "world titles" operated as public relations technology long before they became corporate intellectual property. Most of all, he treats "Scottish identity" as both sincere attachment and strategic performance for the marks, while insisting that sincerity and skulduggery can coexist in the same athlete.

This wonderful book, in the language of marketing, "does what it says on the tin." The Scottish pioneers, Douglass writes, "helped to establish the foundation" of what wrestling and "sports entertainment would ultimately become," with "fingerprints…all over the evolution of wrestling…from the growth of promotional territories and the development of its biggest stars to the legacies of its most prestigious championships." He adds that later Scottish portrayals became "more theatrical," less rooted in Highland sporting tradition and more in outward symbols, but the legacy "still echo[es] into the present." A lineage that powerful should not be left to fade "from memory rather than ascending into legend."

I was happy to have played a small part in its elevation.

Oliver Lee Bateman, J.D., Ph.D.
Editor

ACKNOWLEDGEMENTS

Thank you to my Douglass family members for making Scottish ancestry and identity so intriguing that it instilled the desire in me to explore our family's history even further.

Along these lines, thank you to Ed Sweeney and Robert Battle for helping to close the genealogical loop using both tireless classic research and the marvels of modern genetic science to confirm our Douglass family's patrilineal descent from the ancient Clan MacDougall of the Scottish Highlands.

A long overdue thanks to Alister MacDougall, AKA Alexander Douglass, for surviving both the Battle of Dunbar and your resulting indentured servitude, sowing the seeds for our family to thrive in the New World.

Thank you to Drew and Bradley for their involvement with this project, as they are two of the most credible living links to Scottish wrestling history.

Once again, I'm appreciative of Oliver Lee Bateman — quite possibly the best writer in the world — for allowing me to bug him incessantly with details of this project, and for helping me strategize my approach to tackling this content.

As usual, I'm grateful to the friends and family members who encouraged my writing hobby, including the greatest parents on earth, James and Pauline Douglass, my grandmother Janet Douglass, and of course my wife Teisha, son Isaiah, and wonderful dog Basil.

Finally, I am eternally appreciative to God — Father, Son, and Holy Spirit — for providing me with the time, space, motivation, and healthy outlet to get some of this mental energy out of my system.

"The Lord makes firm the steps of the one who delights in Him; though he may stumble, he will not fall, for the Lord upholds him with His hand." – Psalms 37:23-24

Regards,

Ian C. Douglass

CREDITS

Author
Ian C. Douglass

Editor
Oliver Lee Bateman

Cover Art **Foreword** **Afterword**
Erik Hinton   Drew McIntyre   Bradley Craig

Cover Quotes
Mike Johnson   Tom Lawlor

Additional Aid and Thanks
James Douglass   Ken Bevan
Robert Battle   Jamie Hemmings
Ed Sweeney   Erik Love
Glenn Gilbert
The Clan MacDougall Society of North America
The Scottish Wrestling Network
The Professional Wrestling Hall of Fame for Scotland

ABOUT THE AUTHOR

Ian Douglass has been a contributing writer for *Men's Health Magazine*, *The Ringer*, *Splice Today*, *Cracked*, and *MEL Magazine*, and has had his material curated into the New American History project at the University of Richmond. He has also been a content contributor to *Popular Science Magazine*, *Fixed Ops Magazine*, *The Pro Wrestling Post*, *Pro Wrestling Stories*, The International Pro Wrestling Hall of Fame, and The Bahamas Historical Society.

In addition to writing, Ian was also an on-air reporter for the NBC News affiliate in Flint, Michigan. He is a graduate of the University of Michigan in Ann Arbor, earned a master's degree from Northwestern University's Medill School of Journalism, attended the Specs Howard School of Media Arts, and completed the Executive MBA program at the Quantic School of Business and Technology.

Between 2016 and 2024, Ian co-authored the autobiographies of professional wrestlers Dan Severn, Dylan "Hornswoggle" Postl (along with Ross Owen Williams), Buggsy McGraw, Brian Blair, and Steve Keirn, with multiple books earning "Best Wrestling Book – Finalist" honors from *The Wrestling Observer* and the "Best of the Best" ranking from *The Pro Wrestling Torch*.

He is also the author of "Bahamian Rhapsody: The Unofficial History of Pro Wrestling's Unofficial Territory," published in 2022, and "Gentleman Jack and Rough Rufus: The Rise of Black American Wrestling" and "A Decided Novelty: The Essential Guide to Black Pro Wrestling History, 1880-1950," both published in 2025.

Ian was inducted into the Pro Wrestling Author's Hall of Fame in 2024, and contributed to the 2025 Webby-Award-winning project "Leroy Smith: Michael Jordan's Myth."

Finally, Ian is a card-carrying member of the Clan MacDougall Society of North America, and is a patrilineal descendant of Alister MacDougall, who was taken captive at the Battle of Dunbar in 1650, and brought to the United States to serve out his indentured servitude at the Saugus Iron Works in Saugus, Massachusetts. Upon relocation, Alister MacDougall's name was changed to Alexander Douglass.

www.ingramcontent.com/pod-product-compliance
Lightning Source LLC
Chambersburg PA
CBHW060450090426
42735CB00011B/1962